S0-CFB-434

DATE DUE   APR 14 '96

DEC 11	DEC 27 '94	APR 13 '96
	MAY 12 '92	
MR 27 '84	DEC 01 86	
MR 21 '84	DEC 01 '86	APR 22 '94 DEC 27 '94
RL MAR 22 1984	NOV 15 APR 12 '95	RT'D NOV 21 '95
AP 26 '84		RT'D SEP 13 '93
APR 7 1984	OCT 12 '87	
MY 2 '84	OCT 14 '87	RT'D DEC 09 '94
MAY 3 1984		OCT 22 '93

ILL Boys Town Search Service
for 4 weeks use. Sept 6-28-84

MR 18 '85	AUG 31 1989	RT'D APR 12 '95
MAY 01 1986	SEP 02 89	NOV 12 '93
APR 21 1986	APR 2 1990	DEC 20 '93
OCT 16 86	MAY 6 '91	MAR 12 '94 RT'D DEC 07 '93
OCT 16 1986	MAY 6 1992	APR 13 '94
MAY 15 '97		MAY 19 '94 RT'D NOV 26 '95
MAY 04 '98		MAY 25 '97

DEMCO 38-297

MAY 04 '93

Adolescents,
Sex,
and Contraception

Adolescents, Sex, and Contraception

Edited by
Donn Byrne
State University of New York at Albany

William A. Fisher
The University of Western Ontario

LEA LAWRENCE ERLBAUM ASSOCIATES, PUBLISHERS
1983   Hillsdale, New Jersey   London

HQ
27
A365
1983

#8865894
DLC

2-23-83
JH

Copyright © 1983 by Lawrence Erlbaum Associates, Inc.
  All rights reserved. No part of this book may be reproduced in
  any form, by photostat, microform, retrieval system, or any other
  means, without the prior written permission of the publisher.

Lawrence Erlbaum Associates, Inc., Publishers
365 Broadway
Hillsdale, New Jersey 07642

Library of Congress Cataloging in Publication Data

Adolescents, sex, and contraception.

  Includes Index:
    1. Youth—United States—Sexual behavior—Addresses,
essays, lectures. 2. Birth control—United States—Addresses,
essays, lectures. 3. Youth—United States—Attitudes—
Addresses, essays, lectures. 4. College students—United
States—Sexual behavior—Addresses, essays, lectures.
I. Byrne, Donn Erwin. II. Fisher,William A.
HQ27.A365   1983   306.7'088055   82-18360
ISBN 0-89859-217-8

Printed in the United States of America

Contents

ALUMNI MEMORIAL LIBRARY   v
Creighton University
Omaha, Nebraska 68178

472592

ALUMNI MEMORIAL LIBRARY
Creighton University
Omaha, Nebraska 68178

Preface

According to numerous surveys, an American female who was born at the time of the first world war was very likely to reach her wedding night without previously experiencing sexual intercourse—slightly more than two out of three had sex for the first time after marriage. Most males of that period did not remain premaritally chaste, thanks in large part to the existence of formal and informal prostitution. For those individuals born just after the second world war, the sexual realm had indeed undergone a revolution. By that point, the odds very much favored premarital intercourse for both males and females. In the most recent research on college campuses, it has been found that the two genders are almost indistinguishable in their sexual histories, and only a small percentage are virginal at graduation. Not only are more adolescents engaging in sexual intercourse at some point prior to marriage, but the average age of puberty has been getting gradually lower each decade; the average age of first intercourse has shown a corresponding drop. Recent figures suggest that about one out of ten thirteen year olds in the U.S. are sexually experienced.

Whatever one's reactions to these changes in behavior and moral standards, there is one aspect of the new sexuality about which it is easy to become scandalized. Among teenagers, their first act of intercourse is most likely *not* to involve contraceptives. The impetus to seek such protection is very often either a pregnancy or the false alarm of a late menstrual period. As is documented in various places in this book, the result is about 1,000,000 unwanted teenage pregnancies each year in the United States. Though these data are based on the American experience, the combination of teenage sexuality, the avoidance of contraception, and the consequent unwanted pregnancies are by no means unique to this country. The U.S. birthrate among 15–19 year olds is matched or exceeded by Australia, Hungary, Romania, New Zealand, East Germany, and Bulgaria.

For behavioral scientists, there is an interest in these phenomena that goes beyond the intriguing new sexual mores, the personal tragedies, and the societal costs. First, there is a very puzzling question—*why* do individuals who do not want to conceive offspring engage in behavior that is likely to result in conception? Second, assuming that answers can be found as to the whys of such inconsistent and maladaptive behavior, we must ask: *what* can be done about it?

That's what this book is about—the noncontraceptive sexual behavior of adolescents, the reasons for that behavior, and possible solutions to the problem.

Organized around these three major topics, this book has been written by a group of concerned individuals (psychologists, a sociologist, and a health educator) who are directly involved in research and/or applied activities in the area of adolescent sexuality. The problem is a new one, the search for answers is of recent origin, and the proposed solutions are only just beginning to emerge. This book, as a consequence, is the first of its kind—bringing together theory, research, and application on this important contemporary issue. Our hope is that this collection of original chapters will act to instigate further concentration on the problem, additional scientific inquiry, and increasingly innovative applications so that in future decades there will be no need for a book on this topic.

As editors, we wish to thank each contributor for his and her creative efforts. This volume is obviously a collective product, and any credit must be shared equally by each person involved. We also wish to express our very special appreciation to Lawrence Erlbaum for his support of this venture through a variety of tribulations. Our thanks also to the staff of LEA who contributed to the final product. Finally, we are grateful to Larry Apple for his early support and for his suggestion as to the book's title.

Donn Byrne
William A. Fisher

Adolescents,
Sex,
and Contraception

ADOLESCENT PREGNANCY: THE PROBLEM, AND SOME INITIAL CONCEPTUALIZATIONS REGARDING THE PROBLEM

As individuals who are concerned about teenage pregnancy, there are a number of important tasks before us. First—before any preventive measures may be proposed—it is necessary to describe in detail the social problem that we wish to solve. How many teenagers become pregnant each year? Is teen pregnancy a phenomenon that is limited to inner city minority youth, or is it common among white middle class teens as well? What are the consequences of early childbearing for teenage mothers and their children? To provide some indication of the dimensions of this problem, our volume begins with a description of the teenage pregnancy epidemic and the personal, societal, and global difficulties that are associated with it.

The second task before us is to formulate theory—however tentative—to help explain why teens so often risk pregnancy by having intercourse without contraceptive protection. Is it that teenagers are simply uninformed about sex and contraception? Do they neglect using birth control because it is so difficult to obtain? Or are there additional, psychological barriers to the use of contraception? In the chapters that follow, several conceptualizations are proposed to account for why sexually active adolescents may fail to use contraception. To the degree that these explanations prove to be accurate, they should help us in devising strategies for reducing the incidence of teenage pregnancy, and is with just such solutions that this book is ultimately concerned.

1 Sex without Contraception

Donn Byrne
State University of New York at Albany

Editors' Note

During the past 20 years or so, there has been a much discussed sexual revolution in various advanced societies. For example, it is now the norm—at least statistically speaking—for American teenagers to have sexual intercourse before they get married. Unfortunately, however, it is also the norm for them to do so without using effective means of contraception. To the surprise of few (with the possible exception of some of the teenagers involved), this leads to an enormous number of unplanned and unwanted adolescent pregnancies in the U.S. each year. In Chapter 1, Donn Byrne describes the extent of the teenage pregnancy epidemic and discusses the constellation of social problems that result from it. Then, Byrne provides a social psychological analysis of the several behavioral steps that sexually active adolescents must undertake in order to acquire and use contraception. A theoretical model of sexual behavior is then proposed to explain systematically why teenagers may perform—or fail to perform—these necessary contraceptive behaviors.

In most of the world's industrialized nations, sexual attitudes and sexual practices have undergone truly astonishing changes. The attitudinal changes have been in the direction of greater tolerance and permissiveness with respect to a great many aspects of sexuality. The behavioral changes have been in the direction of earlier, more frequent, and more varied sexual experiences. An elemental, but often ignored, concomitant of the new sexual mores is conception. That sexual intercourse often results in the creation of a new being may not come as a great shock to many of us, but such expectations seem to play a negligible role in our earliest sexual interactions. The simple biological reality of the blind union of sperm and ovum can lead to the profound joy of deliberate parenthood, but it

3

also can lead to the anguish of an unwanted pregnancy and the specter of a critically overpopulated earth. The antecedents of each of these negative consequences involve psychological processes that cause an individual to engage in sexual intercourse or not and concurrently to employ effective contraception or not. The maladaptive choice occurs when those who do not want or need offspring engage in noncontraceptive intercourse. We need to be able to identify the specific determinants of such behavior in order to be able to solve the resulting problems.

The many difficulties posed by unwanted and unneeded pregnancies will be outlined briefly, and then a theoretical model designed to account for contraceptive neglect will be described. The ultimate goals of this inquiry are to understand why individuals behave in such a way as to create unwanted pregnancies and to utilize this understanding to design procedures that alter the maladaptive behavior.

THE PROBLEM: SEXUAL ROULETTE, UNINTENTIONAL PARENTS, AND AN OVERCROWDED PLANET

In order to stress the seriousness of the overall problem, it may be useful to examine what is involved when we speak of unwanted teenage pregnancies and of unneeded pregnancies for any age group.

The Teenage Pregnancy Epidemic: Sex, Yes; Contraception, Maybe

Recent changes in sexual attitudes and in sexual activity are perhaps best documented with respect to Americans. Compared to the samples of U.S. males and females interviewed by Alfred Kinsey and his colleagues in the late 1940s and early 1950s (Kinsey, Pomeroy, & Martin, 1948; Kinsey, Pomeroy, Martin, & Gebhard, 1953) and those studied by Ira Reiss (1961) a decade later, the average individual today is much more sexually tolerant and much more sexually active. Specifically, the majority of young people in this country are newly tolerant of the sexual practices of others, and they are now likely to engage in a wider range of sexual practices more frequently and starting at an earlier age than ever before in our history (Christensen & Gregg, 1970; Curran, 1975; DeLamater & Mac-Corquodale, 1979; Finger, 1975; Hopkins, 1977; Hunt, 1974). The most dramatic changes are with respect to premarital sexuality in that the majority of males and females today engage in intercourse with one or more partners prior to marriage. Included here are 1.3 million cohabiting American couples, a number that doubled between 1970 and 1977, according to the U.S. Census Bureau.

Whatever one's evaluation of this new sexual climate, there is another set of statistics about whose negative meaning there is consensus. It is an established fact that, as they embark on their sexual careers, most teenagers engage in intercourse without using any form of contraception, using contraceptives only sporadically, or using unreliable and ineffective methods to try to prevent conception (Cvetkovich & Grote, 1977; Eastman, 1972; Kantner & Zelnik, 1973, 1977; Miller, 1973).

According to a report by the Alan Guttmacher Institute (1976), one million, mostly unmarried, American teenagers become pregnant each year, including 30,000 annual pregnancies among girls under the age of 15. From 1968 through 1973, the rate of teen pregnancies increased 13.1% among black and Hispanic adolescents and 50% among anglos. Thus, the adolescent pregnancy epidemic is not restricted by racial or class boundaries. White middle-class suburban teenagers are as unprotected from conception and as fecund as those from any economically disadvantaged minority group. Further, 20% of the teenagers who undergo an unwanted pregnancy repeat the process at least once (*Chicago Daily News*, October 20, 1976). According to Joseph A. Califano, Jr., former Secretary of Health, Education, and Welfare, such figures mean that at the present time one out of every ten female teenagers becomes pregnant during any given year.

Most of these pregnancies are terminated by abortions. Over 200,000 result in out-of-wedlock births, even though teenage birthrates have been slowly falling (Klerman & Jekel, 1978), presumably because of the availability of legal abortions (Allgeier, Allgeier, & Rywick, 1979). It might be noted that in Washington, D. C. in 1975, there were more abortions than live births (Raspberry, 1976). Approximately 10% of the adolescent pregnancies lead to hasty, unanticipated marriages characterized by a disruption of educational and vocational plans (Baizerman, Sheehan, Ellison, & Schlessinger, 1971), divorce within 4 years (Semmens, 1970), a high rate of child abuse by unhappy young mothers (Kempe & Helfer, 1968; Starr, 1979), and a suicide rate among these young women that is ten times that of the general population (Cvetkovich, Grote, Bjorseth, & Sarkissian, 1975). To add to this bleak depiction, it is found that teenage mothers face a much greater risk of unemployment and poverty than do comparable mothers in their twenties (McCormack, 1976).

It is impossible to estimate the economic and emotional cost of these unplanned and unwanted pregnancies to the individuals directly involved, to their families and friends, and to society at large. This leads us directly to the primary research question: Why is contraception avoided among sexually active individuals who (1) do not wish to conceive and who (2) can expect to suffer numerous negative consequences should pregnancy occur?

Many individuals working in the areas of family planning and teenage counseling have proposed that the primary reason for unwanted pregnancies is the lack of adequate sexual education and the existence of economic, moral, and legal barriers that interfere with the acquisition of contraceptives, especially for unmarried adolescents (e.g., McCormick et al., 1981; Reichelt, 1979). Both education and availability are unquestionably important factors. For example, only one fifth of the states require sex education as part of the school curriculum, and less than one third of the existing courses on sex deal with birth control. Availability has markedly increased in recent years, largely as the result of legal battles to permit minors to obtain prescription contraceptives without parental knowledge or consent. It must be added, however, that many states still have laws that prevent a young, unmarried individual from receiving the necessary medical examination without parental permission (e.g., Indiana) and/or from actually purchasing contraceptives (e.g., Massachusetts). Among numerous difficulties that are encountered is the fact that only one fifth of the colleges and universities in this country offer birth control as part of their health care for students (Alan Guttmacher Institute, 1976). The barrier of cost must also be considered for the financially disadvantaged.

Despite the importance of improved accessibility to contraceptive education, services, and products, we have obtained some interesting data in our ongoing research with college undergraduates which suggest that these traditional remedies touch on only part of the total story. In a study of 150 unmarried undergraduate females (ages 18 to 23) at Indiana University, we found that 61% report that they are currently engaging in sexual intercourse (Byrne, 1977). What of their contraceptive practices? Note that these are very bright, well-educated, late adolescents and young adults. They attend a university that houses the internationally known Kinsey Institute for Sex Research, that provides birth control as part of its Student Health Service program, and that has an unusually active contraception information service (see Chapter 10). Almost all of the undergraduates we studied indicated awareness of the easy availability of birth control services. Nevertheless, less than one third of these sexually active individuals reported using contraceptives regularly, and over two thirds said that they use contraceptives on an irregular basis or not at all. Astonishingly, their behavior in this respect is very much like that of less intelligent, less well-educated, younger teenagers for whom contraceptive information may be lacking and among whom contraceptives themselves may be much more difficult to obtain. It seems clear that an explanation of these students' behavior must go beyond what has previously been suggested with respect to thorough sex education and easy access to the appropriate technology. That is to say, contraception and noncontraception are behaviors determined by a variety of psychological factors. Our task is to identify the relevant variables that enhance or inhibit adolescent birth control practices.

The World-Wide Baby Epidemic: The Population Grows; the Earth Doesn't

The focus of this book is on unwanted adolescent pregnancies. There is, however, a related problem that should at least be noted. Unplanned, unwanted babies are more than a personal hardship—they also constitute one part of a calamitous present and future disaster that influences each of us (Byrne, 1979).

It is not difficult to generate a list of pressing crises confronting society. There is widespread concern about seemingly endless worldwide emergencies involving energy, food, jobs, inflation, crime, overcrowding, pollution, and the declining quality of life available to most human beings (Zeidenstein, 1978). Though the range of culprits identified as being responsible for our troubles extends from moral rot to the Communist/Capitalist/OPEC menace, a different explanation will be offered here. Let us entertain the hypothesis that overpopulation is at the root of much of our current frenetic malaise (Behrens, 1978). There are simply *too many people* on this planet in relation to our present ability to utilize and distribute available resources (Brown, 1981; Davis, 1981), and the situation is worsening at a rapid rate (Anderson, 1979).

Even the most abstract statistics in this area provide a grim picture. As a group, human beings were once scattered about the globe in tiny bands, barely eking out survival. As recently as 10,000 years ago the entire world population of five million could have been comfortably settled into today's Metropolitan Chicago area (Ehrlich & Ehrlich, 1971). It wasn't until 1800 that the one billion mark was reached (Demeny, 1974). In 1976, the number reached 4,000,000,000. There will be six and one half billion by the turn of the century (UPI, October 23, 1978). Each day, the earth gains as many people as now reside in Des Moines, Iowa—that's a net gain of 70 people every 30 seconds (Cherfas, 1980). At current growth rates (the highest of any mammal), that figure *doubles* approximately every 35 years. That is to say, unless something changes, in 2011 there will be eight billion, in 2046 there will be sixteen billion, and so forth. It helps to concretize such data by noting that every time an additional billion people join us, we must provide the equivalent of 308 new Chicagos complete with dwellings, food supplies, fuel and energy, transportation, education, medical care, jobs, and all the rest. It is almost impossible to visualize a world 350 years in the future populated by four trillion individuals (Coale, 1974).

From some sources, one can hear comforting arguments which suggest that the problem is overstated or even that it is already solved. For example, *Time* and *Newsweek* simultaneously declared the crisis to be over and zero population growth (ZPG) to be achieved, at least for the highly developed Western nations. Among the political responses to this "good news" are efforts such as those by the West German government to encourage parents to begin having more children (Rosenfeld, 1979). Not to be outdone, East Germany also encourages parenthood with monetary credits of $1,000 for one child, an additional $1,500 for the second, and $10,000 for the third (UPI, November 17, 1978).

Even within the limited sphere of the relatively prosperous nations, however, sanguine conclusions about ZPG can be sustained only by making unwarranted assumptions as to the constancy of projected family plans (Sklar & Berkov, 1975) and by totally ignoring legal and illegal immigration from the "overproducing" gestation centers of the world (Eisen, 1978). Though figures are obviously difficult to obtain, the number of illegal immigrants in this country is now estimated to be about 4,000,000. Since the United States is usually cited as a success story with respect to stopping population growth, it may be unsettling to learn that we add almost 5,000 people each day, and that our population showed a *net growth* of 2,000,000 in 1981. Between 1970 and 1980, we grew by 23,200,000 human beings (*ZPG National Reporter*, June, 1981). In 99 years, the U.S. population is expected to double, thus reaching 445 million (Ibrahim, 1980).

Equally elusive good news is provided when one reads of declining birth rates. It must be noted that any reported declines in the *rate* of growth simply indicate that it takes longer for population doubling to occur. For example, if China is miraculously successful in slowing its growth rate to a mere 1% a year, its population will require about 72 years to double. That sounds good until one realizes that this still means there will be 9,000,000 additional Chinese each year (*ZPG National Reporter*, January, 1978). Using even the most optimistic data, we can look forward to the year 2000 with eleven nations having over 100,000,000 citizens and with some enormous new urban centers—for example, Mexico City with 31,600,000, Sao Paulo with 25,800,000, Tokyo-Yokahama with 26,000,000, Shanghai with 22,700,000, Bombay with 17,100,000, Cairo with 16,800,000, and Lagos with 9,800,000.

As with the teenage pregnancy problem, our goal is to seek solutions. Isaac Asimov (1975) suggested the enormity of the problem by calculating that in 6,700 years, all of the matter in the known universe will consist of human flesh. Given such an impossibility, something will and must happen to stop the growth. The real question is whether that something is to our liking or whether it will consist of devastatingly undesirable events. Heilbroner (1974) predicts the inevitability of starvation, disease, and global nuclear war as the result of and as the final solution to the problem of overpopulation. In the few instances where governments have become alert to the necessity for action, the solution all too often entails heavy-handed totalitarianism (Kramer, 1979) which, as in India's forced sterilization program, tends to be both reprehensible and counterproductive. Following the ouster of Indira Gandhi in 1977, the new government policy on the subcontinent led to observations that the "birth-control program is in a shambles there" (Kramer, 1979, p. 40). Now that Mrs. Gandhi has returned to power, attention has again been focused on the problem. In a May, 1981, speech in New Delhi, the prime minister characterized her nation's population growth as "shocking" and indicated a total commitment to voluntary birth control (*New York Times*, May 26, 1981, p. A-10). The goal of halting growth voluntarily is not an impossible one, by the way. Sweden's birth rate is so low that it will be 1,386 years before there is a doubling of its eight and a third million residents (Ibrahim, 1980).

Given the teenage pregnancy epidemic and the world-wide baby epidemic, what should we do? For the behavioral scientist, the key is seen in knowing more about the responses of individuals and of interacting individuals. It is, after all, people who engage in sex or abstain, use measures to interfere with conception or fail to do so, and who do or do not produce offspring. With that in mind, let's turn our attention away from the million unwanted teenage pregnancies in the U.S. and the billions of surplus individuals being added to the world's population and focus instead on the basic human behavior that provides us with such figures.

A THEORETICAL MODEL: UNDERSTANDING THE PSYCHOLOGICAL DETERMINANTS OF CONTRACEPTIVE BEHAVIOR

Most of the research dealing with unwanted teenage pregnancies tends to be concentrated on the use and nonuse of contraceptives. It should be made explicit that this concentration represents a value judgment. It is true, of course, that if all young people who engaged in intercourse were to use effective methods of contraception consistently, the epidemic of unwanted pregnancies would virtually vanish. Nevertheless, that is not the only way to solve the problem. In fact, the traditional stance in Judeo-Christian societies is to preach abstention from sex prior to marriage. Though this message may have the blessing of many religious groups and of most parents, it has obviously not been particularly effective in restraining sexual conduct.

A less generally acceptable, but perhaps more feasible, solution would be the advocacy of various forms of teenage sexual interaction that do not involve genital-genital contact between those of the opposite sex. Though many would find this approach morally culpable, Hamilton (1978) advises her adolescent readers to express their love through manual-genital contact to the point of orgasm. In other words, she advocates the legitimization and institutionalization of "heavy petting" as the end-point of adolescent sexual interaction. A third possible solution is to terminate the life of the new creation either through one of the methods of abortion or in the practice of infanticide. The difficulty is that abortion is a divisively emotional issue for those on both sides of the pro-choice versus pro-life debate, and the killing of babies hasn't had many advocates since Jonathan Swift's satirical solution of the Irish problem in the 18th century (*A Modest Proposal*).

Though there are ethical and practical difficulties associated with each of these ways of dealing with teenage pregnancies, abstention, nonprocreative sex, and extermination are each potential solutions. Three other possibilities should also be mentioned, because they are often proposed as ways of dealing with the immediate crisis of an unwanted pregnancy. It can be argued that they are also less than adequate. It is possible, for example, to continue the unwanted pregnancy to term and then to place the baby for adoption. Though it is true that there is a shortage of adoptive babies (especially those who are white and without handicaps), world overpopulation considerations provide arguments against this

alternatives

option. One might also question on ethical grounds a deliberate policy to employ large numbers of teenagers as societal incubators. There are additional difficulties with the final two possibilities—the unwed mother raising her child or the couple marrying in haste to "give the child a name." In addition to population constraints, there is abundant evidence that the teenage parents and their offspring are likely to suffer in the numerous ways noted earlier.

In brief, then, these various counterarguments—along with the personal values of those conducting the research—have led to a focusing of interest on contraception as the best solution. Acknowledging that this is simply one among several solutions, let us examine precisely what is involved in "contraceptive behavior."

Contraception: A Five-Step Process

Before describing the theoretical model, let us first consider in detail the behavioral steps that are necessary in order for successful contraception to occur. That is, rather than simply lumping the entire process together as contraceptive behavior, analysis suggests that five distinct behavioral steps are actually involved.

Step One: Acquire, Process, and Retain Accurate Contraceptive Information. The first step in the contraceptive process is one of acquiring the necessary factual information about conception and its prevention. It is possible, though unlikely, to reach physical maturity in our culture without being exposed to the basic "facts of life." For example, Loretta Lynn, the country and western star has written in *Coal Miner's Daughter* of her lack of knowledge about sexual intercourse until after she was married and of her subsequent surprise at being told that such behavior had something to do with pregnancy and the birth of babies. Though most of us have been fortunate enough to have been provided with more knowledge than that, the way in which we obtain the relevant information is most often an unsystematic combination of remarks from parents, stories told by older friends, remembered bits of "dirty" jokes, things we read, scattered graffitti, and so forth. Formal sex education is still a luxury available only to a minority. Even when such school programs are available and even when they involve accurate and extensive material, they often are given *after* rather than *before* puberty. For example, my only contact with formal sex education was as a senior in high school. It is also true that such courses tend to avoid the topic of contraception, sometimes by state law. Considering all of this, it is hardly surprising that many teenagers possess a confusing array of information, misinformation, and distorted information with respect to the details of conception and contraception. Part of a 1980 survey of sexually active Canadian college students by William Fisher is shown in Table 1.1. It is clear that even very bright, well educated, late adolescents are in need of more accurate information than they possess.

TABLE 1.1

Misinformation About Conception Among College Undergraduates

Item	Correct Answer	Percent Answered Incorrectly	
		by Males	by Females
A woman's chances of becoming pregnant are greatest if she has intercourse just before her period begins.	False	39%	24%
A woman can become pregnant even if the male does not achieve orgasm during intercourse.	True	33%	21%
The diaphragm should be removed immediately after sexual intercourse.	False	22%	24%
Condoms are not an effective means of birth control.	False	17%	26%
A woman's chances of becoming pregnant are much greater if she experiences orgasm during sexual intercourse.	False	17%	9%
Douching after intercourse is not a good way to prevent pregnancy.	True	11%	0%

Note: In a 1980 survey of Canadian college students (18 males, 34 females), William
Fisher found that a sizeable percentage of these individuals held incorrect beliefs
about various aspects of conception and contraception. It appears that many of
our brightest and best educated adolescents are lacking in some types of knowledge about this topic.

Even when the educational process is optimal as to when it occurs and the
knowledge it imparts, there is another problem. There are two major components
of contraceptive information, each is complex, and each involves individual
differences. First, there are factual details relating to such variables as relative
effectiveness, long-term and short-term side effects, and cost. Second, there are
emotionally relevant details such as degree of interference with an ongoing
sexual interaction, messiness, and loss of sensitivity. Each individual differs
with respect to the importance he or she places on effectiveness versus particular
side effects versus interference with spontaneity, and so forth. Ideally, each of us
would be given all of these details about all types of contraception along with a
means to gauge our personal reactions to each. Because two people are involved,
the reactions of both members of an interacting pair must be taken into account.
The resulting personal equations would indicate that, all factors considered,
condoms are the best bet for couple A and the pill for couple B. In actuality, few
people have acquired a sufficient amount of information in sufficiently realistic
detail to be able to make such rational judgments.

In addition to obtaining and sorting through the information, individuals must
also remember what they have learned in order to utilize the appropriate contraceptives. Among the least facilitative circumstances for retrieving this com-

plex information are very possibly those in which adolescents find themselves as their sexual lives begin. That is, situations combining sexual excitement, fear, and awkward embarrassment are unlikely to facilitate one's ability to remember the comparative benefits of different contraceptive techniques (see Figure 1.1).

Step Two: Acknowledge the Likelihood of Engaging in Sexual Intercourse. There is no need to make contraceptive preparations unless one is going to engage in sexual intercourse. In our society, premarital sex tends to originate in social situations that are not characterized by detailed foreknowledge of what is going to take place. In this respect, males and females have been taught to differ somewhat (Simon & Gagnon, 1969). Males are usually socialized to seek sexual contact, to evaluate each female as a potential sex partner, to initiate a sexual interaction whenever possible, and, if the issue arises at all, to assume that conception and its prevention are matters for the female to worry about. Females are more likely to have learned that love is a prerequisite for sex, that sex has dangerous consequences, and that one shouldn't let a boy (or oneself) go "too far." The usual consequence of such differentially socialized partners is that when sexual intercourse first occurs in adolescence, there is no contraceptive protection and not even much forethought as to possible results (Eastman, 1972).

Males, then, represent a subgroup in which talk of sexual conquests and sexual adventures has been a common aspect of interactions with peers. Social comparison processes leave each male with the secret impression that he must be the last virgin on the block or the least successful would-be lover in town. When, after repeated thoughts of and sometimes half-hearted attempts at "going all the way," sexual intercourse actually occurs, the initiator may actually be as surprised as the target. In this context of lust and hope combined with fears of rejection or inadequacy, the thought of contraceptive responsibility is not ordinarily a paramount concern among adolescent males.

Females, on the other hand, are likely to emerge from a subgroup in which sexual thoughts are blended with images of popularity, love, and finding just the right partner. Even without necessarily knowing all of the precise details, most females have been impressed with the dangers of pregnancy that accompany close contact with males. My mother was a teenager in the early part of this century, and when she was first kissed by a boy in early adolescence, she agonized for weeks as to whether or not she had been made pregnant by that act. With this mixture of desire for romance and fear of pregnancy, few females decide ahead of time that they are about to become participants in the world of interpersonal sex. Instead, they are likely to find themselves "carried away" by love, lust, or liquor. Once again, contraceptive planning is not likely to occur.

Even beyond one's sexual initiation, acknowledgment of sexual plans is most likely to take place within the confines of a stable, ongoing sexual relationship or among older, sexually experienced individuals who have established a consistent pattern of semi-regular sexual encounters in their interpersonal relationships. For the young, inexperienced, uncommitted adolescent, the necessary prescience about a sexual act tends to be absent.

Step Three: Obtain the Relevant Contraceptive.   Given the required information as to how to prevent conception and the necessary self-knowledge as to one's need for contraception, a third step must be taken. Depending on the specific method the individual elects, it is necessary to visit a physician, clinic, pharmacy, and so forth for the appropriate prescription, service, or product.

The negative aspects of this action are rather powerful. At this point, the individual must not only acknowledge his or her own sexuality, but such acknowledgment must now be made to another person—usually a representative of the forbidding adult community. Embarrassment lies not only in revealing this private information to a relative stranger but in anticipating possible negative reactions. For example, the physician, pharmacist, or whoever might respond with a moralistic lecture opposing such activity, might tell one's parents, or (as in *Summer of '42*) might respond with teasing and implicit ridicule. Finally, the possession of any such product (condom, diaphragm, foam, cream, jelly, pills) constitutes concrete evidence of one's sexual involvement. Thus, other people (such as Brenda's mother in *Goodbye, Columbus!*) may discover the product, gain instant knowledge of the individual's intimate affairs, and react in various punitive ways.

Step Four: Communicate with the Sexual Partner about Contraception.   If one individual assumes total responsibility for preventing pregnancy, he or she can simply make the necessary preparations, and communication is not needed. If neither partner assumes that responsibility or silently assigns it to the other person, communication about this topic becomes vitally important.

Many barriers to such communication exist, including the lack of appropriate role models for this behavior. In addition to the general absence of communication behavior to model, there is the belief that talk of conception is counterproductive in the context of either manipulative seduction or storybook romance. The details of contraception seem intrusive, cold, clinical, mechanical, unspontaneous, and overly planful to many individuals. Further, a couple may feel that they know each other well enough to engage in intercourse but not well enough to discuss contraception—that, strangely enough, requires a closer relationship (Foreit & Foreit, 1981). A special problem is that the individual who is contraceptively prepared may very well be perceived as being sexually active and

---

FIG. 1.1   (see pages 14–15). There are many bits of contraceptive knowledge that teenagers must learn, remember, and retrieve at the appropriate time (Reproduced courtesy of Searle Pharmaceuticals, Division of G. D. Searle and Company of Canada Limited).

	Intrauterine Copper Contraceptive	The Pill
WHAT IS IT?	A small plastic object on which a coil of pure copper has been wound.	A combination of synthetic hormones very much like those a woman produces in her own body. There are many varieties of the pill available on prescription. The most commonly used type employs a balanced combination of progestogen and estrogen in each pill. The hormone action of this type of pill is similar to that of the hormones secreted by a healthy woman at times when ovulation is normally inhibited.
HOW DOES IT WORK?	Following insertion into the womb, by a doctor, the copper exerts the contraception action. Exactly how it works to prevent pregnancy is not completely known but it does not prevent the ovaries from releasing eggs.	Prevents the ovary from releasing an egg cell. With no egg cell present, a woman cannot become pregnant.
HOW RELIABLE IS IT?	Intrauterine copper contraceptives are almost as effective as the 'pill' and will prevent pregnancy in most cases. However, they may be expelled unknowingly. They may also be inserted in women who have not had children.	Virtually completely effective if you follow directions. Rates higher in effectiveness than any other method.
HOW DO I USE IT?	Inserted by a doctor and replaced every two years. Patient must check frequently, by feeling thread to make sure it has not been expelled. Do not pull on the thread. It is important that the patient return at least once a year for a thorough examination.	Ask your doctor. The usual schedule is one pill a day for 21 consecutive days each month, beginning five days after the menstrual period starts. Essentially this 21-day cycle is repeated each month until you wish to try to have a baby. Some products contain tablets for a 28-day schedule.
WHAT ABOUT SIDE EFFECTS AND OTHER OCCURENCES?	Most women have no problem. Some may have cramps and bleeding between menstrual periods and the copper contraceptive may be expelled, although these occurrences are less frequent than with other intrauterine devices. (If there is excessive discomfort the doctor will remove the copper contraceptive). Rarely, the device has perforated the womb and entered the abdomen.	The majority of women experience few, if any, side effects. In studies, less than 5 per cent discontinued use of the newer low dose combination pills for this reason. However, occasional side effects, some of them serious, may occur especially in women over 35 years of age, and in women of any age who smoke. If they do, you should discuss them with your doctor. The more common ones usually occur in early cycles of use, then ordinarily diminish rapidly or disappear.
DOES IT AFFECT SEXUAL RELATIONS?	There is little or no feeling of it being in the womb. When properly inserted, neither partner should be aware of it.	Many couples say they enjoy sexual relations more because they do not worry about pregnancy.
WHERE CAN I GET IT OR WHERE CAN I FIND OUT MORE ABOUT IT?	From your doctor, pharmacist or family planning clinic. The doctor will examine you and decide if the intrauterine copper contraceptive is suitable for you.	Consult your doctor, pharmacist or family planning clinic. Your doctor or the clinic doctor will talk with you and examine you before prescribing the pill. The clinic, or a local pharmacy, will fill the doctor's prescription. Your doctor, pharmacist or the clinic, can answer your questions, and will probably give you informative material to accompany your prescription.

Condom	Diaphragm	Other Intrauterine Devices	Chemical Methods	Rhythm
thin sheath or cover made f latex rubber or similar material. It is worn over the penis during sexual intercourse.	A flexible, cupshaped device made of rubber, inserted before intercourse. It is used with vaginal cream or jelly.	A small object (loop, spiral, ring) made of plastic or stainless steel.	A vaginal foam, jelly, cream, suppository or tablet. A special powder or fluid, applied with a sponge, is also available.	A plan of avoiding sexual intercourse during the woman's fertile period - that is, just before and just after an egg has been produced in her body.
catches and holds the man's sperm, so they cannot nter the vagina and fertilize n egg cell.	It is placed in the vagina to cover the entrance to the womb. If properly inserted, it prevents sperm from passing into the womb.	It is inserted into the womb by a doctor and left there indefinitely. Exactly how it works to prevent pregnancy is not completely known but it does not prevent the ovaries from releasing eggs.	Acts in the vagina by coating its surfaces and the entrance to the womb. Destroys sperm cells and may act as a mechanical barrier as well.	Most women release an egg cell about once a month - usually about 14 days before menstruation. This may vary from month to month and it is necessary to determine as accurately as possible when an egg will be produced.
offers good protection if he man uses it correctly and onsistently. Failures are due rimarily to improper handng resulting in tearing of the ondom, improper use or its lipping off during sexual elations.	If used correctly, many women have a high degree of success. Among consistent users, about 2 or 3 women out of 100 become pregnant each year. If diaphragm is improperly placed or becomes displaced during intercourse, pregnancy can result.	Not as effective as the pill, but will prevent pregnancy in a majority of instances. However, it may be expelled unknowingly. Ordinarily not recommended for women who have not had children as it is difficult to insert in such cases.	Not rated as effective as the first five methods described, although some women have used them successfully. Vaginal foams rate somewhat higher in effectiveness than the other chemical methods.	Uncertain unless the menstrual cycle is regular and you can accurately figure out your fertile period. Correct use means having no sexual relations for the specified time - often as long as half of each month.
he man puts it on his penis fter erection, and well beore entry into the vagina. For xtra protection the woman ould use a contraceptive elly, cream or foam.	The doctor will fit you and show you how to insert it. You should return to the doctor at least every two years, and after each pregnancy, to have the diaphragm checked for size.	Inserted by a doctor. It is important to return at least once a year for a thorough examination. Must also be checked frequently, by feeling to make sure it has not been expelled.	Read and follow the instructions. Must be used before each sex act. Provides protection for about an hour.	Consult a doctor or a rhythm clinic for help in determining when your fertile period is likely to be each month. You will need to keep records of previous menstrual periods for a number of months.
No physical side effects. Avoid use of petroleum based lubrication.	None, if properly inserted. Some women do not like to insert a diaphragm. Others find it distasteful to remove and clean.	Many women have no problem. Others have cramps and bleeding between menstrual periods. If there is excessive discomfort the doctor will remove the device. In a relatively few cases, the device has perforated the womb and entered the abdomen.	Usually no side effects.	No physical side effects.
Some couples object to the condom because they must nterrupt activity to use it. Some men dislike it because t interferes with their full exual enjoyment.	If properly inserted, neither partner should feel it.	There is little or no feeling of its being in the womb. If properly inserted, neither partner should be aware of it.	Drainage of the preparation from the vagina is objectionable to some couples. Foaming tablets may cause a temporary burning sensation.	Most couples are unwilling - or unable - to refrain from sexual relations for the length of time required to be "safe".
At any pharmacy. No prescription is required.	Your doctor, pharmacist or family planning clinic can supply you.	Obtained from a doctor, pharmacy or family planning clinic. The doctor will examine you and decide if the device is suitable.	At any drug counter. No prescription required.	Consult a doctor or family planning clinic.

as viewing the current partner as simply one more in a series of partners. The prepared male may be viewed as an overconfident stud ready to bed whomever is available. The prepared female may be viewed as an easy lay who is probably promiscuous. For all of these reasons, the majority of individuals seem to progress toward at least initial acts of intercourse in a relatively nonverbal fashion (except to express love and/or desire) without utilizing contraceptives. Those couples who *do* discuss their sexual plans beforehand and who communicate well about a variety of topics are more likely to utilize a contraceptive such as a condom (Cvetkovich & Grote, 1981).

Irony   It is found that as two individuals get to know one another better within an increasingly serious relationship, contraceptive use is progressively more likely (Fisher, Byrne, Edmunds, Miller, Kelley, & White, 1979; Foreit & Foreit, 1978). In other words, with comparative strangers, it is better to risk pregnancy than to raise the problems related to talking about contraception. With someone sufficiently close to be able to plan an engagement, marriage, or cohabitation, it becomes possible to take active steps to prevent parenthood.

Step Five: Utilize the Chosen Method of Contraception.   The final step in the chain is the actual utilization of a method of contraception. Here, each method has special requirements and raises special problems. Birth control pills are usually taken at a time and place totally separate from the sex act itself, but the individual is required to be precise and regular in her habits. The insertion of an IUD also occurs in a nonsexual setting, and the only requirement is a periodic self-examination to make sure that the device is still in place.

The most sexually intrusive contraceptives involve the use of a diaphragm, condom, or foam. These techniques require careful planning in advance, accessibility during sexual interaction, and the ability to anticipate and/or to interrupt ongoing sexual behavior. There are problems of timing (the use of spermicidal foam or jelly should be followed by intercourse within the next sixty minutes) and of placement (diaphragms must be fitted snugly into place and condoms should leave room for the semen after ejaculation). These methods necessarily require manipulation of one's genitals (as does the IUD checking process), and negative feelings about masturbation can make such acts aversive (Kelley, 1979). The individual also must know such things as the importance of leaving a diaphragm undisturbed for six to seven hours after intercourse. Similarly, detailed information is required if a condom is to be held in place on the penis during withdrawal from the vagina in order to avoid the possibility of slippage that could permit semen to enter the vagina.[1]

---

[1]There are two additional methods of contraception (rhythm and withdrawal prior to ejaculation) that are based on behavioral acts rather than the use of manufactured products. Neither of these approaches to contraception involves Step 3, and withdrawal need not involve Step 2. Because neither method is optimally effective, most research interest has been directed at the use or nonuse of

Contraception Is So Hard to Do.   In outlining the five steps in the contraceptive process, a deliberate attempt was made to emphasize the difficulties involved. The intent was not to discourage contraception but to indicate the general barriers to effective contraception, especially among inexperienced adolescents embarking on their initial sexual explorations.

It would seem that some of these steps could be made easier for the individual and hence more likely to occur by the institution of relatively simple changes in how conception is treated publicly. For example, both sexual and contraceptive education could be universally available, and the requisite information could be provided as an integral part of the school curriculum. It would seem to be important that adolescents have accurate and detailed knowledge about how to avoid unwanted parenthood—such knowledge might be seen to be at least as critical as that routinely provided with respect to driver education, cooking, and woodshop.

At the third step, it is certainly easier and less embarrassing to obtain condoms by mail or from a vending machine than in a drugstore. When buying condoms directly, it is easier to select them or other contraceptive products from an open shelf than to be required to ask a clerk to provide them from behind a counter or from a locked display. In visiting a clinic or private physician, it should be arranged that a female need not discuss the reason for her visit with a receptionist in front of a crowded waiting room audience, and there should be well advertised assurances that the visit is confidential and that the medical practitioners will respond nonjudgmentally.

Even with these and other efforts to erase situational barriers to contraception, problems still remain. There are internal obstacles, some of which were suggested above, and there are vast individual differences in the tendency to engage in each of the five steps. What specific psychological variables are involved? It is to this question that we now address ourselves.

The Sexual Behavior Sequence: Multiple Determinants of Behavior

Most psychological theories are based on the general premise that behavior is determined by external events in our physical and social environments and by internal events ranging from physiological processes to idle fantasies. The fact that we differ from one another with respect to the external events we have

---

physical contraceptives. It should also be noted that throughout the world, the most popular forms of contraception are vasectomy and laporascopic sterilization, methods that have been used by 80,000,000 couples. These techniques *do* involve all five steps, but they are most applicable to individuals who are beyond adolescence. They are most often employed by married couples (three out of ten in the U.S.) who have already had the number of children they desire (United Press International, April 17, 1978).

previously experienced, and with respect to the multitude of resulting internal processes, forms the basis of the concept of *personality*. That is, we are each unique, and each of us tends to be relatively consistent from day to day and year to year in the way we behave, at least *in response to a given stimulus situation*. Behavior change can be brought about by making changes in the external situation, and the fact that we can learn leads to the possibility of alterations in the internal processes over time. In the most general terms, that is the outline within which theories of behavior are constructed.

In our research on sexual behavior, we have found the following conceptualization useful as a way of thinking about what determines sexual responses and the way in which these determinants operate. As shown in Figure 1.2, the behaviors we wish to predict are represented on the right-hand side. Included are *goal responses* such as intercourse and masturbation, and preparatory or *instrumental* acts such as arranging a date, purchasing contraceptives, and so forth. On

---

FIG. 1.2. The Sexual Behavior Sequence

The Sexual Behavior Sequence (Byrne, in press; Byrne & Byrne, 1977), or, more generally, the Behavior Sequence (Byrne & Kelley, 1981) is a theoretical model that attempts to account for sexual behavior as a function of several classes of internal and external events.

On the left of the figure are the external determinants of behavior that consist of stimulation that is innately arousing (such as touching one's genitals) and stimulation to which we must learn to respond (such as a photograph of panties or undershorts).

The six central variables involve internal processes that mediate the effects of external stimulation and that also can initiate behavior. Emotional responses involve momentary positive and negative feelings (such as joy and disgust). Attitudes are based initially on such feelings, but they consist of more long-lasting evaluative dispositions (such as the judgment that one likes heterosexual intercourse and dislikes sadism). Informational responses consist of beliefs that may be true, untrue, or of unknown validity (such as the belief that males need sex more than females do). Expectancies are based on beliefs and refer to probabilities that a given behavior will result in a specific outcome (such as the expectation that continued masturbation will almost certainly cause poor eyesight). Imaginative responses involve self-created fantasies and those borrowed from others (such as erotic dreams and pornographic stories). Physiological sexual responses include the various bodily changes that preceed and accompany sexual excitement (such as increased blood flow to the genitals and the production of lubricating fluids).

The behaviors toward which all of these internal and external factors are directed include actual sexual goals (such as intercourse and masturbation) and a multitude of possible instrumental acts (such as buying a candom or locking a bedroom door).

Finally, a major factor in strengthening a given behavior sequence or in bringing about its alteration is the positive or negative outcome of the sexual act (such as a satisfying orgasm or an unwanted pregnancy).

The various arrows suggest hypothesized relationships between and among the variables in the model, many of which have been confirmed by empirical research. (Source: Byrne & Kelley, 1981)

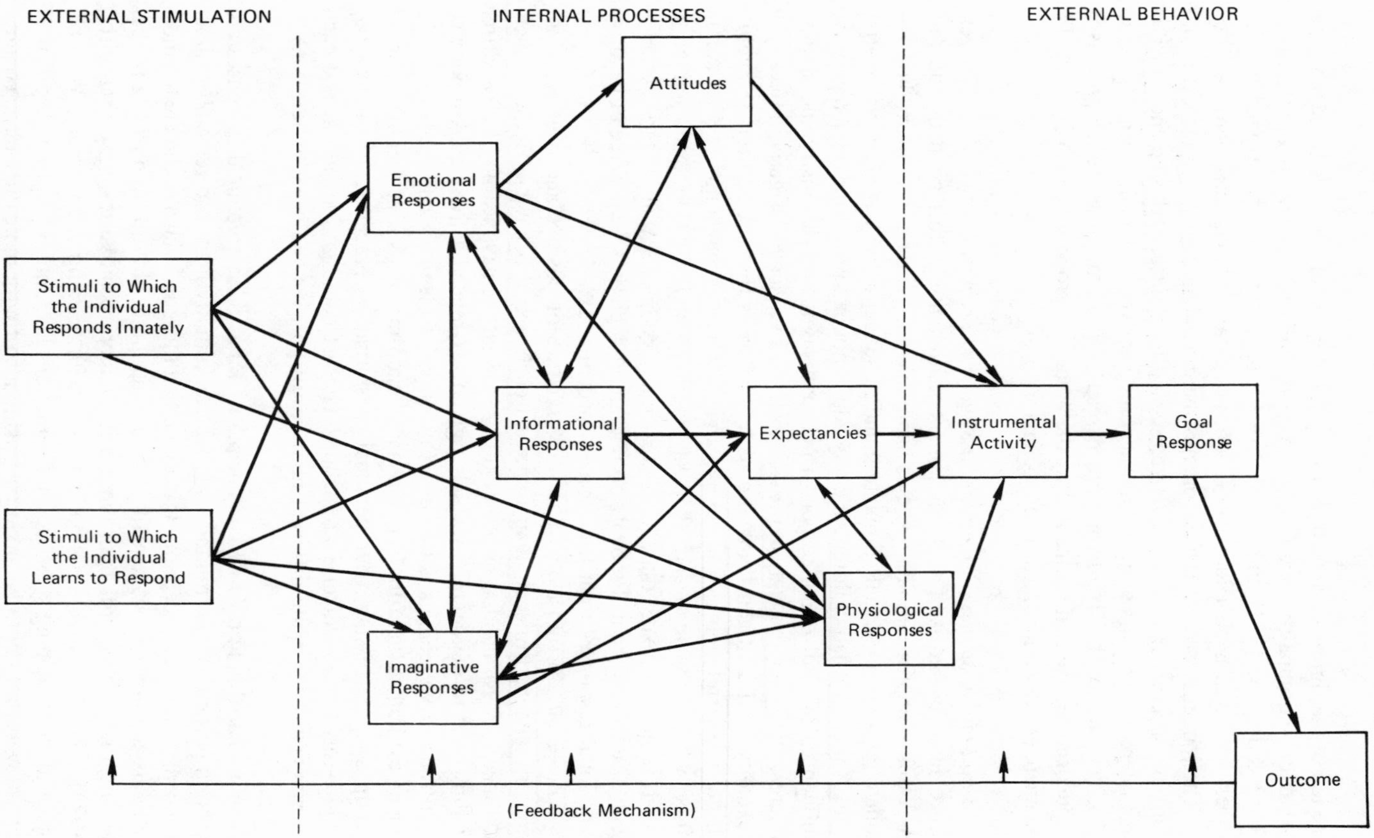
EXTERNAL STIMULATION
INTERNAL PROCESSES
EXTERNAL BEHAVIOR
Attitudes
Emotional Responses
Stimuli to Which the Individual Responds Innately
Informational Responses
Expectancies
Instrumental Activity
Goal Response
Stimuli to Which the Individual Learns to Respond
Physiological Responses
Imaginative Responses
Outcome
(Feedback Mechanism)

FIG. 1.2.

the left of the figure are shown the two types of external events that lead to sexual behavior—stimulation to which we respond *innately* such as a genital caress (Ford & Beach, 1951) and stimuli to which we can *learn* to respond such as shoes with high heels (Rachman, 1966; Rachman & Hodgson, 1968).

The remainder of the figure contains the crucial elements with respect to our current concerns. In order to understand what happens at each step and why it is that intercourse occurs with or without contraceptive protection, it is necessary to consider each of the six internal processes shown in the figure. Each process is influenced by external events and by the other five processes. Each is a partially independent determinant of overt behavior.

Emotional Responses: Positive and Negative Feelings.   Much of one's experience includes an emotional component in that things feel good or bad, are pleasant or unpleasant, and make us happy or sad. With respect to sex, the basic innate response to sexual stimulation and to sexual activity is clearly a positive one. Animals, small children, and any adults not exposed to the often repressive influences of civilization respond to sexuality with joy, curiosity and abiding interest. It is easy enough, however, to learn to associate negative affect with sexuality. Children can learn in a variety of ways that sex is dirty, shameful, disgusting, frightening, nauseating, and so forth. Such things can be taught directly by what parents and others say and indirectly by what they do and fail to do. It is not surprising that, for a great many people, sexual matters are laden with anxiety and guilt. Probably no one in our society is *totally* free of negative emotional responses to at least some aspects of sex.

The result, for most of us, is some mixture of positive and negative emotionality attached to each sexual cue and each sexual behavior (Byrne, Fisher, Lamberth, & Mitchell, 1974). We differ in what we have learned, so we differ with respect to the degree to which a given sex-related activity evokes positive and/or negative feelings within us. How do *you* feel, for example, about watching an explicit sexual film that emphasizes sado-masochistic acts, thinking about group sex, discussing your personal masturbatory practices, or taking your clothes off for a medical examination? The list could go on and on, and each person can report quite different mixtures of positive and negative reactions to each.

What has this to do with contraception? First, these emotional responses are very important in determining what we can initially learn and remember about conception and contraception. It is found that those individuals who are the most anxious and upset about sexuality actually retain less information from a factual lecture on birth control than those with a more positive response (Schwartz, 1973). Thus, negative emotions interfere with learning and memory. With respect to the remaining steps, negative emotions lead, quite simply, to avoidance. Those who find sex to be anxiety arousing also find it more difficult to contemplate their own sexual plans (Fisher, 1978), to acquire contraceptives (Fisher, Fisher, & Byrne, 1977), to communicate about sex (Fisher, Miller, Byrne, &

White, 1980), and to use contraceptives (Allgeier, Przybyla, & Thompson, 1977; Upchurch, 1978). Given all this, it is not surprising to find that, among sexually active college coeds, those who have the most negative feelings about sex are the most likely to become pregnant (Gerrard, 1977).

Attitudes: Positive and Negative Evaluations. According to a well established theory (Byrne, 1971, 1981; Clore & Byrne, 1974), our immediate positive and/or negative emotional responses to a given stimulus blend together to become a relatively enduring evaluation of that stimulus. The details of that blending need not concern us here, but the general idea is that our attitudes toward any "target" are based on the proportion of positive feelings (positive divided by positive plus negative) associated with the target (with each feeling weighted according to its strength). It's as if we carried around a portable calculator in our heads that provided us with our personal net evaluations each time we hear a song, see a movie, meet someone, engage in a sexual act, and so forth. We don't have to examine each blip of positive and negative emotion that occurs; instead, we can summarize our judgments by noting that we hate the song, mildly like the movie, feel neutral about the person, and think that this particular sexual practice is great.

With.respect to sexuality, there is a general tendency to respond to most sexual cues in a consistently positive or negative judgmental fashion. The consistency is such that tests have been developed (for example, Mosher, 1966) to assess where individuals fall along this attitudinal dimension. In our own research, we developed the Sexual Opinion Survey as a way of getting at an individual's general attitudes about a wide variety of sexual matters (White, Fisher, Byrne, & Kingma, 1977). We have labeled the dimension erotophobia-erotophilia (Byrne, 1981) with erotophobes being those who hold primarily negative judgments about things sexual (masturbation, homosexuality, pornography, etc.) and erotophiles being those who respond positively. It should be mentioned that sexual attitudes are not necessarily totally consistent. Despite the generality of responses to sex, it is possible to identify subgroups of attitudes about such topics as masturbation (Abramson & Mosher, 1975; Kelley, 1979) and homosexuality (Kelley, 1981; Lumby, 1976) that are at least partially independent of other sexual attitudes.

As with feelings, negative attitudes tend to interfere with each step of the contraceptive process. That is, the closer an individual is to the erotophobic end of the dimension, the less he or she knows about the factual details of sex such as conception and its prevention (Byrne, Jazwinski, DeNinno, & Fisher, 1977; Mosher, 1979), the less likely to seek contraceptive services or products (Fisher, Byrne, Edmunds, Miller, Kelley, & White, 1979), and the less likely actually to use contraceptives when engaging in sexual intercourse (Fisher, 1978).

In summary, then, both immediate negative feelings in a situation and more enduring negative attitudes about sex can interfere with necessary steps in the contraceptive process. Among those who are sexually active, erotophobia tends

to interfere with the acquisition of contraceptive knowledge and with its utilization. Note, however, that negative emotional-attitudinal responses to sex can be
sufficiently strong that the individual avoids sexual intercourse altogether, especially premarital intercourse (Fisher, Byrne, Edmunds, Miller, Kelley, &
White, 1979; Mosher & Cross, 1971). This inhibition of sexual activity provides
a solution to the problem of unwanted pregnancies, though once again one must
make a value judgment as to whether that is viewed as the optimal way to prevent
adolescent conception. Most of these erotophobes eventually marry. Though
they may continue to feel negatively about sex, may enjoy it less and be less
orgasmic than erotophiles, and may engage in intercourse less frequently, they
nevertheless desire to have more children (Byrne, Jazwinski, DeNinno, & Fisher, 1977; Kutner, 1971). This desire could possibly be explained as a realistic
acknowledgment of the consequences of their avoiding contraception.

Informational Responses: Accumulating Fact and Fiction.   A third internal
process involves the vast array of factual information in addition to the many
inaccurate beliefs that we acquire throughout our lives. This total body of information, whether true or false, is an important determinant of our behavior.

Knowledge about sex is likely to be acquired in a very haphazard and unsystematic manner. Parents and their offspring have a very difficult time communicating about sexual matters (Pocs & Godow, 1977) and the efforts of schools in
this area are limited, as described previously. The result is that individuals differ
in precisely how much they know about the details of sexual functioning and in
the accuracy of the information they do possess. Further, it has been found that
lack of knowledge about sex is associated with negative attitudes about sex
(Byrne, Jazwinski, DeNinno, & Fisher, 1977) and also negative attitudes about
contraception (Allgeier, 1978). One explanation of such findings is that negative
feelings and attitudes about these topics act to interfere with the learning process
and they incline the individual to avoid situations where additional information
could be obtained.

Major subsets of the information-belief domain dealing with sex include the
areas of morality, normality, and legality. We learn to place various sexual
practices, sexual attitudes, and sexual preferences along continua indicating the
degree to which each is good or bad, normal or deviant, lawful or criminal. Such
knowledge and beliefs tend to be associated with corresponding emotions and
attitudes. Thus, words such as "evil," "pervert," and "sex criminal" tend to
evoke strongly negative feelings and evaluative rejection. It has been hypothesized (Byrne, Fisher, Lamberth, & Mitchell, 1974) that—at least in some
instances—the emotions and attitudes are primary determiners of what we
"know" and believe. That is, we seek to *justify* what we feel by amassing
supportive facts and arguments.

With respect to contraception, the information-belief system is likely to range
from specific information about conception and how it occurs to knowledge

about various methods of maximizing or minimizing its probability. Interviews with a small sample of the 33,000 New York City teenagers who gave birth in 1981 revealed many informational gaps: "My friends told me the first time you do it you don't get pregnant," "I thought you had to do it a lot to get pregnant, and I wasn't doing it that often," and "It just never crossed my mind that I'd get pregnant" (Bennetts, 1981). As Fisher (1978) has shown with respect to male beliefs about condoms, there is also a complex network involving what each individual believes about a given contraceptive and its relation to love, convenience, effectiveness, embarrassment, sensual pleasure, and so forth. Such beliefs are found to be associated with contraceptive behavior.

One other set of relevant beliefs should be noted. There are individuals of both sexes who believe, at least in part, that impregnation is a desirable outcome. Included here are ideas that conception is a testament to manhood and womanhood, that it cements a love affair and insures a continuing relationship, and that procreation is actually one's main purpose on earth (Bennetts, 1981). Later on, the baby may not be wanted for very good reasons, but this belief system can nevertheless attest the values of pregnancy itself. Conception can also be favored for a quite different reason. Some suggest that pregnancy, childbirth, and parenthood are just punishments for the sin of deliberately engaging in premarital sex (Allgeier, Allgeier, & Rywick, 1979).

The way in which informational processes influence contraceptive behavior is primarily through the expectancies that are associated with most facts and beliefs, as will be discussed next.

Expectancies: Evaluating the Possible Consequences of Our Behavior.   Our information and beliefs about a given topic very often include elements that lead us to expect relatively specific positive or negative consequences to result from a specific behavior. The content of an individual's expectations, his or her judgment as to the value of obtaining a positive consequence or avoiding a negative one, and the person's subjective probability that behavior X is going to be followed by consequence Y each act to determine whether a given behavior will or will not occur (Davidson & Jaccard, 1979; Fishbein, 1972; Fishbein & Jaccard, 1973; Fisher, 1978; Rotter & Hochreich, 1975).

If two individuals find themselves in a situation in which they might engage in intercourse for the first time, there are numerous ways in which their expectancies operate. For example, if one of the individuals believes that the odds are against conception occurring during first intercourse, noncontraceptive sex is more likely to occur. If they believe that planful acquisition of contraceptives is a sign of heartless, unromantic lust, contraceptives are less likely to be used. If contraception is held to be a greater sin than fornication, the consequences clearly favor indulging in the latter without compounding one's transgression with the former. If there is a belief that conception is prevented by intercourse in a position placing the woman on top, that act is more likely to occur without benefit of contraception. If the male believes that condoms decrease his pleasure or a female believes that the pill endangers her health, the use of such methods becomes less probable. Such expectancies may be true, false, or untestable—the important thing is what the individual *thinks* will happen. Further, the relative effect of each expectancy rests on the value the person places on having a baby, being romantic, committing a sin, enhancing pleasure, avoiding illness, etc. *and* on the odds one places on such events occurring.

It should be mentioned that some theoretical systems (for example, Fishbein, 1972; Jaccard et al., 1981) place a major emphasis on behavior as a more or less rational outcome of decisions based on beliefs and expectancies. As a person weighs the various consequences, the pluses and minuses accumulate until the balance favors one behavior or another. In the present formulation, such processes are also proposed to operate in this manner, but only along with the other, less rational determinants of behavior.

Imaginative Responses: Fantasies as Motivators and Models.   The role of imagination in human behavior has often been neglected, but psychologists to an increasing extent are becoming aware of the power of these pictures and stories that we carry about with us (Kelley & Byrne, 1978; Przybyla, Byrne, & Kelley, in press).

McClelland (1961, 1965) and his associates, working with the need for achievement and other motives, have provided convincing evidence that the desires expressed in our fantasies are also reflected in our overt behavior. There is even evidence of a causal chain such that the motives of the adults in society determine what is deemed appropriate fantasy to be provided for children in the form of elementary school texts, story books, television programs, and so forth. This material, in turn, helps to mold the imaginative fantasies and hence the learned motives of society's young. As these young people grow and develop, they act in response to the motivational factors that have been painlessly instilled in them from their earliest years. On the basis of this line of reasoning, McClelland has been able to predict a society's economic growth by going back a generation to analyze the achievement imagery present in fourth grade readers. If external fantasies, internal imagination, and subsequent external behavior are interrelated with respect to achievement, affiliation, power, and other needs, it seems very likely that sexual motives function in a similar way. Thus, those who fear the consequences of a sexually permissive society as well as those who welcome the liberation implied by such a society are each probably correct in placing stress on the role of sexually explicit books, movies, television programs, and so forth. While cause and effect are difficult to establish in this realm, it is a good bet that the dramatic changes in the sexual content of the media over the past few decades at least contributed to the equally dramatic changes in sexual attitudes and behavior during the same period (Byrne & Byrne, 1977; Hunt, 1974; Przybyla, Byrne, & Kelley, in press).

In addition to its motivational effects, fantasy plays another role. From the earliest stories we were told as children to a program we saw on television last night, these imaginative productions tell us *how* to behave, *what* to feel, and the *way* in which those in our culture are expected to respond. With behavior that we are likely to encounter in everyday life, we can compare the behavior of our imaginative models with the behavior of those around us. Superman may leap tall buildings in a single bound, but that fantasy observation is not matched by the reality of anyone we know. Therefore, we don't use this behavior as a model for our own. Sexual behavior is much more dependent on fantasy than most behaviors because it tends to be a private activity observed only by ourselves and our sexual partners. Heterosexuals, for example, can easily go through life without ever observing another of their own sex become sexually excited or utilize a contraceptive.

In externally and internally produced fantasies, however, we can observe such things—and much more. For that reason, these fantasies can become crucial guides to tell us what to do. Ideas of romantic love (Walster & Walster, 1978) are an example of how an entire culture can learn to experience a particular emotion and to express it in certain prescribed ways (Byrne, 1972).

Contraception is especially interesting in this respect because, for the most part, fantasy models of contraceptive behavior have not existed. Whether in gossamer tales of romantic love or in the grossest pornographic productions, there is ordinarily little or no mention of conception and no mention of con-traception. Two exceptions to this general rule in the late 1970s are sad re-minders of the way we "protect" adolescents from exposure to appropriate contraceptive models. In the television program *James at 16,* writer Dan Wakefield had James preparing for his first sexual experience (with a Swedish exchange student) by obtaining condoms from a friend. The NBC censors would not allow such responsible adolescent behavior; in the rewritten script, James and his girl have intercourse without forethought—afterward they were shown ago-nizing over a late menstrual period. One of the best examples of contraceptive responsibility was in the R-rated *Saturday Night Fever.* John Travolta and a girl are about to have intercourse in an automobile. First he asks her about her use of the pill, diaphragm, and IUD. When she indicates "no" to each question, he zips up his pants and leaves the car. That exceptional model was lost on the under-17 audience because of the movie's "restricted" rating.

In general, then, models showing contraceptive forethought, acquiring con-traceptives, discussing contraception, and using such devices prior to intercourse are absent from our public fantasies. As a consequence, they are also absent from our private fantasies. The end result is that contraceptive behavior is largely reserved for the sexually experienced, often following the trauma of a real or imagined unwanted pregnancy. Appropriate modeling would provide a guide for such behavior where it is badly needed—among the sexually inexperienced young people just beginning to form serious interpersonal relationships.

Physiological Responses: Arousal and Sexual Behavior.   The final internal process in the model is physiological sexual arousal—the bodily changes associated with various stages of the sexual act, as documented by Masters and Johnson (1966). Arousal is instigated by external physical stimulation such as touching various sensitive bodily areas, internal physical stimulation such as pressure on the seminal vesicles of the male, external psychological stimulation such as erotica, and internal psychological stimulation such as an erotic daydream (Kelley & Byrne, in press). As sexual excitement increases, the probability of sexual behavior increases. The major reason for referring to such matters here in a discussion of contraception is to emphasize the fact that arousal propels the individual toward engaging in a sexual act without regard for emotions, attitudes, information, expectancies, or fantasies. In other words, the entire system can be at least partially "short-circuited" by intense arousal. Recognition of the powerful influence of excitement is reflected in booklets for teenagers cautioning against "crossing over the line" when petting. The warning is that too much stimulation leads to getting carried away, being unable to stop, losing one's head, etc. Dealing with the same general phenomenon is the saying that an erection "knows no conscience."

Whether such lack of control is genuine or simply the result of a widely shared belief, its effects are real. That is, even the most contraceptively aware and responsible individual can find himself or herself engaging in sexual intercourse without benefit of contraceptive protection. The association between sexual arousal and sexual pleasure on the one hand and the various contraceptive steps on the other is tenuous at best. It is proposed that to the extent that any of the processes described above are not directing the individual toward contraception, sexual arousal will act to make such behavior even less likely (Schwartz, 1973). The only solution would seem to be to attempt to establish strong links between excitement and contraception (as in the male magazine ads that associate condom use with sexual pleasure and interpersonal popularity) or to attempt to decrease the amount of stimulation available for those who are not contraceptively prepared (as in a repressive society).

CONCLUSION

As has been implied from time to time in the foregoing discussion, three stages are involved in solving the problems of unwanted and unneeded pregnancies. One of these stages is completed, the second is well developed, and the crucial third stage is underway.

First, it was necessary to analyze in detail the steps involved in contraceptive behavior and to isolate the proposed psychological determinants of behavior at each of those steps. The analysis of the steps involved in contraceptive behavior and the hypothesized determinants of each were described in the present chapter.

Second, research had to be undertaken to verify the hypothesized associations among the processes in the theoretical model and each contraceptive behavior. Some of that research has been noted in the present chapter, more will be discussed in the following chapters, and still more will undoubtedly be undertaken. There are enough very promising results at this point to provide solid encouragement that the theoretical explanations have considerable validity.

The third stage is the utilization of the theory and the established relationships among variables to devise procedures that will bring about changes in the contraceptive behavior of individuals. For example, work based on the Fishbein model indicates that exposure to the appropriate messages about contraception will result in positive changes in the reader's intention to use condoms or the pill (McCarty, 1981). Though there is not yet a large body of examples of such efforts, the final stage involves just that. It should be clear that application has from the beginning been a major goal of our conceptual and empirical efforts to deal with the serious personal and societal problems outlined in the first section of this chapter.

This effort is undoubtedly going to be subjected to the criticisms ordinarily leveled at any attempts to modify, alter, or otherwise exert some control over behavior. It would be well for those conducting basic research in this area and for those contemplating applying the fruits of this research to anticipate the possible problems. An essential element is a sincere commitment to the proposition that no attempts should be made to modify anyone's emotions, attitudes, beliefs, fantasies, or whatever unless the individual is both knowledgeable as to what is being done and fully willing to accept the anticipated behavioral changes. Because the area in question involves sex, it seems very likely that painful emotional confrontations lie ahead. The goal of developing foolproof procedures to insure that anyone who engages in sexual intercourse and does not want offspring will behave appropriately appears to be simple and worthwhile. Nevertheless, disagreement about that goal is almost a certainty.

REFERENCES

Abramson, P. E., & Mosher, D. L. Development of a measure of negative attitudes toward masturbation. *Journal of Consulting and Clinical Psychology*, 1975, *43*, 485–490.

Alan Guttmacher Institute. *11 million teenagers*. New York: Alan Guttmacher Institute, 1976.

Allgeier, A. R. *Attitudinal and behavioral correlates of sexual knowledge*. Paper presented at the meeting of the Midwestern Psychological Association, Chicago, May, 1978.

Allgeier, E. R., Allgeier, A. R., & Rywick, T. Abortion: Reward for conscientious contraceptive use? *Journal of Sex Research*, 1979, *15*, 64–74.

Allgeier, E. R., Przybyla, D. P., & Thompson, M. E. *Planned sin: The influence of sex guilt on premarital sexual and contraceptive behavior*. Paper presented at the meeting of the Psychonomic Society, Washington, D.C., November, 1977.

Anderson, D. E. Population of 6 billion may be earth's capacity. *Indianapolis Star*, June 24, 1979, p. 5–4.

Asimov, I. Colonizing the heavens. *Saturday Review,* 1975, *2* (20), 12–13, 15–17.

Baizerman, M., Sheehan, C., Ellison, D. B., & Schlessinger, E. R. *Pregnant adolescents: A review of literature with abstracts 1960–1970.* Washington, D. C.: Consortium on Early Childbearing and Childrearing. Research Utilization and Sharing Project, 1971.

Behrens, S. Perhaps, only one more doubling. *ZPG National Reporter,* 1978, *10* (8), 3–4.

Bennetts, L. Teen-age pregnancies: Profiles in ignorance. *New York Times,* December 20, 1981, p. 57.

Brown, L. R. World population growth, soil erosion, and food security. *Science,* 1981, *214,* 995–1002.

Byrne, D. *The attraction paradigm.* New York: Academic Press, 1971.

Byrne, D. Learning from Andy Hardy. *Sexual Behavior,* 1972, *2* (12), 34.

Byrne, D. A pregnant pause in the sexual revolution. *Psychology Today,* 1977, *11* (2), 67–68.

Byrne, D. The people glut: Societal problems and the sexual behavior of individuals. *Journal of Sex Research,* 1979, *15,* 1–5.

Byrne, D. *The antecedents, correlates, and consequents of erotophobia-erotophilia.* Invited lecture, Society for the Scientific Study of Sex, New York, November, 1981.

Byrne, D. Predicting human sexual behavior. In A. G. Kraut (Ed.), *The G. Stanley Hall lecture series.* Volume 2. Washington, D. C.: American Psychological Association, in press.

Byrne, D., & Byrne, L. A. *Exploring human sexuality.* New York: Harper and Row, 1977.

Byrne, D., Fisher, J. D., Lamberth, J., & Mitchell, H. E. Evaluations of erotica: Facts or feelings? *Journal of Personality and Social Psychology,* 1974, *29,* 111–116.

Byrne, D., Jazwinski, C., DeNinno, J. A., & Fisher, W. A. Negative sexual attitudes and contraception. In D. Byrne & L. A. Byrne (Eds.), *Exploring human sexuality.* New York: Harper and Row, 1977.

Byrne, D., & Kelley, K. *An introduction to personality.* Englewood Cliffs, New Jersey: Prentice-Hall, 1981.

Cherfas, J. The world fertility survey conference: Population bomb revisited. *Science 80,* 1980, *1* (7), 11, 14, 16, 18.

Christensen, H. T., & Gregg, C. F. Changing sex norms in America and Scandinavia. *Journal of Marriage and the Family,* 1970, 32, 616–627.

Clore, G. L., & Byrne, D. A reinforcement-affect model of attraction. In T. L. Huston (Ed.), *Foundations of interpersonal attraction.* New York: Academic Press, 1974.

Coale, A. J. The history of human population. *Scientific American,* 1974, *231* (3), 40–51.

Curran, J. P. Convergence toward a single sexual standard? *Social Behavior and Personality,* 1975, *3,* 189–195.

Cvetkovich, G., & Grote, B. Adolescent development and teenage fertility. Paper presented at the Planned Parenthood Regional Conference on Adolescence. Boise, Idaho, June, 1977.

Cvetkovich, G., & Grote, B. Psychosocial maturity and teenage contraceptive use: An investigation of decision-making and communication skills. *Population and Environment,* 1981, *4,* 211–226.

Cvetkovich, G., Grote, B., Bjorseth, A., & Sarkissian, J. On the psychology of adolescents' use of contraceptives. *Journal of Sex Research,* 1975, *11,* 256–270.

Davidson, A. R., & Jaccard, J. J. Variables that moderate the attitude-behavior relation: Results of a longitudinal survey. *Journal of Personality and Social Psychology,* 1979, *37,* 1364–1376.

Davis, K. It is people who use energy. *Science,* 1981, *211,* 439.

DeLamater, J., & MacCorquodale, P. *Premarital sexuality: Attitudes, relationships, and behavior.* Madison: University of Wisconsin Press, 1979.

Demeny, P. The populations of underdeveloped countries. *Scientific American,* 1974, *231* (3), 148–159.

Eastman, W. F. First intercourse. *Sexual Behavior,* 1972, *2* (3), 22–27.

Ehrlich, P. R., & Ehrlich, A. H. The population crisis. *Britannica book of the year.* Chicago: William Benton, 1971.

Eison, P. Observations from a total-immersion course on illegal immigration. *ZPG National Report-er*, 1978, *10* (6), 1, 6.

Finger, F. W. Changes in sex practices and beliefs of male college students over 30 years. *Journal of Sex Research*, 1975, *11*, 304–317.

Fishbein, M. Toward an understanding of family planning behaviors. *Journal of Applied Social Psychology*, 1972, *2*, 214–227.

Fishbein, M., & Jaccard, J. J. Theoretical and methodological considerations in the prediction of family planning intentions and behavior. *Representative Research in Social Psychology*, 1973, *4*, 37–51.

Fisher, W. A. *Affective, attitudinal, and normative determinants of contraceptive behavior among university men*. Unpublished doctoral dissertation, Purdue University, 1978.

Fisher, W. A., Byrne, D., Edmunds, M., Miller, C. T., Kelley, K., & White, L. A. Psychological and situation-specific correlates of contraceptive behavior among university women. *Journal of Sex Research*, 1979, *15*, 38–55.

Fisher, W. A., Fisher, J. D., & Byrne, D. Consumer reactions to contraceptive purchasing. *Personality and Social Psychology Bulletin*, 1977, *3*, 293–296.

Fisher, W. A., Miller, C. T., Byrne, D., & White, L. A. Talking dirty: Responses to communicating a sexual message as a function of situational and personality factors. *Basic and Applied Social Psychology*, 1980, *1*, 115–126.

Ford, C. S., & Beach, F. A. *Patterns of sexual behavior*. New York: Harper and Brothers, 1951.

Foreit, J. R., & Foreit, K. G. Risk-taking and contraceptive behavior among unmarried college students. *Population and Environment*, 1981, *4*, 174–188.

Foreit, K. G., & Foreit, J. R. Correlates of contraceptive behavior among unmarried U. S. college students. *Studies in Family Planning*, 1978, *9*, 169–174.

Gerrard, M. Sex guilt in abortion patients. *Journal of Consulting and Clinical Psychology*, 1977, *45*, 708.

Hamilton, E. *Sex, with love*. Boston: Beacon, 1978.

Heilbroner, R. *An inquiry into the human prospect*. New York: Norton, 1974.

Hopkins, J. R. Sexual behavior in adolescence. *Journal of Social Issues*, 1977, *33* (2), 67–85.

Hunt, M. *Sexual behavior in the 1970's*. Chicago: Playboy, 1974.

Ibrahim, Y. M. World fertility in rapid decline, according to vast new study. *New York Times*, July 15, 1980, p. C-1.

Jaccard, J., Hand, D., Ku, L., Richardson, K., & Abella, R. Attitudes toward male oral contraceptives: Implications for models of the relationship between beliefs and attitudes. *Journal of Applied Social Psychology*, 1981, *11*, 181–191.

Kantner, J., & Zelnik, M. Contraception and pregnancy: Experience of young unmarried women in the U. S. *Family Planning Perspectives*, 1973, *5*, 21–25.

Kantner, J., & Zelnik, M. Sexual and contraceptive experience of young unmarried women in the United States, 1976 and 1971. *Family Planning Perspectives*, 1977, *9*, 55–71.

Kelley, K. Socialization factors in contraceptive attitudes: Roles of affective responses, parental attitudes, and sexual experience. *Journal of Sex Research*, 1979, *15*, 6–20.

Kelley, K. Heterosexuals' homophobic attitudes and responses to mildly stimulating erotica. Paper presented at the meeting of the Midwestern Psychological Association, Detroit, May, 1981.

Kelley, K., & Byrne, D. The function of imaginative fantasies in sexual behavior. *Journal of Mental Imagery*, 1978, *2*, 139–146.

Kelley, K., & Byrne, D. Assessment of sexual responding: Arousal, affect, and behavior. In J. Cacioppo and R. Petty (Eds.), *Social psychophysiology*. New York: Guilford Press, in press.

Kempe, R. R., & Helfer, C. H. *The battered child*. Chicago: University of Chicago Press, 1968.

Kinsey, A. C., Pomeroy, W., & Martin, C. *Sexual behavior in the human male*. Philadelphia: W. B. Saunders, 1948.

Kinsey, A. C., Pomeroy, W., Martin, C., & Gebhard, P. *Sexual behavior in the human female.* Philadelphia: W. B. Saunders, 1953.

Klerman, L. V., & Jekel, J. F. Teenage pregnancies. *Science,* 1978, *199,* 1390.

Kramer, B. China, in big effort to slow population growth, is likely to impose harsh economic punishment. *Wall Street Journal,* October 3, 1979, p. 40.

Kutner, S. J. Sex guilt and the sexual behavior sequence. *Journal of Sex Research,* 1971, *7,* 107–115.

Lumby, M. E. Homophobia: The quest for a valid scale. *Journal of Homosexuality,* 1976, *2,* 39–47.

Masters, W., & Johnson, V. *Human sexual response.* Boston: Little, Brown, 1966.

McCarty, D. Changing contraceptive usage intentions: A test of the Fishbein model of intention. *Journal of Applied Social Psychology,* 1981, *11,* 192–211.

McClelland, D. C. *The achieving society.* Princeton: Van Nostrand, 1961.

McClelland, D. C. *n* Achievement and entrepreneurship: A longitudinal study. *Journal of Personality and Social Psychology,* 1965, *1,* 389–392.

McCormack, P. Teen pregnancy epidemic cited. UPI, November 26, 1976.

McCormick, N., Wiener, R., Levine, G., Mintz, R., Lebel, K., & Kolberg, L. Rural teenagers' contraception: Arguments for being knowledgeable and sophisticated. Paper presented at the meeting of the Society for the Scientific Study of Sex, New York, November, 1981.

Miller, W. B. Sexuality, contraception and pregnancy in a high-school population. *California Medicine,* 1973, *119,* 14–21.

Mosher, D. L. The development and multitrait-multimethod matrix analysis of three measures of three aspects of guilt. *Journal of Consulting Psychology,* 1966, *30,* 25–29.

Mosher, D. L. Sex guilt and sex myths in college men and women. *Journal of Sex Research,* 1979, *15,* 224–234.

Mosher, D. L., & Cross, H. J. Sex guilt and premarital sexual experiences of college students. *Journal of Consulting and Clinical Psychology,* 1971, *36,* 27–32.

Pocs, O., & Godow, A. G. Can students view parents as sexual beings? In D. Byrne and L. A. Byrne (Eds.), *Exploring human sexuality.* New York: Harper and Row, 1977.

Przybyla, D. P. J., Byrne, D., & Kelley, K. The role of imagery in sexual behavior. In A. A. Sheikh (Ed.), *Imagery: Current theory, research, and application.* New York: Wiley, in press.

Rachman, S. Sexual fetishism: An experimental analogue. *Psychological Record,* 1966, *16,* 293–296.

Rachman, S., & Hodgson, R. J. Experimentally-induced "sexual fetishism": Replication and development. *Psychological Record,* 1968, *18,* 25–27.

Raspberry, W. Washington's teen-age tragedy. Washington Post Syndicate, December 20, 1976.

Reichelt, P. A. Coital and contraceptive behavior of female adolescents. *Archives of Sexual Behavior,* 1979, *8,* 159–172.

Reiss, I. *Premarital sexual standards in America.* New York: The Free Press, 1961.

Rosenfeld, A. Good news on population. *Saturday Review,* 1979, *6* (5), 18–19.

Rotter, J. B., & Hochreich, D. J. *Personality.* Glenview, Illinois: Scott, Foresman, 1975.

Schwartz, S. Effects of sex guilt and sexual arousal on the retention of birth control information. *Journal of Consulting and Clinical Psychology,* 1973, *41,* 61–64.

Semmens, J. P. Marital sexual problems of teen-agers. In J. P. Semmens & K. E. Krants (Eds.), *The adolescent experience.* London: MacMillan, 1970.

Simon, W., & Gagnon, J. H. On psychosexual development. In D. A. Goslin (Ed.), *Handbook of socialization theory and research.* Chicago: Rand McNally, 1969.

Sklar, J., & Berkov, B. The American birth rate: Evidences of a coming rise. *Science,* 1975, *189,* 693–700.

Starr, R. H., Jr. Child abuse. *American Psychologist,* 1979, *34,* 872–878.

Upchurch, M. L. Sex guilt and contraceptive use. *Journal of Sex Education and Therapy,* 1978, *4,* 27–31.

Walster, E., & Walster, G. W. *A new look at love*. Reading, Massachusetts: Addison-Wesley, 1978.

White, L. A., Fisher, W. A., Byrne, D., & Kingma, R. Development and validation of a measure of affective orientation to erotica: The Sexual Opinion Survey. Paper presented at the meeting of the Midwestern Psychological Association, Chicago, May, 1977.

Zeidenstein, G. Population process and improving the quality of human life. *Studies in Family Planning*, 1978, *9*, 198–201.

2 An Intrapersonal and Interactional Model of Contraceptive Behavior

John DeLamater
Department of Sociology
University of Wisconsin-Madison

Editors' Note

In Chapter 2, John DeLamater discusses adolescents' use or nonuse of contraception, as well as their choices of a particular method of birth control. To understand these behaviors adequately, DeLamater suggests that we must consider both an individual's sexual-interpersonal relationship and the person's views concerning sex and contraception. Thus, to explain why adolescents may fail to use contraception, we need to assess the intimacy of teens' sexual relationships, their premarital sexual standards, and frequency of intercourse, as well as adolescents' judgments about the likelihood of pregnancy and their desire to avoid it. With regard to teens' choice of a particular method of contraception—a heretofore neglected subject—DeLamater emphasizes the need to examine their attitudes towards different methods of birth control, their knowledge about each as well as its perceived availability, and finally, their own experiences with various methods of birth control. Throughout this chapter, DeLamater stresses the importance of understanding teens' own point of view and their perceptions with respect to contraception, as well as the basic need to study contraceptive behavior in the context of a sexual-interpersonal relationship.

Studies of sexually active single persons have consistently found substantial nonuse of contraception (Morris, Conn, Stroh, & Gesche, 1976; Sorensen, 1972; Zelnik & Kantner, 1977). However, research has only begun to address the question of precisely *what factors influence the use or nonuse of birth control*. Is it the quality of the individual's heterosexual relationship(s), as proposed by Rains (1971)? Is it acceptance by the person of his/her own sexual activity, as hypothesized by Reiss, Banwart, & Foreman (1975)? Or is it primarily a matter

33

34

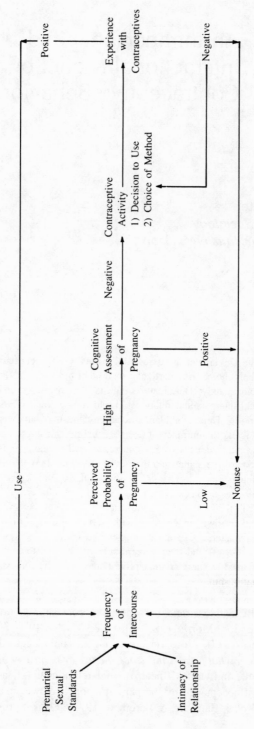

FIG. 2.1. Conceptual Model of Premarital Contraceptive Activity

of access to information and techniques in a supportive social situation, as suggested by Goldsmith, Gabrielson, Gabrielson, Mathews, & Potts (1972)? This chapter will present a model of the determinants of birth control use. The model emphasizes the individual's perceptions of certain aspects of sexuality and aspects of the interpersonal relationships within which sexual activity occurs.

The model also addresses a related question, which has been relatively neglected in the past: given that contraceptives are used, *what factors influence the choice of a particular method?* Since methods vary in effectiveness, and we know that sizeable numbers of young people rely on less effective methods (Zelnik & Kantner, 1977), this is an issue of considerable practical importance. It has been suggested that choice is primarily determined by differential access, where access is defined broadly to include physical, economic and psychological factors (e.g., see Lindemann, 1974). But other factors may influence choice, in particular perceptions of relative safety and effectiveness of various methods, based on experience.

CONCEPTUAL MODEL

The model is summarized in Figure 2.1. It specifies a sociopsychological process whose outcome is (1) the use or nonuse of contraception, and given use, (2) choice of a specific method. Following a brief overview in this section, each component will be discussed, and the relevant literature summarized.

I accept as a working hypothesis Lindemann's (1974) thesis that frequency of intercourse is the "prime mover" (p. 48) in the decision process which determines contraceptive use. She states that as frequency of intercourse increases, a woman becomes increasingly aware of the possibility of pregnancy; as this awareness increases, a woman is more likely to use birth control. Research (DeLamater & MacCorquodale, 1979) indicates that there are two major influences on coital frequency: (1) the individual's premarital standards, and (2) the emotional intimacy of the heterosexual relationship. In general, one's standard determines whether coitus occurs in a specific relationship; both standard and emotional intimacy are positively associated with frequency of intercourse. Changes in standards or in the quality of a relationship should therefore indirectly affect contraceptive behavior, via their direct influence on coital activity.

Given the occurrence of intercourse, I propose that the next factor is the perceived probability of pregnancy; Luker (1975) also stresses this perception, which she calls "likelihood of pregnancy." If a woman believes her sexual activity cannot result in pregnancy, or that the probability of conception is quite low, she will not consider contraceptives. Alternatively, if pregnancy is perceived as a real possibility, the next consideration is her assessment of the consequences of conceiving a child. If she views these as positive on the whole, she is unlikely to use birth control. However, if she views the effects of pregnancy as undesirable, she will consider contraception. Her actual contraceptive activity consists of (1) the decision to not use or use, and (2) the choice of a particular method of birth control. I believe that different factors influence these two aspects, as will be discussed below.

The model assumes that contraceptive activity is the result of an ongoing process over time. Thus, arrows denoting "feedback loops" are included. If use of a particular method results in a generally positive experience, use will continue and coital frequency might increase. If use results in a negative experience, the woman will reassess her choice, and may switch to a different method or stop using birth control. In addition, if change occurs in one or more other components specified in the model, there should be corresponding changes in other components.

Rationale

The rationale comes in part from the extant literature on contraceptive activity by single young women; much of the research has been done with adolescents. In this section, we will (a) consider each component of the model in more detail, and (b) review relevant prior work.

Premarital Sexual Standards.   DeLamater and MacCorquodale (1979) report findings of interviews with random samples of 18 to 23-year-old women, both students at a university (N = 429) and women who were not university students (N = 293). Statistical analyses indicated that premarital standards—the individual's beliefs about the acceptability of various sexual behaviors before marriage—are a major determinant of whether premarital intercourse occurs, and its frequency. Thus, women with permissive standards who believed premarital coitus is acceptable were more likely to engage in it and to do so more frequently.[1] These researchers also found that a variety of factors were correlated with contraceptive use including sexual standards, age of first intercourse, and the frequency of attendance at religious services while in high school; however, regression analyses indicated that these variables were not independently related to use. That is, these factors were associated with birth control use due to their

---

[1]This finding, like all of those which will be discussed in this chapter, is based on "cross-sectional" study, i.e., where measures of many behaviors and attitudes are taken at the same time, e.g. in the course of one interview. In analyzing such data, we can say that two variables, in this instance premarital standard and frequency of intercourse, are associated or correlated meaning that as one increases/decreases the other also changes systematically. However, we often do not know whether one occurs prior to the other; therefore, we usually cannot infer that one causes the other. In this case, one's standard may develop in early adolescence and determine one's subsequent behavior. Alternatively, once a woman engages in a particular behavior, her standard may change to one which is consistent with her behavior. So in this and many other instances we can say two variables are related, but not which is cause and which is effect.

association with frequency of intercourse; when we controlled for the latter relationship, there were no correlations between standards, age of first intercourse and attendance, and use.

The most widely known research on the contraceptive activity of single women is by Zelnik and Kantner (Zelnik and Kantner, 1977; Zelnik and Kantner, 1973). Their national surveys of samples of 15 to 19-year-old single women provide a wealth of information about patterns of contraceptive use. In a recent paper (1977), they report differences in the method used the first time a woman employs birth control. They compared three groups: women who had coitus only once, those who used birth control from their first intercourse experience on, and those who began to use birth control sometime after their first intercourse. They interpret these differences as supporting the theory "that an upgrading of contraceptive practice, i.e., a progression from nonuse to conventional (condom, spermicides, douches, etc.) to medical methods, follows increasing commitment to sex." They attribute this view to Lindemann (1974), but it was also suggested by Rains (1971). "Commitment to sex" in this context essentially means acceptance of intercourse for oneself, which is an aspect of one's premarital standard.

Reiss and his colleagues (1975) collected questionnaire data from two university student groups, women who came to a clinic to get contraceptives, and sexually active women who had never used birth control (the latter completed questionnaires distributed during classes). They found that the premarital sexual standards of clinic attenders did *not* differ significantly from those of non-attenders; however, women who sought birth control were more likely to approve of abortion, extramarital sex and premarital intercourse for a hypothetical daughter. The hypothesis underlying their research is that contraceptive use occurs only when it is congruent with the woman's "sexual life-style." They identify five aspects of lifestyle. The first is called endorsement of sexual choices and includes acceptance of female initiation of sexual activity, approval of premarital and extramarital coitus, and approval of abortion. The other four are self-assurance, early acquisition of information about sex, dyadic commitment (i.e., commitment to one's heterosexual partner) and degree of congruence between one's premarital standard and sexual activity. They argue that an increase in any of these reflects the greater integration of sexuality into a woman's lifestyle which should in turn make her more likely to use birth control.

DeLamater and MacCorquodale (1978) developed operational measures of both the Rain's and Reiss et al. formulations. The measures were included in data from four random samples of 18 to 23-year-old single persons: student men and women, and nonstudent men and women. In general, the results for sexually active single men showed few significant relationships between the measures employed and use of birth control. This was interpreted as a reflection of the fact that most respondents and their sexual partners were using the more effective medically prescribed methods (diaphragm, pill, IUD), and all of these are female linked. Thus, while males may influence the couple's contraceptive activity, they often are not personally using birth control. Since it is the woman who is using the technique, it is not surprising that her characteristics are more closely associated with use. This finding is the basis for excluding males from the discussion in this chapter. Among women, DeLamater and MacCorquodale found that premarital sexual standard was significantly correlated with contraceptive use. Women with more permissive standards, who believed that intercourse was acceptable early in the development of a relationship, were more likely to use birth control.

Thus, there is strong evidence of a relationship between a young person's sexual standard and his/her participation in intercourse. The more one accepts his/her own involvement in sexual activity, the more likely s/he is to engage in intercourse, and the more frequently it occurs. There is also a positive correlation between a permissive standard and birth control use.

Intimacy of Relationship.   DeLamater and MacCorquodale (1979) asked each respondent in their study of 18 to 23-year-olds to classify his/her heterosexual relationship(s) into one of the following categories: engaged, in love and expect to marry, in love but not engaged, emotionally attached, someone you date often, or someone you dated once or twice. Thus measured, intimacy was the most strongly associated of several variables with the type of sexual behavior in which the couple was engaging.

Rains, who presented the first conceptualization of contraceptive use by single women, believes that intimacy plays an important role in the transition from nonuser to user of birth control. Her model is based on a semistructured interview with clients in three homes for unwed mothers; her book (Rains, 1971) does not present systematic quantitative data. Rains asserts that nonuse is caused by "moral ambivalence." She assumes that women in American society are initially socialized to believe premarital coitus is morally wrong. Thus, when a young woman begins heterosexual activity, Rains argues that the woman will be unable to accept her own sexual activity, i.e., she will be "morally ambivalent." Birth control use is presumed to require the resolution of ambivalence, the acceptance by the woman of her participation in sexual intercourse. Rains hypothesizes that a sequence of experiences are involved in this resolution. The first step is falling in love which provides a rationale for coitus in one relationship; however, the woman will not use birth control herself. Next as intercourse continues, the woman comes to accept it as appropriate to that relationship and she begins to use contraception. Thus, for Rains, the quality of the relationship is related directly to intercourse, and indirectly to the use of birth control.

Three studies report findings which are consistent with Rains' view. Reiss et al. (1975) found greater dyadic commitment, as indicated by going steady, being engaged, or having plans to marry among women attending a birth control clinic compared to sexually active nonusers of contraceptives. DeLamater and MacCorquodale (1978) found that exclusivity of the relationship—dating only one person as opposed to more than one—was associated with the use of more effective methods by the women in their study. Thompson and Spanier (1978), in a study of 434 sexually active 17 to 22-year-old young people, found that "involvement" with partner was a major influence on reported use.

Lindemann (1974) discusses a number of factors, including the relationship, which she believes are related to contraceptive activity. She observed and interviewed 2500 single women in a variety of settings: free and public health clinics, and high school and college classes. These interviews became the basis of her theory of the "birth control prescription process." Her basic model is that frequency of intercourse influences "awareness" which determines use. Awareness is comprised of conscious awareness of one's sexual activity, of the possibility of pregnancy and awareness of and information about contraceptives. In addition, she argues that some aspects of the relationship directly influence awareness. She hypothesizes that increases in the duration of the relationship and in commitment of the partner will increase awareness. An increase in awareness is postulated to lead to the use of or more consistent use of effective contraception, while a decrease in awareness leads to reduced consistency of use and/or shifts to less effective techniques. She supports some of these hypotheses with qualitative interview data.

Thus, the emotional quality of the heterosexual relationship has been identified in two conceptual analyses and demonstrated in empirical studies to be related to frequency of intercourse and to birth control activity. The model proposed here assumes that the latter association is mediated by the relationship between frequency of coitus and contraceptive use, to which we now turn.

Frequency of Intercourse.   Coital frequency is the variable which is most consistently discussed in the literature on premarital contraceptive activity. Most authors have found empirically or suggested that there is a substantial correlation between these two variables: as frequency of intercourse increases, the individual is more likely to use birth control.

DeLamater and MacCorquodale (1979), in their data from random samples of student and non-student women, found independent and significant relationships between contraceptive use and two frequency measures: the relative frequency with which she and her current partner engaged in coitus, and her estimate of the number of times in her life she had intercourse. DeLamater and MacCorquodale (1978), in their test of the Reiss et al. and Rains models, also found that number of lifetime coital experiences was correlated with contraceptive use.

Thompson and Spanier (1978), in their study of a "purposive sample" of sexually active college students, found that the frequency with which the couple had intercourse was positively associated with use of birth control.

Goldsmith et al. (1972) obtained questionnaire data from three groups of adolescents: single, never-pregnant women who attended teen clinics to obtain contraceptives, single clinic patients who were seeking an abortion referral, and women in maternity homes. Comparing these known groups, they also found that frequency of sexual activity—mainly frequency of coitus—as well as number of partners were positively associated with use.

Rains (1971) argues that a woman must accept, i.e., perceive as probable, continuing intercourse with her partner before the woman will begin to use contraceptives. Thus, Rains is emphasizing perception or acceptance of continuing coitus, or what she terms "long-term sexual involvement." Reiss et al. (1975) also consider acceptance of intercourse, which they term congruence between one's premarital standard and one's behavior. They assume coitus is occurring and so the issue is whether it is acceptable to the woman. Congruence is hypothesized to be associated with use. However, comparing clinic attenders and sexually active students who were not using birth control, the differences in acceptance of their sexual behavior were not significant. Using a more direct measure of the actual discrepancy between standard and behavior, DeLamater and MacCorquodale (1978) did find a correlation between discrepancy and contraceptive use; the larger the discrepancy between her standard for herself and her sexual activity, the less likely a woman was to use birth control.

As noted earlier, Lindemann (1974) argues that frequency of intercourse is the "prime mover" in the "birth control prescription process" which she describes. Thus, as frequency increases or decreases, awareness (of one's activity, the possibility of pregnancy and contraceptives) will increase or decrease. Awareness, as we have seen, is hypothesized to effect directly the use of birth control. Within this continuous process, Lindemann suggests that there are three distinct stages corresponding to three levels of coital frequency. The first is the "Natural Stage." Here, coitus is infrequent and unpredictable. The woman believes (or rationalizes?) that it will not occur, so her awareness is low. Consequently, she does not use contraceptives. The second is the "Peer Stage." Here, there is an ongoing relationship within which coitus occurs fairly frequently. This produces moderate awareness; particularly if she is single, Lindemann argues the woman will rely on partner or peers for information and devices. At this stage she will use nonprescription methods of birth control, such as the condom, douche, or foam. The third stage is labelled "Expert"; here there is frequent intercourse and thus high awareness. This produces the motivation to get a highly effective method, i.e., to see a health professional and use a prescription technique, i.e. pills, diaphragm, or an intrauterine device. These stages parallel the sequence discussed by Rains (1971), though Rains emphasizes increases in the quality of the heterosexual relationship as the "prime mover" rather than frequency of coitus. As discussed earlier, quality or intimacy of the relationship is positively associated with coital frequency.

Thus, the effect of frequency of intercourse on contraceptive activity is a consistent theme in the literature. The model proposed here suggests that this effect is mediated by the perceived probability of pregnancy.

Perceived Probability of Pregnancy.   The literature reviewed thus far explicitly or implicitly assumes that the important characteristic of a birth control method or device is its effectiveness. The conceptual models of Lindemann (1974), Rains (1971), and Reiss et al. (1975) hypothesize that in general sexually active single women will move toward use of the most effective methods. But this hypothesis is based on an unstated premise that these women do not want to get pregnant. In this context, a woman's perception of the likelihood of conception becomes important. Even if she is highly motivated to avoid conception, she need not use birth control if she believes she cannot get pregnant. The present conceptualization assumes that, in general, single women want to avoid pregnancy; thus, women who are more active sexually are more aware of the possibility of pregnancy and thus more likely to employ birth control.

Goldsmith et al. (1972) found that women who came to the clinic to obtain contraceptives did perceive a greater likelihood of getting pregnant, compared with women seeking abortions and maternity home residents.

Luker (1975), whose model will be discussed in more detail below, emphasizes the *subjective* probability assigned to getting pregnant. She makes the important point that most women view the likelihood of pregnancy as either zero or one. This subjective probability depends partly on their own, their friends', and their parents' experiences with pregnancy. Especially important is a woman's own experience; if she has been sexually active for a long time and has not gotten pregnant, she is likely to assign a low probability to that outcome. Also important is her perception of her partner's ability to impregnate her; if she believes he is sterile then she will perceive pregnancy as unlikely. Lindemann (1974) also identifies the experiences of a woman or her friends as an influence on the woman's awareness of pregnancy. DeLamater and MacCorquodale (1979) report some relevant findings. Young people who had been pregnant/gotten a woman pregnant, or who thought they had for at least one week, reported that the experience resulted in more consistent use of contraceptives or changing to a more effective method. However, there were no differences in the methods they reported using or in the consistency with which they used them.

Thus, there is some data concerning the role of perceived probability of pregnancy in contraceptive activity. These findings suggest that, as the perceived probability of pregnancy increases, a woman is more likely to use birth control.

Cognitive Assessment of Pregnancy.   As noted above, most of the extant literature on contraceptive behavior by single women assumes that they do not want to get pregnant. Thus, the explanatory focus in most work, including several chapters in the present volume, is on identifying barriers to the successful use of effective contraception. However, a recent analysis by Luker (1975) challenges this assumption, and argues that a woman should not be assumed to have a negative attitude toward getting pregnant.

To some extent, Luker's (1975) work is an extension of Lindemann's model. Several of the characteristics or variables identified by Lindemann as influences on awareness are discussed by Luker as factors influencing decisions. Thus, both discuss the influence of her sexual activity on a woman's perception of the need for contraceptives. Both consider the sexual partner's attitude toward birth control a significant influence in the woman's behavior. While Luker consistently portrays a woman as making a "decision" she recognizes that the decision may not be conscious, nor made systematically at a specific point in time. Instead, the decision may be diffuse in time and may not be consciously recognized as a decision.

Luker identifies three stages in the decision process. The first is the assessment of the "utilities" assigned to using birth control and to getting pregnant. The major benefit of contraception is obviously prevention of pregnancy. Against this positive utility she identifies a variety of "costs" of contraception. A major group of potential costs are social and cultural in character. These include the costs of acknowledging involvement in coitus (similar to Rains' discussion of overcoming moral ambivalence), of planning contraception, and of continuing contraception after a particular relationship ends. Such activity can produce guilt to the extent that it forces a woman to recognize her involvement in coitus when she does not accept it for herself. There are also "structural problems and prices"; these refer to the practical difficulties and economic cost of obtaining contraception from medical professionals and/or drugstores. A third category is comprised of "maintaining costs"; major factors here are partner's attitudes toward the woman's use of birth control, and the costs to a relationship of continuing use. Finally there are biological and medical costs, primarily side effects of particular methods/devices, and "iatrogenic effects," concern about the effects of birth control methods on one's fertility.

In addition to these potential costs of contraception, Luker identifies a variety of benefits of pregnancy which may influence the woman's decision. These include the value of pregnancy in affirming a woman's role and self worth, and in symbolizing or proving her fertility. Pregnancy may also have effects on the relationship which a woman perceives as desirable, including testing the male's commitment, creating the possibility of marriage, or "shoring up" a problematic marriage. Pregnancy may force significant others to pay (more) attention to her; it may have this effect on the male (husband, lover), or on parents or surrogate parents (such as an aunt or uncle with whom she is living). Finally, pregnancy may on infrequent occasions be a plea for help, a signal to others of psychological distress.

Luker argues that some or all of these costs and benefits are assessed, depending on a woman's situation or relationships, to arrive at the utilities of birth control use and of pregnancy. The result is a "cost-benefit 'set'" toward risk-taking. If this is unfavorable, e.g., the perceived costs of pregnancy are high relative to perceived benefits, the utility of contraception is high and the woman will use birth control. However, if this risk-taking "set" is favorable—if perceived costs of use are high, relative to perceived benefits and utility of pregnancy is moderate or high—the woman is predisposed to take risks, and not to use contraception.

According to Luker, the next phase of the decision is the subjective probability assigned to getting pregnant. Perceiving a low probability of pregnancy predisposes women to take risks. The third stage is assessing the likelihood of reversing pregnancy, i.e., the possibility of getting an abortion. Thus, nonuse is the result of a process of assessing, not necessarily consciously, various costs, benefits and probabilities.

Luker makes a persuasive case for incorporating a woman's assessment of the consequences of pregnancy in a model of contraceptive activity. Note that she hypothesizes that the cost/benefit assessment of pregnancy precedes the assessment of the subjective likelihood of pregnancy, whereas the order is reversed in the model proposed here. I believe that if a woman thinks she cannot conceive, she will not consider the possible effects of pregnancy; the latter are relevant only if she considers conception as a possible outcome of her sexual activity.

There is little data relevant to the importance of this assessment. Goldsmith et al. (1972) found that contraceptors were more likely to desire a college education and to plan to postpone marriage than pregnant women seeking abortions or maternity home residents. These researchers assume that women with high ambitions will perceive pregnancy as more costly and therefore utilize birth control. It is possible, of course, that women who get pregnant are thereby forced to lower their educational ambitions. Further evidence for the importance of educational and career plans was found in a study of abortion patients by the author; among 450 women receiving abortions, the desire to pursue an education or a career was spontaneously mentioned by 35% as a major reason for seeking the termination of pregnancy.

We need detailed and systematic research on the role of the perceived effects of getting pregnant on a woman's contraceptive activity.

Contraceptive Activity.   Contraceptive activity is assumed to have two components, the *decision* to use contraception, and the *choice* of a method of birth control.

The decision to use is hypothesized to be a result of the process outlined above. Coitally active women who perceive a significant probability of conception and who believe that on balance the effects of pregnancy would be negative should desire to use contraception.

The model proposed here recognizes that the process involved is a dynamic one. The decisions made by a woman can vary over time, depending upon changes in the various components specified in the model. The Rains and Reiss et al. formulations are essentially linear ones. They hypothesize positive relationships between the resolution of "moral ambivalence" and the development of an integrated sexual lifestyle respectively and contraceptive use. They imply that once a woman begins to use one of the most effective methods, she will continue to do so indefinitely.

The proposed model, like those presented by Lindemann (1974) and Luker (1975), explicitly recognizes that patterns of use may evidence either progression or retrogression over time. As we have seen, use is a result of a variety of factors. While "positive" changes (e.g., an increase in coital frequency) may produce increased frequency of use and/or a shift to more effective methods, "negative" changes (e.g., a decrease in the perceived probability of pregnancy) may produce a decrease in frequency of use and/or a shift to less effective methods. In order to test such models we need data concerning patterns of use over time, in relation to variables thought to influence use. Thus we need retrospective, sexual/contraceptive history data, and longitudinal designs.

Choice of method has been relatively neglected in much of the work on contraceptive use. Once we recognize that use does not automatically progress from least effective to the medically prescribed methods, and that women may change methods over time, we need to study explicitly the process of selecting a particular method.

One potential influence on choice is a woman's attitude about particular methods. Goldsmith et al. (1972) assessed a group of general attitudes toward birth control. They found that young women seeking contraceptives had more favorable attitudes toward them. They were more confident that contraceptives would prevent pregnancy, and less frequently agreed that birth control was unnatural, messy and that it took the enjoyment out of sex.

Lindemann (1974) and Luker (1975) stress the influence of knowledge of possible side effects of particular methods on use. Luker argues that a woman may consciously select a less effective method because she perceives it as safer. In addition to the information she possesses about side effects, her assessment of the likelihood that she personally will experience them may affect her choice. In view of the publicity concerning potential side effects in recent years, such influences may be the primary ones for many women.

Lindemann and Luker also include availability of particular devices as factors which may influence choice. Both Lindemann and Rains argue that at one stage, a woman will rely on partners or peers for devices and thus, given a decision to use contraception, will have only non-medically prescribed methods available. Lindemann and Luker suggest that an increase in access to devices via clinic outreach-type programs should produce increased use. Conversely, a reduction in availability may lead to reduced use or the use of less reliable methods rather than additional effort to obtain the device one has been using. Again, however, it is the perceived availability of particular methods which influences behavior; women must be aware of increases or decreases in access in order for these to effect their contraceptive activity.

Once a woman begins to use contraceptives, I believe that the major influence on choice is her own experience; this is represented on the right side of Figure 2.1.

What can we get from using a condom?

Nothing...
but pleasure and protection!

See your pharmacist for free information on family planning and venereal disease prevention.

Sponsored by
Pharmacists Planning Service Inc.
3000 Bridgeway Boulevard, Suite 202
Sausalito, California 94965
(415) 332-4066

For the clinic nearest you call your local Health Department.

FIG. 2.2. Attitudes and beliefs about different methods of contraception—What are the side effects? How easy is it to obtain?—are thought to determine choice of a particular method. This poster seeks to instate positive attitudes and beliefs about the use of condoms. (Reproduced courtesy of Pharmacists Planning Service, Inc., P.O. Box 1336, Sausalito, CA. 94965. Posters are available upon request. © Pharmacists Planning Services, Inc.).

If a woman experiences unpleasant physical or psychological phenomena which she believes are due to her use of a method, she is likely to reassess her choice. Similarly, if she becomes pregnant she is likely to switch methods. As indicated in Figure 2.1 such "negative" experiences are expected to lead to either a new decision/choice of methods or to nonuse. Nonuse in turn may effect frequency of intercourse.

Conversely, a woman's experience may be positive. She may not perceive any undesirable effects as associated with the method, nor become pregnant. This should lead to continued use, as long as other components do not change, i.e. as long as the relationship, frequency of coitus, perceived probability of pregnancy, and assessment of pregnancy remain the same.

These "feedback loops" are an important component of the proposed model. They give it its dynamic character, and differentiate it from the "linear" models proposed by Rains and Reiss et al.

Other Variables.   Lindemann (1974) argues that duration, the period of time over which coitus occurs, should effect use; she hypothesizes that increased length of involvement in coital activity should lead to an increase in the perceived likelihood of pregnancy and therefore stimulate use. On the other hand, Luker (1975) argues that the longer the woman engages in unprotected intercourse without getting pregnant, the less likely she will be concerned with pregnancy and the less likely she will use birth control. Duration is not explicitly included in the present model; its effect appears to be on perceived probability of pregnancy and may vary from woman to woman.

There are two variables which are not related to use according to prior studies and thus are not included in the model. Although Reiss et al. (1975) predicted that religious activity would be related to contraceptive activity, both their results (using percent "inactive" as their measure) and those reported by DeLamater and MacCorquodale (1978) (using frequency of attendance at services as the measure) failed to confirm the hypothesis. More problematic is the role of knowledge about birth control devices. Lindemann (1974) argues that knowledge is a prerequisite to use, and her model asserts a progression in quality and sources of information. Luker (1975) argues that knowledge is not a variable, that all or almost all women possess the basic information. Both Reiss et al. (1975) and DeLamater and MacCorquodale (1978) did not find a relationship between their measures of sources and timing of knowledge and use.

DISCUSSION

It was stated at the outset that the use of contraception by sexually active single women needs to be the focus of more empirical research. Some information is available from studies of premarital sexuality (e.g., Sorensen, 1972; DeLamater and MacCorquodale, 1979), but the utility of such data is limited because these studies were addressed to sexual attitudes and behavior, not the use of birth control.

Zelnik and Kantner (1973, 1977) have collected and published the most extensive data about the contraceptive activity of 15 through 19-year-old single women. Their research thus makes a major contribution; at the same time, their published work has been primarily descriptive. There have been four previous works which present conceptualizations (Rains, 1971; Lindemann, 1974; Reiss et al., 1975; Luker, 1975), of varying degrees of specificity, of premarital contraception. All are based on empirical studies of limited, nonrandom populations. Only one (Reiss et al., 1975) reports quantitative data. All rely on samples of women attending birth control or counseling clinics; such samples do not provide data on those women in comparable situations who choose not to go to a clinic.

The model presented here is much more explicit in specifying basic variables than the previous conceptualizations. It includes more precise statements about the links between these variables. Also, as noted earlier, the present conceptualization assumes that contraceptive use involves a dynamic process rather than a unidimensional progression from nonuse to the use of the most effective, medically prescribed techniques. Finally, this model combines the emphasis of the Luker (1975) and Reiss et al. (1975) models on cognitive variables with the emphasis of Lindemann (1974) and Rains (1971) on heterosexual relationships and coital frequency as determinants of contraceptive behavior.

The paucity of research in this area perhaps reflects, in part, the lack of an explicit model on which to base hypotheses, the selection of instruments, subject samples, etc. To that extent, the present model will hopefully stimulate greater empirical activity. This lack of data is especially striking in view of the need for information about the antecedents of contraception in order to formulate public policy. In particular, given the continuing controversy over the availability of and funding for abortions, it is imperative that we identify the antecedents of contraceptive activity by single women (and men). Such information is basic to the designing of effective programs to reduce premarital conception.

REFERENCES

Center for Disease Control, *Abortion Surveilance, 1973*. Atlanta: 1975.

DeLamater, J., & MacCorquodale, P. Premarital Contraceptive Use: A Test of Two Models. *Journal of Marriage and the Family, 40*, May 1978, 235–247.

DeLamater, J., & MacCorquodale, P. *Premarital sexuality: Attitudes, relationships, behavior*. Madison: The University of Wisconsin Press, 1979.

Goldsmith, S., Gabrielson, M., Gabrielson, I., Mathews, V., & Potts, L. Teenagers, Sex and Contraception. *Family Planning Perspectives, 4*, January 1972, 32–38.

Lindemann, C. *Birth control and unmarried young women*. New York: Springer, 1974.

Luker, K. *Taking chances: Abortion and the decision not to contracept.* Berkeley: University of California Press, 1975.

Morris, L., Conn, J., Stroh, G., & Gesche, M. Sexual Experience, Contraceptive Usage, and Source of Contraception for Never-Married Women: Albany (NY) Health Region. *Proceedings of the American Statistical Association,* 1976, 627–632.

NCHS, Advance Report-Final Natality Statistics, 1974. *Monthly Vital Statistics Report, 24,* (11), Supplement 2, February 13, 1976.

Rains, P. *Becoming an unwed mother.* Chicago: Aldine, 1971.

Reiss, I., Banwart, A., & Foreman, H. Premarital Contraceptive Usage: A Study and some Theoretical Explorations. *Journal of Marriage and the Family, 37,* August 1975, 619–630.

Sorensen, R. *Adolescent sexuality in contemporary America.* New York: World Publishing, 1972.

Thompson, L., & Spanier, G. Influence of Parents, Peers and Partners on the Contraceptive Use of College Men and Women. *Journal of Marriage and the Family, 40,* August 1978, 481–492.

Zelnik, M., & Kantner, J. Sexuality, Contraception and Pregnancy Among Young Unwed Females in the United States. In C. Westoff and R. Parke, Jr. (Eds.), *Demographic and Social Aspects of Population Growth,* (Vol. 1), Washington, D.C.: U.S. Government Printing Office, 1973.

Zelnik, M., & Kantner, J. Sexual and Contraceptive Experience of Young Unmarried Women in the United States, 1976 and 1971. *Family Planning Perspectives, 9,* March/April 1977, 55–71.

3 Implications of the Sexual System

Paul R. Abramson
University of California at Los Angeles

Editors' Note

According to Paul Abramson, adolescents' sexual behavior is governed by hypothetical "cognitive structures" or sets of principles concerning sexuality. Cognitive structures are, on the one hand, the products of past experience (i.e., parental standards, social norms, maturational processes, and one's own sexual experience), and on the other hand, they regulate our future sexual behavior. In Chapter 3, Abramson proposes that many adolescents develop cognitive structures which—reflecting society's own values—are fundamentally ambivalent about sexuality. For these teens, sex becomes a covert activity, and by extension, birth control is also viewed as illegitimate, resulting in teens' failure to use contraception effectively. Moving from the level of theory to the level of the individual teenager, Abramson illustrates this reasoning in the analysis of a case study of contraceptive neglect.

I am sure that every reader knows that there are eye boggling statistics for unwanted teenage pregnancies. In fact, many of those statistics are presented elsewhere in this book. There is also a growing debate as to whether teenage pregnancy is of "epidemic" proportions (Culliton, 1978; Klerman & Jekel, 1978). However, I am going to sidestep all of these figures in order to talk about one person—a teenager with an unwanted pregnancy. I believe that this particular case will provide considerable insight into the process of contraceptive neglect.

The whole issue of contraceptive neglect is obviously independent of the availability of contraceptives. For instance, several authors (Allen, 1968; Finch & Green, 1963; Hines, 1936; Tietze, 1965) have already described the chimeral devices of yesteryear even as far back as ancient China, which by the way

49

include having the woman lie completely still, using vaginal suppositories made of exotic and unmentionable substances, using a hollowed out lemon as a diaphragm to cover the cervix, and so on, suggesting that contraception has had a long, albiet unusual, history. Although modern technology has endeavored to create more efficient and reliable means of contraception, their acceptance seems less related to technological advances or availability than it does to social values. As an example, Reed (1978) points out that reliable contraceptives (i.e. condoms) existed even in the 19th century, but their approval was withheld until they were conceived as a solution to overpopulation. That is, the development of the pill and the intrauterine device were in response to cultural changes during the 1930s when birth control was represented as a means of insuring the monogamous family, as well as limiting the potential for overpopulation. Were contraception to have been presented as an adjunct to "sexual" relations, "the pill would have been dismissed as a dangerous interference with natural processes; the IUD would have been banned as an abortifacient" (Reed, 1978, p. 376).

Although birth control may now be considered a legitimate and necessary aspect of human sexuality, its legitimacy has yet to be established for adolescent use. This latter finding is in some respects analogous to the status of birth control prior to the 1930s. That is, reliable contraceptives are once again readily available, but no defendable rationale exists for their acceptance. In fact, the most obvious and critical reason, that of controlling teenage pregnancy and venereal disease, is excluded because it is assumed to sanction teenage sexuality. Unfortunately this perspective, which ties contraceptive use with public endorsement of sex for teenagers, produces "casualties" in the form of teenage girls with unwanted pregnancies. And before I introduce you to one such case, I want to briefly remark about the value of theory for understanding the psychology of unwanted teenage pregnancies.

There are many important reasons for presenting statistics about unwanted teenage pregnancies. These statistics portray both the extent of the problem and the consequences of this situation. In fact, the availability of such statistics may help to provide a defendable rationale for supporting contraceptive use among adolescents. Yet, in the absence of theory, these statistics only document the problem without providing the means for understanding the process or suggesting solutions. That is, through theory, we derive both order and meaning out of data. And while other chapters in this book will apply theory to these national statistics, the present chapter will utilize theory to convey the significance of one particular case study. In this way, the story of one individual can be extrapolated to a problem confronting many adolescents and their parents.

Although there are several theories (Byrne, 1977; Freud, 1938; Gagnon & Simon, 1973) which are capable of deriving meaning out of this particular case study, it will be interpreted in terms of a theory known as the "sexual system" (Abramson, 1983a). Since this is a relatively new theory, it will be introduced prior to the case material so as to enable the reader to follow the logic of interpretation. This particular theory has been chosen for this purpose because first, I am intimately familiar with it, and second, because it focuses upon standards of "acceptable" sexual conduct, a concern which is also central to the use and misuse of contraceptive agents.

THE SEXUAL SYSTEM

This theory starts with an assumption that all decisions regarding sexual expression are controlled by a hypothetical mechanism referred to as a *cognitive structure*. A cognitive structure does not really exist, it is merely a metaphor used to describe what is perhaps a reservoir of feelings and experience. For instance, our standards for the acceptability of contraceptive use depends upon our individual experiences, although our present behavior may not reflect every single one of those specific happenings. That is, we may forget the occasions we learned about contraception, but each experience has left behind a residue. And it is these "residues" which are organized in a "cognitive structure" which now has regulating and controlling functions (Neisser, 1967).

The *Sexual System* proposes that this cognitive structure is the overseer of all sexual behavior. It has developed as a result of four classes of input: *parental standards; social norms; maturation;* and *previous sexual experience*. Since residues from these inputs exist in the cognitive structure, these residues are in turn organized into a small set of principles, or codes of conduct, which determine how sexual stimuli are perceived and remembered. As an example, let us say that for the first five years of her life, Ms. Y was informed, in one way or another, that sex is reprehensible. However, now that she is 19, there is no reason to suspect that she remembers the occasions whereby she learned that sex deserves censure. Instead, the present theory proposes that a principle exists, in her cognitive structure, which says (sternly pointing its index finger) "SEX IS REPREHENSIBLE AND SHOULD BE INHIBITED", and as such, all of her present experiences which are relevant to sex are perceived, remembered, avoided, or defended against in terms of that principle. These principles, by the way, are manifested in everyday life as attitudes, beliefs, expectancies, and needs related to sexual expression.

Inputs

As I mentioned above, the inputs (parental standards, social norms, maturation, and previous sexual experience) determine how the cognitive structure will develop. First, there are "parental standards", since it is obvious that much of what kids learn, or fail to learn about sex is a direct consequence of their parents. This includes each time that parents scold, chastise, praise, or ignore the child when she or he does something sexual; all of the talks about the birds and the bees, the vaginas and penises, or the seed and the pod; all of the talks about "saving oneself for marriage", "it will grow hair on the palms of your hands", or "if you are going to dance, you are going to have to pay the fiddler"; and so on. In essence, each of these parental values can become internalized and the residues will form principles in the cognitive structure.

Since most kids do not live in parent-created vacuums, they also tend to learn about sex in other ways, the most likely alternative being "social norms". Social norms include peers, religious groups, cultural and community organizations, the media and so on—each of which has the potential of presenting standards which could be incorporated into the cognitive structure. For instance, there are many adolescents whose sexual behavior is guided by peer-induced values, which of course can be inconsistent with their parents' edicts. As is often the case, peer acceptance is a powerful determinant of how an adolescent is going to act.

Other important social norm influences include an especially significant film, magazine, book, or T.V. show which prohibits a sexual activity; or a cultural norm which sets minimum or maximum standards for a particular sexual behavior. In the last case, there are often varying standards, depending upon where you live, where you work, your religious affiliation, and so on.

The remaining two classes of input are *maturation* and *previous sexual experience*. *Maturation* encompasses all of the processes of growing up (physiological, intellectual, personality, etc.), which in turn, create significant transitions in childhood and adolescent development. That is, the changes which occur when you get older (i.e. the transition from virginity to nonvirginity) will often affect sexual standards within the cognitive structure. And last, is *previous sexual experience* which is the "testing ground" for the principles within the cognitive structure, given that once you engage in sexual behavior, you can examine how you feel after it has occured. Where the consequences are consistent with expectations, the principle in the cognitive structure is strengthened. Where the consequences are inconsistent with expectations, conflict emerges, or the principle changes.

Let me give you an example of the effect of *previous sexual experience* on the cognitive structure. You are now 16 years old, madly in love, determined to be perceived as an adult, and striving for your independence (and perhaps, concerned over an acne flare-up which resulted from the 4 previous characteristics). You are also dying to make love, and receiving considerable support (or pressure) from your mate to initiate this activity. But—in your head (i.e. cognitive structure) you keep hearing a voice which says "sexual intercourse is appropriate *only* for married couples" (i.e. a principle). However, despite this concern, you obtain the necessary contraceptives and have safe and satisfying sex. In fact, the sex was so good you wonder why you never did it before, because you are certainly going to do it again. Now, what happens to the principle? It changes because you have obviously learned (through a *previous sexual experience*) that there are no dire consequences to having intercourse before marriage, and in fact, you are receiving a lot of peer support for your "nonvirgin" status. However, had you not used contraceptives, had you been sexual with someone you did not care for, had sex been traumatic, then conflict would have resulted, and the principle would have remained the same. The implication of being that when you confront your principles, allow for your behavior to be as satisfying and productive as possible, because if it is not well thought out, or planned for, you will merely strengthen what you have striven to overcome.

Besides determining whether we are going to be sexual or not, the principles within the cognitive structure also influence how we *perceive* sexual stimuli. That is, if sexual stimuli falls within an "acceptable" principle, then we will be aroused by it. When it is unacceptable, we will either avoid the situation, or perhaps, experience a negative emotional reaction. For instance, one can usually predict what someone's response to a pornorgaphic movie is by merely asking them whether it is acceptable to be sexually aroused to such a movie. If this is an acceptable principle, then the sexual stimuli (i.e. the movie) will be perceived as exciting. If it is not acceptable, then the sexual stimuli will be perceived as disgusting or embarrassing. Let me also mention that this is not necessarily a conscious process, since there are certain types of sexual stimuli which are internal (like hormones) and cannot be observed. Furthermore, there are situations where a fraction of a second intervenes between recognizing sexual stimuli, and monitoring them by the principles within the cognitive structure.

Sexual Stimuli

In addition to creating classes of inputs, I have also grouped classes of sexual stimuli. These include: *endocrinological, physiological, conditioned and unconditioned,* and *situational* stimuli. *Endocrinological* stimuli would be influences due to hormones; *physiological* stimuli would be influences due to the central and autonomic nervous system; *conditioned and unconditioned* stimuli would consist of all of the stimuli which the person associates as erotic (sexual movies and stories, lovers, genital stimulation, clothing, etc.); and *situational* stimuli would be influences due to external or environmental variables (drugs, alcohol, socially permissive environments, etc.).

Figure 3.1 is a schematic representation of the *Sexual System* and can be interpreted as follows: the *inputs* create the cognitive structure by leaving residues of their occurrence. The residues in turn become organized into principles of acceptable sexual conduct. Once this cognitive structure is established, it regulates and controls sexual behavior because it monitors *all* sexual stimuli. That is, any sexual stimulus which could initiate sexual behavior first gets processed by the cognitive structure. When the sexual stimuli (resulting from one of four classes) is categorized as acceptable, a sexual behavior or fantasy will be exhibited. When categorization of sexual stimuli is unacceptable, its effect will

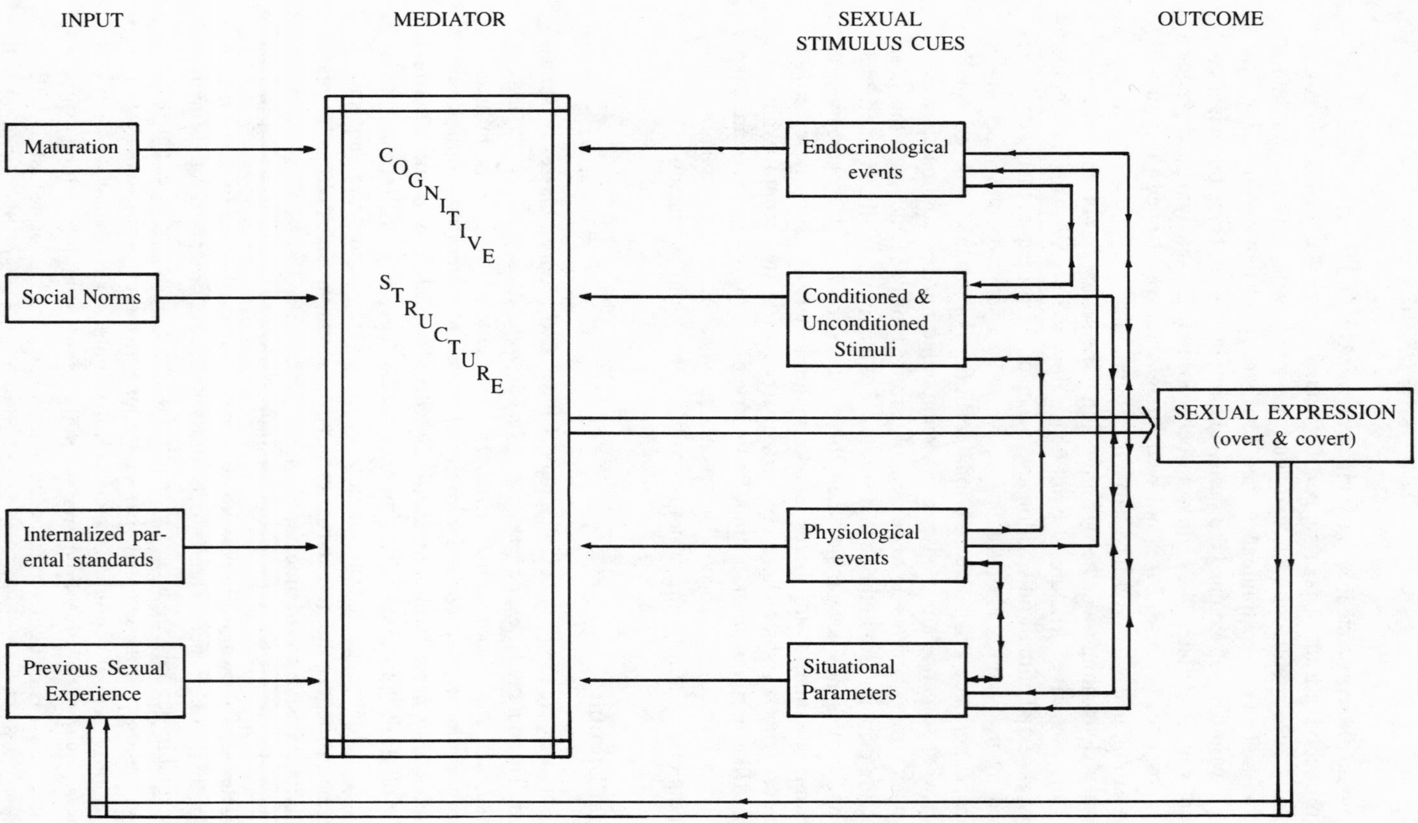

FIG. 3.1.* The Sexual System
*From Abramson, 1983a.

54

either be denied or repressed, or experienced as adversive (disgust, shame, etc.). However, once a sexual behavior is expressed it gets re-entered into the system, through a feedback loop known as previous sexual experience.

Before closing this introduction to the *Sexual System* (1983a), there are several additional points I would like to make. The first is that because learning about sexuality begins during infancy and early childhood, principles are also developing at that time. While there may be nothing earthshattering about this statement, its implications have considerable relevance for child development. That is, the hypothesis suggests that the *foundation* of all sexual knowledge is being established at a time when the child has very limited intellectual skills, yet this training will ultimately be utilized in *all* subsequent sexual interactions. As such, I think it will be helpful if we also consider the *quality* of sexual training at the point where the cognitive structure is being created.

First, there is very little research on the relationship between parental training and the sexual behavior of the child. While this in and of itself is disconcerting, the reluctance of the scientific community to engage in research of this nature has several additional consequences. First, if professionals do not have valid information about sexual training for children, then the same is likely to be true of parents. Certainly the studies presented in this text provide sufficient evidence to suggest that parents know very little about sexual training. Also, parents may perceive the lack of commitment to research on childhood sexuality as a sign that sexual training for a child is an inconsequential matter. Clearly, the near void of literature on this topic, especially in child care manuals, is testimony to its limited consideration. And given the influence child care manuals have on children rearing in this country, it seems reasonable to assume that parents do not really know what constitutes sufficient training for a child in the area of sexual behavior and feelings.

Of course it is not easy to provide sexual training for a child, given society's torment about sex. Parents do not want to do something that will contribute to "promiscuity," "homosexuality," or "sexual deviance" in their children. Consequently, they often do nothing, which unfortunately provides little discussion or labels for sexual feelings, functions, and organs. And when children do not have labels they tend to have an inadequate understanding of their sexuality, since labelling and discussion facilitate learning (Sears, Rau, & Alpert, 1965). Yet, sexual training cannot be considered independent of the social climate for sexual expression. Actually, if we were forced to trace sexual dysfunctions and misunderstandings to one condition, a strong candidate would be the ambivalence and uncertainty about sexual expression which is so pervasive in this culture. That is, this ambivalence creates parents who are uptight about sex, and who in turn, convey this to their children. Moreover, it is also this situation which has turned sex into an excessively complex social encounter, which again makes sexuality a difficult topic to teach a child.

Admittedly, I have been brief in the discussion of this theory. I have also introduced terms which were unfamiliar, and perhaps required re-reading to remember. However I think that it will become clearer as you see the theory applied to a case of contraceptive neglect.

THE CASE OF BETSY M.: CONTRACEPTIVE NEGLECT AND THE SIN OF PREMEDITATION

To me, the crux of the whole matter of adolescents, sex, and contraception evolves around society's ambivalence about approving contraceptive devices to control teenage pregnancy because it may legitamize sex among teenagers. That is, although society may consider unwanted pregnancies to be a tragic and problematic concern, many parents believe that the alternative, that of permitting safe and satisfying sex for teenagers, is an equally appalling consequence. Unfortunately, teenagers are not accorded the dignity of claiming sex as a necessary requirement of their relationships, as was the case with married couples during the 1930s, which incidently led to the acceptance of birth control pills. Instead, they are forced to either inhibit their sexual expression (which is becoming less and less likely), to seek their own contraceptive training and devices, or to have sex without contraceptives. The following case material will describe the dilemma confronting one adolescent (Betsy M.) and her excruciating trauma associated with her contraceptive neglect. After presenting her dialogue, I will then interpret her behavior in terms of the *Sexual System*.

"As I mentioned before I had a very strong Catholic upbringing, so that it wasn't until I was 14 that I learned about dating standards. Actually, after the experience with my first boyfriend I became pretty much of a prude, in that I wouldn't French kiss or pet with anyone. I remember this caused a lot of struggles with the boy I dated next. You know, it would be your typical struggling scene, with the guy wanting to feel me and my moving his hands away, saying no, and so on.

Sometimes I remember that when a date and I would hold or lie down in the car, which by the way I liked because of the feeling of closeness, we would get into verbal hassles about this. They would start coming out with their stories with why I should let them touch me and sometimes it turned out O.K., while other times not. Some boys would call me a "prickteaser", while others would have respect for me saying "Hey, you're a really neat girl." I also remember that a lot of the times I would talk about religion with these boys.

The next significant thing in my dating was when I was 16 and going steady with *John* who, by the way, was my first "sexual experience." *John* lived in the same apartment building that I did and when we started dating we went together for three months. However we then broke up when I had to go back, for a short time, to New York. When I returned home I began dating him again, this time going steady and seeing each other all of the time. And it was 6 or 7 months after this, with seeing each other very much, that we started having sex. You see, we were with each other a great deal, totally unsupervised, since both of our parents were divorced, working, and dating. What started out as just kissing, then turned into petting, then petting under clothes, and finally, getting to the point where we were in his bedroom, during the day, petting on his bed, that we started having intercourse, although he didn't have an orgasm. I remember him putting it into me but I don't remember him moving back and forth, and it was just an insertion. And we did that for a couple of minutes but I don't recall touching him. This experience was a "first" for both of us.

After having sex with *John* I would always go to confession. It was getting to a point where I was having a lot of guilt feelings and I would have to confess having intercourse in order to go to communion on Sunday. This kind of confusion brought us to points where we would break up, but since we couldn't stand it, we would get back together again.

My feelings about that first sexual experience were "Well, now I've done it." Of course, I also experienced a lot of guilt. Even though we had sex after this, I still didn't really know what I was doing. I guess the best way to describe it all was that I had very mixed feelings: that it was wrong and I should feel guilty, and have to go confess this; but it felt good. You know, at that time, I didn't even think I could become pregnant. I guess *John* was in the same place since he never used rubbers or anything, however, he would withdraw.

Each time after *John* and I had intercourse, we would talk about it. And each time we would vow not to do it again. As such, we would go for a week with only petting, but then we would resume having intercourse. You know, I enjoyed sex very, very much with *John*. He had a large penis but intercourse was never painful. In fact, I was always very well lubricated. Yet, there were other complications. You see, we never got together to have intercourse, that is, we could never plan it. I guess this is what I needed to do because of my religious beliefs. So naturally, we never had any birth control at our disposal because that would mean planning or premeditation. It would just have to happen, that is, it would have to get to a point where we were so totally out of control that we couldn't turn back. Actually, we were usually so hot and turned on that we couldn't stand it." (Abramson, 1983b)

What you have just read is only the scenario of Betsy's story, what follows is the tragic epilogue. Fortunately, most instances are not this extreme.

"Having this abortion was a very, very traumatic experience. I had to go with *John* in a car one night to meet this young girl on a designated street, in the east part of Los Angeles, near Watts. We had to follow this girl, in her car, to an empty apartment where she made a phone call. From this apartment this girl took me (alone) to the house where the abortion was to be performed.

I got into the car with her and she started driving toward this house. I really didn't know where I was and can't recall whether I was blindfolded or not, but it was night and very dark. Well, when we got to the house I could see that it was very old and decrepit, and in an all black neighborhood. As I walked into this shanty looking place we were greeted by a large black man who was sitting on the couch watching T.V. and drinking beer. The woman who was to perform the abortion then walked out of the kitchen. She was supposed to be a registered nurse, although I am still not sure about this.

Anyway, this woman and my driver took me into the bedroom. I was not at all comfortable being in a strange room, with two strangers, and a man just outside the door. I remember I was struck thinking—there is this guy watching T.V. while *I'm* getting an *abortion*.

This "nurse" then asked me to remove my clothes and I remember feeling embarrassed—and thinking to myself "my God, I'm embarrassed to take my clothes off, yet I'm here to get an *abortion*—I mean, what am I doing here?" The whole thing was just unreal to me, it was like it wasn't me doing this, it was someone else.

The nurse then spread newspaper on the bed, which I laid on, and then I had my abortion. This night was basically 8 weeks from conception, 8 weeks I really wanted to forget. The abortion itself, using a tube with a needle on the end of it to break the water bag, was very painful. I recall getting cramps right as the water came out and right then and there, I began having contractions. All of this was awful, but that was it. This nurse then stuffed me with gauze and told me to get up and get dressed.

Coming back, I remember I was shaking, and then when I was being driven home, I was crying and again I couldn't stop shaking. I knew I wasn't cold, but it felt like my whole body was in shock. After I got home the pain became so intolerable that I called the doctor who told me to contact him if there were any complications. The doctor came over and looked at me and I remember him telling my mother that I was in a state of shock. I don't know what kind of medication or shots he gave me, but he told me to leave all of the gauze inside of me for at least 24 hours.

Instead of getting better, I got worse. My temperature went down to 95, so the doctor came back and said I'd have to go the hospital right away. Apparently, the fetus did not come all the way out and they made me catch everything, after I took out the gauze, and put it in a jar in the refrigerator and bring it to the hospital.

Now, knowing how I was raised, and being as sheltered as I was, you can imagine what a total nightmare this was. This whole experience was like something you read in a book or saw in a movie which you couldn't believe could actually happen. It was just incredible, a total nightmare, being so disgusting and degrading, and I couldn't believe that I did this," (Abramson, 1983b).

What you have just read is obviously a very dramatic account of the consequences of contraceptive neglect. While the legalization of abortions has presumably precluded the reoccurence of such incidences, it has by no means removed the burden or trauma associated with the termination of a pregnancy.

As I indicated in the discussion on the *Sexual System,* if you want to understand sexual conduct, then you must reconstruct what a child (up to around 12 years of age) learned about sexuality since all subsequent sexual training and experience becomes evaluated in terms of principles deduced from this input. As such, I will first describe Betsy's "principles" and then relate them to the experiences which she just related.

Betsy is one of eight people whose entire lives are presented in a book of mine entitled *Sexual Lives* (Abramson, 1983b). Since I have had the opportunity to obtain a complete record of her experiences and beliefs, I am now able to hypothesize about Betsy's sexual training. First, before Betsy was 10 years of age, her parents did all that they could to convince her that there was no such thing as sex. That is, although she was aware that boys were different than girls, she was led to believe that genitals were only for eliminative functions. After the age of 10 however she had some exploratory sex play with other girls, which elicited mysterious and sensual feelings. Even though Betsy was aware that she should not be doing this, she never considered it sex. This was the case because her parents made her believe that sex is something that you do not think about since it is "bad" and hard to understand. In fact, when Betsy's girl friends told her about reproduction her parents denied that it was true.

By the time Betsy was 14 she had learned, through her sex play, that sexuality could be a positive, albeit ambiguous feeling. However, through religious, peer group, and parental pressure, Betsy also learned that sex must be concealed. As such sex then became an "externalized" object that was happening "out there", which in turn, meant that she could not think about it, although it did feel good. This confusing belief eventually become formalized into a principle which stated: "sex could not be planned, since that would imply thinking about." Therefore, when intercourse did occur, it was the result of an "out of control" experience. That is, Betsy was required (by her principle) to create situations where she would be so overwhelmed and caught up in feelings that her thinking was bypassed. Moreover, since she was "out of control" she was no longer liable for her actions. Unfortunately for Betsy, and other adolescents who follow the same course, the risk is unwanted pregnancies, which in Betsy's case, may have been her *punishment* for losing control.

Although the trauma associated with the illegal abortion tends to make this an extraordinary example, Betsy's sexual style is really not that unusual. In fact it results from the type of sexual training which is very prevalent in our society. That is, when parents provide either few or inappropriate labels for sexual feelings and functions, when parents avoid sincere and open discussions about sexuality, and when parents (or other adult models) appear uncomfortable about sexual matters, then children believe that sex is corrupt and unmentionable. As such, these children never integrate sexuality into their sense of identity, which in turn has the effect of making sex feel like it is "out there". Furthermore, when sex is externalized this way it tends to get relegated to a covert activity, which also means that there is less reason to legitimize it through the use of contraceptives. Moreover since sex is now covert, it engenders ambivalence about being sexual, and it is this ambivalence which creates indecisiveness about contraceptive devices.

It should be clear that most teenagers are not sabotaging themselves with pregnancy as a need to punish themselves for being sexual. Instead, the pregnancies are usually a consequence of inadequate sexual training. However, in the event that *all* children were to receive sufficient sexual educations, there would still be unwanted pregnancies. That is, to be an adolescent is to be impulsive, and to be impulsive is to take risks. Although impulsivity may contribute to growth and development, there are always going to be certain adolescents who will use the "risk" of avoiding contraceptives as excitement for their sexuality.

In concluding, I would like to offer several suggestions for minimizing the risk of unwanted adolescent pregnancies. First, parents must realize that their children have the right to be sexual. Although every reader of this book may not agree with my position, it is still the case that parents need to systematically train their children about sexuality and reproduction. This training should occur simultaneously with all other forms of education, using graduated levels of information for varying age groups. This particular type of training will yield teenagers who are conversant about sexual matters and experienced and comfortable with contraceptives. However, I am by no means implying that parents should avoid training children about love, intimacy, or ethical standards. Instead, I mean only to convey that sex education (whether at home or in school) must also be included since sexuality is an integral part of adolescence.

As far as the impulsivity issue is concerned, contraceptive neglect is less likely to occur if contraceptives are presented as a necessary aspect of hygiene. That is, rather than training children to conceive of contraceptives as "sexual devices", it is more effective to present contraceptives as a hygienic requirement. Given that mothers have little trouble convincing their daughters that precautions are necessary for menstruation, parents are also capable of conveying that contraceptives are required for sex.

REFERENCES

Abramson, P. R. *The sexual system: A theory of human sexual behavior*. New York: Academic Press, 1983, forthcoming. (a)

Abramson, P. R. *Sexual lives*. Under editorial review, 1983. (b)

Allen, C. The long history of birth control. *Sexology*, 1968, Dec., 276–278.

Byrne, D. Social psychology and the study of sexual behavior. *Personality and Social Psychology Bulletin*, 1977, *3*, 3–30.

Culliton, B. News and Comment. *Science*, 1978, *199*, 508.

Finch, G. E., & Green, H. *Contraception through the ages*. London: Peter Owen, 1963.

Freud, S. *The basic writings of Sigmund Freud*. New York: The Modern Library, 1938.

Gagnon, J. H., & Simon, W. *Sexual conduct: The social sources of human sexuality*. Chicago: Aldine, 1973.

Hines, N. E. *Medical history of contraception*. Baltimore: Williams & Wklkins, 1936.

Klerman, L. V., & Jekel, J. F. Teenage pregnancies. *Science*, 1978, *199*, 1390.

Neisser, U. *Cognitive psychology*. New York: Appleton-Century-Crofts, 1967.

Reed, J. *From private vice to public virtue: The birth control movement and American society since 1830.* New York: Basic Books, 1978.

Sears, R. R., Rau, L., & Alpert, R. *Identification and child rearing.* Stanford: Stanford University Press, 1965.

Tietze, C. History of contraceptive methods. *Journal of Sex Research,* 1965, *1,* 69–85.

EXAMINING THE DETERMINANTS OF ADOLESCENT CONTRACEPTIVE BEHAVIOR

In the first section of this book, three conceptual models were proposed to help explain why teens use—or fail to use—contraception. The present section follows up this theorizing with empirical research on some of the determinants of contraceptive behavior. We begin with an overview of the literature on factors that affect teens' use of contraception. A number of general hypotheses emerge from this review, and findings are reported from a large-scale study that tested these hypotheses. Next, we turn to more narrowly focused research on particular antecedents of adolescent contraception. Two chapters adopt a developmental perspective on this issue, and discuss the effects of limited maturity and early socialization experiences on teens' use of birth control. The last three papers in this section consider the roles of sex-related knowledge, beliefs, and emotions in the process of adolescent contraception.

4 Personality and Attitudinal Barriers to Contraception

Stuart Oskamp
Claremont Graduate School

Burton Mindick
Cornell University

Editors' Note

A good deal of research has examined personality and attitudinal factors that may affect teens' use of contraception. Unfortunately, these studies are scattered throughout the disciplinary journals, their results are often enough in conflict, and methodological problems consistently bedevil this line of research. In Chapter 4, Stuart Oskamp and Burton Mindick provide a very useful critical review of the literature that clarifies the research on personality and attitudinal determinants of contraceptive behavior. A general conclusion that emerges from this analysis is that a *longitudinal* approach is most suitable for studying the relationship of personal dispositions to contraceptive behavior. In this approach, an individual's characteristics are measured first and are correlated with contraceptive behaviors that occur later; in this fashion, we can come closer to teasing out cause and effect relations with respect to personality, attitudes, and teens' contraceptive behavior.

Based on their review of the literature, Oskamp and Mindick propose several hypotheses concerning the role of personality factors and attitudes as determinants of teenage use of birth control. Two large-scale longitudinal studies were conducted to evaluate these hypotheses, and the results of this research are reported and discussed in detail. It is especially noteworthy that these investigations followed the contraceptive successes and failures of several hundred teenage women across a long span of time—one and a half to three years—and sampled women from a variety of ethnic groups (black, Hispanic) and socioeconomic levels.

The unintended results of adolescent pregnancy—including illegitimacy, abortion, and ill-advised hasty marriages—comprise major social problems in modern society (Baldwin, 1976; Chilman, 1979). These problems could be drastically reduced if contraceptive programs for teenagers were more widespread and successful. Sexually active young women who never use contraception have about a 60% likelihood of getting pregnant, whereas those who use a method of contraception regularly run only about a 6% risk of pregnancy. Yet about 30% of sexually active adolescents don't use contraception at all, about 40% use it only irregularly, and more than 10% use it ineffectively (Zelnik & Kantner, 1978b). Thus, a very important question is: Why don't adolescents use birth control methods more often and more effectively?

We have been studying factors affecting the success or failure of young women's contraceptive programs for over 6 years. In this research we have typically used a longitudinal design, following each individual's behavior and experiences over a period of several years. Though we have studied demographic variables and information as factors in contraceptive success and failure, the bulk of our attention has been directed to personality, attitudinal, and interpersonal factors. In this chapter we will report our findings which relate specifically to adolescents. But first, let us briefly survey other research studies to gain an overview of previous findings in this area.

OVERVIEW OF PAST RESEARCH

The most representative empirical surveys of U.S. teenagers' sexual and contraceptive behavior have been carried out by Kantner and Zelnik (1972, 1973; Zelnik & Kantner, 1977, 1978a, 1978b). These investigators utilized interviews with national probability samples of thousands of 15 to 19-year-old women in 1971 and again in 1976. The data provide very complete information on the typical sexual, contraceptive, and reproductive experiences of American teenagers and on changes in their sexual and contraceptive behavior in the early 1970s. However, these data are analyzed mostly in terms of demographic factors (i.e., focusing on age, race, social class, etc.), and little information on personality or attitudinal factors is provided.

In studying personality and attitude variables, a longitudinal research design is highly desirable. In such a design, each individual's personal characteristics are measured initially, and then these variables are related to behavior and experiences which occur later on. This approach is especially useful when studying transitional periods in a person's life (such as the beginning of sexual activity) and when investigating criterion behaviors which require a long period of time for correct classification (such as successful versus unsuccessful contraception). A longitudinal design allows a much fuller and more accurate understanding of the factors which influence each individual's behavior. In particular, it can distinguish between pre-existing traits which may contribute to behavior, and later characteristics which may result from it (for instance, it can differentiate between pre-existing low self-esteem as a cause of unwanted pregnancy, and subsequent low self-esteem as its result). However, because of the time, expense, and difficulties involved in long-term follow-up of subjects, it is only very recently that longitudinal research on adolescent sexual and contraceptive behavior has begun. Some prominent examples of such longitudinal research include Vener and Stewart's (1974) study of a Michigan community, Jessor and Jessor's (1975) research on Colorado high school students, Miller's (1976) survey of California undergraduates, and our work with California contraceptive clinic patients (Oskamp, Mindick, Berger, & Motta, 1978).

Most other research on personality and attitudinal factors in contraception and sexual behavior has been concurrent or postdictive in nature. Typically, criterion groups are chosen on the basis of some behavior or outcome of interest (e.g., using contraception versus not using it), and the groups are then compared on other current characteristics. In this type of design, any study of past experiences or personal characteristics which led up to the present state of affairs must rely on *retrospective reports,* with their serious attendant dangers of forgetting, selective reporting, and distortion as time passes. And, as mentioned above, observed personality differences between groups (e.g., between pregnant and nonpregnant individuals) may be a *cause* of their current condition, or simply a *result* of it, and we cannot definitely establish which is the case.

Methodological Problems

In addition to the problems of retrospective reports and difficulties in inferring cause and effect, many studies on contraceptive and sexual behavior have suffered from numerous other methodological liabilities. These problems generally stem either from the *choice of samples* studied, or from the *measurement procedures* used to study them (see Mindick & Oskamp, 1979, for a fuller discussion). A common problem is the use of comparison groups which are nonequivalent in many respects to the main group under investigation (e.g., pregnant clinic patients versus nonpregnant college students). Some even less-adequate studies have used no comparison group at all. And a number of papers present case reports, which describe a very small number of individuals. Another frequently encountered difficulty is the use of impressionistic measurement, through unstructured clinical interviews or unvalidated ratings. This can present a particularly serious problem when investigators know the subjects' criterion classification but do not adopt double-blind procedures in rating other characteristics. For example, girls who are known to have had an unwanted pregnancy are apt to be judged negatively on many ratings, due to a spurious "halo effect."

Even where measurement is objective, it may still be inadequate in scope, depth, or precision, or it may use inappropriate items or scales. The timing of measurement can also create problems of reactivity, since many measures can influence or be influenced by accompanying events—a particularly clearcut example is measurement of anxiety while women are waiting for an abortion. Even careful measurement may be insufficient to obtain valid findings when the samples suffer from the previously mentioned problems of nonequivalence, or small size, or selection from a larger group on the basis of some unusual characteristic (for instance, having repeated abortions). Perhaps the worst aspect of methodological problems in sampling or measurement is that the results of inadequate studies have often been improperly used to make generalizations about groups or circumstances to which they do not apply—such as "all contraceptors" or "pregnant teenagers in general."

No single study can avoid all methodological problems, but numerous studies of fertility behavior have been marred unnecessarily by these and other shortcomings. Also, many studies have focused on women of various ages, so their results may or may not apply to adolescents. Keeping these possible limitations in mind, we will summarize some of the better-supported conclusions about personality and attitudinal factors affecting contraceptive success or failure.

PERSONALITY AND ATTITUDINAL FACTORS AFFECTING CONTRACEPTIVE BEHAVIOR

View of Self as Not Sexually Active

For many individuals, the earliest sexual experiences may occur without advance planning, impulsively, unexpectedly, or even contrary to their expectations and values. Also, on the average, unmarried teenagers are apt to have relatively long periods between one sexual encounter and the next (an average of about a month, according to data from Zelnik & Kantner, 1977). Therefore, it is quite possible for teenagers to view their first few sexual experiences as "accidents" or "slips" that won't happen again—at least not for awhile—and thus to view themselves as not *really* sexually active. Of course, taking such a view drastically lessens the likelihood of having and using contraceptive protection, and thus increases the chance of unwanted pregnancy when intercourse actually does occur. This is one example of the principle that transitions in behavioral stages are apt to be danger points in contraceptive practice (Miller, 1973a).

Research findings confirm that perception of oneself as being sexually active is an important precondition for effective use of birth control (Bardwick, 1973; Goldsmith, Gabrielson, Gabrielson, Matthews, & Potts, 1972; Miller, 1973a). However, there is more debate about the reasons for inaccurate sexual self-perception. Cvetkovich, Grote, Bjorseth, and Sarkissian (1975) ascribe it to normal adolescent immaturity, while Bardwick (1973) and Gerrard (1977) attribute it to excessive sex guilt which inhibits full self-awareness. Whatever the reasons, it is clear that adolescents' denial of being sexually active is a major barrier to their using contraception.

Low Socialization

A second factor which predicts ineffective contraception is low levels of socialization—that is, incomplete learning and/or acceptance of the norms of society. This general concept has been investigated by using scores on a socialization scale and also by studying related variables such as responsibility, stability, acceptance of traditional social values, and avoidance of deviance.

About two decades ago Gough (1960) and Vincent (1961) reported low socialization scores among girls who had illegitimate pregnancies. Gough (1973a, 1973b) has also concluded that socialization scores are related to the choice of particular birth control methods and to success in using contraceptives as well as to preference for certain birth control methods (e.g., women low in socialization preferred the IUD and/or pills).

Even in the "sexy seventies," various aspects of socialization have remained important predictors of fertility related behavior. Oskamp et al. (1978) found that higher socialization scale scores were significantly related to good contraception among family planning patients, and Miller (1976) reported similar findings for college students. Jessor and Jessor (1975) showed that adolescents who were making the transition from virginity to sexual activity had more of an anti-establishment value system than those who were still virgins, as well as a greater tolerance for deviance and more friends who served as models for deviance. Similarly, Vener and Stewart (1974) found that higher sexual activity among teenagers was related to greater use of alcohol and illicit drugs and to a higher number of delinquent acts. In addition to these predictive studies, Ball's (1973) concurrent study also showed a linkage between adolescents' socially acceptable sexual attitudes and their avoidance of pregnancy risks.

Poor Personal Efficacy

Another personality factor related to contraceptive behavior is personal efficacy. This general concept has been widely studied under several different names: competence (White, 1959), internal versus external locus of control (Rotter, 1966), self-efficacy (Bandura, 1977), and its opposite side, passivity or learned helplessness (Seligman, 1975). Efficacy can best be viewed as an individual's sense that they may cause or control events in their lives—an aspect of the broader concept of positive self-esteem—and these concepts have been widely viewed as conducive to better contraceptive practice.

Several studies of birth control outcome criteria have shown self-esteem or self-concept to be higher among effective contraceptors than among women who developed unwanted pregnancies or were at risk of doing so (Ball, 1973; Goldsmith et al., 1972; Mindick, 1978; Slavin, 1975). Measurement methods in these studies have included interviews, psychometric instruments, and observation of nonverbal behavior and speech characteristics.

Turning to more specific measures of personal efficacy, by far the most commonly used such instrument is Rotter's (1966) I-E Scale, measuring internal versus external locus-of-control. Several early studies of low SES subjects found that an external perceived locus-of-control and feelings of powerlessness were related to nonuse or inconsistent use of birth control, and to high fertility (Groat & Neal, 1967; Kar, 1971; Keller, Sims, Henry, & Crawford, 1970). Similarly, studies of sexually active unmarried female college students have shown that contraceptive users were significantly more internal than nonusers (Lundy, 1972; MacDonald, 1970). Yet several other studies with the Rotter I-E Scale have not yielded positive results (e.g., Brown, 1977; Gough, 1973a; Oskamp et al., 1978; Seeley, 1976).

However, it may be unreasonable to expect a global measure such as the Rotter I-E Scale to predict conceptually-related criteria under all conditions and circumstances; narrower, more situation-specific measures may often prove more useful (Rotter, 1975). Several studies have supported this view, showing relationships between effective contraception and more specific aspects of efficacy such as sexual assertiveness, heterosexual initiative, and lack of passivity, submissiveness, or dependency (Brown, 1977; Grunebaum & Abernethy, 1974; Miller, 1973b). In a male sample of urban blacks, Bauman and Udry (1972) found that irregular contraceptive use was associated with self-reported feelings of powerlessness. Similarly, two recent large-scale studies of women have shown that unwanted pregnancy is related to feelings of lack of competence and to general passivity (Oskamp et al., 1978; Slagle, Arnold, & Glascock, 1974). Thus, more specific measures of efficacy may show relationships to particular contraceptive behaviors even when more global measures do not do so.

Poor Cognitive Skills

Another personal characteristic which has been related to contraceptive behavior is the cognitive dimension. This can include cognitive coping style, information gathering and problem solving skills, general intelligence, and more specific measures of sexual and contraceptive knowledge.

Only a few studies have investigated general cognitive skills. Grunebaum and Abernethy (1974) suggested a relationship between problem-solving skills and contraceptive success in married couples, and Steinlauf (1977) reported a similar finding for her adolescent subjects.

A frequently studied aspect of cognitive style is the defense mechanism of denial, which involves avoidance of cognitive focus on one's problems. Several recent studies comparing effective and ineffective contraceptors have found more use of denial as a general response pattern among women with undesired pregnancies (Grunebaum & Abernethy, 1974; Miller, 1975; Rader, Bekker, Brown, & Richardt, 1978; Slavin, 1975).

This emphasis on differences in cognitive skills does not mean that ineffective contraceptors are necessarily less intelligent than other individuals, however. Though Udry (1978) reported an inverse relation between I.Q. and general fertility among urban American white women, this relationship may be mediated by level of education (i.e., brighter women tend to get more education, and their education may account for their lower levels of childbirths). More focused studies comparing successful and unsuccessful contraceptors have failed to find differences in intelligence (Brown, 1977; Oskamp et al., 1978).

The most frequently studied cognitive variables have been specific areas of contraception-relevant knowledge, which may be viewed as the outcome of effective cognitive learning. Furstenberg, Gordis, and Markowitz's (1969) study of pregnant unmarried teenagers concluded that limited knowledge was the most important factor in their failure to practice birth control. Though less extreme in their conclusions, most studies of knowledge have agreed that it is conducive to contraceptive success. Typical examples of this view are many of the KAP studies (focusing on birth control Knowledge, Attitudes, and Practices) done in foreign countries, which have been reviewed by Cernada and Crawford (1973).

The best approach in this area is to use carefully developed scales of sexual and/or contraceptive knowledge rather than subjective interview assessment or sketchy self-reports of knowledge. Three studies which used versions of the same knowledge scale all demonstrated significant differences between successful and unsuccessful contraceptors in the predicted direction (Goldsmith et al., 1972; Hagelis, 1973; Oskamp et al., 1978). Using a similar test of knowledge, Gough (1973a) found that users of coitus-independent types of contraception (pills or IUD) or of surgical types (vasectomy or tubal ligation) had significantly more knowledge than did users of the less-trustworthy coitus-inhibiting methods (rhythm, abstinence, or withdrawal). In an experimental study of a college health education class, Shipley (1974) found that, following the class, birth control knowledge was significantly related to contraceptive effectiveness.

A particularly crucial area of contraceptive information is correct knowledge of the most fertile time in the menstrual cycle as opposed to the "safe period," and several authors have shown abortion seekers to be typically more misinformed than other women about this topic (e.g., Adler, 1974; Miller, 1975).

Some researchers have questioned the link between contraceptive knowledge and practice (e.g., Kane & Lachenbruch, 1973; Lehfeldt, 1971; Luker, 1975). However, this view is much in the minority, and all three of these studies suffer from serious methodological problems, such as highly atypical samples, lack of comparison groups, and/or extremely limited and subjective measures of knowledge (Mindick & Oskamp, 1979).

Nevertheless, it is well to keep in mind that knowledge alone is not sufficient to ensure good contraceptive practice. Fujita, Wagner, and Pion (1971) have described a large group of college students who had good knowledge of sex and birth control, yet frequently used poor contraceptive methods such as withdrawal and rhythm. Byrne (1977) has noted that cognitive processes are closely inter-twined with less rational feelings and emotions in human sexuality. In a similar vein, Cobliner, Schulman, and Smith (1975) have described some of their sample of repeat aborters as having "knowledge without belief"—e.g., they disregarded the clinic information because their friends told them differently—and others as having "belief without knowledge"—they came to believe that they couldn't get pregnant. These descriptions are vivid examples of the mechanism of denial.

In summary, it seems that using birth control knowledgeably requires a fair degree of cognitive-emotional maturity (that is, a clear understanding of oneself), rather than a high level of intellectual ability.

Low Planfulness

A particularly important characteristic in contraception is planfulness. Also conceptualized as future orientation, or as impulse control, its importance to human adaptive functioning has been stressed by such theorists as Lewin (1946) and Freud (1953). Later, Craik (1964) suggested that a limited future time perspective should be associated with a lack of socialization, and thus it should be linked to ineffective contraceptive practice.

Many empirical findings confirm the relationship between planfulness and contraceptive success, as shown in a review of early research by Fawcett and Bornstein (1973) and in several subsequent studies. Drucker (1975) showed that nonusers of birth control had a need to see sex as being unplanned, while Noble (1972) found that aborters were more impulsive in sexual activities than successful contraceptors. Rovinsky (1972) demonstrated lower impulse control in a group of repeat aborters than among first-time aborters, and Cobliner et al. (1975) described repeat aborters as lacking in frustration tolerance and ignoring the foreseeable future effects of their behavior. Spain (1977) found successful adolescent contraceptors to have better future planning ability than unsuccessful ones, while Kar (1971) reported a greater future orientation among low SES families who started using birth control *before* rather than after their first pregnancy.

A number of different scales of planfulness have been developed and used in research. Keller et al. (1970), in a study of black, lower class women, found contraception users higher than nonusers on a scale of planfulness and lower than nonusers on a scale of impulsivity. Miller (1973b) developed the Personal Style Inventory (PSI), having six scales theoretically and empirically related to fertility behavior, and collected validation data from college undergraduates. In our own research, we have proposed a scale of future time perspective as a measure of planfulness (Mindick, Oskamp, & Berger, 1977) and used it successfully in predicting unwanted pregnancy versus effective contraception in later studies (Mindick, 1978; Oskamp et al., 1978).

Neuroticism, Anxiety, and Poor Social Adjustment

Another set of personality characteristics often mentioned as reasons for contraceptive failure are the related characteristics of neuroticism, anxiety, sex guilt, and poor adjustment. Many different measurement methods have been used in this area, and consequently the research findings are often confusing.

Many studies have linked neuroticism and/or anxiety with ineffective contraception, but unfortunately, most of this research is retrospective in nature, with personality assessment after pregnancy is ascertained, or at the time of abortion, or some time after abortion (e.g., Kane & Lachenbruch, 1973; Lehfeldt, 1971). Consequently, it is impossible to know whether any neuroticism or anxiety which may be found is a stable personality trait or simply a situational response to the unwanted pregnancy or abortion. In one of the few studies where measurements were made prior to pregnancy, Brooks and Butcalis (1976) showed that inconsistent pill users were significantly more anxious than consistent pill users; however, the two groups did not differ on several other related dimensions nor on the total neuroticism score of Cattell's Neuroticism Scale Questionnaire. In a study which was truly predictive in nature, some intake ratings of poor adjustment, but not all of them, proved significantly related to later unwanted pregnancy (Oskamp et al., 1978).

Quite a number of studies have investigated the narrower concept of sex guilt, but again most of them have been retrospective, with measurement after a pregnancy or abortion has occurred. In addition, many investigators have used subjective assessment through interviews or projective questions, though several studies have used psychometric scales such as the Mosher Sex Guilt Inventory (e.g., Gerrard, 1977; Schwartz, 1973). Within the limits imposed by these methods, the general findings have been that poor contraceptors are higher in sex guilt than good contraceptors (Brown, 1977; Cobliner, Schulman, & Romney, 1973; Grunebaum & Abernethy, 1974; Lehfeldt, 1971; Rader et al., 1978; Spain, 1977). Gerrard (1977) found that this relationship held for users of each major type of contraception; and in an experimental study, Schwartz (1973) demonstrated that individuals high in sex guilt were poorer than other subjects in remembering birth control information—a failing which certainly might reduce their contraceptive success.

The broader concept of social adjustment has been measured in many different ways, but the results have generally confirmed that better social adjustment is related to better contraceptive practice. For example, avoidance of unwanted pregnancy has been found to be associated with better relationships with parents (Ball, 1973; Jessor & Jessor, 1975), better relationships with peers (Ball, 1973), a better or longer relationship with the sex partner (Noble, 1972; Mindick, 1978), and clearer communication and agreement in decision-making with the partner (Campbell & Barnlund, 1977; Downs, 1976; Grunebaum & Abernethy, 1974). Thus, there is considerable convergence in the findings in this area.

Contraceptive Attitudes and Intentions

A final area, which has been very widely studied, is the influence of attitudes and intentions on contraceptive behavior. Among research reviews in this area, Cernada and Crawford (1973) have summarized the value of the hundreds of KAP studies, which have investigated contraceptive attitudes in many different countries; Werner (1977) has reviewed the attitude-versus-behavior controversy as it touches on sexual behavior and contraception; Chilman (1979) has published an extensive review of research, with chapters on sexual attitudes and behavior, contraception, abortion, and other areas where attitudes and intentions are important factors; and Mindick (1977) has summarized trends in public opinion concerning population growth, family planning, birth control, and abortion over the last 40 years.

Most early research on population issues took a demographic or sociological approach and largely ignored psychological factors like attitudes. If attitudes were measured, the focus was usually on their sociological, rather than psychological, correlates. Even the best recent demographic studies, such as Zelnik and Kantner's (1973) survey of a national sample of teenage girls, still usually include only an occasional attitude item, such as "Whose responsibility is it to use birth control?"

Many psychological studies of sexual and contraceptive behavior have studied attitudes more extensively, but have measured them quite roughly with single items. Recently, however, several authors have increased the reliability and precision of measurement by developing multiple-item scales of contraceptive attitudes (e.g., Cvetkovich et al., 1975; Miller, 1976).

Most of the studies which have used attitude scales have found clear relationships between contraceptive attitudes and various behavioral criteria. For example, Parcel (1974) found a significant correlation of attitudes with effective birth control behavior among unmarried college undergraduates. In several studies of birth control use or nonuse, similar positive relationships with attitude scales have been found for black urban high school students (Ball, 1973), poor black married women in the South (Kothandapani, 1971), and poor urban women in Venezuela (Kar, 1976).

The attitude literature also contains a number of successful studies of other contraceptive behaviors. Cole (1975) developed scales of behavioral intentions and potentially inhibiting extraneous events (ones which might interfere with clinic attendance), and both of these scales were significantly related, in the expected direction, to contraceptive clinic patients' return for their annual appointment. Similarly, Ager, Werley, and Shea (1973) showed that a scale of perceived barriers to using clinic services predicted patients' clinic dropout. Among high school students, both Vener and Stewart (1974) and Jessor and Jessor (1975) found several attitude scales which were significant predictors of sexual behavior.

From a theoretical viewpoint, Fishbein (1967) and Fishbein and Ajzen (1975) have presented formulas for predicting behavioral criteria from individuals' beliefs, attitudes, and intentions, and several studies have tested this theory in the area of contraceptive behavior. The theory's postulate that behavioral intentions should be the best predictors of actual behavior was supported by Kothandapani (1971) in an elaborate psychometric study of regularity of birth control use. In turn, Jaccard and Davidson (1972) demonstrated that attitudes and normative beliefs are excellent predictors of behavioral intentions, as the theory proposes (shown by a multiple correlation above .80); but later they found only a moderate relationship (about .45) between behavioral intentions to use birth control pills and the behavior itself (Davidson & Jaccard, 1976). More recently, the same authors have reported correlations above .60 both for predicting use of birth control pills from behavioral intentions to use them, and for predicting the behavioral intentions from relevant attitudes and subjective norms (Davidson & Jaccard, 1979). On the other hand, Kar's (1976) study found that perceived social support for birth control use and perceived accessibility of birth control services influenced the criterion behavior (level of birth control usage) independently and not just through attitudes and intentions, as Fishbein and Ajzen's theory proposes. Consequently Kar has suggested a revised theory, as have Townes, Beach, Campbell, and Wood (1976).

Clearly, the attitude area has proved to be a fruitful approach to studying adolescent fertility.

OUR RESEARCH APPROACH

We turn now to presentation of our own research methods and findings with adolescent contraceptors. We will describe two major studies separately, though they used the same general approach and had partially overlapping methods and results. In both studies our general aim was to carry out socially relevant research using a large-scale, multivariate, correlational approach in a naturalistic setting, and giving close attention to the interaction of personal and situational determinants of behavior. Such an approach has been advocated with increasing frequency in recent years as an answer to some of the problems of experimental social psychology (e.g., Argyris, 1975; Cronbach, 1975; McGuire, 1973).

The design of the research was a longitudinal one, attempting to predict "real-world," complex, molar behavior using a variety of previously-gathered measures. The criterion behaviors studied were several different indicators of success or failure in using contraception, and the research population consisted of young women who were sexually active and had demonstrated their motivation to avoid pregnancy by attending birth control clinics.

In preliminary archival research on this population, we found that, despite their motivation, many of them were failing in their contraceptive programs and were returning to the clinic to seek help in getting an abortion (sometimes even a second abortion within a brief period). What factors could explain this unfortunate discrepancy between plans and outcomes?

In attempting to answer this question, we have concentrated primarily on attitudinal and personality characteristics as predictors of the criteria of contraceptive success or failure. However, in addition, we have included demographic variables, measures of sexual and contraceptive experiences and practices, and situational aspects of life circumstances.

Based on the kind of research findings which we have summarized in the preceding pages, we hypothesized that contraceptive *success*—in contrast with contraceptive failure—would be related to:

(a) higher levels of socialization,
(b) feelings of personal efficacy, internal control, and lack of social passivity,
(c) higher levels of sexual and contraceptive knowledge,
(d) planfulness and future time perspective,
(e) better adjustment on various measures, such as relationships with parents and sexual partners, and
(f) better communication with parents and partners about sexual and contraceptive matters,
(g) attitudes about sex and birth control which are conducive to careful contraception,
(h) behavioral intentions to use birth control,
(i) past use of contraception, and
(j) relatively low levels of sexual activity, which would allow fewer opportunities for failure; whereas
(k) contraceptive *failure* was predicted to be associated with transitions in behavioral stages (e.g., moving away from home) and/or in relationships (e.g., breaking up with a boyfriend), as suggested by Miller (1973a).

STUDY ONE—METHOD

Subjects

Participants in the study were new contraception-clinic patients who came to four suburban Los Angeles Planned Parenthood agencies between November, 1973 and July, 1974. A randomly-selected group of 630 intake patients was interviewed and tested during the intervals between the regular clinic procedures. Only 2% of the patients refused to take part, though participation was voluntary and did not affect the receipt of clinic services. Subsequent to the initial interview, the research group was carefully followed up for a period of 3 years. These patients ranged in age from 14 to 50 with a mean of 21.6, but this report deals only with the 283 patients who were below the age of 20 at their intake appointment. One-year follow-up findings for the whole sample have been presented by Oskamp et al. (1978), and analyses of their 3-year data are in Mindick (1978). There was also a randomly-selected control group of 431 clinic intake patients who were not tested, interviewed, nor specially followed up, but whose regular clinic records were used for comparison with the follow-up data of the research group.

Instruments

Each research group patient had a 15 to 20-minute interview with a female member of the clinic staff who had been specially trained for this project. Following the interview, subjects received three fairly short questionnaires to answer. Spanish-speaking patients were interviewed and tested in Spanish. Several different sets of questionnaires were used during the course of the research so that a greater number of predictive instruments could be tried out. Consequently the number of patients who responded to the different measures varied rather widely. The instruments utilized were:

(a) Future Events Test (FET), a measure of planfulness adapted from the work of Stein, Sarbin, and Kulik (1968);
(b) Personal Values Abstract (PVA—Gough, 1972), which included a measure of socialization;
(c) Rotter's (1966) Internal-External Locus-of-Control Scale, a measure of personal efficacy;
(d) Miller's (1973b) Personal Style Inventory (PSI), developed to measure personality variables related to pregnancy planning behaviors (e.g., planfulness, behavioral stability, etc.);
(e) Miller's Sexual and Contraceptive Knowledge Questionnaire (no date);
(f) A questionnaire on knowledge and attitudes concerning sexual and contraceptive matters, containing the most discriminating items used by Goldsmith et al. (1972) with teenage Planned Parenthood patients;
(g) Shipley-Hartford vocabulary scale, a brief measure of verbal intelligence (Buros, 1972, p. 321).

The interview probed many diverse areas, particularly the patient's relationship with her parents and her sexual partner. Several behavioral indices of sexual and contraceptive activity were also investigated (e.g., number of recent sex partners, frequency of past birth control usage), as were all the available demographic variables (e.g., age, race, education, marital status, etc.).

Follow-Up Procedure and Criterion Classification

At these clinics, patients using oral contraceptives (88% of the teenagers in the research group) are normally expected to return 3 months after intake for another supply of pills, and IUD patients (3% of the sample) usually return for a check on the IUD's placement about 1 month after its insertion. Diaphragm users and condom-and-foam users (respectively 3% and 5% of the sample) are not expected to return until their next regular medical exams, which are scheduled at 6 months and 1 year after intake for all patients. The clinic routinely sends follow-up letters to patients (unless they have specifically requested no mail contacts) reminding them to make an appointment for the 6-month, 1-year, and subsequent medical exams. Of course patients can come in at any time for help with medical problems, side effects, and method changes, or to get further birth control supplies.

Additional follow-up procedures beyond the regular clinic routine were established for patients in the research group. All nonreturners who had agreed to allow mail contacts were sent a second letter about 2 months after the first one. It again reminded them about returning to the clinic, and it requested information about whether they were getting birth-control help elsewhere or had decided to stop using birth control. If these letters proved to be undeliverable, they were returned to us by the dead-letter section of the post office. Later, patients who had neither returned to the clinic nor answered the letters were followed up by telephone (if they had indicated that phone contacts were acceptable). Up to five phone calls at various hours were made, and if the patient was reached, a brief and diplomatic phone interview asked about her current contraceptive status using questions similar to those in the follow-up letter.

Based on these follow-up procedures, a criterion classification system was established involving several different measures of contraceptive success or failure. It included behavioral indices of patient attrition, amount of delay in return visits to the clinic, and the ultimate outcome measure, occurrence of unwanted pregnancies. Three and one-half years after the time of clinic intake, the patients' 3-year criterion status was classified using the following categories:

1. unwanted pregnancies (45 cases)—about 80% of these women obtained abortions,
2. pregnancies where wantedness was questionable (5 cases), including clear cases of method failure—since contraceptive success or failure was not determinable in these cases, they were omitted from further analyses to reduce error variance,
3. wanted pregnancies (6 cases),
4. unknown status; no recent contact nor information indicating classification in any other category (123 cases),
5. moved away, and no additional information (5 cases),

6. discontinued using birth control (21 cases),
7. getting birth control elsewhere (30 cases),
8. returned to clinic at around 3 years, but had missed or unduly delayed some previous clinic visits (19 cases),
9. regular, prompt returners for the full 3-year period (29 cases).

Two independent raters reached over 92% agreement on assigning patients to a category within this classification scheme. A more precise computation of inter-coder agreement for nominal scale judgments was made using a method recommended by Scott and Wertheimer (1962, p. 194) on a random selection of cases. For 285 judgments by each coder, the value of the π coefficient was .905, a high level of agreement.

Several different analyses of these criterion groups have been made. The one we will report here compares the unwanted pregnancy group (group 1, above) with the patients in groups 3, 7, 8, and 9 above, combined (a total of 84 individuals). The latter combined group is called "birth planners" since they had successfully met their birth control goals, either having continued a contraception program successfully for 3 years without getting pregnant or else having carried on their birth control program until they decided to have a child. (Generally the decision to have a child followed a change of status such as completing school or getting married.) Combination of the wanted pregnancy group together with the three nonpregnant groups was justified partly on these rational grounds, and partly through empirical tests which showed that they were more like the nonpregnant groups than like the unwanted pregnancy cases.

STUDY ONE—RESULTS

Description of Research Group

At the time of clinic intake, the teenagers in the research group had a mean age of 17.2 years (ranging from age 14 to 19) and had completed an average of 10.9 years of school. They included a substantial proportion of ethnic minorities: 17% black, 17% Latin or Spanish surnamed, and 1% Asian, figures which are fairly close to those for Los Angeles County as a whole. About 73% were still living with their families, but most of these were classified as independent by the clinic for purposes of computing income and family size. Thus their average family size was 1.5 persons, and the average family take-home pay was about $4200 per year, though both of these figures are undoubtedly underestimates since they generally omit parents and siblings and parental income. For the total sample, the average income was above the poverty level for 1973–74, so these girls seem to have been largely upper-lower-class, lower-middle-class, and middle-middle-class.

Only 7% of the teenage patients were married, 91% were single, and 2% separated or divorced. However, at intake 27% had been pregnant at least once, 14% had had one or more therapeutic abortions, and 12% had living children. Though almost all of them had had some sexual experience (94%), about 40% had never used birth control before. Fully 64% had not been using contraception in the weeks before they came to the clinic (though only 27% had not been sexually active), while half of the rest had been using pills and the other half some other method. A large majority (76%) stated that they wanted a child or children later on, while only 5% said they wanted no more children.

Comparison of Unwanted Pregnancy and Birth Planner Groups

The present analysis of results compared the most distinct criterion groups: the clear cases of unwanted pregnancies due to human failure, versus the successful birth planners. Omitted from the analysis were the cases having pregnancies where wantedness was ambiguous, including method failures, and the middle categories (groups 4 and 5, above), where contraceptive outcomes were unknown. This procedure held error variance in the criterion classification to a minimum though it also appreciably reduced the number of cases analyzed.

Results for the failure and success groups are shown in Table 4.1, which presents statistically significant[1] differences as well as some nonsignificant differences that have theoretical implications. In discussing these results we will occasionally refer to our past findings for the total sample, which included both teenagers and older women.

The demographic variables in Table 4.1 reveal one striking difference between the two groups: the unwanted pregnancy group had a much higher percentage of ethnic minority women. Related to this was the fact that a higher proportion of the pregnancy group had attended the three satellite clinics (in outlying communities) than was true for the successful contraceptors. Also, as in our previous findings for the total sample, the pregnant teenagers tended to be somewhat lower in education than the successful birth planners. However, there were no significant differences between the two groups in marital status, age, weekly family income, or number of individuals supported by the family income.

The sex and contraception history variables generally showed clearer relationships to the criterion than the demographic variables had. The contraceptive failure group was more likely than the birth planners to have used no contraceptive method previously, and to have obtained some initial method other than pills from the clinic. Though a younger age at first intercourse was a significant

---

[1]Statistical tests reveal whether differences between means or other measures are significant (i.e., not likely to be due to chance) or nonsignificant (i.e., probably due to chance or random fluctuations).

predictor of contraceptive failure for the total sample, it did not reach significance for these teenagers. As with the total sample, the number of previous pregnancies was somewhat higher for the contraceptive failure group, but the two groups did not differ in number of past abortions, and consequently the failure group had significantly more living children when they entered the clinic. The failure group claimed more past pregnancies as being wanted or of uncertain wantedness status, but they did not admit to more unwanted pregnancies than the birth planner group. (Considering their age and marital status, this may be an indication of denial on their part, or possibly of a different value system.) Though frequency of intercourse did not distinguish the two groups, the unwanted pregnancy group reported significantly more sex partners in the last year and significantly less frequent past use of birth control.

As with the total sample, sexual and contraceptive knowledge was significantly higher for the birth planners. Specific items on which they scored better at the intake interview were:

4. If a girl has sexual intercourse for a month or so without getting pregnant, this means she probably isn't too likely to get pregnant for awhile.
5. Once a girl starts taking the birth control pill she probably won't be able to have babies later on, even when she stops the pill.
7. Girls can have V.D. without knowing they have it.

In contrast to the Goldsmith et al. measure of knowledge, Miller's multiple-choice Sexual and Contraceptive Knowledge Questionnaire proved to be too difficult for these patients (the average score was below 50% correct), and perhaps as a result of the low scores, it did not reveal any significant differences between the two groups.

The personality variables in Table 4.1 show a mixed picture. Gough's PVA Socialization scale, which indicated a significantly higher socialization for the birth planners in the total sample, displayed only a small tendency in the same direction for these teenagers. In part this may be due to the relatively small number of girls who received this measure, and the same is true for the PSI scales. However, the PSI Vigilance scale did reach significance, with the birth planners being higher than the pregnancy group in this measure of contraceptive concern (versus risk-taking and denial of risk). As in our past reports, the Rotter I-E scale and the measure of verbal intelligence did not show significant differences, though in this case the vocabulary measure of intelligence almost reached significance in favor of the pregnancy group. As with the total sample, this finding demonstrates that the difference between the two groups in sexual and contraceptive knowledge was not due to differential intelligence.

The interviewers' intake ratings on personality characteristics showed some surprising findings. The rating for "passive, controlled by events" was the only one that paralleled the significant findings on these measures for the total sample. As expected, it was higher for the pregnancy group; but the difference in ratings

TABLE 4.1
Comparison of Birth Planner Group (Successful Contraceptors) with Unwanted Pregnancy Group (Contraceptive Failures)

Measure	Birth Planners Mean	SD	N	Pregnant Group Mean	SD	N	t or X^2
Demographic Variables							
Clinic location							$X^2 = 3.65^{a,b}$
Main clinic			59			24	
3 satellite clinics			25			21	
Ethnic group							$X^2 = 13.34$***
White Anglo			70			24	
Black, Latin, Asian			14			21	
Marital status							n.s.
Single			76			40	
Married			7			4	
Separated, divorced			1			1	
Age	17.21	1.17	84	17.13	1.36	45	n.s.
Education (yrs.)	11.15	1.45	84	10.40	2.56	45	$1.83^{a,b}$
Weekly family income ($)	80.18	3.04	83	78.33	2.04	45	n.s.
No. on family income	1.46	1.02	83	1.71	1.31	45	n.s.
Sex and Contraceptive History Variables							
Previous method							$X^2 = 3.28$*
None			44			31	
Some			40			14	
Method prescribed							$X^2 = 4.94$*^{b}
Pill			77			35	
Other			7			10	
Age at first intercourse	16.06	1.51	48	15.65	1.55	26	n.s.
No. of previous pregnancies	.33	.52	84	.51	.79	45	1.36^a
No. of previous therapeutic abortions	.18	.38	84	.18	.49	45	n.s.
No. of living children	.12	.33	84	.29	.59	45	1.79*
No. of wanted pregnancies	.05	.27	83	.24	.53	42	2.18*^{b}
No. of pregnancies where wantedness unsure	.01	.11	83	.10	.30	42	1.76*
No. of unwanted pregnancies	.27	.44	83	.19	.50	42	n.s.
How often having sex recently	3.90	1.54	30	3.73	1.28	15	n.s.
No. of male sex partners in last yr.	1.48	.99	48	2.11	1.52	28	1.95*
How often used birth control in past	3.04	1.74	47	2.33	1.57	27	1.75*

[a] $p < .10$ (marginal statistical significance)

* $p < .05$ (statistically significant; only 5 chances out of 100 that difference was due to random fluctuation)

** $p < .01$ (statistically significant; only 1 chance out of 100 that difference was due to random fluctuation)

TABLE 4.1 (Continued)

	Birth Planners			Pregnant Group			
Measure	Mean	SD	N	Mean	SD	N	t or X^2

Sex and Contraceptive Knowledge

Sex knowledge scale errors							
(Goldsmith et al., 1972)	2.64	1.63	47	4.15	2.40	26	2.88**
Item No. 4 (1 = wrong, 2 = right)	1.98	.14	48	1.83	.38	29	2.04*
Item No. 5 " "	2.00	.00	48	1.90	.31	29	2.32*
Item No. 7 " "	2.00	.00	48	1.90	.31	29	2.32*

Personality Variables

PVA Socialization scale	20.17	3.64	18	19.22	4.36	18	n.s.
Rotter externality scale	10.47	4.05	34	9.62	3.14	16	n.s.
PSI Planning and Future Orientation scale	6.33	2.66	33	5.38	2.60	16	n.s.
PSI Vigilance scale	7.85	2.05	33	6.69	2.24	16	1.80*
Vocabulary (verbal intelligence) scale	25.24	3.81	25	28.00	3.22	6	n.s.[b]
Interviewer ratings on:							
Passive, controlled by events	2.94	.72	70	3.16	.64	38	1.54[a]
Impulsive, not planful	2.88	.63	69	2.94	.55	34	n.s.
Psychological conflicts	3.29	.60	77	2.95	.90	38	-2.10*[b,c]
Feels inadequate	2.99	.71	78	2.69	.89	38	-1.80[a,b,c]
Guilt about sex or birth control	2.90	.73	82	2.54	.79	39	-2.50*[b,c]
FET mean future age	30.58	10.04	69	27.42	3.68	29	2.28*
FET mean future extension	12.29	5.48	68	10.59	3.53	29	1.83*
FET items (expected ages):							
Lose someone you love	23.15	13.93	39	16.47	3.22	19	2.84**
Buy a home	27.81	5.82	59	23.89	4.44	27	3.11**
Enjoy life your own way	22.74	15.44	58	18.36	5.84	25	1.87*
Have a first child	23.40	3.78	60	21.77	4.02	26	1.80*
Get ticket for fast driving	18.83	3.24	30	17.55	1.37	11	1.79*
Win lots of money	24.05	7.92	21	18.00	2.74	5	2.86**

Attitude Variables

Can talk with man about sex	3.81	.66	80	3.60	1.03	40	n.s.
Relationship with parents	3.18	1.03	82	3.23	1.02	43	n.s.
Discussed V.D. with parents	1.31	.47	48	1.14	.35	29	1.73*
How sure of continuing birth control program	4.10	.54	80	4.00	.73	42	n.s.
Should we avoid mentioning Planned Parenthood (when phoning)?	1.74	.44	53	1.33	.48	21	3.42***[b]

*** $p < .001$ (statistically significant; only 1 chance out of 1000 that difference was due to random fluctuation)

[b] Two-tailed test because no directional hypothesis was made (all other tests were one-tailed because directional hypotheses were made for them).

[c] A negative t value indicates that the difference between means was in the direction opposite to that predicted.

for "impulsive, not planful" was nonsignificant, and three ratings of poor adjustment and sex guilt were all significantly more favorable for the pregnancy group, contrary to prediction (as shown by the negative t values in Table 4.1). These last three ratings were not significant for the total sample, so it appears that the interviewers may have been better judges of somewhat-older women than they were of teenagers.

However, our primary measure of planfulness, the Future Events Test (FET), displayed equally good prediction for teenagers as for the rest of the sample. The two summary scores both showed a significantly longer future time perspective for the birth planner group, and six individual items were also significant in the same direction. These data, together with the results for the conceptually-related PSI Vigilance scale, suggest the importance of planfulness in the successful use of contraception.

Finally, the attitude items used in this study produced only a few significant findings. The respondents' self-reports of relationships with parents and with the sex partner were not appreciably different for the two groups, except that the birth planners more often reported having discussed V.D. with their parents. Contrary to results for the total sample, strength of intentions to continue their birth control program did not distinguish between later contraceptive failures and successes—a possible indication that teenagers' behavior is less consistent and harder to predict than that of older women. The birth planners' markedly more frequent requests that Planned Parenthood not be mentioned when telephoning them seem to fit very well with the interviewers' view of them as higher in sex guilt. This finding may suggest that part of their success in contraception was due to their felt need to conceal from their parents the fact that they were sexually active.

Summary.   We may sum up the group differences in various categories as follows. There were quite strong and consistent differences between the contraceptive success and failure groups in two areas: sex and contraceptive history, and sex and contraceptive knowledge, with the success group showing a more favorable picture in both areas. There were relatively few group differences in the areas of: demographic variables (except that ethnic group and possibly education showed significant differences), and sex and contraceptive attitudes. In the area of personality variables, findings were conflicting (except that the FET measures of planfulness were consistently higher for the successful contraceptors).

Multiple Regression Analysis

In addition to the above significance tests of differences between the contraceptive success and failure groups, an important further analysis was multiple regression, to determine which variables could be combined to yield the best predictions of the birth-planning criterion. Two such analyses were conducted, with the limitation that measures used had to have been given to a majority of the subjects, and with preference given to scale measures which combined several items. These regression analyses were conducted on the total sample, including both teenagers and older women, so their results may not be directly applicable to the teenagers alone. (See the results of Study Two below for further discussion of this point.)

The first multiple regression analysis demonstrated that psychological variables could add significantly to predicting the criterion, *over and above* the contribution to prediction made by the (simpler) demographic variables. The four best demographic measures were selected and arbitrarily entered first into the regression equation, followed by an equal number of selected psychological variables, and results showed that all four of the psychological measures did add significantly to prediction of the criterion.

The second multiple regression analysis investigated which set of predictor measures would explain the maximum amount of criterion variance, so it set no restrictions on the number or type of variables nor on their order of inclusion. The results showed that six variables (five of them psychological and one demographic) gave optimum significant prediction of the criterion, yielding a multiple R of .48. In order, these variables were: sex knowledge scale, a past contraceptive usage scale, PVA Socialization scale, discussion of menstrual periods with parents, ethnic background, and planfulness as shown by the FET mean future age. These findings emphasize the utility of psychological variables, and highlight the particular value of several of the types of psychological variables which we have stressed in our review of the contraception literature (specifically, knowledge, socialization, planfulness, and past behavior).

Comparison of Research Group with Control Group Patients

A final important finding of Study One concerns the control group of 431 randomly-selected clinic intake patients, who were given all the usual clinic procedures and services but were not tested, interviewed, nor specially followed-up as the research group subjects were (until the final criterion determination follow-up). Because high patient attrition is a major concern in many family planning clinics, our inclusion of a control group was designed to test the effect of the research procedures on indices of patient attrition. On one hand, taking the research interview and questionnaires might annoy patients and discourage them from returning to the clinic. Or on the other hand, the greater amount of initial contact and later follow-up might engage patients' interest, causing greater involvement with the clinic and lower attrition rates.

As we had hoped, the latter hypothesis was supported by our findings. The greater amount of staff attention has frequently been perceived by patients as interest and concern for them as individuals. Moreover, the attrition rates at 1 year after intake were 63% for the control group, but only 47% for the research group—a difference significant at the .001 level. Also, at that point 53% of the returning research group patients were on time (within 1 month), while only 44% of the returning control group patients were on time—also a significant difference. These results are impressive evidence that greater initial contact and more intensive follow-up efforts can markedly reduce the rate of patient attrition. In the long run such a change should help more women to achieve their birth planning goals and to avoid unwanted pregnancies.

STUDY TWO—METHOD

In planning this second study we had the benefit of our first study's results for the 1-year criterion point. The second study dealt *solely with teenagers,* focusing on the important early stages of their sexual and contraceptive experience. It was planned as a more extensive and intensive investigation of a broad range of factors which might affect their contraceptive success or failure. In most respects the research design was similar to that of Study One. Both studies were guided by the same general hypotheses, as previously summarized; but the specific questionnaires used were quite different, as indicated below.

Subjects

Sites for the study were eleven different family planning clinics. In addition to the four clinics used in Study One, the sites included two other private suburban clinics run by Los Angeles Planned Parenthood, and five public county-run clinics in different areas of Orange County (a part of greater Los Angeles). A consecutive sample of approximately 700 new contraceptive patients below the age of 20 was contacted at their intake visits starting early in 1977. Because of differences in the demographic characteristics of the patient populations and in the follow-up procedures which we were allowed to use, only the private Planned Parenthood data are comparable to Study One. Therefore the approximately 200 Orange County patients are not included in this report.

Instruments

Data were gathered from clinic records, extensive research questionnaires, and brief interviews by specially trained female research assistants. The major types of variables studied were listed earlier, prior to description of Study One. An attempt was made to develop short scales having from 2 to 10 items to measure each major variable, and in some cases multiple alternative scales or items were used. Specific scales and items were adapted or selected from our own previous research and from studies by Ager (1976), Ball (1973), Bendig (1956), Cole (1975), Goldsmith et al. (1972), Jessor and Jessor (1975), Kantner and Zelnik (1973), Kar (1976), Kothandapani (1971), Miller (1976), Rosenberg (1965), Rotter (1966), Slagle et al. (1974), Stein et al. (1968), Vener and Stewart (1974), and several other investigators.

The items chosen for use were organized by topic into one brief interview and six questionnaires. All subjects received the interview, which dealt mostly with family occupational and educational information, and two questionnaires, which concerned (a) sex and birth control knowledge and (b) sex and birth control experiences. Each subject also received two of the other four questionnaires, with the forms in use being alternated each week. These forms concerned (c) sexual attitudes, (d) birth control attitudes, intentions, and extraneous events which might interfere with those intentions, (e) personality traits and related attitudes, and (f) parental and peer relationships and communication regarding sex, birth control, and deviant behavior. Thus, questions on these last four topics were answered by only about half of the subjects. The interview and four questionnaires took most subjects about an hour to complete, but only 1% of the patients refused to participate.

Follow-Up Procedure and Criterion Classification

The same general follow-up procedure as in Study One was used in the longitudinal study of this sample. About 2 years after their initial clinic visit, the 465 Planned Parenthood teenage patients were followed up—first through a check of clinic records, and then by mailing the same questionnaire as in Study One to patients who had not returned to the clinic for their 1-year visit nor contacted the clinic subsequently. Because past follow-up efforts had shown these young women to be a highly mobile group, we decided that attempts to telephone the patients who had not returned the questionnaire would not be productive.

The final criterion classification was based primarily on the 18-month return visit point, for which data were available on almost all patients. The same basic indices and categories of contraceptive success or failure were used as in Study One, with some minor refinements. Patients were classified into the following criterion categories:

1. unwanted pregnancies (47 cases),
2. pregnancies where wantedness was questionable (7 cases, including 2 cases of possible method failure)—because their contraceptive success or failure was not determinable, these cases were omitted from further analyses to reduce error variance,
3. wanted pregnancies (10 cases),
4. unknown status; no recent contact nor information about their criterion status (216 cases),

5. moved away, and no additional information (5 cases),
6. miscellaneous communications, but no recent return to clinic (6 cases),
7. discontinued using birth control (14 cases),
8. getting birth control elsewhere (25 cases),
9. reported abstinence as their latest method, and had not gotten pregnant since intake (7 cases),
10. returned to clinic at around 18 months, but not completely regular in all return visits (41 cases),
11. regular, prompt returners for full 18 months (87 cases).

As in Study One, a criterion group of "birth planners" was defined, in this case made up of categories 3, 8, 9, 10, and 11 above (a total of 170 individuals). Though many analyses were conducted, the one to be reported here compared the birth planners with the unwanted pregnancy group (category 1, above).

STUDY TWO—RESULTS

Description of Subjects

The patients in Study Two had a mean age of 17.8 years (ranging from age 12 to 19) and had completed an average of 11.2 years of school. They included 13% blacks, 13% Latin or Spanish surnamed, and 1% Asians—a bit lower percentage of minorities than in Study One. About 71% were still living with their families, but again clinic policies in recording the data caused most of these girls to be considered as financially independent. As a result, their average family income was reported as being $2100 per year and their average family size was recorded as 1.2 persons (both of these figures are unrealistically low because they generally omit parents and siblings and parental income). In contrast, the various indices of their parents' income and education shown in Table 4.2 suggest that many of them were in the middle-class range.

As with Study One, almost all these teenagers were still single—92% never-married, 7% married, and 1% separated or divorced. Also much as before, 30% of them had been pregnant, 21% had had at least one therapeutic abortion (more than in Study One), and 8% had living children (somewhat less than in Study One). Only about 6% had never had intercourse, but 43% had never used birth control. Over half (62%) had not been using contraception recently (though only 22% had not been sexually active), while about 20% had been using pills and about 18% some other method. Their clinic prescription was predominantly pills, or pills plus foam and/or condom as an interim or backup method (81%—somewhat less than in Study One), with only 4% being given an IUD, 7% getting a diaphragm, and 8% receiving only foam and/or condom. As before, a heavy majority (72%) of these young women said they wanted a child or children later on, while only 4% were definite in wanting no more children.

Reliability of Predictor Scales

A major emphasis in this study was to develop short but discriminating scales to measure important psychological concepts. For this purpose, the best items were selected from the measures of many other researchers, with the wording adapted whenever necessary in order to be appropriate for the present research subjects. Other items were developed afresh, and for each major concept one or more scales was assembled, each containing 2–10 items.

The reliability[2] of the 66 resulting scales was determined using Cronbach's (1970) alpha coefficient of homogeneity. In general the results were quite satisfactory, particularly in view of the very short length of most scales. Quite a number of even the 2-item scales had alpha coefficients in the .70s and .80s. Overall, there were 13 scales with alphas of .80 or more, 38 scales with coefficients between .50 and .80 and only 15 relatively poor scales with alphas below .50.

Comparison of Birth Planner and Unwanted Pregnancy Groups

Since this study had many more predictors and significant findings than Study One, results are presented in a series of tables. Since the research strategy used was one of extension and conceptual replication, rather than direct replication of Study One, most of the variables used in this study were different from those in Study One. Only the significant findings are presented in the tables, except for Table 4.2.[3]

Table 4.2 shows a comparison of the demographic characteristics of the birth planner group versus the unwanted pregnancy group. As in Study One, many of the variables here showed nonsignificant differences between the groups, with noteworthy similarities on age, marital status, religious preference, gross weekly household income as shown in clinic records, and number of persons on that income. The two major types of variables which *did* differentiate the groups were ethnic background and socioeconomic status measures, particularly the educational level of the main family members. Consistent with the findings of Study One, the contraceptive failure group were more likely to be ethnic minorities and to have lower socioeconomic status. A similar finding appeared in the last two variables in Table 4.2, which showed that the pregnant group were less likely to receive private health care.

---

[2]An estimate of how dependable (in the sense of internal consistency) scores on the various scales were.

[3]As in Study One, most significance tests were based on prior hypotheses, so in all tables they are one-tailed tests unless stated otherwise. All items were coded in an ordinal fashion so that t-tests could be used, and findings opposite to the hypothesized direction are indicated by a negative t value and treated with two-tailed tests.

TABLE 4.2
Demographic Characteristics and Health-Care Indices of Birth Planner
Group (N = 170) vs. Unwanted Pregnancy Group (N = 47)—Study Two

Measure	Birth Planners			Pregnant Group			t
	Mean	SD	N	Mean	SD	N	
Race (1 = white; 2 = other)	1.11	0.32	169	1.19	0.40	47	1.43[a]
Latin Descent (2 = no; 4 = yes)	2.24	0.62	169	2.49	0.83	47	1.94*
Age	17.80	1.37	170	17.65	1.49	47	n.s.
Marital Status (1 = single; 2 = ever married)	1.07	0.26	169	1.07	0.28	46	n.s.
Conservatism of religious group (1-5; 5 = most conservative)	3.43	1.31	166	3.56	1.35	43	n.s.
Patient eligibility (4 = private fee; 5 = other)	4.88	0.33	170	4.91	0.28	47	n.s.
Gross weekly household income	39.37	40.46	170	38.77	37.70	47	n.s.
No. on income	1.17	0.54	169	1.32	1.02	47	n.s.
Anyone in family on welfare (1 = yes; 2 = no)	1.95	0.21	170	1.87	0.34	47	1.56[a]
Highest grade completed	11.29	1.40	169	10.79	1.43	47	2.17*
Highest grade patient expects to complete (a behavioral intention)	14.57	2.03	169	13.48	1.80	44	3.27***
Father's highest grade	13.19	2.86	154	11.97	3.55	38	2.25*
Mother's highest grade	12.69	2.71	162	11.61	2.39	44	2.38**
Father's SES based on job (Warner et al., 1949) (1-7; 1 = highest)	3.41	1.58	158	4.03	1.37	38	2.21*
Patient yearly income to nearest $1000.	2.62	2.01	66	2.71	1.86	14	n.s.
Health-Care Variables							
Where go for health care (1 = private Dr.; 3 = clinic; 5 = nowhere)	2.15	1.47	165	2.66	1.48	41	1.98*
Have private Dr. (1 = yes; 2 = no)	1.34	0.48	167	1.59	0.50	44	3.07***

[a] $p < .10$
* $p < .05$
** $p < .01$ See TABLE 4.1 for interpretation.
*** $p < .001$

In previous sexual and contraceptive experience, shown in Table 4.3, there were substantial differences between the two groups, though many of them were rather surprising. As in Study One, the unwanted pregnancy group had had more previous pregnancies before the time of clinic intake. They also reported having more miscarriages than the birth planners, though the two groups didn't differ significantly in the number of previous abortions nor in their number of living children. Consistent with our hypotheses, the birth planner group had had less sexual experience, having their first intercourse at a later age, and reporting a shorter period of sexual involvement with their current partner.

However, unlike Study One, in this study the birth planner group had had *less* previous experience with several aspects of birth control. They were less likely to have obtained any contraceptive supplies, less likely to have gone to a clinic or a doctor for birth control, and less likely to have used contraceptive pills recently. Only in the use of condoms were the birth planners significantly higher than the pregnant group, and consequently they had more often obtained their birth control supplies from a store. Consistent with this picture, but also contrary to our expectations, the birth planners were more likely to report past *joint* use of birth control and joint decision-making about it with their partners, whereas the contraceptive failure group were more likely to have taken unilateral responsibility for using birth control themselves. In the area of communication with their partner, however, the unwanted pregnancy group reported more past discussions of sex and birth control issues with their partners than did the birth planners, and also more discussions specifically about plans for having children. This finding may simply reflect the pregnant group's greater length of sexual relationships, for they were lower than the birth planners in their past discussions of sex with their parents. In the end, despite their greater past experience with birth control and their more frequent discussions of sexual topics with their partners, the pregnant group turned out to be ineffective contraceptors.

Moving from sexual and contraceptive experience to sexual and contraceptive knowledge (Table 4.4), the differences between the two criterion groups were striking and in the predicted direction. Despite the longer sexual and contraceptive experience of the pregnancy group, the birth planners were significantly higher on several different aspects of knowledge: on self-rated level of information, on the number of birth control methods spontaneously listed (particularly IUD, rhythm, and condom), and on scales of multiple choice items tapping specific knowledge about sexual and contraceptive matters. Not shown in Table 4.4 are eight such items on which the birth planners scored significantly better than the unwanted pregnancy group (for instance, that masturbation is normal and not harmful, that the chances of pregnancy are greater with more frequent intercourse, and that douching won't prevent pregnancy). The only two items on which the pregnancy group scored significantly higher were knowledge of the day in one's cycle on which one should begin taking birth control pills, and of the danger of pregnancy if 3–4 pills are skipped. Logically enough, the atypical

TABLE 4.3
Previous Sex and Contraceptive History of Birth Planner
Group (N = 170) vs. Unwanted Pregnancy Group (N = 47)

Measure	Birth Planners			Pregnant Group			t^c
	Mean	SD	N	Mean	SD	N	
No. of pregnancies	0.36	0.65	170	0.68	0.84	47	2.44**
No. of miscarriages	0.03	0.17	170	0.15	0.47	47	1.73*
Age at 1st intercourse	16.23	1.66	145	15.55	1.67	43	2.37**
Sexual experience (yrs.)	1.50	1.44	159	2.25	1.61	44	2.98**[b]
Months of sex with current partner	6.46	8.45	127	10.67	12.02	36	1.97[a,b]
Obtained b.c. from nowhere (0 = no; 1 = yes)	0.33	0.47	170	0.19	0.40	47	1.83[a,b]
Obtained b.c. from hospital clinic (0 = no; 1 = yes)	0.07	0.26	170	0.17	0.38	47	1.69[a,b]
Obtained b.c. from other clinic (0 = no; 1 = yes)	0.14	0.34	170	0.26	0.44	47	1.73[a,b]
Source of b.c. (2 = clinic or Dr.; 3 = store or other)	2.59	0.49	100	2.32	0.48	31	-2.66**[b]
B.C. in last month—used pills (0 = no; 1 = yes)	0.16	0.37	170	0.32	0.47	47	-2.16*[b]
% of time used condom (0 = 0-9%; 9 = 90-100%)	2.31	3.65	127	1.09	2.15	34	2.48*[b]
Who used b.c. (1 = only me; 3 = both; 5 = only partner)	3.31	1.68	104	2.38	1.50	32	-2.82**[b]
Who decides about using b.c. (1 = only partner; 3 = both; 5 = only me)	3.32	0.70	82	3.60	0.82	25	-1.70[a,b]
No. of times discussed birth plans with partner (1-4; 4 = many times)	2.43	1.10	65	3.36	0.92	11	2.65**[b]
Discussion of sex and b.c. with partner (5-25; 5 = least)	13.57	3.74	65	16.18	3.74	11	-2.14*[b]
No. of times discussed sex with parents (1-4; 4 = many times)	2.31	0.93	67	1.85	0.90	13	1.67*

[a] $p < .10$
*$p < .05$
**$p < .01$ See TABLE 4.1 for interpretation.
***$p < .001$
[b] 2-tailed test (all others are 1-tailed).
[c] Negative t means finding is opposite to direction predicted.

results on these two items are consistent with the pregnancy group's greater past use of birth control pills.

In the area of contraception-related attitudes, shown in Table 4.5, there were many more significant findings than in Study One. First, the pregnancy group members believed more strongly in the effectiveness of IUDs and tubal ligation or vasectomy than did the birth planners. Consistent with this was the rather

TABLE 4.4
Previous Sex and Contraceptive Knowledge of Birth Planner
Group (N = 170) vs. Unwanted Pregnancy Group (N = 47)

Measure	Birth Planners			Pregnant Group			t^c
	Mean	SD	N	Mean	SD	N	
I have good information about getting pregnant (1-5; 1 = definitely true)	2.25	1.14	75	3.07	0.96	15	2.58**
Self-rated information about sex and b.c. (2-10; 2 = least)	7.62	1.79	73	6.47	1.89	15	2.24*
No. of different b.c. methods mentioned	4.95	2.14	168	4.20	2.39	46	2.07*
IUD mentioned (0 = no; 1 = yes)	0.77	0.42	170	0.60	0.50	47	2.42**
Rhythm mentioned (0 = no; 1 = yes)	0.39	0.49	170	0.26	0.44	47	$1.75^{a,b}$
Condom mentioned (0 = no; 1 = yes)	0.85	0.36	170	0.66	0.48	47	$2.49*^b$
No. of correct days circled in indicating most fertile period	2.08	2.15	157	1.41	1.82	44	1.88*
Day of cycle on which one should start taking b.c. pills (1 = wrong; 2 = right)	1.39	0.49	87	1.58	0.50	24	$-1.69^{a,b}$
Total correct on sex knowledge items 2-11 (Scale 1)	6.20	1.82	168	5.46	2.28	46	2.03*
Total correct on sex knowledge items 16-26 (Scale 2)	8.29	2.31	168	7.43	2.55	46	2.18*
Total correct on sex knowledge items 2-26 (Combined scale)	14.49	3.60	168	12.89	3.96	46	2.61**

$^a p < .10$
$^* p < .05$ See TABLE 4.1 for interpretation.
$^{**} p < .01$
$^{***} p < .001$
^{b} 2-tailed test (all others are 1-tailed).
^{c} Negative t means finding is opposite to direction predicted.

TABLE 4.5
Previous Sex and Contraceptive Attitudes of Birth Planner Group (N = 170) vs. Unwanted Pregnancy Group (N = 47)

Measure	Birth Planners			Pregnant Group			t^c
	Mean	SD	N	Mean	SD	N	
% effectiveness of IUD	82.62	19.41	142	88.09	14.23	35	1.88[a,b]
% effectiveness of tubal ligation or vasectomy	93.01	18.85	143	96.58	6.34	33	1.85[a,b]
Mentioned fear that b.c. won't work (0 = no; 1 = yes)	0.09	0.29	85	0.00	0.00	27	-1.66[a,b]
How convenient to use b.c. (1-5; 1 = very)	2.04	1.29	152	1.60	0.93	40	-2.44*[b]
Worry about other people seeing my b.c. (1-5; 1 = strongly agree)	3.49	1.20	85	4.04	0.98	25	2.08*[b]
Youth or readiness mentioned as reason for not having children (0 = no; 1 = yes)	0.28	0.45	170	0.43	0.50	47	-1.97[a,b]
Sex should be spontaneous (1-5; 1 = strongly agree)	2.90	1.07	84	2.42	1.17	25	1.96*
Don't believe I can become pregnant easily (1-5; 1 = strongly agree)	4.36	0.86	84	3.81	1.13	26	2.63**
Had inconvenience and waiting to get b.c. (1-5; 1 = strongly agree)	3.57	1.06	76	3.00	1.16	25	2.26*
Cost of clinic services (1-5; 1 = very good)	1.72	0.77	57	2.11	0.94	19	1.79*
If out of b.c., not use other method (1-5; 1 = strongly agree)	4.22	0.98	83	3.76	1.20	25	1.94*
Miscellaneous pro-b.c. behavior intentions (6-30; 6 = least)	22.94	3.41	80	21.48	3.20	25	1.89*

[a] $p < .10$
* $p < .05$ See TABLE 4.1 for interpretation.
** $p < .01$
*** $p < .001$
[b] 2-tailed test (all others are 1-tailed)
[c] Negative t means finding is opposite to direction predicted.

94

surprising finding that some of the birth planners, but none of the pregnancy group, mentioned having fears that their birth control method wouldn't work. Also unexpected were reports by the failure group that they felt greater convenience in using contraception, less worry about other people seeing their birth control supplies, and greater concern about their youth as a reason for not having children than did the birth planners. On the other hand, the birth planner group professed many attitudes which were consistent with their later contraceptive success. For instance, they were less likely to say that sex should be spontaneous or that they probably couldn't become pregnant easily. They were less likely to criticize contraception clinics for inconvenience and waiting or for high cost. In the area of behavioral intentions, they were more likely to say that they would use a substitute birth control method if their normal method wasn't available. Finally, they scored higher than the failure group on a scale of several pro-contraception behavioral intentions though, as with Study One, the item on strength of intentions to continue their birth control program didn't differentiate the two groups.

Turning from attitudes to personal and contextual characteristics of the subjects (Table 4.6), again there were more significant findings in this study than in Study One. As expected, the birth planner group showed better relationships on a peer relations scale, and they had a reputation for more conventional sexual behavior than did the pregnancy group. Unlike Study One, the birth planners were significantly higher on the scale of internal locus-of-control used in this study, as well as on the system control sub-scale (which involves perceived control over aspects of the national political system). The results were similar to Study One on the FET indices of planfulness, which showed the birth planners to have a greater density of expected future events, a longer future time perspective, and even a longer perspective on past events. The other items listed as personal characteristics indicated that the birth planners had higher levels of socialization and cooperation (shown in their more faithful completion of the questionnaire forms, in more of them having earned a driver's license, and in their willingness to give information which would allow them to be contacted again in the future).

The interviewers' intake ratings of the patients' personality characteristics, also shown in Table 4.6, were much more supportive of our hypotheses than in Study One. Five of the specific ratings and two summary scales all showed that the birth planner group made a generally more favorable personal impression at the time of clinic intake, many months before the groups' criterion classification was determined. Particularly interesting here were the findings that the birth planners were seen as more planful, more mature, more knowledgeable about sex, and less intropunitive.

The last set of items in Table 4.6, labeled contextual characteristics, represent social situational variables, but ones which were personally chosen by the patients themselves. Like the personal characteristics, they also showed interesting contrasts between the two groups. More of the birth planners were still going to

TABLE 4.6
Previously Measured Personal and Contextual Characteristics of Birth
Planner Group (N = 170) vs. Unwanted Pregnancy Group (N = 47)

Measure	Birth Planners			Pregnant Group			t^c
	Mean	SD	N	Mean	SD	N	
Personal Characteristics							
Peer relations scale (2-10; 10 = best)	8.51	1.38	71	7.80	1.47	15	1.78*
Friends think I'm fast (1-5; 1 = definitely true)	4.39	0.91	72	3.93	1.03	15	1.72*
Internality, system control (2-10; 10 = most internal)	6.29	1.76	73	5.38	1.61	13	1.73*
Combined internality scale (12-60; 60 = most internal)	43.00	6.28	73	39.38	6.13	13	1.92*
Number of FET future events	11.22	5.49	76	8.40	5.64	15	1.81*
FET mean future extension	15.03	3.93	66	12.40	4.42	12	2.09*
FET mean past extension	2.13	2.38	57	1.19	0.89	12	2.30*[b]
Form 2 not taken (= 99)	19.58	17.00	170	24.66	18.44	47	1.78*
Has Calif. driver's license (1 = yes; 2 = no)	1.35	0.48	162	1.60	0.50	40	2.91**
Gave driver's license information (1 = yes; 3 = no; 4 = no license)	2.08	1.42	162	2.80	1.49	40	2.85**
Interviewer Ratings							
Avoids eye contact (1-5; 1 = very little, a pos. rating)	1.62	0.79	164	2.05	1.14	44	2.32*
Immature (1-5; 1 = very little, a pos. rating)	1.81	0.90	165	2.23	1.25	43	2.10*
Impulsive, not planful (1-5; 1 = very little, a pos. rating)	2.09	1.25	111	2.57	1.25	30	1.86*
A loser, masochistic (1-5; 1 = very little, a pos. rating)	1.86	1.03	111	2.44	1.19	27	2.59**
Ignorant or naive about sex (1-5; 1 = very little, a pos. rating)	2.04	0.99	108	2.56	1.16	27	2.36**
Negative ratings by interviewer on more-used scales (5-26; 5 = least neg.)	9.31	3.70	162	10.90	4.95	41	1.92*
Combined negative ratings by interviewer (13-66; 13 = least neg.)	23.49	9.20	57	29.56	11.20	16	2.22*

TABLE 4.6 (Continued)

Measure	Birth Planners			Pregnant Group			t^c
	Mean	SD	N	Mean	SD	N	
Contextual Characteristics							
Going to school (1 = full-time; 2 = part-time; 3 = no)	1.55	0.80	164	2.00	0.95	45	3.21***
Living arrangement (1 = with parents; 2 = alone, room-mate, etc.; 3 = with man)	1.34	0.66	165	1.55	0.82	44	1.75[a,b]
Expect to move soon (1 = no; 2 = up to 10 mi.; 3 = yes, unspecified location; 4 = farther)	1.61	1.05	163	1.37	0.76	43	-1.66[a,b]
No. of unmarried girls known who have had sex	20.48	23.65	54	35.10	32.37	10	1.69*
No. of friends who have tried marijuana (1-5; 5 = all)	3.70	1.05	69	4.85	0.38	13	7.03***
No. of friends who use marijuana regularly (1-5; 5 = nearly all)	2.70	1.32	69	3.77	1.48	13	2.64**
No. of friends who tried LSD or psychedelics (1-5; 5 = all)	1.72	0.80	69	2.83	1.27	12	2.93**
Friends' models for deviance (7-35; 7 = least)	18.00	4.34	68	21.36	4.20	11	2.40**

[a] $p < .10$
[*] $p < .05$ See TABLE 4.1 for interpretation.
[**] $p < .01$
[***] $p < .001$
[b] 2-tailed test (all others are 1-tailed)
[c] Negative t means finding is opposite to direction predicted.

high school or college, and more were still living with their parents. These two findings may help to explain the unexpected fact that the birth planners were also more likely to be planning a longer move in the near future. Finally, four items and an overall scale showed that the unwanted pregnancy group had more peer-group models of deviant behavior (in drug usage as well as sexuality) than did the birth planner group—a finding consistent with the differences in their level of socialization.

Summary. We can summarize the various types of differences found between good and poor contraceptors in Study Two as follows. There were quite marked differences between the groups in three categories: (1) In sexual and

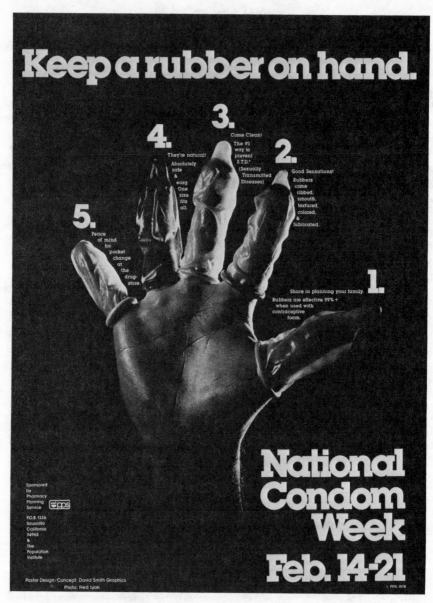

FIG. 4.1. According to results presented in this chapter, *planfulness* is consistently linked with contraceptive success. This poster uses humor to remind teens of the need for such planfulness. (Reproduced courtesy of Pharmacists Planning Service, Inc., P.O. Box 1336, Sausalito, CA. 94965. Posters are available upon request. © Pharmacists Planning Service, Inc.).

contraceptive knowledge the good contraceptors were superior on many measures. (2) In personal and contextual characteristics the good contraceptors were superior on measures of peer relationships, internal locus-of-control, planfulness, socialization, the impression that they made on interviewers, and their avoidance of socially deviant friendships. (3) In sexual and contraceptive attitudes the good contraceptors were higher on many attitudes and intentions which were consistent with effective use of birth control, though they were also unexpectedly higher on several items concerning worries about the possible ineffectiveness or inconvenience of using birth control. In a fourth area, sexual and contraceptive experience, there were substantial differences between the two groups, but some were in unexpected directions: as predicted, the good contraceptors had had less sexual experience, fewer pregnancies, etc.; but unexpectedly, they had also had less experience with several aspects of birth control and less discussion of sexual topics with their partners. Finally, in the area of demographic variables, there were relatively few differences between the two groups, except that the poor contraceptors were more likely to be ethnic minorities and to have lower levels of education and socioeconomic status.

Sub-Group Analyses

Another type of analysis which we carried out was to compare the significant predictors of contraceptive success for one sub-group of patients with the significant predictors for other sub-groups. As an example, it is possible that, even within the limited age group of teenagers, there could be different predictors of birth planning success for younger teenagers (below age 18) than for older teenagers (ages 18–19). If large differences of this sort were found when using age as a moderator variable, then it would be necessary to make predictions separately for each age group in order to approach optimum levels of prediction.

In fact, that is exactly what was found in the analysis using age as a moderator variable. These results confirmed the suggestions of other researchers (e.g., Cobliner, 1970) that there are differing bases for contraceptive failure in the teenage years, depending on the age of the teenager. Specifically, we found that only 50% of the younger group's significant predictor variables would be useful in predicting contraceptive success for the older teenagers, while 42% of the predictors would not be useful due to their very low correlations ($r < .10$) for the older group, and 8% of the predictors would be incorrect since they operated in opposite directions for the two groups.

Actually this result for age as a moderator variable showed one of the *highest* degrees of commonality of predictors across sub-groups that was obtained in 9 different analyses which we carried out, using several types of moderator variables (demographic variables, sex experience, sex attitudes, and contextual variables). For instance, using ethnic background as a moderator variable, there were considerably fewer common predictors for the racial sub-groups than for the age sub-groups mentioned above. A fairly typical example here showed that trying to apply the Anglo sub-group's significant predictors to the Black sub-group would yield only 24% useful predictors, 46% which were not useful due to their small size, and 30% which would predict in the reverse direction. Thus, Blacks and Anglos had more significant predictors that worked in opposite directions than in the same direction. Hence, it would be hopeless to try to make predictions for one racial sub-group based on the significant predictors for a different racial sub-group.

Results for the other moderator variables which we investigated were never appreciably better than those for age mentioned above, and a number of them were about as unsuccessful as the illustration given for the racial sub-groups. Consequently, we concluded that adequate prediction of each sub-group could only be done by using its own significant predictor variables, and not by using a prediction equation based on the whole sample of patients. Therefore we did not attempt to carry out multiple regression analyses for the total sample of patients, as we had done in Study One.

Results of Clinic Educational Programs

A final question of interest in this study concerned the effectiveness of the clinics' standard programs of sexual and contraceptive education. All of the clinics involved in the study had such informational sessions as one part of the regular clinic routine. Normally our interviewers were able to contact patients and give them the sex and contraceptive knowledge questionnaire to answer before the education session began. However, sometimes the education session was held early, or patients arrived late, so that there was no time for testing beforehand. As a result, we were able to conduct a quasi-experimental study of the impact of the clinic educational programs, a topic completely separate from any of our previous analyses.

The research design for this study compared 269 patients who took the sex knowledge questionnaire before the education session with 83 who took it afterward. The results were quite clearcut and favorable regarding the effect of the educational program. The posttest group scored significantly better than the pretest group at the .001 level on both subtest scores and on the total sex knowledge scale. Thus, it appears clear that they learned a substantial amount in the education session. On individual items the increase in knowledge ranged from 0% on some items to 20% on others, with a mean difference of exactly 10%. The two items (stated in abbreviated form) which showed practically no effect of the session were:

A good indication of a girl's fertility is: (the regularity of her period).
Birth control pills will really mess a girl up inside.

while the three items (abbreviated) which displayed the greatest effect were:

No birth control method can be trusted.
Men can almost go crazy if they don't have sex.
A girl's not having a climax helps prevent pregnancy.

Fifteen of the 21 items showed a substantial superiority in scores (> 5%) for patients who were tested after the education session (versus before it), so it appears that the learning in these sessions was relatively broad in scope.

DISCUSSION

The results described above provide some clear evidence of convergent validity in specifying factors which will predict contraceptive success or failure. Yet in interpreting these findings and comparing them to those of other studies, it is important to keep in mind the differences in the research populations used. In particular, our studies of clinic patients have focused on young women who have recognized and publicly admitted that they are, or are about to become, sexually active. In contrast, some studies have included many girls who had not yet reached that perceptual watershed, and other studies have included more older women and/or married women. Consequently, the factors which predict success or failure in avoiding pregnancy are apt to be somewhat different for these differing groups.

From a methodological perspective, the present findings once again clearly demonstrate the value of a psychological approach to contraception research as a supplement to the previously heavily-emphasized demographic approach. In fact, in these studies, demographic factors were generally not useful predictors, with the exception of ethnic group and measures of socioeconomic status. One reason for this may be the fact that sociocultural differences in fertility norms among U.S. urban groups are rapidly disappearing, so that predictions based on demographic variables alone are likely to be increasingly inadequate (Sweet, 1974).

Another methodological point highlighted by our findings is the importance of using behavioral outcome measures. In the past many psychological studies have used contraception attitudes or intentions as the criteria to be predicted, instead of overt behavior. Our research shows that, though attitudes and intentions are important, they are just one of several domains which must be considered in understanding contraception behavior and outcomes.

Parallel to this conclusion is our demonstration that personality and attitudinal variables are useful in predicting contraceptive behavior. This is contrary to the views of writers such as Mischel (1968), who has claimed that situational variables are more important than personological ones. However, in studying complex social behaviors longitudinally over a period of years, our research has found relatively few situational variables which are good predictors, whereas it has shown that many personality and attitudinal variables are useful in predicting contraceptive behavior.

Among the psychological factors studied, we have found general support for: (a) the importance of experiential and cognitive variables (particularly sexual and contraceptive knowledge), (b) the utility of personality measures and social-context variables such as peer-group influences toward deviancy, and (c) a fair degree of consistency between overt behavior and attitude or behavioral intention measures.

Another conclusion from the present research is based on data from the randomly-selected control group of clinic intake patients in Study One. Compared with these control subjects, the research group's greater amount of initial contact and later follow-up produced significantly higher rates of clinic retention and of promptness in return visits. This finding has important practical implications for intensive clinic intake programs and follow-up campaigns.

Results Bearing on Specific Hypotheses

Before concluding, let us briefly summarize the results relevant to each of the hypotheses concerning predictors of contraceptive success stated earlier in this chapter. For hypotheses (a) and (b), regarding greater socialization and higher personal efficacy, we found little support in Study One but substantial support in Study Two.

For hypotheses (c) and (d), concerning greater sexual knowledge and greater planfulness, we found support in both studies and particularly strong support in Study Two.

Hypothesis (e), about better psychological adjustment, met with opposing evidence from the interviewer ratings in Study One but received support from them in Study Two. Other measures of adjustment were nonsignificant, so no clear conclusions can be drawn. Hypothesis (f), concerning better communication, also produced mixed results. It received a little support in Study One, but in Study Two it was supported regarding communication with parents but contradicted regarding communication with the sexual partner.

Hypotheses (g) and (h), concerning attitudes and behavioral intentions conducive to careful use of contraception, received no support in Study One, but some support in Study Two.

Hypothesis (i), about greater past contraceptive use, was supported in Study One but contradicted in Study Two (except for the item about past use of condoms). However, hypothesis (j), regarding low past levels of sexual activity, received some support in Study One and stronger support in Study Two. Finally, hypothesis (k), linking life transitions with contraceptive failure, received no clear support in either study.

Conclusion

In summarizing the value of these studies, we would stress that they share both the strengths and weaknesses of naturalistic, longitudinal, multivariate research designs. They have investigated socially important questions, studied them in real-life situations, and tracked the research subjects for several years in order to develop stable measures of their behavior. On the other hand, in this kind of research there are many complex interrelationships among the variables, and there is no possibility of experimentally controlling the conditions and experiences of the subjects. Since the design is correlational in nature, it is more difficult to demonstrate causal connections between variables. However, despite these inevitable limitations, we have found support for a number of hypotheses based on past research studies, and we have had some success in predicting important contraceptive behaviors on a longitudinal basis.

Finally, from a practical point of view, these methods and findings may not only have predictive value, but they may also suggest new approaches to planning treatment strategies in family planning agencies, both public and private. A basic goal in such intervention programs must be to break the web of relationships between low socialization, poor personal efficacy and adjustment, insufficient information, poor planning, unfavorable attitudes and intentions, and responsiveness to external pressures toward deviancy—all of which can contribute to inadequate contraceptive behavior in which society and the unfortunate adolescent both lose. Future research should continue to be directed toward breaking this chain of relationships.

ACKNOWLEDGMENTS

We are grateful for the help of countless people in carrying out this research: particularly the 2000 or so young women whose contraceptive progress we have studied; the dozens of interviewers, coders, clinic staff members, research assistants, and secretaries who have contributed to the work; and the Center for Population Research of NICHD which provided six years of support under research grant HD-08074 and research contract HD-82842.

REFERENCES

Adler, N. E. *Factors affecting contraceptive use.* Paper presented at the American Psychological Association meeting, New Orleans, August 1974.

Ager, J. *Comparison of participants and dropouts from a contraceptive teen program.* Paper presented at the American Psychological Association meeting, Washington, D.C., September 1976.

Ager, J. W., Werley, H. H., & Shea, F. P. Correlates of continuance in a family planning program. *Journal of Obstetric, Gynecologic, and Neonatal Nursing,* 1973, *2*, 15–23.

Argyris, C. Dangers in applying results from experimental social psychology. *American Psychologist*, 1975, *30*, 469–485.

Baldwin, W. H. Adolescent pregnancy and childbearing—Growing concerns for Americans. *Population Bulletin*, 1976, *31*(2), 1–34.

Ball, G. W. *A method of identifying the potential unwed adolescent.* Unpublished doctoral dissertation, University of California at Los Angeles, 1973.

Bandura, A. Self-efficacy: Toward a unifying theory of behavioral change. *Psychological Review*, 1977, *84*, 191–215.

Bardwick, J. Psychological factors in the acceptance and use of oral contraceptives. In J. T. Fawcett (Ed.), *Psychological perspectives on population.* New York: Basic Books, 1973.

Bauman, K. E., & Udry, J. R. Powerlessness and regularity of contraception in an urban Negro male sample. *Journal of Marriage and the Family*, 1972, *34*, 112–114.

Bendig, A. W. The development of a short form of the manifest anxiety scale. *Journal of Consulting Psychology*, 1956, *20*, 384.

Brooks, G. G., & Butcalis, M. R. Psychometric testing as a basis for counseling patients choosing a method of contraception. *American Journal of Obstetrics and Gynecology*, 1976, *124*, 85–87.

Brown, L. S. *Do users have more fun: A study of the relationship between contraceptive behavior, sexual assertiveness, and patterns of causal attribution.* Unpublished doctoral dissertation, Southern Illinois University at Carbondale, 1977.

Buros, O. K. (Ed.). *The seventh mental measurements yearbook.* Highland Park, N.J.: Gryphon Press, 1972.

Byrne, D. A pregnant pause in the sexual revolution. *Psychology Today*, July 1977, *11*(2), 67–68.

Campbell, B. K., & Barnlund, D. C. Communication style: A clue to unplanned pregnancy. *Medical Care*, 1977, *15*, 181–186.

Cernada, G. P., & Crawford, T. J. Some practical applications of social psychology to family-planning programs. In J. T. Fawcett (Ed.), *Psychological perspectives on population.* New York: Basic Books, 1973.

Chilman, C. S. *Adolescent sexuality in a changing American society: Social and psychological perspectives.* Washington, D.C.: U.S. Government Printing Office, 1979.

Cobliner, W. G. Teen-age out-of-wedlock pregnancy: A phenomenon of many dimensions. *Bulletin of the New York Academy of Medicine*, 1970, *46*, 438–447.

Cobliner, W. G., Schulman, H., & Romney, S. L. The termination of adolescent out-of-wedlock pregnancies and the prospects for their primary prevention. *American Journal of Obstetrics and Gynecology*, 1973, *115*, 432–444.

Cobliner, W. G., Schulman, H., & Smith, V. Patterns of contraceptive failures: The role of motivation re-examined. *Journal of Biosocial Science*, 1975, *7*, 307–318.

Cole, S. G. *Critical factors in family planning participation.* Final progress report for NICHD grant, Texas Christian University, 1975.

Craik, K. H. *Social and asocial patterns of temporal behavior.* Unpublished doctoral dissertation, University of California, Berkeley, 1964.

Cronbach, L. J. Beyond the two disciplines of scientific psychology. *American Psychologist*, 1975, *30*, 116–127.

Cvetkovich, G., Grote, B., Bjorseth, A., & Sarkissian, J. On the psychology of adolescents' use of contraceptives. *The Journal of Sex Research*, 1975, *11*, 256–270.

Davidson, A. R., & Jaccard, J. J. *Application of the Fishbein behavioral-intentions model to fertility behavior.* Paper presented at the American Psychological Association meeting, Washington, D.C., September 1976.

Davidson, A. R., & Jaccard, J. J. Variables that moderate the attitude-behavior relation: Results of a longitudinal survey. *Journal of Personality and Social Psychology*, 1979, *37*, 1364–1376.

Downs, P. E. *Examining the intrafamily decision-making process with respect to contraceptive behavior.* Unpublished doctoral dissertation, The University of North Carolina at Chapel Hill, 1976.

Drucker, C. A. *The psychological aspects of contraceptive choice among single women.* Unpublished doctoral dissertation, Adelphi University, 1975.

Fawcett, J. T., & Bornstein, M. H. Modernization, individual modernity, and fertility. In J. T. Fawcett (Ed.), *Psychological perspectives on population.* New York: Basic Books, 1973.

Fishbein, M. Attitude and the prediction of behavior. In M. Fishbein (Ed.), *Readings in attitude theory and measurement.* New York: Wiley, 1967.

Fishbein, M., & Ajzen, I. *Belief, attitude, intention and behavior: An introduction to theory and research.* Reading, Mass.: Addison-Wesley, 1975.

Freud, S. Formulations regarding the two principles in mental functioning. In *Collected papers* (Vol. 4). London: Hogarth, 1953.

Fujita, B., Wagner, N., & Pion, R. Contraceptive use among single college students: A preliminary report. *American Journal of Obstetrics and Gynecology,* 1971, *109,* 787–793.

Furstenberg, F., Jr., Gordis, L., & Markowitz, M. Birth control knowledge and attitudes among unmarried pregnant adolescents: A preliminary report. *Journal of Marriage and the Family,* 1969, *31,* 34–42.

Gerrard, M. Sex guilt in abortion patients. *Journal of Consulting and Clinical Psychology,* 1977, *45,* 708.

Goldsmith, S., Gabrielson, M., Gabrielson, I., Matthews, V., & Potts, L. Teenagers, sex and contraception. *Family Planning Perspectives,* 1972, *4,* 32–38.

Gough, H. G. Theory and measurement of socialization. *Journal of Consulting Psychology,* 1960, *24,* 23–30.

Gough, H. G. *Manual for the personal values abstract.* Palo Alto, Calif.: Consulting Psychologists Press, 1972.

Gough, H. G. A factor analysis of contraceptive preferences. *Journal of Psychology,* 1973, *84,* 199–210. (a)

Gough, H. G. Personality assessment in the study of population. In J. R. Fawcett (Ed.), *Psychological perspectives on population.* New York: Basic Books, 1973. (b)

Groat, H. T., & Neal, A. G. Social psychological correlates of urban fertility. *American Sociological Review,* 1967, *32,* 945–959.

Grunebaum, H., & Abernethy, V. Marital decision making as applied to family planning. *Journal of Sex & Marital Therapy,* 1974, *1,* 63–74.

Hagelis, J. P. *Unwed adolescent pregnancy and contraceptive practice.* Unpublished doctoral dissertation, California School of Professional Psychology, Los Angeles, 1973.

Jaccard, J. J., & Davidson, A. R. Toward an understanding of family planning behaviors: An initial investigation. *Journal of Applied Social Psychology,* 1972, *2,* 228–235.

Jessor, S. L., & Jessor, R. Transition from virginity to nonvirginity among youth: A social-psychological study over time. *Developmental Psychology,* 1975, *11,* 473–484.

Kane, F. J., Jr., & Lachenbruch, P. A. Adolescent pregnancy: A study of aborters and non-aborters. *American Journal of Orthopsychiatry,* 1973, *43,* 796–803.

Kantner, J. F., & Zelnik, M. Sexual experiences of young unmarried women in the United States. *Family Planning Perspectives,* 1972, *4*(4), 9–17.

Kantner, J. F., & Zelnik, M. Contraception and pregnancy: Experience of young unmarried women in the United States. *Family Planning Perspectives,* 1973, *5*(1), 21–35.

Kar, S. B. Individual aspirations as related to early and late acceptance of contraception. *The Journal of Social Psychology,* 1971, *83,* 235–245.

Kar, S. B. *Consistency between fertility attitudes and behavior: A conceptual model.* Paper presented at American Psychological Association meeting, Washington, D.C., September 1976.

Keller, A. B., Sims, J. H., Henry, W. E., & Crawford, T. J. Psychological sources of "resistance" to family planning. *Merrill-Palmer Quarterly of Behavior and Development,* 1970, *16,* 286–302.

Kothandapani, V. *A psychological approach to the prediction of contraceptive behavior.* Chapel Hill, N.C.: Carolina Population Center, 1971.

Lehfeldt, H. Psychology of contraceptive failure. *Medical Aspects of Human Sexuality,* 1971, *5,* 68–77.

Lewin, K. Behavior and development as a function of the total situation. In L. Carmichael (Ed.), *Manual of child psychology.* New York: Wiley, 1946.

Luker, K. C. *Taking chances: Abortion and the decision not to contracept.* Berkeley: University of California Press, 1975.

Lundy, J. R. Some personality correlates of contraceptive use among unmarried female college students. *The Journal of Psychology,* 1972, *80,* 9–14.

MacDonald, A. P., Jr. Internal-external locus of control and the practice of birth control. *Psychological Reports,* 1970, *27,* 206.

McGuire, W. J. The yin and yang of progress in social psychology: Seven Koan. *Journal of Personality and Social Psychology,* 1973, *26,* 446–456.

Miller, W. B. Psychological vulnerability to unwanted pregnancy. *Family Planning Perspectives,* 1973, *5,* 199–201. (a)

Miller, W. B. *The personal style inventory.* Unpublished manuscript, Stanford University, 1973. (b)

Miller, W. B. Psychological antecedents to conception among abortion seekers. *Western Journal of Medicine,* 1975, *122,* 12–19.

Miller, W. B. *Some psychological factors predictive of undergraduate sexual and contraceptive behavior.* Paper presented at the American Psychological Association meeting, Washington, D.C., September 1976.

Miller, W. B. *Sexual and contraceptive knowledge questionnaire.* Unpublished manuscript, Stanford University, no date.

Mindick, B. Attitudes toward population issues. In S. Oskamp, *Attitudes and opinions.* Englewood Cliffs, N.J.: Prentice-Hall, 1977.

Mindick, B. *Personality and social psychological correlates of success or failure in contraception: A longitudinal predictive view.* Unpublished doctoral dissertation, Claremont Graduate School, Claremont, California, 1978.

Mindick, B., & Oskamp, S. Longitudinal predictive research: An approach to methodological problems in studying contraception. *Journal of Population,* 1979, *2,* 259–276.

Mindick, B., Oskamp, S., & Berger, D. E. Prediction of success or failure in birth planning: An approach to prevention of individual and family stress. *American Journal of Community Psychology,* 1977, *5,* 447–459.

Mischel, W. *Personality and assessment.* New York: Wiley, 1968.

Noble, L. D. *Personality characteristics associated with contraceptive behavior in women seeking abortion under liberalized California law.* Unpublished doctoral dissertation, California School of Professional Psychology, San Francisco, 1972.

Oskamp, S., Mindick, B., Berger, D., & Motta, E. A longitudinal study of success versus failure in contraceptive planning. *Journal of Population,* 1978, *1,* 69–83.

Parcel, G. S. *A study of the relationship between contraceptive attitudes and behavior in a group of unmarried university students.* Unpublished doctoral dissertation, Pennsylvania State University, 1974.

Rader, G. E., Bekker, L. D., Brown, L., & Richardt, C. Psychological correlates of unwanted pregnancy. *Journal of Abnormal Psychology,* 1978, *87,* 373–376.

Rosenberg, M. *Society and the adolescent self-image.* Princeton, N.J.: Princeton University Press, 1965.

Rotter, J. B. Generalized expectancies for internal versus external control of reinforcement. *Psychological Monographs,* 1966, *80*(1, Whole No. 609).

Rotter, J. B. Some problems and misconceptions related to the construct of internal versus external control of reinforcement. *Journal of Consulting and Clinical Psychology,* 1975, *48,* 56–67.

Rovinsky, J. J. Abortion recidivism: A problem in preventive medicine. *American Journal of Obstetrics and Gynecology,* 1972, *39,* 649–659.

Schwartz, S. Effects of sex guilt and sexual arousal on the retention of birth control information. *Journal of Consulting and Clinical Psychology*, 1973, *41*, 61–64.

Scott, W. A., & Wertheimer, M. *Introduction to psychological research.* New York: John Wiley & Sons, 1962.

Seeley, O. F. Field dependence-independence, internal-external locus of control, and implementation of family-planning goals. *Psychological Reports*, 1976, *38*, 1216–1218.

Seligman, M. E. P. *Helplessness: On depression, development, and death.* San Francisco, Calif.: Freeman, 1975.

Shipley, R. R. *Changes in contraceptive knowledge, attitudes and behavior in a college current health problems class.* Unpublished doctoral dissertation, Temple University, 1974.

Slagle, S. J., Arnold, C. B., & Glascock, E. *Self competence: A measure of relative risk of unwanted pregnancy?* Paper presented at the American Psychological Association meeting, New Orleans, 1974.

Slavin, M. E. *Ego functioning in women who use birth control effectively and ineffectively.* Unpublished doctoral dissertation, Boston University School of Education, 1975.

Spain, J. S. *Psychological dimensions of effective and ineffective contraceptive use in adolescent girls.* Unpublished doctoral dissertation, City University of New York, 1977.

Stein, K. B., Sarbin, T. R., & Kulik, J. A. Future time perspective. *Journal of Consulting and Clinical Psychology*, 1968, *32*, 257–264.

Steinlauf, B. *Attitudes and cognitive factors associated with the contraceptive behavior of young women.* Unpublished doctoral dissertation, Wayne State University, 1977.

Sweet, J. A. Differentials in the rate of fertility decline: 1960–1970. *Family Planning Perspectives*, 1974, *6*, 103–107.

Townes, B. D., Beach, L. R., Campbell, F. L., & Wood, R. J. *Values, behavioral intentions and fertility behavior.* Paper presented at the American Psychological Association meeting, Washington, D.C., September 1976.

Udry, J. R. Differential fertility by intelligence: The role of birth planning. *Social Biology*, 1978, *25*, 10–14.

Vener, A. M., & Stewart, C. S. Adolescent sexual behavior in middle America revisited: 1970–1973. *Journal of Marriage and the Family*, 1974, *36*, 728–735.

Vincent, C. E. *Unmarried mothers.* New York: Glencoe Free Press, 1961.

Warner, W. L., Meeker, M., & Eells, K. *Social class in America.* Chicago: Science Research Associates, 1949.

Werner, P. D. Implications of attitude-behavior studies for population research and action. *Studies in Family Planning*, 1977, *8*, 294–299.

White, R. W. Motivation reconsidered: The concept of competence. *Psychological Review*, 1959, *66*, 297–333.

Zelnik, M., & Kantner, J. Sexuality, contraception and pregnancy among young unwed females in the U.S. In C. F. Westoff & R. Parke, Jr. (Eds.), *Demographic and social aspects of population growth and American future research report,* No. 1. Washington, D.C.: U.S. Government Printing Office, 1973.

Zelnik, M., & Kantner, J. F. Sexual and contraceptive experience of young unmarried women in the United States, 1976 and 1971. *Family Planning Perspectives*, 1977, *9*, 55–71.

Zelnik, M., & Kantner, J. F. First pregnancies to women aged 15–19: 1976 and 1971. *Family Planning Perspectives*, 1978, *10*, 11–20. (a)

Zelnik, M., & Kantner, J. F. Contraceptive patterns and premarital pregnancy among women aged 15–19 in 1976. *Family Planning Perspectives*, 1978, *10*, 135–142. (b)

5 Adolescent Development and Teenage Fertility

George Cvetkovich and Barbara Grote
Western Washington University

Editors' Note

What is it like to be young and in love? According to George Cvetkovich and Barbara Grote, an adolescent's transition to sexual activity may cause such conflict and denial as to make it impossible for them to plan for contraception. It is pointed out that, during adolescence, teens must eventually come to accept their own sexuality and learn to think about it rationally. Many teenagers, however, begin to have sexual intercourse *before* they develop the psychosexual maturity that is required for contraceptive planning. This may result in contraceptive neglect for as long as teens are unable to see themselves as sexual beings with contraceptive needs. A longitudinal study of high school students was conducted to examine these assumptions, and the findings reported in this chapter confirm the hypothesized links among maturity, teens' acceptance of their own sexuality, and the responsible use of contraception.

In one sense it is paradoxical that there is a heightened concern about teenage fertility at this time. Statistics show that there has actually been a recent drop in the rate of fertility for women under the age of twenty (Baldwin, 1976). A high point in teenage fertility was reached in 1957 when 97.3 births for every 1,000 women between the ages of 15 to 19 years occurred. In 1974 the rate was 58.7 per 1,000, a little more than half of the 1957 rate. There has even been a slight decline in the absolute number of children borne by teenage mothers. While the number of women between 15 and 19 years of age increased dramatically between 1960 and 1974, owing to the declining fertility rate, the annual number of births decreased from 609,000 to 608,000. We can expect that as the proportion of teenagers in the population decreases (a certainty given current trends) so too will this age group's contribution to the total fertility rate.

Can it be that concern for the "epidemic" of teenage pregnancies is another media hype devised more to keep TV audiences tuned in on the six o'clock news between commercials than to direct attention and concern towards a real social problem? Seemingly not. While the last two decades have witnessed declines in both the relative and absolute levels of teenage fertility, detailed analysis of these figures reveals ample reason for concern. Fertility declines for teenagers have not kept pace with those for women of older age groups (U.S. Department of Health, Education and Welfare, 1979). A majority of pregnancies to teenagers, at least 60% by conservative estimates, are not intended (Zelnik, Kim, & Kantner, 1979). The observed fertility declines noted above have been largely restricted to older (18 and 19-year-olds) and married teenagers. Fertility has not fallen for women under the age of 15 years. Also, teenagers are increasingly utilizing abortion as a method for handling unwanted pregnancies. Thirty-three percent of all abortions on American women are performed on teenagers. There is growing evidence that if a teenager carries her pregnancy to term and keeps the child, she will suffer many physical, psychological, and social and economic costs which are avoided by older mothers (Baldwin & Cain, 1980; David & Baldwin, 1979). If a teen mother and her child are to escape these hazards a great deal of help is needed from her family and other resources (Furstenberg, 1976; Furstenberg & Crawford, 1980). An indication of just how much help is needed is graphically shown by current levels of aid given to teenage mothers by the government. About half of the funds distributed under federal and state programs of Aid to Families with Dependent Children goes to households containing women who bore their first child as a teenager (Moore, Hofferth, Wertheimer, Caldwell, & Waite, 1979). In 1975 this amounted to $4.65 billion!

Concern for teenage fertility therefore certainly seems justified. A large number of women have early pregnancy and perhaps motherhood and their incumbent problems as part of their adolescent experience. Additionally, though obviously not unrelated, an even greater number of American women and men are experiencing premarital intercourse at an unprecedented age. How are we to understand the phenomenon of early parenthood, sexuality, fertility? The avenue of understanding taken by this chapter is to examine teenage fertility and sexuality from a developmental perspective. A major task of the adolescent years, roughly beginning at the onset of puberty, is the achievement of psychosexual maturity and competence. This achievement involves the ability to think about one's sexuality in an objective and rational manner. The very young adolescent may be as yet unable to live up to this demand of adult sexuality (Cvetkovich, Grote, Bjorseth, & Sarkissian, 1975). Indeed there are some who are probably uncertain that they want anything to do with the whole business of sex. The adolescent may not be ready, cognitively or emotionally, to accept his or her sexuality to the degree that allows planning for sex. The hypothesis examined here is that many American teenagers are beginning their sexual careers before psychosocial maturity and competency have been fully achieved.

Surprisingly, when one examines the literature on adolescent sexuality and fertility there is little discussion of developmental issues (cf. Chilman, 1980). On the one hand there are national or smaller sample surveys investigating attitudes and self-reported sexual and contraceptive behavior (Kantner & Zelnik, 1973; 1977; Sorensen, 1973; Miller & Simon, 1974). These "one-shot" surveys do not provide the longitudinal evidence needed to adequately discuss developmental trends. On the other hand, more traditional developmental research and theory assumes that sexual intimacy occurs after the individual has passed through other developmental events such as the completion of secondary education or the selection of an occupation (e.g., Erikson, 1961). As we know, it is increasingly common that sexual intimacy in its full physical sense precedes these events.

Description of the Study

The study described in this chapter was initially designed to develop personal and other individual predictors of teenagers who are at high risk of experiencing (or causing) a pregnancy (Lieberman, 1976; Cvetkovich, Grote, Lieberman, & Miller, 1978; Miller, 1978a, b; 1979a, b, c).

It was coordinated by the American Public Health Association and was conducted in two large metropolitan areas: Washington, D.C., and Atlanta, Georgia; and one smaller urban area, Bellingham, Washington.[1] Only the 120 women and the 101 men in the Washington State sample will be discussed. It might be noted, however, that very few important differences between sites were found. A slight difference was found in average sexual attitudes. The Washington, D.C. sample held the most accepting attitudes towards premarital intercourse, the Washington State sample the least, and the Atlanta sample was in between. There are no large differences in sexual or contraceptive behavior. At any rate, the teenagers discussed in this paper are white, mostly middle class and between the ages of 15 to 19 years. When they were first interviewed most were either 16 or 17 years of age while at the time of the second interview most were 17 or 18 years old.

In the first year of the study, 1975, the teenagers, mostly eleventh graders at the time, were interviewed and completed questionnaires relating to activities and attitudes on sex, family, education, personality, and a variety of other topics. Each interview took 1 to 1 1/2 hours. Approximately 50% of the students listed on current rosters of the two city high schools were randomly selected and

[1]Other investigators in the study were: E. James Lieberman and Sarah Brown (American Public Health Association), Warren Miller (American Institutes for Research), Paul Poppen (George Washington University), and Fred Crawford (Emory University). This research was supported under Grant R01 HD09813, Center for Population Research, National Institutes of Health.

contacted to participate in the study. Sixty-three percent of those selected actually participated in the study. The major reasons for nonparticipation were inability to contact the teenager and other conflicting commitments. The regular high school sample was supplemented by interviews with 14 students attending two alternative high schools. Approximately one-fourth of the "first year" participants were again interviewed 12 to 18 months later.

SEXUAL ACTIVITY

The information obtained on premarital sexual activity for females is in line with national survey statistics reported by Kantner and Zelnik (1977). In 1976, 57% of the women in our study reported that they were sexually experienced, having their first sexual intercourse, on the average, at about 16 years of age. This degree of experience is slightly higher than the national statistics for 18 and 19-year-olds. Kantner and Zelnik report 45% and 55% for these ages, respectively. This difference may be the result of the selection technique used which gave participants more time to consider whether they wished to be in our study than did that of Kantner and Zelnik. Thus we may have been slightly more likely to *ex*clude virgins than to *in*clude sexually active persons. Only a slightly higher percent of males than females, 62.4%, had ever had sexual intercourse. This supports the common observation of a decline in a double standard of sexual activity for the sexes (Chilman, 1980). Comparisons between the sexes on other aspects of sexual activity are presented in Table 5.1.

The terms "sexually active" and "sexually experienced" refer to those individuals who have had full sexual intercourse at least once. "Active" does not refer either to frequency or to recency of intercourse. Our statistics, as do those from other studies, indicate that sexual experience among teenagers is infrequent relative to that of older individuals. In the 3 months prior to the interview only 23% of the women classified as sexually active had intercourse more than once a week, 59% had sex fewer times, and 17% did not have intercourse at all during this period. Regrettably, in spite of the relatively low frequency of activity, the

TABLE 5.1
Comparison of Males and Females on Characteristics of Early Sexual Activity
(1976 data)

	Males	*Females*
Age at first sexual intercourse	15.3 years	16.1 years
Median frequency of intercourse	1 to 2 times in last three months	same
Mean number of sexual partners	3.0	2.4

number of pregnancies for our study group is high. Nearly one quarter of the sexually active women have been pregnant at least once. Over 20% of the ever-pregnant women have had more than one pregnancy.

As might be expected from the pregnancy statistics, contraceptive use is generally low. Thirty-three percent of the women in our study have been protected less than 50% of the time or never during their sexual experience. Eighty percent have been unprotected at least once. Conversely, this means that 20% have always been protected. Contraceptive protection is defined as the use of any of the effective methods such as pill, IUD, diaphragm, or condom. Additionally, correct and consistent use of rhythm or withdrawal was considered contraception since we are interested in assessing intentions and behavior, not biological risk of pregnancy. However, it was found that the more consistent the contraceptive use, the more likely it was that the individual did not rely solely on rhythm or withdrawal.

The Sexual Revolution and Attitudes: The (Somewhat) Permissive Teenager

One of the most common explanations of teenage sexual activity is that American society has experienced a sexual revolution. The image contained in this explanation is one of teenagers uncritically accepting sexual permissiveness as a personal attitude. It is certainly true that there has been a shift to permissiveness in sexual attitudes and behavior, but the sexual revolution as a singular explanation of adolescent behavior misses the important point that not all teenagers accept sexually permissive attitudes. Also there are notable inconsistencies between teenagers' sexual attitudes and behavior.

An index of sexual liberalism was computed based on responses to questions concerning premarital sex. The participants were asked if they accepted premarital intercourse for males and for females at three levels of relationship (when in love, with affection only, just physical attraction). Liberal attitudes were found to be significantly related to sexual activity ($r = .61$; $p < .05$). Sexually liberal women and men were more likely to be sexually active than are those who hold relatively conservative attitudes. But the difference in attitudes is not great. The mean attitude score for the sexually active women is 3.08 on a 7-point scale ("somewhat approve" of premarital sex). The mean score for virgins is 4.80 ("somewhat disapprove"). The relationship between attitudes and activity is less than it might be because of two groups of women who hold attitudes discrepant with their behavior: the sexually liberal women who were virgins, and the conservative women who were nonetheless sexually active.

Our interviews indicate that one reason why some virgins endorse premarital intercourse, but do not engage in it themselves, is that for them permissiveness is an abstraction. Their initial tendency in answering the attitude items was to be nonjudgmental. Essentially they seem to be saying "Yes, premarital intercourse is O.K., if it fits the standards of the person doing it." They may not be liberal when it comes to assessing the acceptability of premarital intercourse for themselves or their friends.

A second important reason for the less than perfect congruence between permissive attitudes and sexual activity results from the woman's assessment of her emotional and social development. An important reason given by many women for not being sexually active is the judgment that she is not yet mature enough to handle the emotions and responsibility which she reasonably connects with sexual activity. Self-assessed maturity was equally or more important than family background such as socioeconomic status or religion as a reason for not beginning sexual activity.

Virgin males also often reported that they had not had sexual intercourse because they were not ready for it. But, rather than emphasizing responsibility and emotional readiness, the males were more likely to say that they lacked the necessary interpersonal skills to seduce a partner. Reasons for not becoming sexually active demonstrate the persistence of traditional stereotyped sex roles. In the area of sexual activity, as in other areas of heterosexual relations, traditional roles specify that males initiate (or at least try to do so) and females regulate (or try to do so) (Peplau, Rubin, & Hill, 1977).

There are few sexually actives who hold conservative attitudes about premarital sex. Their number is much smaller than that of the liberal virgins. This pattern seems to be very recent. In a 1962 study Christensen (1966) found more conservative actives than liberal virgins in the U.S. A generally restricted moral atmosphere surrounded premarital sex at the time. A person might engage in premarital sex, but still not condone this activity. To do so would be to accept a deviant attitudinal value and to mark oneself as immoral. The recent pattern of activity and attitudes found in our study is similar to that found by Christensen for Denmark in 1962 which traditionally has had an accepting attitude towards premarital sex. Thus, at present it may be attitudinally deviant to be sexually conservative. Today—as in the late 1950s—adolescents are bringing their attitudes (but not necessarily their sexual behavior) into line with prevailing social mores.

While based on a relatively small sample, the material we have collected on conservative actives is instructive. These individuals, mainly women, may best be described as erotophobic (Byrne, Jazwinski, DeNinno, & Fisher, 1977; Fisher et al., Chapter 9, this volume). They hold negative attitudes towards sex, tend to deny their own sexual activity and avoid contraceptive responsibility. Erotophobia is often manifested in the circumstances of their sexual encounters. The woman often places herself in situations in which she will lose personal control and critical judgment and thus also lose personal responsibility for sexual conduct. Becoming drunk is one example. However, such "controlled" loss of control is not restricted to those with inconsistencies between their attitudes and behavior. It seems to be generally related to early sexual experience and probably provides a period of time in which to negotiate a new self-concept incorporating the facts of sexual activity. This period of psychological adjustment may account for the extreme length of time usually reported between first sexual intercourse and first use of effective contraception (i.e., between becoming sexual and self-admission of this fact).

CONTRACEPTIVE USE AND MATURITY

Protection at first intercourse.   There is a strong relationship between age at first intercourse and birth control use at first intercourse. The longer a woman postponed first intercourse, the more likely she was to be protected (see Table 5.2). Better contraceptive protection among older adolescent women can be accounted for by their greater acceptance of their sexuality, including the possibility of becoming pregnant if one has unprotected intercourse. For some of these women, a degree of acceptance of sexuality seems to predate the initiation of sexual intercourse. Of those who became active between the 1975 and 1976 interviews (i.e., became active at a later age) all but four had stated on the first interview that they either "definitely would," or "might" become premaritally active.

An acceptance of one's sexuality requires an ability to think about it objectively and rationally. The adolescent may be so tied up in reacting to believed opinions of others that it is very difficult for him or her to dispassionately examine goals, behavior, and alternative actions. In our research we find denial to be a typical adolescent reaction to the newly faced heterosexual situation.

For the sexually inactive we have found many cases of blatant denial of sexuality. This is particularly interesting in the case of teenagers who have active heterosexual social lives, but who are still virgins. The case of one female high school respondent is not unrepresentative. She and her steady boyfriend engaged in heavy petting, drank a lot (illegally), and had even slept together (without having intercourse) one night after a "wild party" at the house of a friend whose parents were out of town. In spite of such apparent advanced heterosexual activity, she denied having any desire to have sexual intercourse before she was

TABLE 5.2
Women's Age and Contraceptive Protection at
First Sexual Intercourse

N	Age at First Sex	% Protected at First Sex
24	13–15	17%
22	16	45%
22	17–18	55%

married, and she did not plan to marry for at least 6 years. She talked a lot about "reputation" and "respect" and what her parents would think if she were not a virgin. She did not openly worry about what her parents would think or her reputation vis-a-vis her illegal drinking, going to wild parties, and staying out all night, although she had said that neither her parents nor several of her "goody-goody" friends knew about this, and that they would be upset and shocked if they did. The dual standard she had developed for thinking about her own behavior did not seem to bother her.

Not only did she deny having any sexual desires herself, but when asked how her boyfriend felt, she stated that he agreed with her that intercourse should be saved until after marriage. While she admitted that they had never talked about this, she was nonetheless sure that he respected her for not letting him have intercourse with her. She said that the more a boy loves a girl, the more he does *not* want to have intercourse with her. Further, when a boy tries to "see how far he can go," he wants the girl to stop him. If the girl did not stop the boy's advances, he would probably just "see what all he could do and then drop her." She estimated that "almost no one" in her high school had had sex, and explained, "Just because people go to bed together, adults assume they are doing something wrong," i.e., that they are having sexual intercourse. She obviously did not assume so. When asked about the cases she knew of high school girls getting pregnant, she said she knew of several cases, and that she had been very surprised; she had not thought they were "that kind of girls."

After having discussed her ideas about premarital intercourse, the interviewer was discussing her perception of others' ideas. When talking about her siblings, this respondent revealed that she did not *really* believe that her oldest brother, who had been married for 2 years, had sexual intercourse with his wife! She thought some more and said, "Maybe they have a few times, but I won't believe it until she gets pregnant."

Such denial of sexuality should not be too surprising. The parents of many, if not most, young teenagers probably behave towards them as if they were asexual children. The young woman above made several references to her parents' thinking that she was "pure" and "innocent." What about her peers? The expected status of girls studied appears to be virginity. When talking about the sex education and family life classes they had had, many sexually active girls mentioned avoiding class discussions, or disguising their true ideas out of fear that classmates would discover they were not virgins.

Given the advanced state of her heterosexual activity as a 15-year-old high school sophomore, it seems highly unlikely that the young woman discussed above will avoid sexual intercourse until she is 21 (when she plans to marry). However, it seems probable that the cognitive and emotional conflict that will be aroused if she does engage in premarital intercourse will practically preclude the possibility of her using contraception. The conflict and denial will make it extremely difficult for her to objectively, rationally, analytically consider her behavior and its possible consequences, and make a decision to use effective contraception. More probably, there will be an extended period of unprotected intercourse during which she will try to think as little as possible about her sexual involvement or the possibility of becoming pregnant.

This is the kind of denial we have observed with several sexually active high school girls. Consider the following protocol from an interview with a 16-year-old junior girl: *typical attitude*

> *Interviewer:* (After discussing relationship with current boyfriend.) Is this a sexual relationship?
> *Respondent:* Well, sort of.
> *I:* I mean, have you had sexual intercourse with your boyfriend?
> *R:* Well, yes: but not every time we go out.
> *I:* Do you use any method of birth control?
> *R:* Well, no.
> *I:* Do you ever worry about becoming pregnant?
> *R:* I try not to think about that. I guess you could say I use the HOPE method. I hope I won't get pregnant. Every month I hope my period comes. But I really can't imagine me getting pregnant.

While we believe that the observed relationship between age at first intercourse and birth control use is due to maturity, there may be an historical effect operating as well. Since all participants were approximately the same age at the time of the interviews, those who were older at first intercourse experienced this event at an historically more recent date. For example, those who were 17 or 18 at first intercourse experienced this event sometime in 1976 or late 1975. On the other hand, the first intercourse for those who were 13 or 14 at the time occurred in the early 1970s. Thus the observed relationship between age and protection at first intercourse may reflect the compound effect of maturity, as well as historical improvement in general attitude toward birth control, availability of contraceptive services, and normative support for birth control use by teenagers.

Protection Last Three Months. In the spring of 1975, when the average age of participants was 16 1/2 years, age at first intercourse was one of the stronger predictors of current birth control use, defined as protection during the 3 months prior to interview. Two personality and social relationship variables were also moderately strong predictors of birth control use at this age: Better contraceptors disagreed with several social risk-taking items, such as "I am willing to try almost anything once" and "How I behave depends completely on the people I am with and the situation I am in." The more protected women tended to be involved with male partners who showed a greater emotional commitment to the relationship than was true of the partners of unprotected women. Interviews

indicate that the male partner was very influential in determining the contraceptive practices of the couple by either taking the responsibility to use condoms or
by suggesting that the woman obtain other methods.

The second interviews were conducted in the summer and fall of 1976, after
the participants had graduated from high school. By this time, overall contraceptive use had improved. In the 1975 sample approximately 25% of the sexually
active women had consistently used a birth control method during the 3 months
prior to interview. In 1976 the comparable proportion was 76%. Additionally, in
1976 different variables were associated with birth control use than in 1975.
Strong associations were found between good birth control use and the perception of birth control as effective, safe, and available. Higher frequency of intercourse (which tends to occur in more stable and serious relationships) was also
associated with better birth control use. Interviews indicate that older women
relied less on the male partner to provide the initiative for birth control use. In
sum, these data indicate that for younger, immature women, contraception use is
influenced by factors which are not readily susceptible to intervention; the most
important of these are personality traits, the emotional commitment of the male
partner to the relationship, and his attitude toward contraception. The picture 15
to 18 months later is somewhat more encouraging. There is a higher level of
protection which includes both a shift to more effective methods and more
women using a method 100% of the time. Also, the variables influencing birth
control use are more similar to those found among adult women. The older
women are less likely to abdicate responsibility for contraception to their male
partners. What is important to protection at this later age are responsible contraceptive attitudes and knowledge of services, and a relationship within which
sexual intercourse is predictable and relatively frequent. Finally, at the time of
the second interview, age at first intercourse no longer predicts current birth
control use; the very early active women have finally reached the higher level of
protection characteristic of the women who were more mature at first
intercourse.

RELATIONSHIPS TO PARENTS AND MATURITY

Much has been said about parent-child relationships during the adolescent years,
most notably about the presumed rebellion by children during this period. Many
writers caution that terms such as "rebellion" are overgeneralizations, since
most people seemingly pass very uneventful and relatively peaceful adolescent
years (e.g., Douvan & Adelson, 1966). However, there have been several attempts to relate sexual behavior to various forms of rebellious adolescent behavior. For instance, studies by Jessor and Jessor (1975), in Colorado, and Miller
and Simon (1974), in Illinois, have found a correlation between sexual activity

and "delinquent" acts: e.g., shoplifting, car joy-riding, beer drinking, marijuana smoking and the like.

Such results are suggestive at best, since they do not provide much evidence from the teenager's point of view about the motivations for the behavior. Sexual activity may be a form of rebellion, but it is also a way of seeking intimacy, having fun, doing what in some cases most others are doing, and an expression of individuality. Questions about rebellion would seem to be settled by examining whether the behavior is autonomous of the parents or not. That is, did the individual use sexual activity as a way of acting against the parent? There are three pieces of information in our study which allow us to examine this possibility: parents' attitudes on premarital sex, parents' disciplinary practices, and the quality of communication between parent and child. All of this information is based on teenagers' reports during the interview.

If teens are having sexual intercourse as a way of acting against their parents, one should find strong opposition to premarital activity among parents of the sexually active. One can hardly rebel against parents with behavior they condone or at least accept. By this logic, rebellion was not found in our study. In fact, if anything, the reverse was true. Parents of sexually active teenagers were reported to be more likely to hold liberal attitudes on premarital sex than were the parents of virgins. And in a sense, that sexually liberal parents have sexually liberal children should be no more surprising than the fact that Democratic parents have children who eventually vote Democratic themselves.

No differences were found between the actives and the virgins in the perceptions they have of their parents or in the interactions they have with them. Both groups feel "mostly good" about their parents. They report that their parents are moderately lax in their rules and somewhat inconsistent in their enforcement. Moderately open communication with mothers was reported by both groups, both for general topics and for marriage and sex. Slightly less communication was reported with fathers, but again virgins and actives did not differ on the average. Only one difference in parental behavior was found to be related to birth control use. Good birth control users reported that their parents were *less* strict in the enforcement of rules than did those with less effective birth control histories.

These findings indicate that early sexual experience is for many adolescents, not primarily a form of rebellion against parents. Rather it is an expression of personal preference and individuality.

Of course we do not wish to imply that rebellion is never a motivation for sexual activity. It is in some cases that seem mostly restricted to those women who have early sexual experience. Very early initiation of sexual activity (13 years old and younger) is often associated with promiscuity and very poor contraceptive use. Some of the early-active women report that they wanted to get pregnant so that they would have a baby to love, or so that they would be "grown up" and could leave home. Such young women often report having had very open communication with their mothers. However, the content of this "open communication" consists in good part of the daughter reporting to her mother every aspect of her misbehavior. The daughter was trying to demonstrate her independence from the mother, but her behavior was motivated by the mother's negative reactions. Such relationships are not typical of good parent-child interactions, where some degree of privacy and mutual respect of attitudes is found.

Parents and Sex Education.   Interview information on relationship to parents also has implications for sex education. In many communities, sex education programs have been opposed by individuals who hold that sexual topics should be taught in the home. The evidence we have speaks both to the possibilities and the limits of sex education in the home. Parental attitudes and values are important to teenagers. However, many teenagers report that discussions are limited because their parents cannot think of them as sexually capable people. Sometimes, interactions with nonfamily members offer a much less threatening atmosphere for the discussion and exploration of sexual attitudes. Teenagers seek out such contacts and have as their confidantes, not only counselors and sex education instructors, but also other teachers who have befriended them, older neighbors, relatives, and even persons for whom they babysit (see Fisher, Miller, Byrne, & White, 1980 on this topic).

SEXUAL AND CONTRACEPTIVE KNOWLEDGE

It is a frequent conclusion that the problems of premarital conception can be solved by increasing sexual and contraceptive knowledge. The President's Commission on Population Growth and the American Future (1972) summed up this thinking when it stated: "One characteristic American response to social issues is to propose educational programs, and this commission is no exception." The transmission of accurate sexual information is important, but our study results indicate that it is not a sufficient response to the problems of teenage fertility control. More and better education along lines other than conventional "information providing" is called for. Several points from our study are pertinent in this regard.

Results for the total sample on a five-item test of basic sex knowledge are given in Table 5.3. Sexually active individuals, both male and female, more often answered correctly and were certain of their answers than were virgins. The actives were also better able to recall or recognize different forms of birth control. This may indicate that because of their activity they are more alert to contraceptive information.

Among women at both ages studied, no differences in sex knowledge or contraceptive knowledge were found between good versus poor contraceptive

TABLE 5.3
Percent of Males anf Females Correctly Answering
Five Sex Knowledge Questions

	Percent Correct			
	1975		1976	
	Males	Females	Males	Females
Pregnancy can occur with the very first sexual intercourse.	85.7%	89.6%	93.6%	96.7%
Pregnancy cannot occur with the withdrawal method.	38.4%	52.6%	59.7%	65.7%
Chances of pregnancy are reduced if the woman is not sexually excited during intercourse.	89.9%	96.6%	96.2%	99.2%
Pregnancy will probably not occur if intercourse is only once in a while.	97.0%	100.0%	98.7%	100.0%
The safe time to have intercourse is the days just before and during the menstrual period.	47.4%	63.2%	65.0%	58.5%

users. All of the sexually active females were equally knowledgeable about the risk of unprotected coitus, and about specific contraceptive methods and their effectiveness. Among men at the first interview, knowledge of specific contraceptive methods was related to better contraceptive use. By the time of the second interview, however, all sexually active males were equally informed about various birth control methods.

The teenagers in our study probably have had sex education which is as good as, or better than, the national average. They have almost all had a required health course which devotes some time to human reproduction and birth control. This is better than 61% of such classes across the nation where the topic of "family planning" is not even discussed (Alan Guttmacher Institute, 1977). At any rate, their educational experience is uniform and thus does not allow assessment or any effects (on birth control practices) of differences in education.

The results do suggest that improvement lies not in better *informational* programs, but better *educational* ones. The need is not only for increasing information, but for adopting educational strategies which emphasize the application of information to one's own life. We see from our study that while relatively well informed, the sexually active still too often fail to use contraceptives. We have recently had the opportunity to conduct a preliminary investigation of a school which not only has a health course required by state law, but also provides an elective family planning course. Both of these courses not only provide information, but they also allow students the opportunity to actually explore, through discussions, lectures and programmed instruction units, their own feelings and attitudes, and the thinking of others about human sexuality. They are courses in sexual decision making. Our findings are tentative, but indicate that this program has the results it should. The students are accurately informed concerning factual aspects of sex and contraception, and seem to have a high degree of sexual responsibility. More of these students plan to postpone their initial coital experience until they are older. Contraception use is high among those who are sexually active. The program is possible because of concerned administrators who are willing to take sensible steps in developing educational programs, and because of faculty who are qualified to conduct the courses and dedicated to the success of the program.

CONCLUSION

Our study began with the question of how adolescent development is related to teenage fertility. It leads to the question, "Are teenagers really different from older individuals?" Our findings indicate that in some respect they are. Detailed here are some of the ways in which sexual experiences are influenced by social and emotional maturity, and some of the problems which result from the need to coordinate development on the levels of biology, individual differences, and social interactions. Many of these problems will never again concern the individual to the great extent that they do during adolescence.

It is well to remember, however, that in a larger sense, teenage fertility regulation is not greatly different than at later ages. Human fertility decisions always demand a blend of emotion and logic. This is an overriding characteristic of human sexuality. The ability to combine both feelings and facts in making life's decisions develops during the adolescent years. If we are to understand the dynamics of psychosexual development, this characteristic must be central to our thinking.

REFERENCES

Alan Guttmacher Institute. *11 Million Teenagers.* 1977.
Baldwin, W. Adolescent pregnancy and childbearing-growing concerns for Americans. *Population Reference Bureau.* 1976, *31,* 2, (Sept.).
Baldwin, W., & Cain, V. S. The children of teenage parents. *Family Planning Perspectives.* 1980, *12,* 1, 34–43.
Byrne, D., Jazwinski, C., DeNinno, J. A., & Fisher, W. A. Negative attitudes and contraception. In D. Byrne & L. Byrne (eds.), *Exploring human sexuality.* N.Y.: Crowell, 1977.
Chilman, C. S. Adolescent sexuality in a changing American society: Social and psychological perspectives. Washington, D.C.: U.S. Government Printing Office (NIH publ. no. 80-1426), 1980.

Christensen, H. T. Scandinavian and American sex morals: some comparisons with sociological implications. *Journal of Social Issues*. 1966, *22*, 60–75.

Commission on Population Growth and the American Future. *Population and the American Future*. New York: Signet, 1972.

Cvetkovich, G., Grote, B., Bjorseth, A., & Sarkissian, J. On the psychology of adolescents' use of contraception. *Journal of Sex Research*. 1975, *11*, 256–270.

Cvetkovich, G., Grote, B., Lieberman, E. J., & Miller, W. Sex role development and teenage fertility-related behavior. *Adolescence*, 1978, *8*, 50, 231–236.

David, H. P., & Baldwin, W. H. Childbearing and child development: demographic and psychosocial trends. *American Psychologist*. 1979, *34*, 10, 866–871.

Douvan, E., & Adelson, J. *The adolescent experience*. New York: Wiley, 1966.

Erikson, E. *Identity, youth & crisis*. New York: Norton, 1961.

Fisher, W. A., Miller, C. T., Byrne, D., & White, L. A. Talking dirty: Responses to communicating a sexual message as a function of situational and personality factors. *Basic and Applied Social Psychology*, 1980, *1*, 115–126.

Furstenberg, F., Jr. *Unplanned Parenthood: The Social Consequences of Teenage Childbearing*. The Free Press, 1976.

Furstenberg, F., & Crawford, A. G. The social implications of teenage childbearing. In P. B. Smith & D. M. Mumford (Eds.), *Adolescent pregnancy: Perspectives for the health professional*. Boston: C. K. Hall & Co., 1980.

Jessor, R., & Jessor, S. L. Transition from virginity to nonvirginity among youth: A social-psychological study over time. *Developmental Psychology*. 1975, *11*, 4, 473–484.

Kantner, J. F., & Zelnik, M. Contraception and pregnancy: experience of young unmarried women in the U.S. *Family Planning Perspectives*. 1973, *5*, 1, 21–25.

Kantner, J. F., & Zelnik, M. Sexual and contraceptive experience of young unmarried women in the United States, 1976 and 1971. *Family Planning Perspectives*. 1977, *9*, 2, 55–71.

Lieberman, E. J. *From innocence to experience*. Paper presented at the Scientific Session of the American Public Health Association meeting. October, 1976.

Miller, P., & Simon, W. Adolescent sexual behavior: Context and change. *Social Problems*. 1974, *22*, 1 (Oct.).

Miller, W. B. Teenagers' sexual careers. *Transitions*. 1978, *1*, 1, 12–14. (a)

Miller, W. B. First sexual intercourse. *Transitions*. 1978, *1*, 2, 7–9. (b)

Miller, W. B. Teenagers' decisions to begin and discontinue prescription contraception. *Transitions*. 1979, *2*, 3, 4–5. (a)

Miller, W. B. Teenage marital and childbearing plans. *Transitions*. 1979, *2*, 4, 2–3. (b)

Miller, W. B. Societal responses to teenage sexual, contraception, marital and reproductive needs. *Transitions*. 1979, *2*, 5, 8–9. (c)

Moore, K. A., Hofferth, S. L., Weathermen, R., Caldwell, S. B., & Waite, L. J. Teenage child bearing: consequences for women, families and government welfare expenditures. Paper presented at the 87th Annual Convention of the American Psychological Association, Sept., 1979. New York.

Peplau, L. A., Rubin, Z., & Hill, C. T. Sexual intimacy in dating relationships. *Journal of Social Issues*. 1977, 33, 86–109.

Sorensen, R. *Adolescent sexuality in contemporary America*. New York: World Publishers. 1973.

U.S. Department of Health, Education and Welfare. National Center for Health Statistics. "Final National Statistics, 1977," *Monthly Vital Statistics Report*, vol. 27, no. 11, Supplement, Feb. 5, 1979.

Zelnik, M., Kim, Y. J., & Kantner, J. F. Probabilities of intercourse and conception among U.S. teenage women, 1971 and 1976. *Family Planning Perspectives*. 1979, *11*, 3, 177–185.

6 Adolescent Sexuality: The First Lessons

Kathryn Kelley
State University of New York at Albany

Editors' Note

In Chapter 6, Kathryn Kelley uses the concepts of learning theory to explain how early socialization experiences may affect the use of contraception in the teenage years. Specifically, it appears that individuals learn emotional responses to sexual cues while they are very young, and such emotional responses may remain influential as the person enters adolescence. According to Kelley, these learned emotional responses to sexuality will generalize to *contraceptive* behavior, since such behavior is essentially sexual in nature. Thus, an individual who has learned a negative emotional response to masturbation should generalize this negative response to contraceptive methods that require genital manipulation (i.e., inserting a diaphragm, putting on a condom, etc.); the person in question should dislike and hence avoid these methods of birth control. By the same token, a person who has acquired ambivalent feelings about heterosexual activity in general should also be ambivalent about contraception in general. In the chapter that follows, Kelley presents research findings that are consistent with these assumptions and discusses how the principles of learning theory may be applied to reduce the negative emotional responses that interfere with contraception.

Sexuality occupies a special place in the lives of most people living in Western society. Individuals are curious about the topic, and will at times exert unusual effort to find answers to their questions. Anyone familiar with the tattered, soiled edges of references to sex in the card catalogs of university libraries can gauge fairly accurately the popularity of such information. Sex sells—witness the relatively recent surge in the number of articles and reports on sexual behavior in periodicals and newspapers. If asked to supply reasons for such general interest, psychologists might offer as an explanation the absence of the ordinary mechanisms for communicating about an important matter when attention shifts from "acceptable" topics to sex. The processes of social comparison allow the individual to build personal standards for behavior, but data about others' sexual activities is generally hidden from observation. So much of what we gain from socialization of our sexual attitudes and behavior is accomplished indirectly, by applying contradictory, misleading, and often confusing guidelines to ourselves.

The process of how individuals learn about sexuality has unfortunately not been described in the same detail as other areas such as the development of moral conscience, intellectual skills, and social behavior. Comprehensive theories and data bases have treated each of those aspects of personality and behavior. Theories from Kohlberg on morality, Piaget on intelligence, and Bandura on social learning have stimulated hundreds of studies of these phenomena, with the result that impressive, comprehensive descriptions of their development and operation now exist. But can the reader name even one major theory of that stature that has done the same for the area of sexuality? Research on Freud's psychosexual stages and Gagnon's developmental descriptions of the role scripts learned about sexuality (Gagnon, 1977) has not produced impressive displays of supportive evidence, despite the interesting ideas presented in these theories.

In the absence of either a major theory or backlog of useful information, some have suggested applying what is already known to the unknown by using analogs of human behavior. For example, moral decision-making occurs with respect to sexuality, so one could use general information about conscience and morality to understand how choices about sexual behavior are made. Cognitive functions change in fairly predictable sequences, so educational efforts directed at sexuality could utilize that knowledge and become more effective. However, the application of social learning principles to this area has distinct possibilities for untangling the web of hidden socialization that has grown up around sexuality as an important although relatively secret aspect of our lives.

This chapter will describe the application of learning theory processes to the socialization of sexuality. We know that behavior can be analyzed into stimuli and responses, but what might we discover about the development of sexuality if those terms were applied to the topics that stimulate our curiosity? Since we know how reinforcements and punishments work in producing aggressive, altruistic, or other kinds of behavior, some of the same principles found in learning theory should also help identify determinants of the diverse experiences of mate choice, contraception, and even dysfunction. Sexuality is a special area in the sense that not much is known or communicated individually about it, but general learning principles can still provide useful information to help guide our understanding of the topic. Sutton-Smith and Abrams (1978) provided an illustration of this in the increasing complexity that occurs in children's sexual stories as they age, a process similar to other areas of their education.

SPECIAL INTERESTS OF LEARNING THEORY

Sometimes learning theory and related research are described as a cold, mechanistic view of human personality and behavior. But they actually emphasize the moods and feelings in the reinforcement process instead of the informational flow described by more cognitive theories. This distinction between affect and information has provided lots of material for scientific debate, but current thinking (e.g., Zajonc, 1979) points out how our tendency to evaluate everything makes information the tool of affect. So while dog-eared reference cards indicate intense interest in sexual information, be assured that those who retrieve it experience emotional reactions to it such as relief or increased worry.

Another criticism of learning theory charges it with ignoring the person who exists somewhere between the intensely scrutinized stimuli and responses. Most recent formulations of reinforcement principles emphasize the role of internally produced stimuli and responses in modifying the external ones. Modern learning theories are definitely eclectic enough to encourage their disciples to study imagination, judgment, and even attribution as evidence that individuals internally process and even drastically change the meaning of incoming information. This style of permissiveness in identifying the proper area for study has produced a potential law in psychology: the personality × situation interaction. For any aspect of behavior, both individual characteristics and the context will jointly contribute to it. For example, a general liberal or conservative orientation to sexuality may become evident only in favorable circumstances for expressing those attitudes. A given adolescent may express relatively conservative, straight-laced attitudes in the presence of authorities like parents or teachers, but switch to liberal, free-wheeling opinions in peer groups. Rather than ignoring characteristics of the individual, learning psychologists have made special efforts to identify when those tendencies are more likely to appear in certain contexts.

The First Exposure

The provision of models occupies an important place in socialization according to learning theory. More effective models encourage a warm, friendly relationship with the youngster learning from direct, deliberate teachings which do not contradict the model's actual behavior. The important characteristics of parental attitudes toward sexuality agreed with that description. Parents with positive attitudes reportedly did not display disgust about the biological aspects of reproduction or negativity about the emotional aspects of sexuality. Both mothers and fathers whom the students described as negative toward sex showed less physical affection toward their spouses in their children's presence and less often encouraged sex to be the general topic of family conversation. More direct exposure to parental sexuality is usually accidental in our culture. Hoyt (1979a) has analyzed primal-scene experiences as recalled by young adults, and found that neither psychopathology nor sexual dissatisfaction necessarily resulted. Imagery concerning parental sexual activity often stimulated college students to have thoughts about incest and isolation (Hoyt, 1979b). A more common sexual experience within the family is that between siblings, which has apparently few negative effects unless force or dominance is involved (Finkelhor, 1980).

Parents may become concerned about influencing their children's attitudes about sexuality in a negative direction because of their own problems in talking about sex or displaying affection toward their partner. Personal change can involve a long, difficult process of substituting new behaviors for well-established habits. In one study, mothers reported that their college student daughters were agents of their own change toward sexual liberality, and that their resultant sexual communication and overall relationship with their daughters had improved (Yalom, Brewster, & Estler, 1981). Awareness of one's potentially undesirable influence on a youngster's sexuality could motivate such change. An alternative solution could consist of avoiding the kinds of parent-child interactions which might create problems in learning about sexuality while providing a more positive source like a book. Rindskopf (1981) has analyzed the content of sex education books for young children, and found evidence of two major themes of traditionality in sex roles and avoidance of explicitly discussing intercourse. Thus such books can typically be expected to portray males as masculine and females as feminine, and to give few details about sexual activity. Parents could role-play with their partners scenes in which they attempt to respond to their youngster's questions about sex to reduce apprehension about an unfamiliar experience or to improve the teaching habits presently in use. Spontaneous discussion of sexuality within the family could be stimulated by the increasingly numerous references to sexual behavior and contraception found in the media such as television shows. Examples include episodes of *White Shadow* in which a high school basketball coach encouraged responsible contraception and *One Day at a Time* in which a female adolescent contemplating the possibility of her first heterosexual experience obtained a diaphragm. The range of sexual situations that could involve children with their parents increases as their adolescence approaches (Gilbert & Bailis, 1980), placing additional demands on the parents' knowledge and comfort with respect to sexuality. Difficulties in discussing sexuality persist through adolescence (Fox & Inazu, 1980), and such problems may in some cases be symptomatic of more generalized discordance in the home (Uddenberg, 1976). Parent-child relationships can change drastically during and after puberty (Steinberg, 1981), with significant implications for transforming sexual education within the family as well. When parents take responsibility for this area of their children's knowledge, adolescents eventually express more satisfaction with both the education and with the rapport developed with their parents (Bennett & Dickinson, 1980). Few parents undertake the process of sex education, leaving by default the influence of peers and others to assume this role. Adolescent females, for example, are more likely to engage in premarital sex if they have nonvirgin peers (Herold & Goodwin, 1981).

One of the earliest processes by which we learn about sexuality has an affective basis that is acquired by the process of classical conditioning. An illustration of this is an aspect of sexual behavior which can make even the most sexually experienced adults blush and change the topic: masturbation has for centuries been variously labeled as a degenerate perversion and as a pleasant, self-indulgent pastime. Masturbation can have strong emotional associations, depending on its definition by others from very early times in our lives. It provides a good example of a behavior which results in immediate feelings of physical gratification. But that naturally occurring behavior also may eventually become associated with the knowledge that engaging in it is defined as disgusting by many people including, very possibly, one's parents. The association of that information input, or conditioned stimulus, of disgust by masturbation can result in the young child's learning a personal reaction of distaste for it, completing the associational chain with a conditioned emotional response. The result of pairing these two strongly emotional responses, the physical pleasure of masturbating and the learned disgust for it, provides the basis for a sexually guilty conscience.

This learned emotional reaction to masturbation has existed for centuries, according to sex historians (Bullough, 1977). Negative attitudes toward masturbation are learned as early as infancy when the problem behavior has been treated by widening the infant's diaper or by tying her legs to the crib to keep them apart (Bakwin, 1952). Other devices designed to discourage masturbation have included spike-lined rings fitted over the penis before bedtime to make masturbation and erection quite painful (Schwarz, 1973). A contraption patented in the United States in 1908 of "Sexual Armor" consisted of a jacket encased in steel armor with perforations, a hinged trapdoor with bolts and a padlock and optional handcuffs. The promised goal of these contraptions was to avoid diseases purportedly caused by masturbation, which included brain damage, general paralysis, and insanity. MacDonald (1967) traced this popular idea to the 1707 publication of the work, *Onania, or, the Heinous Sin of Self-Pollution, and all its Frightful Consequences in Both Sexes consider'd & c.* by an unknown author writing during sexually repressive times. Since then, Boy Scouts in 1922 and medical students in 1959 (Greenbank, 1961) have believed that masturbation frequently caused mental illness.

The reaction to masturbation as a dirty, disgusting habit has occupied a place in history for some time. Most parents probably did not use such extraordinary means to stop it from ruining offsprings' lives. Less intrusive ways can communicate their distaste for that method of sexual self-reinforcement. Verbal methods of conveying disapproval may consist of an overtly negative response by instructing the child, "Stop that," or "That's dirty." Nonverbal means of accomplishing this include spanking, or the parent's facially communicating disgust or even by notably ignoring the practice in contrast to all other of the youngster's behaviors which somehow deserve parental comment. The message in these reactions conveys disapproval mysterious to the child because an initially pleasant, apparently harmless pastime of playing with one's genitals now may evoke intense dislike by socialization agents.

While lessons such as these may be puzzling and upsetting to the child, he or she also conducts trial-and-error experimentation within the limits set for acceptable behavior. Some may make the accidental discovery that masturbation can safely be performed in private. Many societies approve of this context for occasional masturbation for children, adolescents, and frustrated adults (Byrne & Byrne, 1977). Behavior modification techniques can be used to increase the frequency of socially acceptable acts as alternatives to public masturbation (Ferguson & Rekers, 1979). But even adults with acceptable sexual outlets may still suffer from the guilt learned early in their erotic careers (Greenberg & Archambault, 1973). Most college students will admit that they still masturbate in spite of the resultant guilt, and a few continue to label their autosexual experiences positively because of a reinforcing reduction in sexual tension (Arafat & Cotton, 1974). Negative attitudes toward the habit still predominante over positive ones in Western Cultures (Abramson & Mosher, 1975).

A major determinant of a negative reaction to masturbation consists of a corresponding parental attitude toward it conveyed during the individual's childhood. This learning provides a source of the emotional component to sexuality which persists in later years as a basis for responses to personal sexual behavior. As an illustration of this, college students in late adolescence and early adulthood who reported negative attitudes by their parents toward sexuality also indicated that they felt guilty about their own sexual behavior and expected negative consequences for engaging in it (Kelley, 1976). Compared to those who reported positive parental attitudes toward sex, these students continued to feel worse about almost every aspect of their sexual behavior, from masturbation to contraceptive use. They also were identified as the ones most likely to engage in sexual intercourse without the effective use of contraceptives.

Effects on the Contraceptive Process

The personal emotional reactions to sexual behavior learned by such means as these continue to have effects among sexually active adolescents and adults, by generalizing to the use of certain contraceptives. That is, negative feelings about masturbation learned in childhood appear in adulthood as disapproval in their attitude toward using contraceptives which involve genital manipulation (Kelley, 1979). In order to use contraceptive methods such as the diaphragm, condom, foam, abortion, IUD, or withdrawal, genital manipulation occurs in some form. With respect to the condom, foam, diaphragm, and withdrawal, genital manipulation necessarily occurs when they are rolled on the penis, sprayed into or pushed inside the vagina, or removed from it, respectively. Abortions usually involve surgical manipulation of the genital area. In order to use an IUD, a physician must first insert it into the uterine cavity, and then instructs the woman to check periodically for the presence of a string in her vagina. Even if the use of the method did not involve direct manipulation of the genital area, an individual still recognizes the device is present there so that imaginary manipulation occurs in thoughts about it.

Clusters of contraceptive methods on the basis of acceptability ratings support the distinction of genitally manipulative from nonmanipulative forms. Gough (1973) placed the intrauterine device and pill in the category of coitus-dependent. However, Miller and Bowker (1975) found that while females preferred to use the more effective pill and IUD, they actually used the pill most often and the IUD the least.

Both Chilman (1973) and Ford (1973) described the importance of positive feelings toward the genital aspects of sexuality among unmarried females using contraceptives. A female who lacked acceptance of masturbation and menstrual periods was described as passively responsive to preferably romantic sexual encounters, which excluded planning for contraceptive use in favor of being "swept off her feet." Calderone (1960) cited genital manipulation as a factor in reluctance to use some contraceptive methods, and some such as the pill could be highly preferable for use by women who do not like to touch themselves sexually.

Personal distaste toward masturbation becomes associated with the use of genitally related contraceptives, producing the classically conditioned negative affect toward using such methods. The negative response produced by masturbatory stimuli provides the unconditioned response (UCR) evoked by the unconditioned stimulus (UCS) of masturbation. Elements of masturbation performed in the use of these methods become associated with that link, so that a negative, guilty attitude results as the conditioned, negative emotional response (CR) whenever the conditioned stimulus (CS) is present in thoughts about such techniques of contraception. Not surprisingly, this learned relationship appeared the strongest among those students who described their parents as the most negative toward sexuality. By linking the negative emotions of disgust and guilt about masturbation with these genitally manipulative contraceptives, individuals disapprove of their use and use them less often and more ineffectively than a method such as the pill.

With responses to masturbation as a basis for learning about sexuality, socialization processes continue to build a framework for individual responses to a variety of sexual topics. Another major source of this learning consists of each persons's reactions to a heterosexual world of couples, sexual intercourse, and one's performance in it. Positive affective reactions to such heterosexual cues encourage the development of attitudes toward these factors in a relatively nonthreatening manner which is partially independent of one's responses to the other, autosexual base. The orientation of approval or disapproval of heterosexual cues extends to the same reaction to contraceptive use. In the same sense that responses to masturbation and to genitally-manipulative contraceptives corresponded, attitudes toward heterosexual cues such as sexual intercourse and the use of contraceptives in general and the pill in particular have something in common. Negative feelings about non-genital contraceptive use appeared among individuals who expressed less positive reactions to heterosexual erotic cues such as oral-genital sex and intercourse (Kelley, 1979). While the use of genital contraception may prove difficult and unacceptable to some, their positive responses toward heterosexual stimuli may allow them to use more easily a hormonal, non-genitally manipulative method such as the pill.

Of course, certain behavioral steps must occur in order to use any contraceptive. Its use entails planning, acquiring both information and the appropriate equipment, and following through with the plans. In learning theory these steps are known as instrumental responses. Cvetkovich (1979) has found that adolescent males tend to begin using condoms for this purpose either consistently or not at all. The present research points out that a major reason for such different styles in contraceptive use consists of personal and emotional reactions to masturbatory and heterosexual stimuli. Even the steps necessary for accomplishing birth control become related to these general affective bases. Consequently, the distinction between the genitally and non-genitally manipulative forms of contraception persists when the behavioral chain involved in their use is examined. For example, responses to masturbation would even be related to one's reaction toward buying a condom, foam, or diaphragm, while heterosexual feelings would predict that toward buying a packet of pills or asking a doctor for the prescription.

Personal experience can modify these patterns of responses to masturbation, heterosexual acts, and subsequent approval of and comfort with contraceptive use. Degree of sexual experience provides a source of this change in an interactive way with the factor of parental attitudes toward sexuality. In effect, positive experiences with sex in adolescence can counteract the roles of negative attitudes of one's parents in encouraging an individual to develop less disgust and discomfort with both masturbation and related contraceptive activity. Among those who report a lot of sexual experience and positive parents to begin with, little change in their autoerotic-related attitudes occurs, since they mainly have relatively few negative associations to them. Others can develop similar attitudes by providing themselves with different experiential information through their own positively rewarding sexual behavior, about the reinforcing characteristics of sexuality and related behaviors such as contraception. It is therefore possible to experience a counterconditioning of the original effect of negative attitudes of one's parents, or even to become *more* uncomfortable about such matters when punishment results from sexual activity. A punishing outcome can result from embarrassment, ridicule from one's partner or peers, contracting venereal disease, becoming pregnant, or even self-punitiveness for not achieving some desired goal of responsiveness. Events like this may even heighten the unpleasant aspects of sex and reinforce the initially disagreeable characteristics of it for a particular individual. So socialization agents in the form of parents, peers, or one's own real or imagined sexual experiences can slowly change the affective bases for sexuality and related behaviors such as contraception.

The information for parents that emerges from this research concerns the long-term implications of messages communicated to children about their early sexual behavior. Once parents know about these effects of their attempts to teach about sex, they still have a choice to instill positive or negative feelings about masturbation in their children. But most parents probably don't realize that such teaching will influence their youngsters in the distant future, producing a relationship between these early lessons and their eventual preferences for contraceptive use and emotional readiness to use them effectively. Behavioral scientists do know that simply presenting such information in a nonjudgmental, unpressured way can influence a later behavior change. It is possible, although probably idealistic, to say that informing parents about these effects of early sex training can produce beneficial effects in the development of several aspects of their youngster's sexuality.

The bases for expressions of disapproval and personal dislike of genitally manipulative methods of contraception can undergo changes by means of increasing sexual experience and exposure to such stimuli. The IUD provides a good example of how stimuli related to genital manipulation help determine its use or nonuse. Even though it possesses both high theoretical and practical effectiveness rates it has not been the method of choice. But recently practitioners have begun reporting the more frequent use of the device in the United States (Westoff, 1976), possibly as a result of the disenchantment with the pill and all its physiological side effects. But in order to use the IUD effectively, there would also have to be greater comfort with genital manipulation as a correlate of approving this method for personal use. Sources of this cultural change could consist of the increased knowledge of the harmless nature of private masturbation and even because of more frequent media presentations of the facts about contraceptives. Even though the message accompanying the picture of an IUD on the television screen warns about possible uterine perforation and other infections, it may help initiate females' thoughts about it in relation to sexuality and genital manipulation. More positive attitudes enabling it to be used someday could be stimulated by such a presentation.

Decision-making and Adolescent Contraception

These associations between sexual responses and contraception do not involve rational, deliberate planning by the individuals who learn them. When attempting to make a personal decision about whether to engage in a sexual activity or to use a specific contraceptive, they usually operate spontaneously and emotionally rather than coldly and calculatingly. They would not be expected to outline the

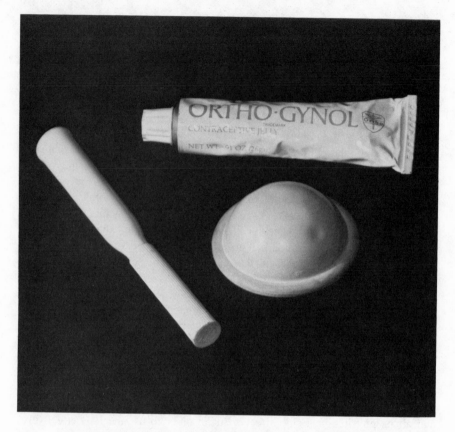

FIG. 6.1. Negative feelings about masturbation generalize and inhibit the use of
contraceptive methods such as the diaphragm, which requires frequent and direct
genital manipulation in order to insert and remove it.

reasons for their behavior in computer-program fashion at any time during or
after the decision process. Even when questions of morality enter the picture, the
quick, first reaction based on feelings about the matter can outweigh the unemo-
tional facts of the situation. When a moral judgment concerns us personally, the
decisions are made at a more rudimentary, self-interested level. If the question is
cast in an abstract, third-person way, individuals begin to use more sophisticated, principled styles of reasoning (Byrne & Kelley, 1981). To the extent that
questions of morality concern very important matters for adolescents like
whether to engage in a first sexual experience, or to initiate sex with a new
partner, or to take steps to avoid an unwanted pregnancy, more emotional, less
reasoned, and more self-interested thinking would probably prevail.

Moral conscience and the decisions and behavior that result from it have been
described by Kohlberg's theory (1964). The particular arrangement in this theory

for the bases of conscience involves a value judgment, since the levels of morality proceed from self-interest to principled thought. But the theory does a good job of differentiating styles used to justify decisions, and may provide some guidelines for understanding how sexual and contraceptive decisions are made. The immediate rewards to be gained or punishments to be avoided form the basis for judgments at the least sophisticated level of conscience. Physical gratification as a positive reward and the loss of one's partner for not complying as a potential punishment qualify as evidence for operation at this level of reasoning about sexual behavior. So does avoiding condom use because of reduced sexual pleasure. At the next major level of moral decision-making, concerns with social rewards and authority characterize the reasons given for undertaking or avoiding different acts. Since most adolescents and adults operate at this level in Western society, most of the reasons for engaging in sexual or contraceptive behaviors will concern these topics. Avoiding embarrassment, seeking spontaneity, obeying social authority, proving one's masculinity, femininity, or love for the partner all can be motivations used to seek social rewards at this middle level of conscience. Beginning one's sexual career because of peer pressure or independence needs also indicates that social rewards are the determining reasons for behavior. At the most sophisticated level of conscience, social principles transcend individual needs or self-interest. Even individuals who regularly reason at this level may regress to a former mode of thought when faced with highly personal, emotional situations like those involving sex and contraception. But for those able to maintain such standards of conscience, world overpopulation might, for example, provide a motivation to remain childless.

Even though the behavior connected with these different levels of moral reasoning may be the same, the reasons given for the activity differ. Avoiding contraceptive use might result whether the reason concerned the messiness of the method, imitating the crowd, or preserving new or potential human life. These reasons may not even be articulated until the individual is asked to supply them. After behavior such as sex without contraception has occurred, reconstruction of the immediate context for the decision would probably not be possible. So the reasons given for the earlier behavior might differ from the actual determinants of the spontaneous decision. The individual may not even be verbally aware of the judgment process while being swept along by a stimulating experience.

The decision to engage in sex and contraception can involve still another complication—that of gender differences. However the reasoning styles may differ, they depend on previous learning about sexuality for their appearance. Even experiences with masturbation, a basis for this learning, vary with gender, because the erect penis is a more highly discriminable stimulus than the retracted clitoris. Evidence for sexual arousal in the male is usually obvious, while the female may have to resort to guessing about her arousal from situational cues. In addition, young females may experience socialization about their sexuality aimed at neutral feelings of denial rather than positive feelings of enjoyment.

Their learning about them would often represent new lessons about their sexual responses which may diverge from their previous experiences with sex. If there is new learning involved for females in the area of sexuality, one would expect them to use less sophisticated levels of reasoning than they usually do in explaining their behavior to themselves and others.

Whether the decision to engage in sex with or without contraception is examined by looking at gender differences or moral conscience, no explicit guidelines from any theory appear in the thoughts and feelings actually experienced by the individual. The youngster about to have a first sexual experience doesn't stop to analyze carefully the immediate versus delayed rewards and punishments. Behavioral research will not soon intervene in such ongoing activity, but once the sexual career is started, or the unwanted pregnancy begun, those involved or observing the results may wish to have it explained to themselves.

Learned Inhibition of Adolescent Contraception

As the interpretations of adolescent sexuality in this volume suggest, a wide range of possibilities for explaining and understanding its development exist. Learning theorists would prefer to apply experimental manipulation of important variables to its study in order to support their case. But obvious ethical and moral considerations make it difficult or impossible to undertake research which might randomly assign youngsters to experimental groups experiencing premarital intercourse, the nonuse of contraception, or unwanted pregnancy, for example. They must often settle for retrospective descriptions of the events in correlational fashion in order to determine whether learning principles explain the facts of these phenomena. Recognizing that other explanations may also apply to a given set of findings, how does this theory fare in an attempt to provide a suitable framework for understanding the adolescent experiencing these life events?

According to learning theory, the establishment and maintenance of behavior occurs mainly in either of two ways. First, by the processes of association and generalization of affect, approval or reluctance with respect to certain contraceptive choices involving masturbatory stimuli can result. Second, responses that are instrumental to the use of these methods can lead to positive reward in facilitating the enjoyment of a sexual experience. Negative reinforcement can occur in the case of the removal of uncomfortable elements in a situation after making the appropriate response, as in ascertaining that one's partner is indeed using a contraceptive. Depending on the reward contingencies present in the environment, individuals could be either positively or negatively reinforced for making similar instrumental responses. Approval of others such as parents for contraceptive choices can thus become associated with the promotion of a more rewarding parent-adolescent relationship, depending on the parents' attitudes and concerns about the topic. If mothers encouraged the use of birth control by specifically instructing their daughters in its methods, they not surprisingly began to contracept (Furstenberg, 1976). If, on the other hand, the maternal side of the family disapproved of contraception, as in Ladner's (1971) study of black St. Louis ghetto residents, the female adolescents avoided effective contraception.

Other possibilities for sources of socialization about contraception include peer influence by the processes of modeling and observational learning. Valued peer relationships can help establish a personal style of attention to planning the need for contraception, or disregard for it. When sexual encounters consist mainly of spontaneity and impulsiveness, adolescents gain much of their information from their peers having the same sorts of experiences (Lindemann, 1974). Using their peer's possibly misinformed behavior as a guide for one's own activities, they may model the ineffective use of the less reliable contraceptives or observe its unwanted effects such as pregnancy. With the model thereby punished for such behavior, steps to correct the individual's similar actions could be taken. But the existence of so few positive references to contraception in the adolescent culture creates another problem, since no basis for the acceptance of the trouble involved in contraception has been presented. Direct training in the advantages of birth control is rare for adolescents before they visit abortion clinics. Some observers have urged deliberate attempts to associate contraceptive use with enjoyed sexual experiences in making commercial advertisements ("Sexy contraceptive ads urged," 1977).

Whether a positive orientation to one's sexuality is referred to as a commitment to it (Goldsmith, Gabrielson, & Gabrielson, 1972) or acceptance of it (Chilman, 1977), that construct helps determine the responses to learning from parents and peers. The net enjoyment of sexual activity depends partially on the physical and psychological pain associated with it, with a corresponding influence on one's reactions to contraception. Accordingly, Bardwick (1973) found in clinical interviews that adolescent females often described their sexual experiences as unsatisfying and painful at times. With such negative reactions to sexual activity, an unsurprising resentment of their responsibility for contraception resulted. As in other areas of human behavior, a moderate amount of anxiety or uncomfortable, negative feelings of arousal about sexuality facilitates appropriate behavior. To the extent that effective contraception involves rational planning and action, high or low levels of anxiety about sexuality debilitated the appropriate responses needed for contraception (Miller, 1976). The motivation to contracept is apparently facilitated by a moderate degree of concern about the prospect of unwanted pregnancy, for example, but either lack of concern or intense worry may inhibit effective contraception.

An additional source for anxiety about sexuality may consist of the adolescent's conflicts about dependence needs and the development of independence (Chilman, 1977). While involvement in a sexual relationship advertises to parents and peers his or her steps toward independence, it also reduces the comfortable dependence upon parental responsibility for the outcome of such an experience. One implication of moves toward independence by sexual activity is to diminish a formerly attractive dependence upon parents. A temporary sexual partner in an uncommitted relationship is an unlikely substitute for parental protection of the adolescent, so that anxiety about the effects of such a relationship mount. The contraceptive process may suffer in being lost someplace by the other seemingly momentous concerns present in the adolescent's experiences.

The time factors in these concerns also influence the motivations and emotions involved. The rewards of immediate dependence upon another adolescent for a date or for affection may not match in value the delayed loss of comfort in the parental relationship. Learning theorists have long recognized the importance of the immediacy of punishments and rewards as they follow the responses that produce them. Long delayed punishments control behavior poorly. While the costs of neglecting contraception might include eventual pregnancy, abortion, or single parenthood, the immediate rewards in most cases must outweigh these since most sexually active adolescents avoid effective contraception. So one takes risks for the imminent benefits from sexual activity in preference to the long-term costs. Whatever the content of the expectations about the immediate versus delayed rewards and punishments involved in sexual activity and contraception, a learning theorist would expect a correspondence between them and the eventual behavior.

The Psychotherapeutic Learning Experience

It is the individual adolescent who responds with effective or ineffective contraception to the need for it during a prospective sexual interaction. To facilitate a more effective response, individual change must occur on the bases of more positive affect, judgment, and appropriate action. Some of the same learning conditions that create sexual dysfunction may contribute to the lack of adolescent contraception as well as less enjoyment of sexuality.

Learning theory has practical value in its application to human problems that require sex therapy. If the conditioning and learning about sexuality has produced sexual dysfunction for an individual, often successful behavioral change can result from a program to modify the problem behavior and to maintain the outcome. Because anxiety, lack of adequate stimulation of the clitoral area, and lack of experience with orgasm may help produce this problem, practitioners have found that direct intervention into the sexual response pattern help women relearn it in a way that becomes satisfying to them. A typical attitude toward orgasmic dysfunction of this sort chides and punishes women for low responsivity and lack of motivation. But if the sexual response pattern becomes associated with sufficient anxiety and other negative affect, temporary absence of a satisfying response becomes readily understandable.

Some therapies have focused on the conditioned emotional response learned about masturbation as a central variable in such dysfunction. Specific programs are designed to aid the relearning of the maladaptive response to this naturally occurring and pleasure-producing sexual behavior, often in the context of an ongoing marital relationship (LoPiccolo & Lobitz, 1972; Zeiss, Rosen, & Zeiss, 1977). Early steps in the therapeutic process help the client to reestablish the pleasurable aspects of self-stimulation, perhaps in the presence of the partner. Eventually the couple may cooperate in discovering how to produce the sexual response together, without pressures for achieving success in the form of orgasm emphasized at any time during the therapy. A primary mechanism for enabling the person to experience sexual satisfaction is the transfer of sexual pleasure experienced during manual stimulation to that during intercourse. Once stimulation and satisfaction occur manually, the response may be produced by the couple using another means such as a dildo to simulate intercourse. From this intermediate step in the process, they may proceed to intercourse as a way to stimulate the woman's orgasm, which does not vary physiologically with the type of stimulus used to produce it. But the goals of this therapy depend on the client's desire to experience orgasm with intercourse, and such methods have achieved impressive success rates.

When the initial stage of behavioral program intervention involves relearning of a pleasurable association to masturbation, the therapist must gauge the client's reaction to this step. If the individual has a positive response to the self-stimulation, the therapy can continue with the remaining exercises. But if the client's reaction is strongly negative, the progress of the program can be set back with consequences for inhibiting further improvement. Such an unfortunate occurrence can be prevented by detecting its likelihood before such a procedure begins, so that the idea, fantasy, and behavioral approach to self-stimulation can be introduced gradually to the person. Information about the client's background, such as attributions of her parents' attitudes toward sex and her own degree of sexual experience, could help predict a highly negative reaction to this topic. If the sexually inexperienced client classified her parents' attitudes toward sex as highly negative, this may indicate the possibility of an adverse reaction to the suggestion of self-stimulation.

At least one clinician objects on moral grounds to the use of such procedures in the treatment of orgasmic dysfunction (Bailey, 1978). Posing the threat of unknown negative side effects of such a procedure, he urged that it be proved much more effective than traditional verbal methods of psychotherapy in order for its establishment as a legitimate treatment method. But others pointed out its beneficial by-products for increasing marital satisfaction (Wilson, 1978) and the futility of dredging up the centuries-old fear of masturbation for any positive use (Wagner, 1978). Apparently for some, even obvious benefits from the use of masturbatory practices do not justify a disregard for the original teachings about the morality of onanism.

CONCLUSIONS ABOUT THE SEXUALITY LEARNING EXPERIENCE

Current data on the socialization of sexuality highlight the importance of learned emotional reactions to even early sexual behavior in differentiating the attitudes and behaviors of individuals. Tendencies to engage in activities like intercourse and contraception are strongly related to basic feelings about sexuality. But these dispositions can be changed by future learning experiences that present other rewards or punishments added to the affective base from which the responses emanate.

The use of learning principles to explain sexuality has some resemblance to a one-night stand. It has no moral guidance to provide and lacks concern about the past except as it influences the interesting present. Just as the potential partner in a singles' bar tries to size up the probability for success with one person and not another, learning principles attempt to assess the affective content of clues to behavior in order to predict and understand it. But it doesn't "love 'em and leave 'em" when it comes to dissecting phenomena. From past experience with its treatment of other areas of behavior, it will follow through with as thorough an examination as the facts permit. As the bar's closing time approaches, the theory may even begin to look more attractive due to its impressive explanatory power.

REFERENCES

Abramson, P. R., & Mosher, D. L. Development of a measure of negative attitudes toward masturbation. *Journal of Consulting and Clinical Psychology,* 1975, 54, 485–490.

Arafat, I. S., & Cotton, W. L. Masturbation practices of males and females. *Journal of Sex Research,* 1974, 10, 293–307.

Bailey, K. G. Psychotherapy or massage parlor technology? Comments on the Zeiss, Rosen, and Zeiss treatment. *Journal of Consulting and Clinical Psychology,* 1978, 46, 1502–1506.

Bakwin, H. Masturbation in infants. *Journal of Pediatrics,* 1952, 40, 675–678.

Bardwick, J. Psychological factors in the acceptance and use of oral contraceptives. In J. Fawcett (Ed.), *Psychological aspects of population.* New York: Basic Books, 1973.

Bennett, S. M., & Dickinson, W. B. Student-parent rapport and parent involvement in sex, birth control, and venereal disease education. *Journal of Sex Research,* 1980, *16,* 114–130.

Bullough, V. L. Sex education in Medieval Christianity. *Journal of Sex Research,* 1977, *13,* 185–196.

Byrne, D., & Byrne, L. A. *Exploring human sexuality.* New York: Crowell, 1977.

Byrne, D., & Kelley, K. *An introduction to personality.* Englewood Cliffs, N. J.: Prentice-Hall, 1981. 3rd Edition.

Calderone, M. S. The acceptability of contraceptive methods to their users. In L. Rainwater (Ed.), *And the poor get children.* Chicago: Quadrangle Books, 1960.

Chilman, C. S. Why do unmarried women fail to use contraceptives? *Medical Aspects of Human Sexuality,* 1973, 7(5), 166–168.

Chilman, C. S. *Adolescent sexuality in a changing American society: Social and psychological perspectives.* Report of United States Department of Health, Education, and Welfare, Public Health Service, National Institutes of Health. Publication Number (NIH) 79–1426, 1977.

Cvetkovich, G. Panel discussion on Adolescent Sexuality presented at the meeting of the American Psychological Association in New York City, September, 1979.

Ferguson, L. N., & Rekers, G. A. Non-aversive intervention in public childhood masturbation: A case study. *Journal of Sex Research*, 1979, *15*, 213–223.

Finkelhor, D. Sex among siblings: A survey on prevalence, variety, and effects. *Archives of Sexual Behavior*, 1980, *9*, 171–197.

Ford, C. V. Why do unmarried women fail to use contraceptives? *Medical Aspects of Human Sexuality*, 1973, 7(5), 162.

Fox, G. L., & Inazu, J. K. Patterns and outcomes of mother-daughter communication about sexuality. *Journal of Social Issues*, 1980, *36*, 7–29.

Furstenberg, F. F., Jr. *Unplanned parenthood: The social consequences of teenage childbearing.* New York: Free Press, 1976.

Gagnon, J. H. *Human sexualities*. Palo Alto, California: Scott, Foresman, 1977.

Gilbert, F. S., & Bailis, K. L. Sex education in the home: An empirical task analysis. *Journal of Sex Research*, 1980, *16*, 148–161.

Goldsmith, S., Gabrielson, M., & Gabrielson, I. Teenagers, sex and contraception. *Family Planning Perspectives*, 1972, 4(1).

Gough, H. G. A factor analysis of contraceptive preferences. *Journal of Psychology*, 1973, 84, 199–210.

Greenbank, R. K. Are medical students learning psychiatry? *Pennsylvania Medical Journal*, 1961, 64, 989–992.

Greenberg, J. S., & Archambault, F. X. Masturbation, self-esteem, and other variables. *Journal of Sex Research*, 1973, 9, 41–51.

Herold, E. S., & Goodwin, M. S. Adamant virgins, potential nonvirgins, and nonvirgins. *Journal of Sex Research*, 1981, *17*, 97–113.

Hoyt, M. F. Primal-scene experiences: Quantitative assessment of an interview study. *Archives of Sexual Behavior*, 1979, *8*, 225–245. (a)

Hoyt, M. F. An experimental study of the thematic structure of primal-scene imagery. *Journal of Abnormal Psychology*, 1979, *88*, 96–100. (b)

Kelley, K. Attitudes toward pornography and contraception. Paper presented at the meeting of the Midwestern Psychological Association in Chicago, May, 1976.

Kelley, K. Socialization factors in contraceptive attitudes: Roles of affective response, parental attitudes, and sexual experience. *Journal of Sex Research*, 1979, 15, 6–20.

Kohlberg, L. Development of moral character and moral ideology. In M. L. Hoffman & L. W. Hoffman (Eds.), *Review of child development research*. New York: Russell Sage Foundation, 1964.

Ladner, J. A. *Tomorrow's, tomorrow: The black women*. Garden City, N. J.: Doubleday, 1971.

Lindemann, C. *Birth control and unmarried young women*. New York: Springer, 1974.

LoPiccolo, J., & Lobitz, W. C. The role of masturbation in the treatment of orgasmic dysfunction. *Archives of Sexual Behavior*, 1972, 2, 163–171.

MacDonald, R. H. The frightful consequences of onanism: Notes on the history of a delusion. *Journal of the History of Ideas*, 1967, 28, 423–431.

Miller, W. Some psychological factors predictive of undergraduate sexual and contraceptive behavior. Paper presented at the convention of the American Psychological Association in Washington, D. C., September, 1976.

Miller, W. B., & Bowker, C. Summary of a longitudinal study of standard undergraduate sexual behavior. Unpublished manuscript, Stanford University, 1975.

Rindskopf, K. D. Subtle signals: A content analysis of sex education books for young children. Presented at the national meeting of the Society for the Scientific Study of Sex, New York City, November, 1981.

Schwarz, G. S. Devices to prevent masturbation. *Medical Aspects of Human Sexuality*, 1973, 7(5), 140–153.

"Sexy contraceptive ads urged," *Journal and Courier*, Lafayette, Indiana, November 3, 1977.

Steinberg, L. D. Transformations in family relations at puberty. *Developmental Psychology*, 1981, *17*, 833–840.

Sutton-Smith, B., & Abrams, D. M. Psychosexual material in the stories told by children: The fucker. *Archives of Sexual Behavior*, 1978, *7*, 521–543.

Uddenberg, N. Mother-father and daughter-male relationships: A comparison. *Archives of Sexual Behavior*, 1976, *5*, 69–79.

Wagner, N. N. Is masturbation still wrong? Comments on Bailey's comments. *Journal of Consulting and Clinical Psychology*, 1978, 46, 1507–1509.

Westoff, C. F. Trends in contraceptive practice: 1965–1973. *Family Planning Perspectives*, 1976, 8(2), 54–57.

Wilson, G. T. Ethical and professional issues in sex therapy: Comments on Bailey's "Psychotherapy or massage parlor technology?" *Journal of Consulting and Clinical Psychology*, 1978, 46, 1510–1514.

Yalom, M., Brewster, W., & Estler, S. Women of the fifties: Their past sexual experiences and current sexual attitudes in the context of mother/daughter relationships. *Sex Roles*, 1981, *7*, 877–887.

Zajonc, R. B. Feeling and thinking: Preferences need no inferences. Paper presented at the meeting of the American Psychological Association in New York City, September, 1979.

Zeiss, A. M., Rosen, G. M., & Zeiss, R. A. Orgasm during intercourse: A treatment strategy for women. *Journal of Consulting and Clinical Psychology*, 1977, 45, 891–895.

7 Informational Barriers to Contraception

A. R. Allgeier
Northwest Center for Human Resources, Inc.

Editors' Note

Experience teaches us that it is difficult to find anyone over the age of three who will admit to serious gaps in their sexual knowledge. Nevertheless, it is clear that many teenagers *are* uninformed about sex and contraception, and such ignorance may place a limit on the effectiveness of the adolescent's use of birth control. In Chapter 7, A. R. Allgeier describes factors which prevent teens from learning the essentials about sex and contraception, including legal prohibition of sex education, parents' reluctance to discuss sexuality with their children, and the failure of the schools to provide instruction on sexual or contraceptive topics. His discussion then turns to a review and critique of research on sex education and its impact (or lack of impact) on students' attitudes and behavior. This chapter concludes with some innovative suggestions for improving the sex education of the future.

LEGAL BARRIERS TO SEXUAL AND CONTRACEPTIVE INFORMATION

The effects of accurate information about sexuality and contraception on the recipient's behavior have been the subject of an ongoing debate in this country that has spanned the last two centuries. Proponents of sex education have generally put forth a rationale that is best reflected in the position taken by the World Health Organization that "ignorance, not knowledge, of sexual matters is the cause of 'sexual misadventure'" (Calderone, 1965). The assumption is that people will make rational decisions about their sexual behavior if they are ade-

143

quately informed about sexuality. At the other end of the spectrum are those individuals who believe that sexual information will lead to experimentation. If children are taught "how to do it" they will, in fact, "do it." The assumption here is that children will not become "sexual" unless they are explicitly told about this type of behavior.

The chief arbitrators of this debate have been the courts and legislatures of the land where learned justices and elected officials have pondered the implications of the dissemination of sexual information. Although the battle has waxed and waned between the opponents and proponents of "sexual education," it appears that the advocates of sex education have been gradually overcoming their opposition. In fact, it might be germane to present a very brief overview of this struggle over the dissemination of sexual information, particularly birth control information, before examining contemporary problems.

Many of the 19th century birth control advocates were primarily social reformers who believed that the regulation of fertility was one means of helping people to achieve a better life. Challenging attitudes and behavior molded by centuries of religious thought, the socialist utopians such as Robert Dale Owen advocated romantic love and the use of coitus interruptus to achieve fewer and better nurtured children. Suffragists, agitating for change in the social and legal status of women, emphasized the necessity for women to have fewer children so that they could take a more active part in social, political and economic life. According to Reed (1978), women in the 19th and early 20th centuries controlled their fertility through extensive use of withdrawal, spermicidal douches, the vaginal diaphragm, condoms, and periodic abstinence.

Any use of contraception, however, roused the ire of those who considered themselves the guardians of public morals. The most effective of these 19th century moralists was Anthony Comstock whose intensive lobbying efforts led to Congressional passage of a comprehensive "anti-obscenity" bill in 1873. The law prohibited the mailing of obscene matter within the United States, as well as advertisement for obscenity which included material for the prevention of conception. He also initiated the passage of a similar law in New York state which even made it illegal to give contraceptive information, verbally, and many other states followed suit. Despite Comstock's efforts, however, native-born Americans became reasonably successful practitioners of the methods of birth control that were available. U.S. fertility fell from about seven children per woman in 1800 to 3.5 children by the end of the century (Reed, 1978). However, immigrants who came to America in large numbers during the latter half of the 19th century continued to have large families. The first half of the 20th century witnessed the emergence of such leading birth control advocates as Margaret Sanger, Robert Litous Dickinson, and Clarence Gamble whose efforts were largely responsible for removing the stigma of obscenity legally associated with contraception.

It was the U.S. v. One Package case that was litigated at the instigation of Margaret Sanger's National Committee on Federal Legislation for Birth Control that partially undid the legacy of Comstock. In 1936, Justice Augustus Hand issued his historical ruling which permitted contraceptive materials intended for physicians to be sent through the mails. Hand reasoned that if the Congress of 1873 had modern (i.e., circa 1936) clinical data on the dangers of pregnancy and the usefulness of contraceptives, they would not have classified birth control as obscenity.

Unfortunately, the Supreme Court, like most other social institutions, has not shown itself to be as responsive to clinical or scientific evidence regarding these issues as was the venerable Justice Hand. It was not until the landmark decision regarding Griswold v. Connecticut in 1965 that the United States Supreme Court began to develop a line of reasoning that emphasizes the constitutional right of sexual privacy. In this case, the Court invalidated a state law under which a physician was prosecuted for providing information, instruction, and medical advice about contraception to a married couple. The Court essentially told the government to stay out of the marital bedroom. A few years later, the Court expanded this ''marital right of privacy'' in the 1972 case of Eisenstadt v. Baird which invalidated a Massachusetts law forbidding the dissemination of contraceptive information to the unmarried. In 1973, the Roe v. Wade case held that the right of privacy was so fundamental that the state could not prohibit abortions during the first trimester. In Planned Parenthood of Central Missouri v. Danforth, the Court declared as unconstitutional laws that required parental consent prior to an abortion for a minor. And, finally, on June 9, 1977, in the case of Carey v. Population Services International, the Court struck down a New York statute which prohibited the sale or distribution of nonprescription contraceptives to minors under the age of sixteen. The Court held that the right of privacy in connection with decisions affecting procreation extends to minors as well as adults, and that restriction burdened minors' access to contraceptives without serving any significant state interest. The state had contended that the prohibition might deter minors from engaging in sexual activity by increasing the hazards attendant on it. The Court pointed out, however, that the same argument could be made to restrict minors' access to abortion or to prevent unmarried persons of any age from obtaining contraceptives.

In addition, the Court invalidated New York state's prohibition on advertising and display of contraceptives. The ruling applied to the advertising and display of prescription, as well as nonprescription methods, at least when the advertising is done by persons licensed to sell drugs. This ruling affected 12 other states that had laws which in some manner restricted the sale or distribution of contraceptives. Most of these states had previously imposed limitations on who could sell or distribute contraceptives (usually limited to pharmacists, physicians, hospitals, clinics, and health agencies) and prohibited distribution of contraceptives by vending machine. Thirteen states in addition to New York had laws restricting or regulating the advertising of contraceptives and seven states had restricted or regulated their display before the Court's ruling.

At the same time as these judicial changes were taking place, substantial legislative changes regarding sexual regulation were also occurring. As of 1980, 21 states (Arkansas, California, Colorado, Connecticutt, Delaware, Hawaii, Illinois, Indiana, Iowa, Maine, New Hampshire, New Jersey, New Mexico, North Dakota, Ohio, Oregon, South Dakota, Washington, West Virginia, and Wyoming) had completely decriminalized private sexual behavior among consenting adults (Vetri, 1980).

Of more direct concern to the problems addressed by this book was the enactment of Public Act No. 226 which was passed by the Michigan legislature on November 30, 1977. This law culminated a long and frustrating battle to have contraception included among the topics taught in sex education courses in the state of Michigan. Before the passage of this bill, teachers were prohibited from discussing birth control with students, even in private. In fact, they could not direct students to clinics or any other place for answers to their inquiries. The debate over the pros and cons of this bill generated the type of accusations and rancor that, unfortunately, are typical of the arguments over contraception and sex education. The hostility between the contending sides was illustrated in a newspaper article (Detroit Free Press, September 22, 1975, page 1-C) in which the then president of Zero Population Growth, a group favoring the bill, accused a female member of Happiness of Womanhood (HOW), a group opposed to the bill, of threatening to have him killed. The article continues ". . . Each side claims the other is being manipulated by sinister forces. NOW (National Organization of Women), proponents of the bill, claim HOW is just a front for the John Birch Society and HOW claims NOW is being manipulated by fascist and communist elements in the government. Both groups compared the other side's tactics with Hitler's.'' The eventual passage of the bill left Louisiana as the only state which forbids sex education and family planning education in its public schools. Thus, the legal barriers to the dissemination of sexual information appear to be eroding gradually. This is not to say, however, that trends toward more liberal sex education policies represent an irreversible process. For instance, sexual reform laws were operative in Arkansas for one year, and then its legislature reenacted felony provisions for private homosexual behavior, retaining decriminalization of sexual practices only for heterosexuals (Coleman, 1978). This same type of regression could happen with respect to the types of information that may be legally taught in a public school sex education course.

Although the legal barriers to sex education have, in large part, been removed, there is still no widespread movement toward sex education in the schools. As of 1976, only six states and the District of Columbia required some type of sex education (Alan Guttmacher Institute, 1976) and only about one-half the states plus the District of Columbia permit the delivery of contraceptive counseling and services to minors without parental consent (Paul, Pilpel, & Wechsler, 1976). The majority of states have adopted a variety of formal positions in relation to sex education. The most popular approach appears to be the issuing of formal guidelines on the topic. The guidelines developed by the state of Pennsylvania are fairly typical. The purpose of sex education is described as contributing to the process by which children and youth develop standards of acceptable behavior, self-control, and a realization of the role of sex in one's adult life. The long-range, over-all objective of sex education is the acquisition by students of personal maturity. The development of constructive values of sexuality in human living, familial roles, and the acceptance of oneself is vital (Pennsylvania Department of Education, 1969). Not many would find fault with these laudable goals. It is the implementation of these goals, however, that can be troublesome and is usually left to the discretion of local school districts but not without a bit more guidance by the state. It is somewhat informative to mention those topics that the Pennsylvania State Board of Education states should be excluded from the classroom:

1. Sexual techniques should not be included in sex education.
2. The consequences of the sex act in terms of pregnancy and the possibility of venereal disease must be explained. However, the teaching of specific methods of birth control and venereal disease prophylaxis should not be included in classroom sex education.
3. In matters of varying moral, ethical, and religious beliefs, the schools and teachers should be especially mindful of individual differences. Such matters should be referred to parents, family, physician, or clergyman (Pennsylvania Department of Education, 1969).

For many sexologists, the material that has been excluded by these guidelines would undermine the effectiveness of sex education. For our purposes, it is pertinent to note that teaching of birth control methods is often forbidden. This author has found that what the state of Pennsylvania has formalized is also the informal position of many junior and senior high school educators and administrators. Although viewing "sex education" favorably, they often balk at the inclusion of topics such as birth control and abortion. In my experience, part of their hesitancy is due to their fear that these topics would raise the ire of members of the school board and certain members of the community. Although this may be true, it is a shame that a small minority of individuals can determine whether sex education is included in the curriculum and, if it is included, what kinds of material should be taught. I refer to this group as a minority because survey research has revealed that a substantial majority of Americans are in favor of sex education in the schools.

PUBLIC ATTITUDES TOWARD SEX EDUCATION

According to a national survey conducted for the Commission on Obscenity and Pornography (Abelson, Cohen, Heaton, & Suder, 1971), there appears to be a clear majority of citizens who do favor sex education in the schools. Sex education programs in public schools was approved by 58% of the men and 54% of the women, with an additional 13% and 16% of men and women giving a qualified approval. A minority of 23% were totally opposed to sex education in the schools. These data also suggest that a substantial number of parents are dissatisfied with the present methods for the transmission of sexual information and are looking to public education for a more effective solution. In a more recent poll (Gallup, 1978) that consisted of 1518 personal interviews of people over the age of 17 in 300 locations selected to represent the United States census, 77% felt that sex education should be taught in schools (compared to 65% in a 1970 Gallup poll). Discussion of contraceptives in sex education courses was supported by 69% of the population—up from only 36% in 1970—and 56% of those interviewed favored making "birth control devices available to teenage boys and girls." Of some note, given the Roman Catholic Church's official position on artificial means of birth control, Catholics were just as likely as Protestants to approve of sex education classes in the schools, approve of having these classes discuss birth control, and favor making birth control devices available to teenagers. In a questionnaire on sexuality developed by *Better Homes and Gardens* magazine, and presented in two consecutive 1977 issues, over 300,000 people responded out of a total readership of 8,000,000. While this study suffers from obvious sampling deficiencies in that the 10,000 respondents whose questionnaires were analyzed were younger, better educated, and more prosperous than the average American, it is interesting to note that in this group 80% felt that contraceptive information and services should be available to everyone including teenagers, and that 82% favor sex education in the schools. Thus, from a variety of sources we find that most Americans are in favor of sex education including contraceptive information being taught in the schools. These figures obviously reflect the changes in attitudes toward sexuality that have occurred in the past two decades, but they also reflect to some extent the failure of the family unit to meet the child's need for information about sexuality.

The Failure of the Family

There is rather convincing evidence that a majority of individuals would prefer to receive their sex education from their parents rather than from other available sources. However, what one prefers and the reality of the situation are two different matters, as is apparent when one considers two surveys that differed markedly in their sampling techniques but whose results showed considerable convergence. Abelson, Cohen, Heaton, and Suder (1971) interviewed 2,486 adults and 700 young persons selected as a national probability sample, whereas Athanasiou, Shaver, and Tavris (1970) collected data from 20,000 adults who responded to a questionnaire appearing in *Psychology Today* magazine. The subjects were asked to indicate what they considered to be the best source of sex education information and then to name the source from which they had actually received their information. Table 7.1 presents both sets of data.

It is apparent that there is a discrepancy in this data between what these respondents considered to be the best source of information and where they actually received their information. In both studies the preferred source of information was parents, while the most common actual source was peers. The distribution of this data did not change significantly when the effect of age of respondent was controlled for statistically. Most respondents did not, and still do not obtain direct sexual information in their home from their parents. Most received, and continue to receive, their sex information from peers who they would not recommend as a source to future generations.

Sorensen (1973), using a national probability sample of adolescents, reported that 50% of male adolescents and 63% of female adolescents wanted to be able to talk to their parents about sex, and this percentage increases as they grow older and acquire sexual experience. However, only 18% of the boys and 16% of the girls reported having been told about masturbation by their parents, and 18% of

TABLE 7.1
Preferred Versus Actual Source of Sex Education Information

Abelson et al. (1971) data[a]		
Locus	Preferred Source	Actual Source
Parents	80–90%	25-46%
Family Doctor	60%	5%
School	40%	8–9%
Church	26%	5%
Siblings	10%	N/A
Peers	5%	35–53%

Athanasiou et al. (1970) data[b]		
Locus	Preferred Source	Actual Source
Parents	48.8%	12.1%
School	22.7%	2.8%
Church	1.1%	0.5%
Peers and friends	4.5%	53.6%
Books	14.0%	18.6%
Pornography	N/A	3.6%
Other	8.9%	8.8%
	100 %	100%

[a] Figures are approximate; several sources were recorded for each subject.
[b] Respondents were allowed to check only one response.

the males and 31% of the females said their parents had told them about birth control. In this sample, 72% of the boys and 70% of the girls reported that they and their parents do not talk freely about sex. A more recent study by Gebhard (1977) supplies more specific information concerning topics that are included under the general heading of sex education. He compared a small sample of undergraduates at Indiana University to white males and females with at least some college education from the original Kinsey sample. Table 7.2 presents six of the ten items from the original study with the most frequently cited sources of information for both groups. Inspection of the table reveals that same sex peers have lost some of their dominance to other sources, particularly mothers for issues regarding conception and, to some extent, contraception. It is also appar-

TABLE 7.2
Comparison of the Main Sources of Sexual Information of the
Kinsey and Gebhard Samples (Gebhard, 1977)*

		Male		Female	
Topic	Source	Kinsey	Gebhard	Kinsey	Gebhard
Coitus	Same-sex peer	73.3	50	49.1	48
	Mother	3.1	9	17.7	15
	Mass media	3.9	12	9.8	5
Fertilization	Same-sex peer	17.8	0	11.5	3
	Mother	4.4	13	14.6	14
	Mass media	24.1	23	19.9	22
	School and other formal training	39.5	45	43.4	44
Pregnancy	Same-sex peer	52.7	3	33.5	6
	Mother	14.2	53	35.7	70
Menstruation	Same-sex peer	51.5	27	18.7	17
	Mother	9.3	16	46.6	36
	Experience or sight	.4	4	19.2	8
	Mass media	13.8	14	2.6	6
	School and other formal training	5.9	16	.5	9
Abortion	Same-sex peer	no data	8	36.1	17
	Mother	no data	20	17.7	24
	Mass media	no data	31	19.2	11
	School and other formal training	no data	8	9.0	13
Condoms	Same-sex peer	89.7	67	66.8	51
	School and other formal training	1.5	5	6.8	16

*Percentages do not add up to 100% because those sources with small percentages were not included.

ent that the mass media is beginning to exert influence as a provider of sexual information. The accuracy of the information provided by these sources, however, was not assessed and this remains an area that needs to be investigated.

Historically, it seems that parents, particularly the father, have given little information to their children about sexuality. This is especially true in the area of contraception. In the Gebhard (1977) study, no females and only 2% of the males reported their father as their main source of early sex information. Why is there such a lack of parent-child communication about sex, when research indicates that most persons would prefer their parents as their main source of sexual information? There are a number of plausible explanations for this phenomenon.

No news is good news or "benign neglect".   Sorensen (1973) found that many adolescents feel they are left to fend for themselves in sexual matters without any supervision or overt assistance. As long as their sexual behavior is not explicitly brought to the attention of their parents, their parents will continue to remain silent in this area. The parental orientation seems to hinge on the hope that "things will take care of themselves" and if they are lucky, no great calamities will be visited upon them—pregnancy, venereal disease, or perversions. It is as if silence about sexuality will somehow envelop their children and whisk them through their adolescent years to the plateau of "responsible" adult sexual behavior. Although this is obviously not a very realistic appraisal of adolescent sexuality (see the statistics presented in Chapter 1), it does serve to avoid parent-child confrontation over sexual values and behavior. For many adults who are uncomfortable or confused about sexuality, this may appear to be the only avenue open to them.

Incest taboo.   Another possible factor affecting the lack of sexual communication within families is the incest taboo. Given the very strong societal prohibition against incestuous relations, parents and children may feel more comfortable in considering the other as relatively asexual. That this can be a two-way street is suggested in a study by Pocs and Godow (1977) where many college students were found to be quite upset at the prospect of even thinking about the sex life of their parents. They greatly underestimated the sexual practices of their mothers and fathers and the frequency with which they engaged in sex. Parents and their offspring may try to avoid perceiving or thinking about one another's sexuality as such a perspective might lead to anxiety-producing thoughts about each other as potential sexual partners. It is of some interest to recall that fathers are almost non-existent as suppliers of sexual information, particularly in relation to their female offspring. Given the fact that father-daughter incest is more frequently reported than mother-son incest (Hyde, 1979), one might venture the hypothesis that the more intense the sexual attraction a parent feels toward a child or vice-versa, the less comfortable that individual feels in communicating to them about sexuality.

Agents of Socialization.   Traditionally, parents have been the main conduits for the transmission of social norms to their children. A culture that discourages or prohibits adolescent sexuality will produce parents who feel it is their duty to support the views of the larger society in the hope that their children will conform to societal standards. Although many parents' private views may differ from the prevailing public morality, they may still feel that they have to influence their children toward conformity so that they will not be seen as deviant. If there is a noticeable discrepancy between parents' private and public views of sexuality, then their children may perceive them as hypocritical and resist their socialization attempts. Parents may also feel a conflict in walking the tightrope between private and public morality and try to keep discussions about sexuality to a minimum.

The Schools

Whatever the reason for parental reluctance to take responsibility for their children's sex education, it appears that the school system is the most viable alternative for transmitting sexual information, and a majority of adults approve of this function. Unfortunately, while there has been a dramatic increase in the percent of Americans who approve of school sex education, there has not been a corresponding rise in the extent to which most states require even the most basic education in sexuality, particularly contraception. Basic information about the extent and types of formal sex education available to students in the United States has not been systematically investigated. In response to this lack of data, the Center for Disease Control awarded a contract to Mathtech, Inc. of Bethesda, Maryland in 1978 to compare successful and unsuccessful sex education programs in this country (Scales, 1979). Perhaps this research effort will be able to outline the types, extent, and effects of sex education available to American teenagers.

A study by Spanier (1976) does provide some indirect information about sex education courses in the 1960's. A national probability sample of 1177 college students was interviewed in 1967 about the role of formal or informal sex education in their sexual lives. Approximately 18% of the males and 23% of the females reported that they attended a sex education course in junior or senior high school. In most cases, the course was taught by a physical education, health education or home economics teacher for females and a physical education or health education teacher for males. About 20% of these students claimed that sex was the sole subject of the course. Of those respondents who took a course in sex education, 33% of the males and 17% of the females claimed that the course contained instruction on contraceptive methods and 60% of the males and 51% of the females reported that the course contained some information on sexual intercourse. Over two-thirds of those attending sex education courses maintained that they received little or no new information about sexuality. Not surprisingly,

Spanier (1976) found that formal sex education had little effect on premarital sexual behavior.

Hopefully, the Mathtech project will find an improvement in the quality of education in the 1970s. If not, there is little reason to believe that sex education will have registered any substantial effect on adolescent sexual or contraceptive behavior.

The Need for Effective Sex Education.   A lack of accurate information, as well as distorted perceptions about sexuality are apparent long before adolescence in the United States. Koch (1978) attempted to compare reproductive knowledge of Swedish third graders with second graders in a suburb of Pittsburgh, Pennsylvania. Students were asked to draw pictures of "where babies came from and how babies are born." The youngsters could score a total of four points; one point was awarded for each of the following criteria if depicted in the child's picture: (1) reference to sexual intercourse; (2) reference to both male and female involvement in conception and birth; (3) accurate account of prenatal development; and, (4) accurate knowledge of birthing through the female birth canal. The Swedish group scored significantly higher than the Pennsylvania children on total scores and each of the four criteria. The spectrum of the raw data is rather striking. The 16 Swedish students obtained a composite score of 40 out of a possible 64 points whereas the 22 Pennsylvania students registered a composite score of 1 out of a possible 88 points. According to the author, the Pennsylvania community felt that the sex education of primary school children should be left to the parents. In this particular case, the parents did not do a very good job. Some of the comments the American children made to their teacher about their drawings are quite instructive:

"I don't know how the baby gets in, but the doctor will have to put holes in the stomach to get it out." "A baby grows when a lady gets fatter, then the doctor cuts the baby out." "Mom has a baby when she eats a certain kind of food, then the doctor has to cut her open. It hurts a lot." In contrast, after the Swedish children were told the results of the study, they expressed a great deal of sympathy for their Pennsylvania counterparts, and one remarked, "It ought to be a human right to know where you come from."

Lest we think that these rather painful visions are limited to a small sample of American children, a study of 185 Israeli kindergarten children whose parents were born in a potpourri of various countries had similar ideas about conception and birth (Kreitler & Kreitler, 1966). The majority of children felt that the baby was either formed from the food the mother eats or was swallowed through the mouth. In addition, the majority of males and females felt that delivery of the baby came through the mother's belly which had to be cut open. The authors, in discussing their findings, warn that "infantile concepts are generally not corrected by knowledge acquired later, but are merely covered up by it. For instance, the infantile concept of birth through opening of the belly may possibly lie at the core of the neurotic anxiety of pregnancy, or the concept of creating the baby through the mouth may underlie complaints about digestion, etc.'' (p. 377).

Perhaps one of the reasons that the Swedish children have a more veridical view of sexuality than their American and Israeli counterparts is that sex education is compulsory in Swedish schools beginning in the first year and continuing through the last year of school. It ranges from first year instruction on how sexes differ to intermediate instruction on contraceptives and abortions at the 14 to 16 year age level. These topics are taught as parts of regular courses such as biology and history, and there is a strong emphasis on the moral and ethical aspects of sexuality. Whatever the cause(s) of the superior knowledge of the Swedish children, for their American counterparts the envelope of ignorance and misperception continues into adolescence even as pubertal changes irrevocably signal entry into the sexual arena. There is accumulating data that adolescent knowledge of sexuality and birth control is often inadequate and distorted, primarily acquired from unreliable sources such as peers, and obtained well after sexual interest and activity have begun (Finkel & Finkel, 1975; Kantner & Zelnik, 1973; Reichelt & Werley, 1975; Schwartz, 1969; Thornburg, 1972).

Even for those who go to college, there is a continuing lack of knowledge. Malcolm (1971) reported that over one-fourth of a sample of sexually active university women failed to answer *any* question correctly on a sex knowledge test and 59% answered only half the questions correctly. To what extent effective sex education can rectify this situation is an empirical question. And, beyond the question of increasing knowledge is the more complex question of the relationship of knowledge to sexual behaviors and attitudes. Can accurate knowledge of sexuality reduce two of the more pressing social problems associated with adolescent sexuality—pregnancy and venereal disease?

Teenage Pregnancy and Venereal Disease.   Early childbearing is strongly associated with decreased educational attainment, even when other factors associated with school achievement are considered. Young mothers are never able to catch up educationally with their former classmates who postpone childbearing (Moore & Caldwell, 1977). This gap in educational attainment and subsequent reduction in potential earning power is likely to be passed on to the child. Espenshade (1979) has estimated that the cost of bearing a child, caring for it to age 18, and financing a public college education ranges from about $77,000 to $107,000 including direct maintenance costs and earnings women might have had but sacrificed to care for their children. Thus, a young mother already at a disadvantage educationally with her peers, is going to have a more difficult time absorbing this cost which may limit the potential upward mobility of her child. If this information is placed in the context of their potential earning power for the next 18 years, then these dull economic figures may become more meaningful. In present day figures, the child could cost them an average of $3,000 a year (no college) to almost $6,000 a year (4 years at a public college) depending upon their aspirations for the child.

Births by very young adolescent girls have a greater incidence of infant mortality and morbidity, as well as increased possibility for maternal complications than is characteristic of births by women in their twenties (Osofsky, 1968). There is also a 50% higher mortality rate for babies when they are spaced 1 year apart as compared to 2 years apart (Alan Guttmacher Institute, 1976). Marriages following a teenage birth have high dissolution rates, as do marriages that follow an out-of-wedlock birth. Even if women remarry, those who experienced a teenage birth have a much higher risk of having the marriage dissolve than do those who postponed childbearing beyond age 20 (McCarthy & Menken, 1979). And, finally, teenage mothers have a suicide rate ten times higher than the general population (Cvetkovich, Grote, Bjorseth, & Sarkissian, 1975).

Another of the unfortunate results of sexual activity among teenagers is venereal disease. Of all the communicable diseases, gonorrhea ranks second in prevalence (the common cold holds down first place) and syphilis fourth. The rapid increase of gonorrhea in recent years has alarmed public health officials. In 1971, there were 620,000 *reported* cases of gonorrhea in the United States and this figure increased to 1,000,000 in 1976. Since public health officials believe only about 25% of these cases are reported, it is estimated that there were approximately 4,000,000 cases in that year. In comparison, there were about 25,000 *reported* cases of syphilis in 1971. Most of these cases are in the 15–29 age group, and it is currently estimated that 50% of American youth contract either gonorrhea or syphilis by the age of 25 (Hyde, 1979).

The problems associated with adolescent sexual activity are all too real. The question that remains to be answered is whether sex education can help to alleviate unwanted pregnancy and venereal disease. At the present time, there is not enough systematic evidence that can be brought to bear on these issues. There has been, however, a notable increase in research in this area and we will examine the available evidence.

RESEARCH ON SEXUAL AND CONTRACEPTIVE KNOWLEDGE

What does one measure in looking for the effects of sex education? To want adolescents to become sexually responsible human beings is an admirable goal but what does this really mean? For most public health educators and social scientists it would mean taking precautions to avoid venereal disease, unwanted pregnancy, and, to some extent, engaging in relatively non-exploitative sexual relationships. To others it may mean avoiding sexual involvement until a stipulated age, or marriage. The educator's own sexual values will obviously play a determining role in selecting the content of what is taught and how it is taught.

Methodological Limitations. There is enormous variation in the type of formal instruction available to adolescents in the United States (Voss, 1980).

This continuum ranges from none through the mandatory one-to-three lectures on the horrors of venereal disease sandwiched into a health course taught by the high school football coach, to sophisticated semester long courses that utilize audio-visual techniques, values clarification exercises, group discussions and lectures. Unfortunately, it is impossible at this point in time to assess the differential impact that they may have on students' attitudes, knowledge, and behavior. Much of the research that has been conducted on the influence of birth control knowledge and, more generally, sexual knowledge, has not focused on the methods used to transmit this information (Kilman, Wanlass, Sabalis, and Sullivan, 1981). In addition, this research has utilized older adolescents and college students because of the difficulties in carrying out this type of research with young teenagers. This discontinuity in the age of the individuals studied obviously restricts the generalization of the results in most studies. Thirteen year-olds and nineteen-year olds are subject to different circumstances that may differentially affect their sexual thinking and decision making.

Another problem encountered in interpreting the body of research on "sex education" is the variety of ways in which investigators have measured sexual knowledge and, more specifically, birth control knowledge. Several studies have measured "knowledge" by a single factor—accurate estimate of the "fertile" period during the menstrual cycle—and other researchers have employed a large inventory of items from which a composite score is derived. These "sexual IQs", except in a few cases, do not meet most of the psychometric requirements of standardized tests. Often, the investigators construct a test for a specific study and fail to establish, or, at the very least, do not report, reliability estimates or normative data. The plethora of sex knowledge measures also contributes to the difficulty of comparing various studies, and many of the investigations in this area suffer from methodological deficiencies that leave open to question the authors' conclusions. Measures of the accuracy of contraceptive information are frequently nested in more general measures of sexual knowledge and are often not "teased out" in the reporting of data. There are a number of exceptions to this assertion and where appropriate, I will review those studies employing measures of contraceptive knowledge. In general, however, most of the studies to be reviewed are concerned with "general" sexual knowledge of which contraceptive knowledge is but one facet. Keeping these caveats in mind, let us consider the research that has been carried out in the area of sexual and contraceptive education.

Kirkendall and Miles (1968) in their review of the literature on the effects of sex education were struck by "an amazing paucity of research. . . . That which is available is for the most part simplistic and often narrow in scope. The questions are there but the data for answering them often are not." (p. 528).

Since that review 14 years ago, there has been a marked increase in the amount of research devoted to this topic. Nonetheless, many of the questions alluded to by Kirkendall and Miles remain unanswered.

Sex Knowledge and Formal Sex Education.   What are the most effective methods of educating teens about sexuality? In general, most studies have utilized some combination of lecture and discussion in modules that run from one session to a semester long course. Students are usually pretested on a measure of "sexual knowledge" and an attitude inventory before the material is presented, and then afterwards receive a post-test using the same measures. Changes in knowledge scores and attitudes are then compared to a control group of students who respond to the same tests, but receive no formal instruction. Differences between groups on the post-tests are then assumed to be a function of the "treatment" (sex instruction).

One of the better examples of this type of research was conducted by Monge, Dusek, and Lawless (1977). Ninth-grade students enrolled in a 6-week Family Life and Living Class were presented material on adolescent sexuality through classroom presentation and assigned readings, and were compared to a control group not enrolled in the course on a 24-item multiple choice test of sexual knowledge. The results indicated that the students who took the course showed a significant increase over the control group in the accuracy of their knowledge about sexuality. On the whole, girls performed better than boys, particularly on those items dealing with female biology and birth control–reproduction. The pretesting also revealed that students in the study were misinformed about many aspects of sexuality, especially vocabulary.

Other studies utilizing an educational "rap" session with teenagers seeking family planning services (Reichelt & Werley, 1976), a one-semester course on human sexuality for college students (Allgeier, 1978a) and various other populations and combinations of instruction (Mims, Brown, & Lubow, 1976; Mims, Yeaworth, & Hornstein, 1974; Woods & Mandetta, 1975) reported significant gains in sexual knowledge as a result of "formal" education.

However, only one study that this writer is aware of has attempted to compare methods of instruction as opposed to comparisons of education versus no education. Watts (1977) compared three teaching methods (lecture, independent study combined with small group discussion, and audiovisual) for knowledge gain and attitude change. College students at Indiana University enrolled in personal health classes were exposed to one of the above three methods for five consecutive class meetings that covered an instructional unit on human sexuality. Comparison of their scores on a sex knowledge and attitude questionnaire before and after the instruction revealed that the lecture method was superior to the audiovisual method in producing a gain in sexual knowledge. None of the three methods produced any significant attitude change. Thus, with the research presently available, it appears that knowledge gain accompanies most of the tried and true pedagogical methods utilized in sex education with the lecture method the most well-established at present.

Attitude Change.   As mentioned earlier, Watts found that none of his three experimental methods of instruction produced attitudinal change in students.

Woods and Mandetta (1975a, 1975b) also reported similar results with a group of college students who were enrolled in a course in human sexuality. A number of other studies (Geidt, 1951; Mims, Brown, & Lubow, 1976; Redfering & Roberts, 1976; Rees & Zimmerman, 1974; Soares & Soares, 1970; Voss & McKillip, 1979; Zuckerman, Tushup, & Finner, 1976), however, all found that attitudes changed in a more permissive direction following some type of formal sexual instruction.

Using a longitudinal approach, Story (1979) followed students for 2 years after they had completed a human sexuality course. In comparison to a control group of students who did not take the course, they displayed a pattern of increasing acceptance of a variety of sexual behaviors over this period of time. Interestingly, the sex education students became steadily more accepting of sexual behaviors for others than they did of those same sexual behaviors for themselves. The control group, on the other hand, tended to become less accepting of behaviors for others than for those same behaviors for themselves. This is the first study to demonstrate that the effects of a human sexuality course on sexual attitudes may persist over an extended period of time. It also suggests the importance of a human sexuality course in developing tolerance for the sexual behavior of other people.

Although there is not unanimity in the studies reviewed, I think it is safe to conclude that formal sex instruction can change attitudes about sexuality, and when this occurs, it is in a more permissive or tolerant direction. What effect this attitude change has on behavior is a question that has not been addressed by available research.

Behavioral Change.   Rees and Zimmerman (1974) reported no changes in sexual behavior among college students following a semester long course in sexuality. However, a well-designed study conducted by Zuckerman, Tushup, and Finner (1976) did find some changes in behavior. College students (mean age = 20.63) who enrolled in a large course on human sexuality were administered questionnaires on sexual experience and sexual attitude scales during the first week of the course, and were readministered these scales during the last week of the class. The same procedure was applied to a control group of students enrolled in another psychology course. The sex course appeared to have significantly changed sexual behavior in the males only, when compared to the control group. Specifically, males who took the course reported more heterosexual, homosexual, masturbatory and orgasmic experience as well as an increase in the number of homosexual partners from pre- to post-test than did control group males. It should be noted that there was no concomitant increase in heterosexual partners so that the increase in heterosexual experience was probably due to increased activity with the same partners. There were no data reported concerning attitudes, knowledge or use of contraception.

Also of potential importance was the finding that students who elected to take the course in human sexuality were more sexually experienced and held more permissive attitudes before they took the course than the control group students. This, combined with Allgeier's (1978b) finding that college students taking a sex course are more knowledgeable going into the course than a comparable group of control students suggests that voluntary sex education programs may have the disadvantage of only reaching a selected part of the population. That is, if the results of these studies with college students can be generalized to younger adolescents, then those likely to take advantage of a sex education course will be more sexually experienced, more knowledgeable about sexual matters, and more likely to hold permissive attitudes about sexuality than their peers who avoid such a course.

Finally, a study by West (1976) did not find any dramatic behavioral change as the result of a course on sex education. West compared high school students in the London, Ontario public schools who had taken a course in sex education which included handling diaphragms, condoms, etc., to a control group of students who did not take the course. Post course questionnaires indicated no difference between the groups in contraceptive behaviors. There was a significant difference in the number of sexual partners, however, with the control group reporting 1.75 partners and the sex education group reporting 1.79 partners (1 = none and 2 = one partner) in the last 6 weeks. This seems to be one of those instances where a statistically significant difference has little implication for the real world.

Correlates of Sexual/Contraceptive Knowledge.   While the foregoing studies have attempted to assess the general effects of formal sex education, there has been another strategy employed by investigators in an attempt to shed some light on the relationship between sexual knowledge and sexual attitudes and behavior. This strategy circumvents the issue of how sexual information is transmitted and focuses on the product—sexual or contraceptive knowledge—which is usually assessed by some psychometric inventory. Basically, this approach reduces the debate over the pros and cons of sexual education to one essential question: What is the relationship between sexual or contraceptive knowledge and sexual attitudes and behavior? This approach from an empirical point of view avoids putting the cart before the horse. That is, it examines the relationships if any, of sexual and contraceptive information to sexual attitudes and behaviors before becoming involved in whether or not sex education should be formally established in the school system. It would be a waste of time and effort to become involved in extensive teaching programs if accurate sexual information has no discernible effect on subsequent attitudes and behavior.

Fortunately, there is some preliminary research in this area that offers some tentative conclusions. Allgeier (1978b) administered the Sexual Knowledge Survey (Allgeier, 1978a), a 40-item true-false inventory (see Table 7.3) of sexual and contraceptive knowledge, and a questionnaire assessing sexual attitudes,

TABLE 7.3
Sexual Knowledge Survey*

This is a test of the accuracy of your knowledge about human sexual behavior. Each of the following statements can be answered true or false. Please answer all questions.

1. A female can become pregnant during sexual intercourse without the male achieving orgasm. (True)
2. The imbalance of sexual hormones is the most frequent cause of homosexuality. (False)
3. Women can become sexually aroused when breast-feeding an infant. (True)
4. A woman's chances of becoming pregnant are much greater if she experiences orgasm during sexual intercourse. (False)
5. Direct contact between the penis and the clitoris is necessary to produce female orgasm during sexual intercourse. (False)
6. There are no physiological differences in orgasms attained through sexual intercourse, masturbation, or any other technique. (True)
7. Males do not develop the capacity to attain an erection until they reach puberty (adolescence). (False)
8. The incest taboo is a result of social learning. (True)
9. Women are biologically more capable of multiple orgasms than are men. (True)
10. A hysterectomy (removal of the uterus) reduces a woman's sexual drive. (False)
11. There are two different types of physiological orgasms in women; clitoral and vaginal. (False)
12. The most sensitive area to sexual stimulation in most women is the clitoris. (True)
13. Erection of the nipples is often a sign of sexual arousal in the male. (True)
14. Homosexual behavior, masturbation, and fetishism occur among other species of animals besides man. (True)
15. Different positions in sexual intercourse are practiced most often by persons of lower socioeconomic classes. (False)
16. In this culture some homosexual behavior is often a normal part of growing up. (True)
17. A male is incapable of orgasm until he reaches puberty (adolescence). (False)
18. Sexual intercourse after the first six months of pregnancy may be practiced without endangering the health of the mother or the fetus. (True)
19. Sex criminals use pornographic material more often in their youth than the average person in their culture. (False)
20. Most prostitutes are nymphomaniacs. (False)
21. A majority of the sexual crimes committed against children are by adults who are friends or relatives of the victim. (True)
22. Almost all cases of impotency are of a psychological origin. (True)
23. The rhythm method is just as effective as the birth control pill in preventing conception. (False)
24. Social rather than biological factors determine the manner in which an individual's sexuality is expressed. (True)
25. Relatively few cases of frigidity are of a biological origin. (True)
26. Masturbation by a married person is usually related to marital problems. (False)
27. For a short period of time following orgasm, men are usually not able to respond to further sexual stimulation. (True)
28. Frequent masturbation is one of the most common causes of premature ejaculation in the male. (False)

TABLE 7.3 (Continued)

29.	During lovemaking it usually takes the female less time to become sexually aroused and reach climax than it does the male. (False)
30.	An intact hymen (maidenhead, "cherry") is a reliable indicator of virginity. (False)
31.	Sexual stimulation often causes erection of the nipple of the female breasts. (True)
32.	Sexual gratification associated with the infliction of pain is called sadism. (True)
33.	Circumcision makes it more difficult for a male to control ejaculation. (False)
34.	Nocturnal emissions or "wet dreams" are indicative of sexual problems. (False)
35.	Central nervous system damage can be one of the results of untreated, advanced syphilis. (True)
36.	Transvestites are individuals who derive sexual excitement from dressing in the clothes of the opposite sex. (True)
37.	The castration of an adult male results in a loss of his sex drive. (False)
38.	Almost all homosexuals can be identified by their physical characteristics. (False)
39.	Certain foods have been shown to be aphrodisiacs (sexual stimulants). (False)
40.	The most important factor in being able to maintain sexual activity during old age is a history of regular sexual activity. (True)

*Source: Allgeier. (1978a)

sexual behavior, and demographic characteristics to a group of college students at Purdue University. In this study there was no difference between males and females with respect to the accuracy of their sexual knowledge. Students were divided into low and high knowledge scorers based on the accuracy of their responses on the Sexual Knowledge Survey. An overview of the results revealed a substantial number of differences between the two groups. Specifically, high scorers in contrast to low scorers reported attending church less frequently, indicated more approval of birth control techniques, desired fewer children, and claimed that sex was discussed more frequently as a part of general family conversation. In reference to behavior, the more knowledgeable individuals reported that they began masturbating and engaging in sexual intercourse at a later age than less knowledgeable students. In general, however, once high scorers began their sexual activity, they tended to engage in these activities more frequently and with a greater number of partners than did low scorers. High scorers were also more likely to report having had some high school sex education than were low scorers. These results are particularly interesting in light of the studies reported in Chapter 4 by Oskamp and Mindick. They compared a group of adolescent females who had successfully met their birth control goals ("birth planners") to a group of adolescent females who experienced unwanted pregnancies. In their study, sexual and contraceptive knowledge was significantly higher for the birth planners than it was for the unwanted pregnancy group. The birth planners also reported beginning sexual intercourse at a later age than did the females who experienced unwanted pregnancies.

That those who demonstrated more accurate knowledge reported that sex was more often a part of family conversation and delayed their sexual activity in contrast to less knowledgeable individuals also provides an indirect link to other studies. Kantner and Zelnik (1973) and Miller and Simon (1974) have found that parents who discuss sexuality and accept their children's interest in it have children who tend to delay initial sexual intercourse and, when they do begin sexual activity, employ contraception. Perhaps parental tolerance for their offspring's sexuality creates an atmosphere conducive to the acquisition of accurate information and judicious decision making.

Finally, it is of some interest to note that even though there was a relatively large difference between their scores on the Sexual Knowledge Survey, low scorers rated their sexual knowledge as very adequate, just as high scorers did. Thus, those students who demonstrated that they possessed the least accurate fund of information still rated their knowledge as very adequate.

Contraceptive Knowledge. A number of studies have attempted to measure directly contraceptive knowledge among adolescents and/or college students. A significant relationship has been found between knowledge of contraceptive devices and techniques and premarital sexual permissiveness—the more accurate the knowledge, the more permissive the attitudes toward premarital sexuality (DelCampo, Sporakowski, & DelCampo, 1976). Females were found to be more knowledgeable than males and whites tended to be more knowledgeable about contraception than blacks. I should note here that the more permissive one's attitude toward sexuality, the more one is likely to engage in sexual activity. Thus, the link between permissiveness and birth control knowledge is an important one in considering unwanted pregnancy.

Hansson, Jones, and Chernovetz (1979), using a different measure of contraceptive knowledge also reported that female college students were more knowledgeable than their male counterparts. Those individuals who reported more formal or expert sources of knowledge (physician, sex education in schools, etc.) knew more about birth control. In addition, less conventionally sex-typed (androgynous) females were more knowledgeable than those females who adhered to traditional sex role expectations whereas there was no relationship between this variable and knowledge for males.

As mentioned previously, Oskamp and Mindick found that adolescents described as birth planners possessed more accurate contraceptive knowledge than adolescents experiencing unwanted pregnancy. Other studies (Cvetkovich & Grote, Chapter 5, Fisher, Byrne, Edmunds, Miller, Kelley, & White, 1979; Kane & Lachenbruch, 1973), however, have not found a relationship between contraceptive knowledge and use of contraception.

An overview of the attempts to find correlates of sexual and/or contraceptive knowledge reveals that females and males are comparable on general tests of sexual information but that females are superior in their knowledge of contraceptive techniques. This is not surprising in that most contraceptive devices involve intervention in the female's anatomy or physiology and may motivate her to find out more about contraception. Accurate contraceptive knowledge appears to be correlated with more sexually permissive attitudes and less endorsement of traditional sex-typed traits among females.

Sexual knowledge appears to be related to sexual behavior. The more knowledgeable an individual, the longer they wait before commencing sexual activity. Once they begin sexual activity, however, they report engaging in sex more frequently and with more individuals than their less knowledgeable peers. Why individuals with a relatively high degree of sexual knowledge postpone their baptism into overt sexuality is certainly a question worthy of further investigation.

What is also in need of further investigation is whether these sexual behaviors "cause" sexual knowledge or vice versa. That is, within a particular group of individuals, as their sexual knowledge increases or decreases, are there concomitant behavioral effects. Or, as a particular group of individuals begin to engage in sexual behavior, do they experience a concomitant increase in the accuracy of their sexual knowledge? The former question or hypothesis is the preferred direction that most "sex educators" assume for the relationship between knowledge and behavior. There is, however, the possibility that teaching adolescents about sexuality with the intention of influencing their behavior is no more effective than encouraging them to engage in sexual activity with the intention of increasing their sexual knowledge. The crux of the problem at this point in time is that we do not know the direction of the relationship.

Most of the research surveyed has been conducted with college students and older adolescents and is fragmentary at best. What we can say with some certainty is that some forms of sex education do increase sexual/contraceptive knowledge, do change attitudes in a more permissive direction, and do rather mildly affect sexual behavior, at least in males. Sexual behavior is complex, and it is influenced by many factors, not the least of which are changing sexual norms. The role that sexual education and, more precisely, contraceptive education plays in sexual decision making is still vague. Research has as yet failed to establish a clear and direct relationship between sex education and use of contraception. This may, in part, be due to the lack of precision with which the term sex education is employed since the quality and content of sex education have not been studied in relation to contraceptive use. In the same vein, we have almost no data on the relationship between sex education and venereal disease, or between sex education and sexual adjustment.

The evidence at this point in time does, I think, allow for two general conclusions to be drawn. The first conclusion is that a lack of sexual/contraceptive knowledge does not inhibit sexual activity. The second conclusion is that a lack of sexual/contraceptive knowledge can inhibit contraceptive behavior. Thus, the failure to instruct adolescent high school students about contraception may not prevent them from engaging in sexual activity, but such a strategy could limit their use of birth control.

SEX EDUCATION IN THE FUTURE

It seems rather trite to emphasize that sex education courses must concern them-selves with more than the recitation of sexual "facts." Teaching sex education as a solely academic subject fails to address the more personal aspects of sexu-ality which are of prime concern to the adolescent. This approach does not take into account earlier learning experiences involving emotional as well as informa-tional components. Byrne and his colleagues (Byrne, 1977; Byrne, Fisher, Lam-berth, & Mitchell, 1974; Byrne, Jazwinski, DeNinno, & Fisher, 1977) have found that individual differences in learned emotional responses to sexuality are generalized to such diverse topics as pornography, censorship, sexual adjust-ment, premarital intercourse, contraception, and family planning. For some indi-viduals, sexual cues seem to be associated primarily with positive emotions, pleasure, and approach tendencies, whereas for others, the same cues seem to be associated primarily with negative emotions and avoidance tendencies. This latter group is the most likely to be untouched by traditional sex education approaches. Schwartz (1973) has demonstrated that sexual guilt can interfere with the retention of sex-related information. In this study, students listened to a lecture on birth control and then took an exam based on the lecture. The results indicated that those high in sex guilt retained less lecture information than low guilt students. Presumably, sex information was anxiety producing to the high guilt students and interfered with their ability to acquire and recall the information.

Any attempt at successful sex education is going to have to develop means of encouraging discussion about sexuality among adolescents. Accurate informa-tion and good intentions do not necessarily lead to rational decision making in the area of sexuality. Partners need to communicate their intent, particularly in regard to contraceptive use. To the extent that an educational forum can contrib-ute through group discussion or simulated role playing of various sex-related situations, it would help to enhance communications among adolescents. Al-though most young people don't talk about contraception, there is some evidence (Misra, 1966) that males who talk comfortably about birth control are more effective users. As was reported earlier, adolescent males seem to possess less contraceptive knowledge than females. Males need to have more attention paid to their role in contraception. Scales (1977) has described the persistence of a sexual double standard that has tended to discourage and devalue the male role in contraceptive planning. Sorensen (1973) reported that nearly twice the percent-age of females as males reported that their parents had told them about contracep-

FIG. 7.1.   Negative emotional responses to sexuality can interfere with the learn-ing of contraceptive information. In this advertisement, a rather lighthearted tone is used to help allay anxieties that might arise from a more serious presentation of facts about condoms. (Reproduced courtesy of Julius Schmid of Canada Limited).

Julius Schmid
would like to give you some straight talk about condoms, rubbers, sheaths, safes, French letters, storkstoppers.

All of the above are other names for prophylactics. One of the oldest and most effective means of birth control known and the most popular form used by males. Apart from birth control, use of the prophylactic is the only method officially recognized and accepted as an aid in the prevention of transmission of venereal disease.

Skin Prophylactics.

Skin prophylactics made from the membranes of lambs were introduced in England as early as the eighteenth century. Colloquially known as "armour"; used by Cassanova, and mentioned in classic literature by Richard Boswell in his "London Journal" (where we read of his misfortune from not using one), they continue to be used and increase in popularity to this very day.

Because they are made from natural membranes, "skins" are just about the best conductors of body warmth money can buy and therefore their effect on sensation and feeling is almost insignificant.

Rubber Prophylactics

The development of the latex rubber process in the twentieth century made it possible to produce strong rubber prophylactics of exquisite thinness, with an elastic ring at the open end to keep the prophylactic from slipping off the erect penis. Now these latex rubber prophylactics are available in a variety of shapes and colours, either plain-ended, or tipped with a "teat" or "reservoir" end to receive and hold ejaculated semen.

Lubrication

And thanks to modern chemistry, several new non-reactive lubricants have been developed so that prophylactics are available in either non-lubricated or lubricated forms. The lubricated form is generally regarded as providing improved sensitivity, as is, incidentally, the NuForm® Sensi-Shape. For your added convenience, all prophylactics are pre-rolled and ready-to-use.

Some Helpful Hints

The effectiveness of a prophylactic, whether for birth control or to help prevent venereal disease, is dependent in large measure upon the way in which it is used and disposed of. Here are a few simple suggestions that you may find helpful.

Packaging

First of all, there's the matter of packaging. Skin prophylactics are now packaged premoistened in sealed aluminum foil pouches to keep them fresh, dependable and ready for use. Latex rubber prophylactics are usually packaged in sealed plasticized paper pouches or aluminum foil.

All of these prophylactics, at least those marketed by reputable firms, are tested electronically and by other methods to make sure they are free of defects. Prophylactics are handled very carefully during the packaging operation to make sure they are not damaged in any way.

Prophylactic Shapes

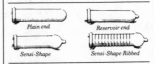

Plain end

Reservoir end

Sensi-Shape

Sensi-Shape Ribbed

Storage and Handling

It is equally important that you store and handle them carefully after you buy them, if you expect best results and dependability. For example, don't carry them around in your wallet in your back pocket and sit on them from time to time. This can damage them and make them worthless. Next is the matter of opening the package. It's best to tear the paper or foil along one edge so that the simple act of tearing doesn't cause a pinhole. And of course, one should be particularly careful of sharp fingernails whenever handling the prophylactic.

Putting Them On

The condom, or prophylactic, should be put on before there is any contact between the penis and the vaginal area. This is important, as it is possible for small amounts of semen to escape from the penis even before orgasm.

Unroll the prophylactic gently onto the erect penis, leaving about a half of an inch projecting beyond the tip of the penis to receive the male fluid (semen). This is more easily judged with those prophylactics that have a reservoir end. The space left at the end or the reservoir, should be squeezed while unrolling, so that air is not trapped in the closed end.

As mentioned earlier, you may wish to apply a suitable lubricant either to the vaginal entrance or to the outside surface of the prophylactic, or both, to make entry easier and to lessen any risk of the prophylactic tearing.

Taking Them Off

When sexual relations are completed, withdraw the penis while the erection is still present, holding the rim of the prophylactic until withdrawal is complete, so as to stop any escape of semen from the prophylactic as well as to stop it from slipping off. Remove the prophylactic and, as an added precaution, use soap and water to wash the hands, penis and surrounding area and also the vaginal area to help destroy any traces of sperm or germs.

And now for a commercial.

As you've read this far you're probably asking yourself who makes the most popular brands of prophylactics in Canada?

The answer to that is Julius Schmid. And we'd like to take this opportunity to introduce you to six of the best brands of prophylactics that money can buy. They're all made by Julius Schmid. They're all electronically tested to assure dependability and quality. And you can only buy them in drug stores.

RAMSES *Regular (Non-Lubricated) & Sensitol (Lubricated).* A tissue thin rubber sheath of amazing strength. Smooth as silk, light as gossamer, almost imperceptible in use. Rolled, ready-to-use.

FOUREX *"Non-Slip" Skins*–distinctly different from rubber, these natural membranes from the lamb are specially processed to retain their fine natural texture, softness and durability. Lubricated and rolled for added convenience.

SHEIK *Sensi-Shape (Lubricated) & Regular (Non-Lubricated).* The popular priced, high quality reservoir end rubber prophylactic. Rolled, ready-to-use.

NuForm *Sensi-Shape (Lubricated) & Sensi-Shape (Non-Lubricated).* The "better for both" new, scientifically developed shape that provides greater sensitivity and more feeling for both partners. Comes in "passionate pink." Rolled, ready-to-use.

EXCITA Gently ribbed and sensi-shaped to provide "extra pleasure for both partners." Sensitol Lubricated for added sensitivity. Also in "passionate pink." Rolled, ready-to-use.

Fiesta Reservoir end prophylactics in an assortment of colours. Sensitol lubricated for added sensitivity. Rolled, ready-to-use.

We wrote the book on prophylactics. If you would like to read it and get some free samples of what we've been talking about, fill in the coupon below and we'll send you everything in "a genuine plain brown envelope."

Name _____

Address _____

City _____ Prov. _____ PC _____

JULIUS SCHMID OF CANADA LIMITED
32 Bermondsey Road
Toronto, Ontario M4B 1Z6

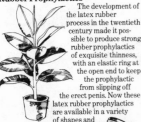

165

tion, yet almost half of the time that contraception is used by teenagers, it involves male responsibility—condoms and withdrawal (Kantner & Zelnik, 1972; Schofield, 1965; Sorensen, 1973). An emphasis on communication and affective education may also help the adolescent to accept and integrate his or her own sexuality in a more positive manner. Goldsmith, Gabrielson, Gabrielson, Mathews, and Potts (1972) concluded from the results of a survey of girls going to teen centers in the San Francisco Bay area that acceptance of one's own sexuality was a more important correlate of contraceptive use than was exposure to sex education or sexual knowledge.

In the same context, one might encourage adolescents who are sexually active to engage in noncoital activities such as mutual masturbation and oral-genital contact. Although this would not necessarily affect venereal disease rates, it could have a beneficial effect on reducing unwanted pregnancy. Justification for this approach could be built upon the reports that most women prefer noncoital methods of stimulation to intercourse, and respond more intensely to them (Hite, 1976; Kinsey, Pomeroy, & Martin, 1948; Kinsey, Pomeroy, Martin, & Gebhard, 1953; Masters & Johnson, 1966). Sex of any sort is rarely encouraged in a sex education course. Information is usually presented in a ''factual'' supposedly value free framework. Students who feel that sex is pleasurable and exciting may disregard the information presented by the teacher because they perceive the information as biased toward a sexually restrictive and inhibitory point of view. Perhaps what is taught about the biological processes and techniques of sexuality is not as important as what is conveyed to students in an emotional sense.

Finally, we should keep in perspective our expectations concerning sex education. Even the most effective and efficient approach to sex education is only a part of a much larger sexual environment and cannot be expected, in and of itself, to remedy all of the sexual problems emanating from the larger system. As Scales (1976) has pointed out:

> The lesson of sex education is clear: though education can encourage responsible sexual behavior, it will not help reduce V.D. and unwanted pregnancy if we continue to lace teenage sexual behavior with a good dose of guilt, fail to break down myths of normal sexuality and neat sex-role differences, make it difficult for young people to use sexual health care services and comfort ourselves with the destructive notion that ignorance is bliss (p. 3).

Formal sex education is to some extent a reflection of the cultural attitudes and beliefs of a particular society. The confusion about what to teach and how to teach it mirrors the ambivalence of our society toward adolescent sexuality. As such, effective sex education programs that involve teenagers, parents, or other community interests working together are still in the experimental stage. The role that sex education, and more particularly, contraceptive education plays in sexual decision-making will remain vague until we have developed innovative programs and the means to evaluate them. Those who see sex education as a panacea for various sex related problems are probably overly optimistic in terms of their expectations. Those who view it as an unnecessary frivolity or, worse, a threat to the sexual status quo are probably unduly pessimistic. Our culture has espoused education and knowledge as the major means by which we can come to understand ourselves and our world in a more precise, and hopefully, more beneficial manner.

REFERENCES

Abelson, H., Cohen, R., Heaton, E., & Suder, C. National Survey of public attitudes toward and experience with erotic materials. In *Technical Report of the Commission on Obscenity and Pornography*. Vol. VI. Washington, D.C.: U.S. Government Printing Office, 1971. 1–137.

Alan Guttmacher Institute. *11 Million Teenagers*. New York: Planned Parenthood Federation of America, 1976.

Allgeier, A. R. *The sexual knowledge survey*. Paper presented at the Eastern Regional Meeting of the Society for the Scientific Study of Sex, Atlantic City, New Jersey, April, 1978. (a)

Allgeier, A. R. *Attitudinal and behavioral correlates of sexual knowledge*. Paper presented at the meeting of the Midwestern Psychological Association, Chicago, May, 1978. (b)

Athanasiou, R., Shaver, P., & Tavris, C. *Psychology Today*, 1970, *4*, 37–52.

Byrne, D. Social psychology and the study of sexual behavior. *Personality and Social Psychology Bulletin*, 1977, *3*, 3–30.

Byrne, D., Fisher, J. D., Lamberth, J., & Mitchell, H. E. Evaluations of erotica: Facts or feelings? *Journal of Personality and Social Psychology*, 1974, *29*, 111–116.

Byrne, D., Jazwinski, C., DeNinno, J. A., & Fisher, W. A. Negative sexual attitudes and contraception. In D. Byrne and L. A. Byrne (Eds.), *Exploring Human Sexuality*. New York: Crowell, 1977.

Calderone, M. The sex information and education council of the U.S. *Journal of Marriage and the Family*, 1965, 27, 533–534.

Coleman, T. F. Sex and the law. *The Humanist*, 1978, *38*, 38–41.

Conceptual Guidelines for School Health Programs in Pennsylvania. Harrisburg: Pennsylvania Department of Education, 1969.

Cvetkovich, G., Grote, B., Bjorseth, A., & Sarkissian, J. On the psychology of adolescents use of contraceptives. *Journal of Sex Research*, 1975, *11*, 256–270.

Delcampo, R. L., Sporakowski, M. J., & Delcampo, D. S. Premarital sexual permissiveness and contraceptive knowledge: A biracial comparison of college students. *Journal of Sex Research*, 1976, *12*, 180–192.

Espenshade, T. J. The cost of children. In J. Wells (Ed.), *Current Issues in Marriage and the Family*. New York: McMillan, 1979.

Finkel, M., & Finkel, D. J. Sexual and contraceptive knowledge, attitudes and behavior of male adolescents. *Family Planning*, 1975, *7*, 256–260.

Fisher, W. A., Byrne, D., Edmunds, M., Miller, C., Kelley, K., & White, L. Psychological and situation specific correlates of contraceptive behavior among university women. *Journal of Sex Research*, 1979, *15*, 38–55.

Gallup, G. Reflects epidemic of teenage pregnancies: Growing number of Americans favor discussion of sex in classroom. *The Gallup Poll*, Princeton, N.J., January 23, 1978, news release.

Gebhard, P. The acquisition of basic sex information. *Journal of Sex Research*, 1977, *13*, 148–169.

Geidt, T. Changes in sexual behavior and attitudes following class study of the Kinsey report. *Journal of Social Psychology*, 1951, *33*, 131–141.

Goldsmith, S., Gabrielson, M. O., Gabrielson, I., Mathews, V., & Potts, L. Teenagers sex and contraception. *Family Planning Perspectives*, 1972, *4*, 32–38.

Hansson, R. O., Jones, W., & Chernovetz, M. Contraceptive knowledge: Antecedents and implications. *Family Coordinator*, 1979, *28*, 29–34.

Hite, S. *The Hite Report*. New York: McMillan, 1976.

Hyde, J. S. *Understanding human sexuality*. New York: McGraw-Hill, 1979.

Kane, F. J., Jr., & Lachenbruch, P. A. Adolescent pregnancy: A study of aborters and nonaborters. *American Journal of Orthopsychiatry*, 1973, *43*, 796–803.

Kantner, J., & Zelnik, M. Sexual behavior of young, unmarried women in the United States. *Family Planning Perspectives*, 1972, *4*, 9–18.

Kantner, J., & Zelnik, M. Contraception and pregnancy: Experience of young unmarried women in the United States. *Family Planning Perspectives*, 1973, *5*, 21–35.

Kilmann, P. R., Wanlass, R. L., Sabalis, R. F., and Sullivan, B. Sex education: A review of its effects. *Archives of Sexual Behavior*, 1981, *10*, 177–205.

Kinsey, A. C., Pomeroy, W. B., & Martin, C. E. *Sexual behavior in the human male*. Philadelphia: Saunders, 1948.

Kinsey, A. C., Pomeroy, W. B., Martin, C. E., & Gebhard, P. H. *Sexual behavior in the human female*. Philadelphia: Saunders, 1953.

Kirkendall, L., & Miles, G. Sex education research. *Review of Educational Research*, 1968, *38*, 528–544.

Koch, P. B. *A comparison of the sex education of primary-aged children as expressed in art in Sweden and the United States*. Paper presented at the Eastern Regional Meeting of the Society for the Scientific Study of Sex, Atlantic City, New Jersey, April, 1978.

Kreitler, H., & Kreitler, S. Children's concepts of sexuality and birth. *Child Development*, 1966, *37*, 363–378.

Malcolm, A. H. Sex goes to college. *Today's Health*, 1971, *26*, 26–29.

Masters, W. H., & Johnson, V. *Human sexual response*. Boston: Little, Brown, 1966.

McCarthy, J., & Menken, J. Marriage, remarriage, marital disruption and age at first birth. *Family Planning Perspectives*, 1979, *11*, 21–30.

Miller, P. Y., & Simon, W. Adolescent sexual behavior: Context and change. *Social Problems*, 1974, *22*, 58–76.

Mims, F. H., Brown, L., & Lubow, R. Human sexuality course evaluation. *Nursing Research*, 1976, *25*, 187–191.

Mims, F., Yeaworth, R., and Hornstein, S. Effectiveness of an interdisciplinary course in human sexuality. *Nursing Research*, 1974, *23*, 248–253.

Misra, B. D. Correlates of male attitudes toward family planning. In D. J. Bogue (Ed.), *Sociological Contributions to Family Planning Research*. Chicago: Chicago Press, 1966.

Monge, R. M., Dusek, J. B., & Lawless, J. An evaluation of the acquisition of sexual information through a sex education class. *Journal of Sex Research*, 1977, *13*, 170–184.

Moore, K., & Caldwell, S. B. *Out of wedlock childbearing*. Washington, D.C.: The Urban Institute, 1977.

Osofsky, H. J. *The pregnant teenager*. Springfield, Illinois: Charles C. Thomas, 1968.

Paul, E. W., Pilpel, H. F., & Wechsler, N. F. Pregnancy, teenagers and the law. *Family Planning Perspectives*, 1976, *8*, 16–21.

Pocs, O., & Godow, A. Can students view parents as sexual beings? *Family Coordinator*, 1977, *26*, 31–36.

Redfering, D., & Roberts, R. Personality correlates and the effects of a human sexuality course on sexual attitudes and information retention of college students. *Journal of Sex Education and Therapy*, 1976, *2*, 34–39.

Reed, J. *From private vice to public virtue.* New York: Basic Books, 1978.

Rees, B., & Zimmerman, S. The effects of formal sex education on the sexual behavior and attitudes of college students. *Journal of the American College Health Association,* 1974, *22,* 370–371.

Reichelt, P. A., & Werley, H. H. Contraception, abortion and venereal disease: Teenagers' knowledge and the effect of education. *Family Planning Perspective,* 1975, *7,* 83–88.

Reichelt, P. A., & Werley, H. H. Sex knowledge of teenagers and the effect of an educational rap session. *Journal of Research and Development in Education,* 1976, *10,* 13–22.

Scales, P. How we guarantee the ineffectiveness of sex education. *Siecus Reports,* 1976, *VI,* 1–3.

Scales, P. Males and morals: Teenage contraceptive behavior amid the double standard. *The Family Coordinator,* 1977, *26,* 211–222.

Scales, P. The context of sex education and the reduction of teenage pregnancy: Some theoretical issues and model program approaches. *Child Welfare,* 1979, 58, 263–273.

Schwartz, M. S. A report of sex information knowledge of 87 lower class 9th grade boys. *The Family Coordinator,* 1969, *18,* 361–371.

Schwartz, S. Effects of sexual guilt and sexual arousal on the retention of birth control information. *Journal of Consulting and Clinical Psychology,* 1973, *41,* 61–64.

Schofield, M. *The sexual behavior of young people.* Boston: Little, Brown, 1965.

Soares, L., & Soares, A. A study of students' sex attitudes and teachers' perception of students' sex attitudes. *Psychology in the Schools,* 1970, *4,* 172–174.

Sorenson, R. C. *Adolescent sexuality in contemporary America: Personal values and sexual behavior.* New York: World Publishing, 1973.

Spanier, G. Formal and informal sex education as determinants of premarital sexual behavior. *Archives of Sexual Behavior,* 1976, *5,* 39–67.

Story, M. D. A longitudinal study of the effects of a university human sexuality course on sexual attitudes. *Journal of Sex Research,* 1979, *15,* 184–204.

Thornburg, H. D. A comparative study of sex information sources. *Journal of School Health,* 1972, *42,* 88–91.

Vetri, D. The legal arena: Progress for gay civil rights. *Journal of Homosexuality,* 1980, *5,* 25–34.

Voss, J. R. Sex education: Evaluation and recommendation for future study. *Archives of Sexual Behavior,* 1980, *9,* 37–59.

Voss, J. R., & McKillip, J. Program evaluation in sex education: Outcome assessment of sexual awareness weekend workshops. *Archives of Sexual Behavior,* 1979, *8,* 507–522.

Watts, P. R. Comparison of three human sexuality teaching methods used in university health classes. *Research Quarterly,* 1977, *48,* 187–190.

West, N. W. The effect of instruction in family planning on knowledge attitudes and behavior of London (Ontario) senior secondary school students. Unpublished doctoral dissertation. Ohio State University, 1976.

Woods, N., & Mandetta, A. Changes in students' knowledge and attitudes following a course in human sexuality: A case-control comparison. *Journal of Sex Education and Therapy,* 1975, *2,* 47–59. (a)

Woods, N. F., & Mandetta, A. Changes in students knowledge and attitudes following a course in human sexuality: Report of a pilot study. *Nursing Research,* 1975, 24, 10–15. (b)

Zuckerman, M., Tushup, R., & Finner, S. Sexual attitudes and experience: Attitude and personality correlates and changes produced by a course in sexuality. *Journal of Consulting and Clinical Psychology,* 1976, *44,* 7–19.

8 Ideological Barriers to Contraception

Elizabeth Rice Allgeier
Bowling Green State University

Editors' Note

If ignorance were the only obstacle to teens' use of contraception, it would be relatively easy to educate adolescents and to realize a swift reduction in the incidence of teenage pregnancy. Unfortunately, however, there appear to be other barriers to adolescent contraception as well. In Chapter 8, Elizabeth Allgeier points out that many teens are committed to beliefs or belief systems which are entirely incompatible with responsible contraception. Such an "anticontraception ideology" may hold that contraception is immoral; that it is dangerous to one's health, or one's fertility, or one's sex drive; or that the use of birth control contradicts one's religious beliefs. In the present chapter, Allgeier describes five clusters of beliefs that act as barriers to the use of birth control by teenagers; the validity of these beliefs is discussed as well, and the chapter closes with suggestions for changing beliefs that inhibit adolescent contraception.

If a girl truly doesn't want to have a baby, she won't get pregnant even though she may have sex without taking any birth control precautions. (Sorensen, 1973, p. 323)

If a girl uses birth control pills or other methods of contraception, it makes it seem as if she were *planning* to have sex. (Sorensen, 1973, p. 322)

Pregnancy, under any conditions, is one of the most significant and wonderful experiences a woman can have. You must not let your experience be marred by the problems that surround it. (Cowart & Liston, cited in Ambrose, 1978)

These quotations are examples of some of the beliefs held by adolescents which inhibit their use of contraception. In this chapter, I will review five major

171

ideological barriers to effective contraceptive use by adolescents, including the beliefs that: (1) contraception is unnecessary; (2) contraceptive use is immoral; (3) acquisition of contraception is difficult; (4) contraceptives cause a variety of immediate and long-term problems; and, (5) pregnancy is desirable, regardless of the conditions under which it occurs. Each of these beliefs will be examined in order to determine the extent to which they are supported by empirical evidence. In addition, I will describe Fishbein's (1972) theoretical model in terms of its usefulness for predicting the relationship between holding particular beliefs and using (or not using) contraceptives. Finally, I will suggest several directions for future research aimed at increasing contraceptive use by sexually active adolescents.

OVERVIEW OF RESEARCH ON ADOLESCENT SEXUAL AND CONTRACEPTIVE BEHAVIOR

Before describing the specific effects of particular beliefs on the contraceptive behavior of young people and the extent to which these beliefs are supported by factual evidence, it may be helpful to understand how, and from whom, the research evidence has been gathered. Examination of the psychological determinants of contraceptive use is relatively recent, as Pohlman (1969) noted in his extensive review of the birth planning literature. This decade has witnessed a substantial increase in the amount of research done on the topic and in the availability of federal, state, and private funds for contraceptive research and services. Since 1970, when the Family Planning Services and Population Research Act was passed, federal funds for family planning have more than doubled (Alan Guttmacher Institute, 1976a). For Fiscal Year 1979, the Carter administration planned to spend $142 million dollars for the prevention of initial and repeat pregnancies among adolescents (Digest, 1978).

The strategies that have been used to examine the effects of beliefs on contraceptive use have run the gamut from studies involving the administration of questionnaires or interviews to thousands of adolescents living all over the United States, through more carefully controlled studies conducted in laboratories examining psychological or biological variables involved in contraceptive attitudes and behavior, to analyses of actuarial data on rates of premarital pregnancy, abortion, contraceptive side effects, and so on. Evidence emerging from the studies by Sorensen (1973) and Zelnik and Kantner (1972, 1974, 1977; Kantner & Zelnik, 1973) has provided a wealth of information about contraceptive attitudes and behavior on the basis of responses of national samples of adolescents, so their methods will be described in some detail.

In his book, *Adolescent Sexuality in Contemporary America,* Sorensen reported the results of his carefully conducted study with about 400 13 to 19-year-old males and females. One of the difficulties of working with adolescents is that researchers must obtain informed consent from parents, as well as from the adolescents themselves, before asking them questions. Sorensen appears to have followed this ethical guideline quite faithfully, and was able to obtain the consent of over 60% of parents of adolescents in the samples. Comparisons of the cooperating parents with the non-cooperating parents on geographic location, community size, race, family income and family size showed no differences. Nonetheless, there may have been some attitudinal differences between the two groups of parents that might affect the sexual and contraceptive behavior of their offspring. As with all research on sensitive topics, generalizations are limited to those adolescents who would consent to participate and who have parents who would give their consent as well. Sorensen reported, however, that the composition of the sample that he obtained conformed quite closely to the composition of the entire adolescent population of the United States in the 1970 census. The self-administered questionnaire used in Sorensen's study was developed on the basis of intensive interviews lasting up to 3 hours conducted with several hundred adolescents. These interviews were conducted to provide information regarding appropriate language to be used in the questionnaire, possible alternative responses, and appropriate areas for study. Unlike some of the other books reporting major studies of sexual behavior (e.g., Kinsey, Pomeroy, & Martin's *Sexual Behavior in the Human Male,* 1948; Masters & Johnson's *Human Sexual Response,* 1966), Sorensen's material is presented in a highly readable fashion with statistical descriptions presented in a manner understandable to the reader with no specialized knowledge of statistics or research methodology.

The studies by Zelnik and Kantner (1972; 1974; 1977; Kantner & Zelnik, 1973) have involved interviewing two independent national samples of 15 to 19-year-old women in 1971 and 1976. Each of the samples contained over 4,000 women. The purpose of these studies was to obtain information on the incidence and frequency of premarital sex, the extent and type of contraceptive use, and the incidence and outcomes of premarital pregnancies occurring to women within this age group. Further, comparisons of the sexual and contraceptive behavior of women at the two different time periods (1971 and 1976) have given us some idea of the changes which have occurred during the intervening 5 years.

Both Sorensen (1973) and Zelnik and Kantner (1977) relied on data from the 1970 U.S. census in determining the extent to which their samples were representative of the adolescent population as a whole. In 1970, there were 13.7 million males and 13.4 million females in the 13–19 age category. Research has repeatedly found that by the time they reach the end of adolescence, the majority of these 27.1 million young people are sexually experienced. For instance, in a study conducted with college students in Virginia, 66% of the women and 73% of the men were sexually experienced (Maxwell, Sack, Frary, & Keller, 1977). King, Balswick, and Robinson (1977) found that 57% of the women and 74% of the men were sexually experienced in their research at a college in Georgia. Among freshmen at a college in western New York, 57% of the women and 84% of the men were sexually experienced (Allgeier, Przybyla, & Thompson, 1977). Zelnik and Kantner's 1977 study of 15 to 19 year-old-women in 1976 indicated that 55% had experienced intercourse by the time they were 19. The median age of first intercourse found in their sample was 16.2. That is, among the sexually experienced women in their sample, half had begun having sexual intercourse before the age of 16.2, and the other half had first intercourse after that age. In a recent sample of rural high school students having an average age of 16.6, 40% were nonvirgins (McCormick, Folcik, & Izzo, 1979). Finally, in Sorensen's (1973) sample of 13 to 19-year-old males and females, 52% were nonvirgins. Of these, 56% of the nonvirgin girls and 71% of the nonvirgin boys had had intercourse by the age of 15. First intercourse had occurred at the age of 12 or under for 13% of the experienced adolescents in his sample. Only 17% of the sexually experienced girls and 5% of the experienced boys waited until they were 18 or 19 to engage in sex for the first time.

The problem, of course, is that although the majority of adolescents have had intercourse before they reach the age of 20, the majority begin doing so in the absence of any protection against pregnancy. This was the case with 63% of the girls in Sorensen's (1973) sample. Among college students, 60% of the sample in Bauman's (1970) study and 76% of the sample in Maxwell, Sack, Frary, and Keller's (1977) study either used no contraception at first intercourse, or used an unreliable (withdrawal, rhythm, or douche) method. And although Zelnik and Kantner (1977) reported that respondents in their 1976 sample were more apt to use a reliable contraceptive than were the respondents in their 1971 sample, they also reported that there is no evidence that the gap between age at first intercourse and age at first contraception has narrowed during the 5-year period. In addition, they found that only 30% of their sample consistently used contraception, as inspection of Table 8.1 demonstrates.

As I sit at the typewriter, describing these statistics, I can hear my 14-year-old daughter's phone conversation regarding how her pregnant girlfriend is going to break the news of a "positive" pregnancy test to her parents. My daughter had a similar conversation with the same girl about 2 months ago, however, that time, it turned out to be a "false alarm." Apparently, the fear that she felt at that time did nothing toward encouraging her to use contraception, although she did ask my daughter what the "safe" time of the menstrual cycle was.

Given the number of teenagers at risk of pregnancy due to nonuse or inconsistent use of contraception, it is perhaps not surprising that over a million of them do become pregnant each year. About 600,000 of these adolescent girls give birth. In fact, one in five adolescent mothers have given birth at least twice (National Center for Health Statistics, 1976; 1977). Another 280,000 of the pregnancies are resolved through abortion.

TABLE 8.1
Percent of Sexually Experienced Never-Married Women Aged 15-19
According to Contraceptive Use Status and Age in Their 1976 Sample*

Age		Use Status			N
	Never	Sometimes	Always	Last time[a]	
15-19	25.6	44.5	30.0	63.5	786
15	38.0	32.5	29.5	53.8	89
16	30.9	38.7	30.5	56.3	139
17	29.4	41.4	29.3	61.8	192
18	20.8	49.1	30.1	70.3	202
19	15.1	54.4	30.5	68.8	164

*Table adapted from Table 9 in Zelnik, M. & Kantner, J. F., 1977.

[a] "Last time" includes always-users plus sometimes-users who used contraception at time of last intercourse.

Combining the annual abortion rate and the out-of-wedlock birth rate, we could conclude that there are about two million unwanted conceptions each year in the United States. This is, of course, a conservative conclusion because it doesn't take into account the nonmarital conceptions which culminate in spontaneous abortion, stillbirth, or hasty marriage by the conceptors.

Movement from *description* to *explanation* of these statistics is quite easy at one level. That is, in the vast majority of cases, nonuse or misuse of contraception is the *cause* of the alarmingly high unwanted conception rate. But in order to reduce this rate, we need to determine the *cause* of inadequate contraceptive use. Explanation at this level is exceedingly difficult. Most of the research I will be reviewing demonstrates that a particular belief is *related* to contraceptive behavior. For instance, those who believe that premarital sexual activity is immoral are less likely to report using birth control when they do engage in sex than are those who believe that premarital sexual activity is normal and healthy under certain conditions. On the basis of findings such as these, though, we can't say that the belief that premarital sex is sinful *causes* nonuse of contraception. Such a causal relationship may exist, but the design of most of the studies done on the relationship between beliefs and contraceptive behavior don't permit us to predict that holding a particular belief causes an increase in the likelihood of engaging in a particular behavior. Instead, we are limited to assertions that particular beliefs vary with, or are related to, particular behaviors. A third variable (another belief, or other unidentified factors in the situation) may be the cause of both the belief and the extent of contraceptive use. Unless otherwise noted, the review which follows will describe findings regarding the extent to which particular beliefs are related to (rather than causing or predictive of) contraceptive use or nonuse. Some studies which are exceptions to this will be noted at the end of the chapter.

BARRIERS DUE TO THE BELIEF THAT
CONTRACEPTION IS UNNECESSARY

Despite the statistics which underline the importance of adolescent contraceptive use, large numbers of teenagers engage in unprotected intercourse and report the belief that contraceptives are not necessary for them for a variety of reasons. Many adolescents believe that conception is unlikely or impossible for them because they don't want to have a baby, they are too young to conceive, they are having sex infrequently, or they are having sex at the "wrong" time of the month. Other young people may believe that luck or fate has more effect on what happens to them than their own efforts do. Finally, some adolescents believe that abortions are so easily obtained that there is no need to worry about possible pregnancy.

Pregnancy is unlikely or impossible.   In Sorensen's (1973) study, 46% of the girls who had sex during the preceding month without always using contraception agreed with the statement quoted at the beginning of this chapter: "If a girl truly doesn't want to have a baby, she won't get pregnant even though she may have sex without taking any birth control precautions." Kantner and Zelnik (1973) found that 56% of the 15 to 19-year-old girls in their sample who did not use contraception at last intercourse reported that they did not believe that they could become pregnant. Among their reasons for this belief were that they were too young to become pregnant, or that they did not have sex that often, or that they were having intercourse at an infertile time of their cycle. About 70% of the girls who strongly believed that they would not easily become pregnant did not use contraception at last intercourse.

For 90% of the population, there is very little support for the notion that conception is unlikely or impossible. That is, only 10% of couples are unable to become pregnant (McCary, 1978). Further, if one hundred women have unprotected intercourse (that is, intercourse without contraception) for a year, 80 of them will conceive babies (Hyde, 1979). In addition, although teenage mothers and their offspring have a higher incidence of life-threatening problems than do women in their twenties, as will be seen below, women are also most fertile in the teenage years (McCary, 1978). Whether or not the use of "truly" not wanting to have a baby works as a contraceptive has not been systematically explored. The statistics indicate, however, that neither the sperm nor the egg has any way of knowing a woman's feelings about the matter when she and her partner are giving them the opportunity to unite; even among married couples, one fifth of the babies are unwanted (Bumpass & Westoff, 1970). Further, over a million conceptions have been terminated by abortion each year since 1975 (Tietze, 1979), presumably because they were not wanted.

Regarding the belief that pregnancy is impossible because of being "too young,'' girls are usually not fertile until about 2 years after first menstruation, although there are individual differences in the length of time between first menstruation and first ovulation. There is an authenticated case of a 5-year-old girl giving birth to a healthy baby (Hyde, 1979), so unless the girl using her youth as an excuse for failure to use contraception is under 5 years of age, the belief that she is too young to conceive is not supported by the evidence. Although males do not typically ejaculate sperm until they reach puberty, Hyde (1979) notes that an 8-year-old girl and a 9-year-old boy have given birth to a son. In addition, girls 10 to 14 have approximately 12,000 births a year and another 16,000 terminate their pregnancies through abortion in the United States.

The belief that infrequent sex reduces the likelihood of conception is correct. For that matter, very frequent sex also reduces the likelihood of conception insofar as the man's sperm count is lowered. To rely on either extremely frequent or infrequent intercourse as a method of contraception is invalid, though, since frequency per se is far less important than timing.

The use of timing, or the belief that one can avoid conception by the use of the rhythm method, is quite problematic for most adolescents. To begin with, only 41% of a national sample of 15 to 19-year-olds have correct information regarding the onset of the fertile period in the menstrual cycle (Zelnik & Kantner, 1977). Second, the effectiveness of this method for the individual woman is dependent on the accuracy with which she can determine the date of her ovulation. The adolescent interested in considering the use of this method may want to consult *Sexual Interactions* (The Allgeiers, 1983) for a description of ways to increase the effectiveness of the rhythm method. The use of rhythm as a contraceptive method is ineffective for many women, though, because: (1) very few women have regular menstrual cycles; in fact, fewer than 13% have cycles which vary less than 6 days in length from the shortest to the longest cycle; (2) unless a woman has a perfectly regular cycle (in which case, she must still maintain chastity for a minimum of 8 days) she should keep a record of her cycles for at least 6 months to a year to determine the date of ovulation, and, of course, she should use another method of contraception during that period; (3) the part of the cycle which is most apt to vary due to individual differences, psychological stress, colds, etc., is the period from menstruation to ovulation, making prediction of the date of ovulation more difficult; and, (4) fluctuations in the menstrual cycle and the date of ovulation are even more common during the first few years of adolescence than they are thereafter. In short, rhythm is not a particularly effective contraceptive method for adolescents. More specifically, every year, 35 out of every 100 women relying on the rhythm method conceive. At best (using an accurate method for pinpointing the date of ovulation and then engaging in intercourse *only* during the period following ovulation until the next menstrual period), as many as 7 out of 100 women become pregnant each year (Federal Register, 1978).

Individuals have little effect on what happens to them.   Observations in working with students have led me to speculate that some individuals are convinced that God, or fate, or the timing of their own birth (that is, the astrological sign under which they were born) has more influence on their risk of pregnancy than do their own actions. There is a fatalism among some adolescents which precludes their active intervention (or taking of responsibility) in their own lives. For such individuals, events are determined or foreordained by some power outside themselves, and if they are "meant to be pregnant" it will occur, regardless of what sorts of contraceptive steps they may take to attempt to influence or control their own destinies. If the Virgin Mary had used a diaphragm, it would have been ineffective in preventing the conception of Jesus, since God, presumably, did not take the usual route in impregnating her. For the rest of us, however, the statistics bear out the fact that we *can* have an effect on whether or not we conceive. As noted previously, 80% of those engaging in unprotected intercourse become pregnant within a year as compared to 1% to 5% of those who consistently and correctly use the pill, the IUD, the diaphragm, or the condom. Those having little confidence in their own power to determine what happens to them, however, would be more prone (pun intended) to accept passively whatever happens to them. Zongker's (1977) study of premaritally pregnant high school girls indicated that their confidence in themselves was very low compared to a group of students matched for age, academic achievement, etc. In addition, adolescent girls who believe that their own actions determine what happens to them (high "internal" locus of control) are less likely to experience unplanned pregnancy than are those who perceive their fates as determined by luck or by the choices of others (MacDonald, 1970; Steinlauf, 1979). It is possible, of course, that pregnancy in and of itself is partially responsible for these findings. That is, premarital pregnancy may result in lower feelings of self confidence and an increased belief that one's fate is controlled by chance. This possibility is somewhat supported by the absence of a relationship between contraceptive behavior and locus of control in a number of studies (Brown, 1977; Gough, 1973; Harvey, 1976; Oskamp, Mindick, Berger, & Motta, 1978; Seeley, 1976). Nonetheless, the hypothesis that contraceptive behavior is related to the extent to which one feels effective and self-confident in controlling one's own destiny seems worthy of further investigation, perhaps using measures other than locus of control. A longitudinal study of adolescents would be particularly useful in resolving the issue as to whether feelings of non-effectiveness are a cause or a result (or neither) of premarital pregnancy (see Chapters 4 and 5).

All problems are readily solved.   The majority of the 13 to 19-year-old women in Sorensen's (1973) sample agreed that "Abortions are so easy to get these days that I don't really worry about getting pregnant." Of those adolescents who had engaged in sexual intercourse during the previous month without always using contraception, over a fourth agreed with that statement. In addition,

59% of the nonvirgins in his study agreed that, "If two people are going to have a baby that neither person really wants, it is all right for the girl to have an abortion."

It could be argued that these attitudes are a subset of a more general belief that the consequences for choices or actions can ultimately be delayed or eliminated. In support of that position, the experience of many adolescents in contemporary America is replete with examples of impunity for their choices. If a class is failed due to insufficient time spent on studying, students on many campuses may withdraw without penalty for a certain period of time, and if they plead with instructors, many students will be withdrawn with a "passing" grade beyond the deadline for such action. If they are doing poorly in most of their courses in a given semester, there is now a policy in some schools which allows the individual to claim "academic bankruptcy" and have the entire semester's grades removed from the record. The judicial system in many states also sees it as appropriate to protect adolescents who are convicted of criminal acts from public knowledge of their behavior, and from punishment as severe as that meted out to an adult convicted of the same behavior. I am not particularly comfortable with labeling an individual for life on the basis of one minor act of wrongdoing, however, in a number of our institutions, there appears to be some tendency to accede to adolescent demands for adult status regarding freedom to make choices, with simultaneous support for the position that these same adolescents should not be held responsible for their choices. Ultimately, this is likely to lead to insufficient socialization regarding the connection between the choices one makes and the consequences attached to these choices. Thus, although I agree with the majority of Sorensen's sexually experienced adolescents that unwanted babies should not be brought into the world, a more important question to be asked, given our present contraceptive technology, is why do people conceive a baby that neither person really wants? Despite the fact that abortions are safer and less expensive now than ever before in our history, there are still risks involved in the procedure, and abortions are still more expensive ($180 to $400) than reliable contraceptives ($10 to $60 per year) (Hyde, 1979). Further, a comparison of financial costs doesn't take into account the social and psychological costs of going through the procedure for the individual, the couple, or the parents of the adolescent. As an extreme example of such costs, until recently women were legally required in Akron, Ohio to go from the abortion procedure to a licensed funeral director to deposit their aborted fetuses (*Newsweek*, June 5, 1978).

Perhaps out of concern for the legal status of abortion as an alternative to bringing unwanted children into the world, various scholars have pointed out that the availability of abortion does not reduce contraceptive use. For instance, Somers and Gammeltoft (1976) examined the abortion rate before and after legalization of the procedure in Denmark in 1973. They found that the mean annual rate for women aged 15–44 was 15 abortions per 1,000 women during the

15 months preceding legalization and 23 per 1,000 in the 15 months following legalization. They concluded that although use of abortion had increased, the rate was not of a magnitude to indicate that large scale abandonment of contraception had occurred. Kantner and Zelnik (1973) also examined the relationship between attitudes toward abortion and contraceptive use. After determining which respondents had used contraception at last intercourse, they asked the women what a young, unmarried girl should do if she finds she is pregnant by a boy she likes but doesn't love. Of those who chose the abortion alternative, 63% had used contraception, compared to a contraceptive use incidence of 35% of those who chose marriage, 44% of those who advocated keeping the baby, and 49% of those who were for adoption. Their data suggest, then, that those who are more favorable toward abortion are also more likely to be current users of contraception. Several recent studies (Allgeier, Allgeier, & Rywick, 1979, 1981) suggest that we tend to hold these attitudes for others as well: undergraduates who approved of premarital contraceptive use were more likely to favor abortion for a pregnant adolescent than were those who regarded premarital contraceptive use with less favor. In addition, these students were far more likely to favor abortion for girls whose pregnancy resulted despite conscientious contraceptive use (that is, the method rather than the user had failed) than they were for girls who had been negligent regarding contraception.

In summary, then, it is difficult to know to what extent the belief in abortion as a ''solution'' results in ineffective or nonuse of contraception. On the basis of the responses of adolescents in his sample, however, Sorensen (1973) makes the following recommendation to parents, schools, churches, and birth control organizations who want to discourage pregnancies among young people: ''Wage a substantial campaign against depending upon abortion as a form of birth control. Abortion should be offered as a last resort to prevent unwanted births. Emphasize the possibility of sterility from repeated abortions'' (p. 372).

BARRIERS DUE TO BELIEFS THAT CONTRACEPTION IS IMMORAL

Moral objections to adolescent contraceptive use appear to be based on two different beliefs. One of these is that the provision of contraceptive services for young people encourages premarital sex and promiscuity. The other is a more general adherence to the Catholic ban on contraception which we will examine in terms of its potential influence on adolescent contraceptive behavior.

Contraception leads to premarital sex and promiscuity. One of the barriers to effective contraceptive use by adolescents is lack of an adequate contraceptive education, as is documented in A. R. Allgeier's chapter in this book on Informational Barriers to Contraception. There are a number of adults who believe that if accurate information is provided, adolescents will make use of it, and begin to engage in sexual intercourse, premaritally and promiscuously. As Udry (1971) put it, there is fear that knowledge of contraceptive techniques will lead to the wholesale collapse of premarital sexual controls. Similarly, Sorensen (1973) suggests that a popular belief is that birth control has increased sexual intercourse among adolescents, and that young people who would formerly have abstained are having sex because they have little threat of pregnancy. This claim is not only made by adults. In Sorensen's sample, two-thirds of the nonvirgins agreed with the statement: "The main reason why people are more casual about sex these days is because birth control is easily available to everyone."

At the outset, there is a great deal of evidence documenting the increase in the proportion of adolescents who are now engaging in premarital intercourse (Hunt, 1974; Kinsey, Pomeroy, & Martin, 1948; Kinsey, Pomeroy, Martin, & Gebhard, 1953). Some assumed that the increase in premarital sex observed in the 1960s was part of a more general protest and rebellion that was going on during that decade (Bell & Chaskes, 1970). Surveys conducted during the 1970s, however, suggest that the trend toward an increase in the proportion of male and female adolescents engaging in premarital sex did not end with the 1960s (Chilman, 1976; Croake & James, 1973; Robinson, King, & Balswick, 1972). In fact, data gathered in 1965, 1970, and 1975 by King, Balswick, and Robinson (1977) has led them to suggest that the premarital sexual revolution that began in the late 1960s has actually accelerated during the 1970s. References to the "virginal marriage bed" will undoubtedly be obsolete within the next few decades, since sex with one's marital partner prior to the exchange of wedding vows is now normative. Further, there is little reason to expect any reversal in this pattern (Hyde, 1979). The notion that contraception is the "culprit" in this trend, however, simply does not mesh with the evidence. The belief that the availability of reliable contraceptives for adolescents has caused the increase in premarital sex rests on the assumption that fear of pregnancy formerly inhibited individuals from engaging in premarital sex. If this were the case, presumably, individuals would refrain from engaging in intercourse in the absence of contraception due to pregnancy fears, or would have sex only after having obtained a reliable method of contraception.

Does fear of pregnancy inhibit adolescents from engaging in premarital sex? A number of researchers have explored this idea. Sorensen (1973) found that half of the nonvirgin girls aged 13 to 15 and 36% of the 16 to 19-year-old nonvirgins in his sample agreed with the statement: "Sometimes I don't really care whether or not I get pregnant." Udry (1971) noted that few men and women who are virgins cite fear of pregnancy as a major reason for remaining chaste. Further, he found that there was no relationship between the amount of confidence his respondents held in contraceptives and their premarital sexual permissiveness or virginity. Bauman (1970) asked a sample of college students who were virgins: "If you or your partner could obtain a 100% effective contraceptive, would you have intercourse?'' About one-third of the male virgins said no, another third said only if they were in love, and the remaining third said that they would even if they were not in love. Among the female virgins, 80% said that they would not, with the remaining 20% indicating that they would if they were in love. Finally, Zelnik and Kantner (1974) noted that among those adolescents experiencing premarital pregnancies who had not wanted to become pregnant, only 13 to 16% had used contraception in an attempt to prevent the pregnancy.

Thus, there is not much evidence to suggest that pregnancy fear inhibits adolescents from engaging in premarital intercourse. There is even less evidence to support the belief that acquisition of contraceptives leads adolescents to become sexually active. Data from surveys based on national samples (Schofield, 1965; Sorensen, 1973; Zelnik & Kantner, 1977) indicate that the first experience with sexual intercourse is rarely accompanied by the use of a contraceptive. Zelnik and Kantner (1977) point out that although the use of contraception has been increasing among adolescents in the past few years, few of the sexually experienced adolescents in their sample began to use contraception until *after* they had begun engaging in sexual intercourse, with many of them first acquiring contraceptives *after* they had experienced a premarital pregnancy. Further, as was seen in Table 8.1, most teens who are sexually active do not always use contraception. Therefore, *lack* of contraception doesn't necessarily *inhibit* sexual activity, even among those who sometimes do use contraceptives.

The statistics from various studies conducted in clinics are even more depressing. Of the 16,470 teenagers (almost 3,000 of whom were 16 or under) seen at family planning clinics in Illinois during an 8-month period, almost half had already been pregnant prior to coming to the clinic. Although they were sexually active, the majority of them had never used contraception (Wilson, Keith, Wells, & Steptoe, 1973). In their study of 502 unmarried 13 to 17-year-olds in California who were seeking contraception for the first time, Settlage, Baroff, and Cooper (1973) found that most of the girls had been sexually active for more than a year. Similarly, three-fourths of the girls visiting a pediatric clinic in Atlanta, Georgia, were sexually active, with 13.5 years the average age of first intercourse. Two-thirds of these girls had never used contraception, and the average length of sexual activity before coming to the clinic was just under a year (Digest, 1974). Studies with pregnant teenagers (for instance, Furstenberg, Gordis, & Markowitz, 1969) indicate that their contraceptive knowledge is inadequate with most of them being aware of the inadequacy of their information, and eager to learn about contraception.

If the availability of contraceptives for adolescents were the causative factor in the increase in premarital sex, it is unlikely that our society would be experiencing the enormous surge in the rates for adolescent abortion and illegitimacy. For instance, between 1972 and 1975, the teenage abortion rate rose from 19 to 32 abortions performed per 1,000 girls aged 15 to 19 years. Furthermore, approximately one out of every five abortions in 1975 were given to women who had previously had abortions, and Washington, D.C. led the nation in repeat abortions (i.e., 30% of abortion patients seen were having a second, third, etc., abortion) (Digest, 1977). This "recidivism" rate is somewhat staggering since clinics typically make an attempt to provide contraceptive education and devices to their abortion clients. Nonetheless, the abortion procedure has, in effect, become a method of birth control, slowing the population growth rate by about a quarter (Stokes, 1977). Even so, Cutright's (1972a) review of illegitimacy rates from 1920 to 1968 indicates that although the number of out-of-wedlock births has decreased for most groups, the illegitimacy rate has continued to increase for adolescent women throughout that period. At present, approximately 10% of all 15 to 19-year-old women in the United States become pregnant each year, and over half of them give birth. In 1975, for instance, there were almost 13,000 babies born to 15 to 19-year-old women. Further, 30,000 girls aged 14 or under become pregnant each year (McCary, 1978). In short, the claims that contraceptive availability has caused the increase in the incidence of premarital sex do not appear to be supported by the evidence. Actually, given the problems posed by premarital pregnancy, both for the individual and society, the portrait of the virginal adolescent acquiring contraception and *then* embarking on a sexual adventure would represent a distinct improvement over the reality that currently exists.

An additional concern of the opponents of contraceptive education for adolescents is that there will be no restraints on their sexual expression. That is, contracepting adolescents will have sex as often (a "frequency" hypothesis) and with as many partners (a "promiscuity" hypothesis) as they can. There is evidence from several different studies to support the "frequency" hypothesis. Vincent and Stelling (1973) found that 59% of the females who were very sexually active used oral contraceptives, and 44% of the partners of very active males used the pill. The less the sexual activity rate, the more likely these college students were to use unreliable contraceptive methods. The number of students who seriously and carefully planned contraceptive practices with their partner increased as the level of sexual activity increased. Kantner and Zelnik (1973) also reported an association between coital frequency and pill use. Garris, Steckler, and McIntire (1976) compared college females who had been using the pill for 6 to 8 months with females who were just beginning to use the pill, and found that sexual activity rates were higher for the former. Thus, frequency of intercourse does appear to be positively related to the reliability of contraceptive methods.

However, with respect to the "promiscuity" hypothesis in the Garris et al. (1976) study, there was no increase in the number of partners in the group of women who had been using the pill for 6 to 8 months over that for the group which was just beginning pill use. In fact, evidence from several studies suggests that reliable contraceptive use is associated with strong commitment to one's partner rather than with promiscuous sexual activity with a number of different partners. For instance, Reiss, Banwart, and Foreman (1975), defining dyadic commitment as going steady or being engaged with someone, reported that the greater the degree of commitment, the greater the adoption of contraceptive methods among college women. Similarly, Maxwell, Sack, Frary, and Keller (1977) found that among couples who were in love or planning to marry, there was greater use of reliable contraception (72%) than among couples who were less involved with one another (61%). This relationship existed even at first intercourse; the greater the degree of involvement the couples had the first time they had sex, the more likely they were to use a reliable contraceptive. Thus, the available evidence suggests that although there is support for the hypothesis that use of contraception is related to greater frequency of sexual intercourse, there does not appear to be support for the notion that contraception is related to promiscuous sexual behavior.

Contraceptive use contradicts religious teachings. In the 13th century, St. Thomas Aquinas maintained that the use of birth control was against nature. Since that time, Catholic theologians have rejected the use of contraception by artificial means under any circumstances (Himes, 1970). Himes suggests that the Biblical story about the refusal of Onan to impregnate the widow of his dead brother (for which God is supposed to have killed him) is regularly used in contemporary discussions of the Catholic prohibition of contraceptives. In his review of the birth planning literature, Pohlman (1969) wrote that:

> As the present manuscript goes to press at the start of 1967, a papal decision on the possibility of modifying the Catholic Church's historical stand on contraception is awaited almost daily. The Second Vatican Council established a commission to consider birth planning questions. A report from this group has been submitted to Pope Paul VI, who has delayed official pronouncements on the matter while giving the document and the problem further study. According to certain Catholic acquaintances of the present writer, some parish priests in the United States have acquired more liberal views about contraception. Individual Catholics are reported to be encouraged in their use of non-approved contraception by the general climate of change, controversy, and re-examination within the Church (p. 369).

Pope Paul VI's eagerly awaited encyclical letter, *Humane Vitae* (1968) did not justify the optimism of Pohlman or his acquaintances regarding the possibility of modification of the Church's stand on contraception. The Pope maintained the absolute prohibition of the use of contraceptives by the 700 million Catholics of the world. In his view, the act of sexual intercourse may not be separated from the possibility of conception. In addition, the U.S. Conference of Catholic Bishops has recently reaffirmed this position (Westoff & Jones, 1977). Pope John Paul II supported mandatory celibacy for Catholic clergy (*Newsweek*, November 20, 1978, p. 84) in his first public address on church discipline, and there is little to suggest that any modification of the Church's ban on contraception is imminent.

Although the Church appears to have retained some of its influence on students who are majoring in theology and religion (Coughlin, 1976), and among Catholic nurses (Elder, 1976), its influence elsewhere has eroded. In their review of factors affecting population growth, Russo and Brackbill (1973) noted that religion was a powerful variable in predicting contraceptive use, but they noted that recent studies indicated that the influence of the Catholic position on this issue has been declining in recent years. In fact, some have suggested that the Catholic ban on contraception has resulted in a decrease in allegiance to the Church. For instance, Greeley, McCready, and McCourt (1976) reported declines of 54% in the proportion of Catholics confessing monthly, and 30% in the proportions attending mass weekly. They attributed these declines almost entirely to a negative response to the birth control encyclical *Humane Vitae*. Westoff and Bumpass (1973) predicted that by the end of the decade, birth control practices of Catholics and non-Catholics would not differ. And research has already confirmed this prediction among married couples (Westoff & Jones, 1977). Even among couples in their sample who received communion at least once a month, only 12.5% remained obedient to the Church ban on contraception.

Among adolescents, the Catholic Church's ban also appears to be ineffective. In fact, in Kantner and Zelnik's (1973) sample of 15 to 19-year-old women, Catholics reported slightly higher levels of recent contraceptive use (51%) and of use ever (85%) than did nonfundamentalist Protestants (46% and 83%, respectively) and those who professed no religion (50% and 80%, respectively). Among Sorensen's (1973) adolescents, Catholics (16%) were no different from all adolescents (16%) in their position that they wouldn't use contraceptives for religious reasons. Further, in spite of the strong antiabortionist stance taken by the Catholic Church, the majority of the Catholics in Sorensen's sample favored abortion if neither the girl nor the boy really wanted to have a baby that had been conceived. Finally, among rural high school students in McCormick et al.'s (1979) sample, religiosity was unrelated to both extent of sexual experience and contraceptive use.

In examining most beliefs which influence contraceptive behavior, research is available to allow us to determine whether or not the belief has any factual support. In the area of religious beliefs, however, empirical support is obviously difficult to obtain. Therefore, Cohen (1975) has examined the position on birth control taken by the Catholic Church from the standpoint of its internal logic, and his argument is as follows: The Church takes the position that sexual intercourse and procreation are universally and indivisibly cojoined. Cohen refers to this as the "inseparability" premise. The Church categorically prohibits all control of the sex act, once begun, and all efforts or devices which have as their object the blocking of conception. Cohen points out that the fact that rhythm and abstinence are allowed is inconsistent with their position against the use of any efforts to block conception. He goes on to suggest that maintaining the argument against all control of the sex act once begun is an untenable position, since there are instances in which control is appropriate (arousal in public places, with inappropriate persons, and so forth). Finally, he suggests that the document whose name is 'human life' (Humane Vitae) will reap human death as its harvest. This statement is probably a bit inflammatory as far as Catholics are concerned. On the other hand, such factors as the overpopulation problem, the 50% higher mortality rate for babies when they are spaced 1 year apart as compared to 2 years apart (Guttmacher, 1947), and the fact that births by young adolescent girls have greater incidence of infant mortality and morbidity as well as increased probability for maternal complications than is characteristic of births by women in their twenties (Osofsky, 1968) does support the idea that the mortality rate is increased by failure to use contraception.

BARRIERS DUE TO BELIEFS REGARDING PROBLEMS IN CONTRACEPTIVE ACQUISITION

Some adolescents engage in unprotected intercourse because they believe that getting contraceptives is difficult, illegal, or expensive. Further, acquisition of contraception requires the admission that they are sexually active. Such acknowledgement carries with it the risk of social disapproval.

Acquisition is difficult because of inaccessibility, expense, or legal problems.   In Sorensen's (1973) sample, almost half of the 13 to 15-year-old girls and 18% of the 16 to 19-year-old girls indicated that there was not any place where they could go to get pills or contraceptives. A number of girls in his sample indicated that they were unaware of Planned Parenthood or other organizations where they could get pills free or at cost, with 15% of the girls who had sex during the previous month without contraception maintaining that they couldn't afford pills or any other reliable contraceptive.

Accessibility appears to be declining as a problem, with teenage enrollment in family planning clinics rising from 453,000 in 1971 to 1.1 million in 1975 (Alan Guttmacher Institute, 1976b). The expense of contraception is less from clinics (and is generally based on one's income) than it is from private doctors. However, some adolescents may assume that contraceptives cost more money than they, in fact, do. Hyde (1979) has provided a table of costs of contraceptive purchase and this information might be useful to adolescents who make the assumption that contraception is expensive. She indicates that on an annual basis, the pill costs about $40, insertion of an IUD ranges from $25 to $50, diaphragm and jelly costs between $15 and $30, condoms range from $18 to $60, and vaginal foam ranges between $10 and $30. In considering expense, of course, engaging in unprotected intercourse is likely to far more expensive than is any form of contraception, with a legal abortion costing between $160 and $400, and pregnancy and childbirth costing in excess of $1,000.

With respect to the legal status of contraception, barriers have been breaking down since 1934 when liberal federal court decisions began the reversal of the absolute ban on contraception under the 1873 Comstock Law (Stokes, 1971). Since 1970, there has been a significant liberalization of laws and policies affecting teenagers' access to contraceptive services (Paul, Pilpel, & Wechsler, 1976). In 1977, in their first consideration of the rights of minors to contraception, the U.S. Supreme Court struck down a New York State statute which had prohibited the sale or distribution of nonprescription contraceptives to minors under the age of 16 (Digest, 1977). The Court also invalidated the prohibition of advertising and display of contraceptives by persons licensed to sell contraceptives. According to the Digest (1977) report, 12 states which had laws restricting the sale and/or distribution of contraceptives, 13 states which restricted or regulated contraceptive advertising, and seven which restricted or regulated their display are affected by these rulings. The result of these decisions by the high court is to eliminate legal barriers to contraceptive acquisition regardless of age.

Acquisition of contraception involves the risk of social disapproval.   In the movie *The Summer of 42,* a young boy goes through a series of approach-avoidance interactions with a pharmacist in his attempt to purchase a condom. Although this scene produced a great deal of laughter in theatres, beliefs that societal agents (pharmacists, doctors, nurses, and parents) will censure or punish attempts to get contraceptives deters some adolescents from attempting to obtain reliable protection from conception. On the basis of his study of English adolescents, Schofield (1965) concluded that risk of social disapproval results in the absence of adequate precautions against pregnancy.

In their investigation of reactions of males to purchasing contraceptives, Fisher, Fisher, and Byrne (1977) found that a proportion of their sample believed that the pharmacist would make negative attributions about them. A study of pharmacists' attitudes, published 9 years ago (Roffman, Speckman, & Gruz, 1973) does not support the belief, although it should be noted that only 40% of the sample of pharmacists returned the questionnaires that the authors mailed to 710 community pharmacies in Maryland. Among those who did respond, the sale of contraceptives to both married and unmarried patrons was nearly universal. The pharmacists explained their contraceptive sale policy as a desire to prevent both illegitimacy and venereal disease. It is interesting that the majority of the pharmacists did not openly display contraceptives over the counter at that time. They indicated that they did not do so because they thought it was in poor taste (45%), or because they expected negative community response (35%), or theft (12%).

Beliefs that doctors and nurses may disapprove of them if teens approach them for contraception may also inhibit contraceptive acquisition. Among the girls in Sorensen's (1973) sample who did not always use birth control, 24%

indicated that they were made very "uptight" by the attitude of doctors and clinics from whom they sought contraceptives. Some of the girls reported that they thought that doctors or clinics had been patronizing or almost abusive to them.

Several studies support the perceptions of these girls that some health care professionals hold anticontraception attitudes for unmarried adolescents. For instance, Ager (1976) found that the students and teaching faculty from schools of nursing, medicine and social work view unmarried women as less appropriate recipients of family planning services than married women. Elder (1976) found that less than 33% of senior nursing students approved of placing nonprescription contraceptives in vending machines or food markets. These students disapproved of the provision of contraceptive services for very young teenagers, with half of the students indicating that contraceptive education was best begun at the age of 15 or older. This attitude is unfortunate in the extreme since 30,000 girls under the age of 15 become pregnant each year. Accordingly, Bickness and Walsh (1976) have recommended that contraceptive delivery systems be designed to reduce the amount of motivation currently required for people to avail themselves of birth control services.

Parents are also seen as a potential source of disapproval or punishment for contraceptive use. In a study of how the use of oral contraceptives influenced sexual behavior in unmarried girls aged 15–20, Garris, Steckler, and McIntire (1976) found that the Before group (those just beginning to use pills) felt more strongly that their parents would disapprove of their sexual behavior than the After group (those who had used the pill for 6 to 8 months). Furstenberg (1976) found more effective contraceptive use by adolescent females whose parents were aware of their daughters' sexual behavior than by those whose parents were not aware. He speculated that the latter group may try to neutralize their family's sexual prescriptions by avoiding the issue of contraception. The potential importance of restrictive parental attitudes as contributors to the adolescent pregnancy epidemic will be discussed more thoroughly at the end of the chapter.

Acquisition of contraception requires acknowledgment that one is sexually active.   Some adolescents avoid acquisition of contraception because they believe that this would be an explicit admission that they are engaging in intercourse. As one of Sorensen's subjects put it:

> Pills? That's what I should have taken. But I didn't want them. I didn't want them because that's like coming right out and admitting, 'I am fucking,' you know. I don't want to admit that to myself. I was trying so hard to think I wasn't fucking that the thought I might get pregnant never entered my mind (1973, p. 324).

Lindemann (1975) suggested that failure to redefine one's self concept as sexually active was a contributing factor in unwanted pregnancies among teenage girls. She suggested that their self-concepts would allow a spontaneous sexual episode, but planned, predictable, or intentional intercourse was too dissonant with their self perceptions to allow realistic and rational appraisals of the consequences of unprotected intercourse. Thus, by refusing to admit to themselves that they were sexually active persons, many girls avoided a decision to use contraception and subsequently became pregnant. Fox (1977) has also discussed the effect of self-concept on sexual behavior, suggesting that trying to conform to normative values regarding being a nice girl encourages a lack of responsibility for one's own sexual behavior.

The absence of a self-concept that one is a sexually active person, of course, makes the planning that is necessary to have a reliable contraceptive out of the question. This is particularly problematic with first intercourse; Bauman (1970) found that 75% of males and 89% of females in his college sample did not plan their first intercourse (see Chapter 5).

BARRIERS DUE TO BELIEFS REGARDING THE EFFECT OF USING CONTRACEPTIVES

Unprotected intercourse takes place among some adolescents because they believe that concern with contraception will inhibit spontaneity in their sexual relations and reduce the amount of sexual pleasure. Some young people also believe that oral contraceptives, in particular, will damage their health and their capacity for later fertility.

Use of contraception causes problems in relationship. Some adolescents avoid dealing with contraception because of beliefs that such concern would indicate that they are too sexually experienced, would show that they are not sufficiently in love with and/or impassioned by their lovers to lose all reationality, or would reduce the "naturalness" and "spontaneity" of the act. For instance, 71% of all nonvirgin girls in Sorensen's (1973) sample indicated that if a girl uses contraception, it makes it seem as if she were planning to have sex, and 74% of the girls who didn't always use birth control when having sex during the preceding month also agreed with that idea. This is closely related to the problem with self-concept (that one is not sexually active) covered in the last section, however, it is also possible that some women may see themselves as sexually active, but be reluctant to let partners know that they considered intercourse a possibility, and therefore acquired some contraceptive protection ahead of time. Belief that sex should be spontaneous resulted in an absence of advance planning for 31% of the students engaging in first intercourse without contraceptive protection in Maxwell, Sack, Frary, and Keller's (1977) college student sample.

Jazwinski and Byrne (1978) attempted to determine responses to films of a couple having intercourse under several different contraception conditions including contraception via the pill, no contraception, and no information regarding contraception. They found that males reported the greatest positive emotional response to the film when the couple was depicted as single and using contraception, but they also perceived the couple as caring the least for one another when they were using contraception. In contrast, females perceived the contraceptive use as positive evidence of mutual caring, and in Finkel and Finkel's (1975) study, 60% of the teenage males believed that condom use indicated respect for one's partner.

Contraception affects sex drive and pleasure.   Some authorities have warned women to expect some loss of sex drive after protracted use of the pill because of its interference with normal hormone production (Trainer, 1965), and Masters and Johnson (1967, cited in McCary, 1978) reported a reduction in women's sex drive after taking the pill for 18–36 months. On the other hand, reports of increases of frequency of sexual intercourse associated with pill use have appeared. Kantner & Zelnik (1973) found that women using the pill, matched on race, age, religion, and education with women not using the pill, appeared to have sex with more frequency.

Contraception threatens health.   Kantner and Zelnik (1973) found that one-fourth of sexually experienced unmarried girls regarded pills as unsafe for their health, and reported that this belief influenced their contraceptive behavior. That is, the pill was used by 31% of contraceptors who believed that it was safe, whereas, only 7% of those who believed it unsafe reported current pill use. A majority (56% of boys, 70% of girls) of adolescents in Sorensen's (1973) study agreed that birth control pills could be harmful to a girl. Among the reasons listed for not using the pill by adolescent girls were that the pill causes weight gains, cancer, headaches, and malfunctioning of one's sexual organs. As noted earlier, it is difficult to determine, of course, whether the belief (in this case, that the pill is "dangerous") is influencing the action (non-use of the pill) or whether the action leads to a reported belief that the pill is unsafe as, perhaps, a justification for not using it.

With respect to the prescription of oral contraceptives for very young girls, Lane (1973) has noted the concern that the pill may inhibit growth. She stated that it has been claimed that hormones contained in the pill may preclude the growth of long bones, or may suppress pituitary activity such that the pituitary may be incapable of stimulating ovulation and ovarian hormone production when the pill is discontinued. In her practice as an MD working with adolescents, however, she states that pregnancy and delivery complications pose a far greater risk. Therefore, she says that she has no qualms abour prescribing the pill for young girls, provided that the pill is the best method for their situation. She reports evidence (Cutright, 1972b) that should a young girl become pregnant during the early post-menarchal period, as increasing numbers of young girls are doing, her many times higher estrogen level would have a much greater potential for limiting her long bone growth then would the low amount of estrogen in the pill.

Arguments that the pill has dangers associated with its use certainly do not support the belief that *all* contraceptives are dangerous, since there are reliable contraceptives (condom, diaphragm with jelly) which carry no long term health risk for anyone. There are data to support the belief that pill use is dangerous for *some* women. Smokers should not use the pill (or, better yet, should give up smoking, of course!) and those with circulatory problems should be sure that their doctors are aware of these difficulties. On the other hand, the pill has proved to be safe for the great majority of young women when its use is supervised by a doctor (McCary, 1978).

Contraception causes a reduction in later fertility.   Concern has been voiced by some women that pill use may decrease their ability to become pregnant when they do desire a baby. In an attempt to investigate the effects of pill use on later fertility, an ongoing study of 17,000 women is being conducted by the Oxford Family Planning Association in Britain (Vessey, Doll, Peto, Johnson, & Wiggins, 1976). They have found that use of the pill does not reduce the likelihood that women can become pregnant after going off the pill. Among women in this study who hadn't previously had children, all but 16% of those who were using the pill had given birth within 30 months of going off the pill, as compared with 11% of those who had been using other contraceptive methods. Within 42 months, the percentages had dropped to 11% and 10%, respectively (Digest, 1977). Among women who had previously had children, regardless of whether they had used the pill or some other form of contraception, all but 8% had given birth within 30 months, and all but 4% had given birth within 42 months of stopping contraceptive use. Thus, there is no evidence to support the belief that pill use causes sterility. Whether or not it produces a short term reduction in fertility remains to be determined.

BARRIERS DUE TO THE BELIEF THAT PREGNANCY IS ACCEPTABLE

In each of the preceding sections, the focus has been on adolescents who do not wish to become pregnant, but who are inadequately protected from conception due to a variety of beliefs which function as barriers to their acquisition and consistent use of reliable contraceptives. It has been relatively easy to review, one at a time, the barriers to effective contraceptive use by adolescents who *don't* want to conceive. Increasing numbers of adolescents, however, are having, keeping, and trying to raise babies (Nye, 1976). Many of them view nonmarital pregnancy in positive terms rather than as the catastrophic ruination of life suggested by the afternoon soaps on television. In fact, almost half (45%) of the male and female nonvirgins, and 29% of all the adolescents in Sorensen's (1973) study agreed with the statement: "Someday, I will probably want to have children, but it won't matter whether or not I get married first." Sorensen found that the willingness to consider becoming a single parent increased substantially with age among both boys and girls, although boys were considerably more positive about the idea than girls were.

The task of identifying and examining each of the beliefs which lead unmarried adolescents to accept the possibility of nonmarital pregnancy is quite complicated. To begin with, we have a general pronatalist (literally, "for birth") ideology, as exemplified by the third quote at the beginning of this chapter to the effect that birth is *always* a positive event, *regardless* of the conditions under which it occurs. In addition, there are assorted other assumptions and ideals which emanate from our pronatalist ideology. Among these are beliefs that impregnation confers adult status and proves a man's masculinity, demonstrates a woman's femininity and permits her to realize what many regard as a woman's most important function: conceiving and raising babies. Some people hold this belief with such intensity that they view the married man and woman who wish to avoid the responsibilities and rewards of reproduction as emotionally disturbed or deficient in some way.

The pronatalist views have been criticized heavily in the past few years (Bernard, 1974; Bem, 1976; Frieden, 1963; Millett, 1970). For instance, Shpunt (1974) has suggested that, "Pronatalism, like racism and sexism, is a more-or-less invisible evil structured into the very thought processes of men and women—particularly women—in all phases of our culture" (p. 28). On the other hand, the position that pronatalism and sexism are malevolent inventions of 20th century American male chauvinists demonstrates, at the least, a lack of historical perspective. Pronatalist values have existed, as far as we know, throughout the history of our species. And, in general, pronatalist and sexist ideologies were highly functional for both species and individual survival until this century. A failure to perceive their historical importance, and the reasons for their necessity, undercuts the importance of contemporary demands for a reduction in adherence to these beliefs. Therefore, after reviewing the research relevant to the effect of pronatalist beliefs on contraceptive behavior, I will describe pronatalism in terms of its historical usefulness and its present threat to the survival of society and the species.

Pregnancy proves that one is a normal man or woman. For those producing many children, "Mother of the Year" awards are granted, and reproductively active couples are commonly (and sometimes, leeringly—a la Johnny Carson) assumed to be very sexually active. Actually, research (Byrne, Jazwinski, De-

Ninno, & Fisher, 1977) has shown that married couples with highly positive attitudes toward sex want fewer children than do those with less positive sexual attitudes. Nonetheless, pregnancy has been seen as a method of proving health and normalcy. We might question the wisdom of unmarried teens seeking conception to prove their normalcy; for those who value pregnancy for that purpose, though, contraceptives are not likely to be sought. As one of Sorensen's (1973) adolescent girls speculated, "Maybe its the experience of being pregnant I need—a motherhood kick. I think that has a lot to do with it. You're not a womanly person in society until you know you can have children. Sometimes in the back of my head it would be nice to know I'm a normal person and can have a baby" (p. 321). Throughout the world, the idea that conception—particularly of sons—demonstrates a man's sexual health and virility has long been popular. More recently, the belief that impregnation proves heterosexual "normalcy" was illustrated in the movie "The Turning Point" in which the male ballet dancer acknowledged to his wife that he impregnated her to silence gossip that he was gay.

Having children is the most important thing a woman can do. The definitions of normalcy described above of course, are actually subsets of a larger belief system—that there are appropriate, and different, behaviors and purposes associated with being male and with being female. Stereotypically, the truly feminine woman is yielding, passive, and demonstrates her love for her man (who is the center of her existence) by raising *his* children. Although supposedly difficult to arouse (Hyde, 1979), she can demonstrate to the male his sexual prowess by being so overcome with passion as to lose all concern with consequences. When the consequences involve premarital pregnancy, she may further demonstrate her "love" by relinquishing all other goals and plans to devote herself to carrying, bearing, and raising the child that they have conceived. This view of womanly love and devotion has been eulogized in song by Paul Anka in which an apparently unmarried woman is told, "Having my baby; what a lovely way to tell me how much you love me," and, with a passing reference to abortion, "You could have swept it from your life, but you wouldn't do it."

To the extent that a woman may be concerned with educational and occupational attainment, she is somehow less than feminine; in fact, she may be perceived as rather masculine. Ironically, although many of the qualities that are associated with masculinity are given greater value than many of the qualities associated with femininity by both psychologists and lay persons (Broverman, Broverman, Clarkson, Rosenkrantz, & Vogel, 1970), when females exhibit some of these valued qualities, they are at times devalued (Goldberg, 1968; Goldberg, Gottesdiener, & Abramson, 1975). Until quite recently, definitions of mental health regarding the dimensions of masculinity and femininity carried with them the assumption that the healthy individual clearly identified with *either* masculine *or* feminine characteristics and traits depending upon their biological gender (Constantinople, 1973). The individual who identified with *both* masculine *and* feminine traits was, then, presumed to be emotionally disordered. Although this assumption has been questioned (Bem, 1974), its impact has been far-reaching; even artists are not immune from its effects. Erica Jong described how the dichotomy between creative (male) and generative (female) processes has affected her (*The New Republic,* January 13, 1979). She pointed out that females, in general, have been expected to choose between exercising their talents and their reproductive organs. She noted that some childless artists even refer to their books or works of art as their babies. She contested this view (having had her first child at 35) and maintained that the two processes are not analogous at all, and that the individual can do both things if she chooses (I am quite sympathetic to this view as I began writing this chapter a few months after the birth of our son, whose care is shared by my husband and me). She makes, however, the crucial point that it is difficult to develop one's vocational skills if one begins having children at an early age. She maintains that it is far easier to combine the two after one's skills at a career or vocation are well-developed than it is to attempt the combination of development of new vocational skills with new parenthood. That amounts to an argument for delayed marriage and parenthood, and it is well supported by the fact that early parenthood, in addition to leading to welfare dependency, frequently results in premature entry of the mother and/or father into the labor market, and shortened educational training for future job competencies (Klerman & Jekel, 1973).

Unfortunately, though, young girls receive more training in, and rewards for, those skills relevant to the task of servicing others than for skills relevant to the development of their own talents. Stein and Bailey (1973) have suggested that the achievement needs of females may be as strong as those of males, but the arena in which females are expected to achieve is that of family and child-centered activities. And Russo and Brackbill (1973) argue that ". . . current patterns of sex-role socialization propel females toward accepting marriage and childbearing roles and toward rejecting other sources of self-fulfillment as improper" (p. 398).

At this point, the evidence is quite overwhelming that a belief in traditional sex-role norms has a strong impact on reproductive desires and behavior. Eagly and Anderson (1974) found that females who endorsed an equivalent pattern of sex role behaviors for males and females wanted smaller families than those who endorsed a more stereotyped pattern of sex role behaviors. Similarly, Allgeier (1975) found that females who give equally high endorsement to masculine and feminine traits as descriptive of themselves wanted fewer children and placed more importance on the development of competence in their work than did females who give significantly stronger endorsement to feminine traits as self-descriptive. The more importance women place on educational and/or career achievement, the less likely they are to desire early marriage and/or children

(Almquist & Angrist, 1971; Blake, 1969; Freedman & Coombs, 1966; Pratt & Whelpton, 1958; Ridley, 1959; Russo & Brackbill, 1973).

As might be expected, these differing beliefs in what is important have their impact on contraceptive behavior. Joestling and Joestling (1974) have found a positive relationship between modern attitudes toward contraception and equalitarian views of women's place among college students, and Miller (1974) found a positive relationship between modern role orientation and adequate contraceptive use. Reliable contraceptive use is also related to the desire for present and future achievements among female college students (Harvey, 1976). In summary, those girls with developmental goals beyond the exercise of their biological capacity are more motivated to avoid premarital conception than are those girls who believe that their main function is that of sperm and baby repository, and the imminence of potential marriage appears to reduce contraceptive use among some teenagers (Miller, 1973; Shah, Zelnik, & Kantner, 1975).

Regardless of the circumstances, the arrival of a baby is always a blessed event. As noted earlier, in the past it has been crucial for species survival that humans regard reproduction as a desirable activity. Beyond the rewards inherent in the process of conception (at least for those who enjoy sexual intercourse), when it occurs under appropriate conditions, news of a first pregnancy is universally greeted with congratulations, and birth itself is rewarded with gifts and attention. So much value has been placed on the parenting process that little girls in our society begin thinking about how many children they would like to have as early as elementary school (Gustavus & Nam, 1970).

In nonindustrialized, preliterate cultures, such as the *So* of Northeastern Uganda, with whom I lived for a year, pregnancy is seen as appropriate for a couple when the girl is capable of taking full responsibility for building and caring for a hut and a garden, making charcoal, and doing the other things that adult women do to help their mates support the family union. Similarly, the responsibility of fatherhood is seen as appropriate for a man when he is able to hunt, acquire and care for his own herd of goats and cows, and participate in intertribal warfare (Laughlin & Allgeier, 1979). Such adult skills have been completely acquired by the time young people reach their mid-teens in most nonindustrialized societies, and marriage and childbearing are seen as appropriate from that time on. That is, adult responsibilities are expected of young people and they are accorded adult status very shortly after they are biologically capable of reproduction. Given the marginal existence of most preliterate groups, coupled with the extremely high (until the intervention of Western medicine and public health measures) mortality rate, it has been important that young people begin the process of conceiving children as early as possible in order for the society to maintain its population. Even within our own society a short 200 years ago, the life expectancy was half (35 years) what it is now (Coale, 1974). Many of the children born to Colonial women (an average of 7.5 per woman) were dead before they reached reproductive maturity so that a high fertility rate was necessary to ensure that a certain proportion of people lived long enough to maintain the population. In the past 200 years, however, there has been a drastic decrease in the mortality rate; decreases in fertility rates have lagged behind. Consequently, we are faced with incredible population pressures. At present, the earth is doubling its population every 35 years, and the length of time it takes for us to double it is decreasing with each generation. Indeed, contraception is presently as necessary for our survival as pronatalism once was (see Chapter 1).

There is another reason, however, which makes it essential in modern industrialized societies, that we reduce the effects of beliefs that lead young people to value adolescent parenthood. As noted above, in nonindustrialized societies, adulthood and all the skills and privileges that go with it, is reached just after the development of the capacity to reproduce. In complex, industrialized societies, however, there are a huge number of technological, legal, economic, and social barriers to adulthood before individuals reach—at a minimum—the age of 18. In many cases, adulthood is delayed until the mid or later twenties, due to protracted education. Unfortunately, our society has supported decisions by an increasing number of adolescents to become parents when they are too young and unskilled to care independently for themselves or their children. The burden for the financial, and, in some cases, the physical and emotional care of infants born to children and adolescents, therefore, has tended to fall both on the families of the adolescents and on the society as a whole through government supported aid programs. If the necessity of the adolescents' families and the society as a whole to provide support for these children raising children were the only cost—that is, if such support enabled adolescents to continue normal development so that they could eventually take their place as emotionally, educationally, and technologically skilled adults prepared to cope with complex decision-making even as they reared healthy children, then the situation would not be so tragic. That is not, however, the outcome of most adolescent decisions to become parents. In addition to the previously noted permanent limits that are generally placed on their educational and occupational attainment, the most frequent outcome of marriage of premaritally pregnant girls is divorce. As Furstenberg (1979) commented in his description of the outcome of teenage parenthood in a sample of 400 adolescent mothers, "Poorly educated, unskilled, often burdened by several small children, many of these women at age 20 or 21 had become resigned to a life of economic deprivation" (p. 156). Faced with such frustration, it is hardly surprising that adolescent mothers have been more likely to abuse their offspring than are older mothers (Kempe & Helfer, 1968).[1] Finally, shared responsibility for childrearing with a husband eludes many adolescent mothers. Sarrel and Davis' (1966) follow-up study of 95 unwed mothers found that they had pro-

---

[1]Whether or not this difference will persist in an era of legalized abortion remains to be seen.

duced a total of 340 children in the 5 years following the birth of their first illegitimate child, but only four of them were married. In short, dreams of love, as suggested by Paul Anka's song "Having MY Baby" and fantasies of having a rosy infant nestled in one's arms, frequently become nightmares from which the adolescent mother is unable to awaken.

DIRECTIONS FOR FUTURE RESEARCH: MANIPULATING INTENTIONS

Earlier in this chapter, I noted the difficulties inherent in most of our accumulated knowledge regarding the relationship between beliefs and contraceptive behavior. It is frequently problematic to determine whether a reported belief was the cause or the result of a particular contraceptive behavior. In their attempt to develop a method for studying belief-behavior links, Fishbein and Ajzen have proposed one of the most sophisticated models for understanding and predicting social behavior (Ajzen & Fishbein, 1970, 1972, 1973; Fishbein, 1967, 1972; Fishbein and Ajzen, 1975). For our purposes a simplified description of the basic hypotheses of this model will be given so that we can focus on aspects of it that are relevant for reducing the adolescent conception epidemic. Fishbein and Ajzen's basic assumptions are in italic. The parenthetical examples represent my hypothetical application of these assumptions to the contraceptive behavior of a teenaged, sexually active girl.

1. *A person's behavior is a function of his or her intention to perform that behavior.* (A girl's use of a diaphragm and spermicidal jelly whenever she engages in intercourse is a function of her intention to use her diaphragm and jelly on all occasions of intercourse)
2. *Behavioral intentions, in turn, are a function of:*
    (a) *a person's attitude toward an act* (A girl's intention to use her diaphragm and jelly consistently is a function of her attitude—positive or negative—toward using her diaphragm and jelly), and
    (b) *her subjective norms, that is, her perceptions of what significant others think should be done with respect to the act in question* (A girl's perception of the opinion of people who are important to her with respect to using the diaphragm).

Fishbein has broken down *attitudes toward the act* and *subjective norms*—the determinants of intention (and hence behavior)—into basic psychological components that are amenable to change.

3. *An individual's attitude toward an act is a function of:*
    (a) *his or her beliefs about the consequences of performing the act* (A girl's attitude toward consistent use of her diaphragm and jelly is a

function of her beliefs about the consequences of using them; for instance, she may believe the consequences will include the prevention of pregnancy, increased liquid in her vagina, perception by her partner that she is prepared, etc.), and

(b) *the person's evaluation of these consequences* (all of the above consequences may be evaluated positively or negatively depending on whether she doesn't or does want to become pregnant, sees the additional liquid as sensual or messy, and desires her partner to see her as an experienced, responsible woman or as a naive, virginal woman).

4. *Finally, a person's subjective norms are a function of:*

(a) *his or her perception of what specific reference persons think should be done regarding the behavior* (A girl believes that her boyfriend, parents, girlfriends, etc. want her to protect herself from conception by using the diaphragm and jelly), and

(b) *his or her motivation to comply with these referents* (she does—or doesn't—want to comply with what she perceives as her boyfriend's, parents', or girlfriend's wishes).

Preliminary support has been provided for all four of these proposals in the context of research on contraceptive behavior (Davidson & Jaccard, 1975, 1979; Fisher, 1978; Jaccard & Davidson, 1972). With the success of this model for *predicting* contraceptive use, hypotheses may be generated for applying the model to programs for *increasing* contraceptive use. That is, the model suggests particular strategies for intervening in the socialization of adolescents, and, for that matter, in the socialization of adults for their roles as the parents of adolescents who are (potentially) sexually active. The goal of such interventions, of course, is to reduce the number of unwanted conceptions. Now, as Fisher (1978) found, those males who reported an intention to use condoms every time they had intercourse were more likely to do so during the month following the measurement of their intentions than were males who didn't intend to use condoms every time. This finding suggests that we can increase consistent contraceptive use by increasing adolescents' intention to use contraceptives. Although that may sound rather vague, Fishbein and Ajzen's model is quite specific in giving clues as to how this might be done. That is, they suggest that intentions may be influenced by altering:

(a) beliefs about the consequences of an act;
(b) evaluations of the consequences of an act;
(c) perceptions of the beliefs of important others; and
(d) motivation to comply to others' beliefs.

More concretely, as a society, we could provide educational programs at the junior and senior high school level designed to alter beliefs about the consequences of using contraception. For instance, if adolescent males' intention to use condoms is inhibited by the belief that condoms produce a marked reduction in sexual sensation, they should be told about cecum condoms (cecum condoms are made from the intestinal tissue of lambs) which, though more expensive than rubber condoms, result in more natural sensations in that they are very thin and don't inhibit the transfer of heat. If condom use is inhibited by the belief that their female partner(s) will view them as callous or uninvolved, the adolescent males might be told about Jazwinski and Byrne's (1978) study showing that females perceive contraceptive use as a demonstration of mutual caring.

A second approach could involve attempts to alter the evaluations of the consequences of using contraception. As noted earlier, having and using reliable contraceptives may be perceived as an indication that the adolescent is sexually experienced and has planned to have sexual intercourse. This may be evaluated negatively (loss of spontaneity, the contraceptive user has "been around") or positively (the couple can be more relaxed and responsive without the worry of unwanted conception, the contraceptive user is a "responsible" person). Parents and sex education teachers could stress the positive aspects of planning both sexual and contraceptive behavior. For example, they could point out that lovers are apt to be most appealing and responsive when they can anticipate sexual interaction. With such anticipation, they may both bathe, allowing for less inhibited interaction, and they can be more responsive if the male needn't worry about trying to "pull out" in time and if the female isn't worried about whether or not he will be able to accomplish this feat. Impulsive and unprotected intercourse, on the other hand, could be equated with immaturity and selfishness about the effects of one's behavior on both the partner and potential offspring.

Some writers have suggested that increases in adolescent pregnancy are due to increased *societal liberalness* toward both premarital intercourse and illegitimacy (c.f. Chilman, 1978). It is clear, of course, that you can't have an increase in premarital conceptions in the absence of an increase in premarital intercourse (assuming that you hold contraceptive behavior constant). But part of the increase in nonmarital conception may be due to a transition in attitudes about the permissibility of engaging in premarital sex in combination with *societal conservatism* in responding to that transition. Viewed from the vantage point of the Fishbein model, to the extent that (a) contraceptive behavior is influenced by behavioral intentions, and (b) intentions are influenced by perceptions of significant others' opinions regarding contraceptive behavior, societal conservatism may have the powerful, if indirect, effect of increasing nonmarital conception. When adolescent females, for instance, are inhibited in their intention to use reliable contraception by fears that significant others will discover and disapprove of their behavior (find their pills, diaphragms, etc., and punish them for it), we see the effect of the perception of parental conservatism.

Accordingly, we could attempt to alter the attitudes of "significant others" toward contraceptive behavior. Just as most teenagers are inexperienced in dealing with the issues and decisions facing them as they move into adolescence, most adults are equally inexperienced in dealing with their new role of providing guidance to their sexually maturing offspring. Many parents are lacking knowledge about sex and contraception and practice in discussing these issues. A few years ago, I offered a continuing education class called "Adolescent Sexuality for Parents." As it happened, the initial motivation for most of the parents who enrolled was to pick up tips on how to keep their teenagers "chaste" (or in some cases, how to stop them from being sexually active) until marriage. I used the first few sessions to review basic sex education—anatomy, physiology, processes involved in sexual response and reproduction, etc. We then reviewed normative information regarding the incidence of masturbation, premarital sex, and adolescent pregnancy. Toward the end of the class, I asked the parent-students to think back to their own adolescence in terms of what information they wish their parents had given them and what information their parents had actually given them. The responses of these middle-aged parents were very similar to those given by adolescents in research on this issue (Gagnon, 1965). Although their primary preference for the source of their sex education was their parents, most of their information came from other sources. During the remaining sessions of the course, the parents eagerly participated in a series of role-play exercises. Half the parents played the part of teenagers and the other half played the role of parents. In addition to producing some hilarious interactions, this process gave the parents practice in talking openly about sex and birth control.

Such courses could be set up for parents (with appropriate control groups of parents) to see if changes in the attitudes of important reference persons (parents) can be produced, and if, in turn, these changes are accurately perceived and reflected in the contraceptive behavior of their offspring. Presumably, adolescents who are raised by parents who discuss sexual and contraceptive responsibility are more likely to perceive their parents as approving the use of contraception than are those who are raised by parents who bend their energies toward trying to ignore or prevent any sexual expression by their offspring.

REFERENCES

Ager, J. W. Multiple-regression and facet techniques in psychological research on population. In S. H. Newman & V. D. Thompson (Eds.), *Population psychology: Research and educational issues*. Washington: U.S. Government Printing Office, 1976.

Ajzen, I., & Fishbein, M. The prediction of behavior from attitudinal and normative variables. *Journal of Experimental Social Psychology, 1970, 6*, 446–487.

Ajzen, I., & Fishbein, M. Attitudes and normative beliefs as factors influencing behavioral intentions. *Journal of Personality and Social Psychology, 1972, 21*, 1–9.

Ajzen, I., & Fishbein, M. Attitudinal and normative variables as predictors of specific behaviors. *Journal of Personality and Social Psychology, 1973, 27*, 41–57.

Alan Guttmacher Institute. *11 million teenagers*. New York: Planned Parenthood Federation of America, 1976. (a)

Alan Guttmacher Institute. Data and analyses for 1978 revision of DHEW five-year plan for family planning services, New York, 1976 (b)

Allgeier, A. R., Allgeier, E. R., & Rywick, T. Orientations toward abortion: guilt or knowledge? *Adolescence*, 1981, *16*, 273–280.

Allgeier, E. R. Beyond sowing and growing: The relationship of sex-typing to socialization, family plans, and future orientation. *Journal of Applied Social Psychology*, 1975, *5*, 217–226.

Allgeier, E. R. & Allgeier, A. R. *Sexual Interactions*. Lexington, MA: D. C. Heath, 1983.

Allgeier, E. R., Allgeier, A. R., & Rywick, T. Abortion: Reward for conscientious contraceptive use? *Journal of Sex Research*, 1979, *15*, 64–75.

Allgeier, E. R., Przybyla, D. P. J., & Thompson, M. E. *Planned sin: Sex guilt and contraception*. Psychonomic Society Convention, Washington, November, 1977.

Almquist, E. M., & Angrist, S. S. Role model influences on college women's career aspirations. *Merrill Palmer Quarterly*, 1971, *17*, 263–279.

Ambrose, L. Misinforming pregnant teenagers. *Family Planning Perspectives*, 1978, *10*, 51–57.

Bacon, L. Early motherhood, accelerated role transition, and social pathologies. *Social Forces*, 1974, 52.

Bernard, J. *Future of motherhood*. New York: Dial Press, 1974.

Bauman, K. E. Selected aspects of the contraceptive practices of unmarried university students. *American Journal of Obstetrics and Gynecology*, 1970, 108, 203–209.

Bell, R. R., & Chaskes, J. B. Premarital sexual experience among coeds. *Journal of Marriage and the Family*, 1970, *32*, 81–84.

Bem, S. L. The measurement of psychological androgyny. *Journal of Consulting and Clinical Psychology*, 1974, *42*, 155–162.

Bem, S. L. Probing the promise of androgyny. In A. G. Kaplan, & J. B. Bean (Eds.), *Beyond sex-role stereotypes*. Boston: Little, Brown, 1976.

Bickness, F. O., & Walsh, D. C. Motivation and family planning: Incentives and disincentives in the delivery system. *Social Science and Medicine*, 1976, *10*, 579–583.

Blake, J. Population policy for Americans: Is the government being misled? *Science*, 1969, *158*, 730–739.

Blake, J. The teenage birth control dilemma and public opinion. *Science*, 1973, *180*, 708–712.

Broverman, I. K., Broverman, D. M., Clarkson, F. E., Rosenkrantz, P., & Vogel, S. R. Sex role stereotypes and clinical judgments of mental health. *Journal of Consulting Psychology*, 1970, *34*, 1–7.

Brown, L. S. *Do users have more fun: A study of the relationship between contraceptive behavior, sexual assertiveness, and patterns of causal attribution*. Unpublished doctoral dissertation, Southern Illinois University at Carbondale, 1977.

Bumpass, L., & Westoff, C. F. The "perfect contraceptive" population. *Science*, 1970, *169*, 1177–1182.

Byrne, D., Jazwinski, C., DeNinno, J. A., & Fisher, W. A. Negative sexual attitudes and contraception. In D. Byrne & L. A. Byrne (Eds.), *Exploring human sexuality*. New York: Crowell, 1977.

Chilman, C. S. *Possible factors associated with high rates of out-of-marriage births among adolescents*. Unpublished manuscript, University of Wisconsin-Milwaukee, School of Social Welfare, 1976.

Chilman, C. S. *Adolescent sexuality in a changing American society: Social and psychological perspectives*. Washington, D.C.: U.S. Government Printing Office, 1978.

Coale, A. J. The history of the human population. *Scientific American*, 1974, *231*, 40–51.

Cohen, C. Sex, birth control, and human life. In R. Baker & F. Elliston (Eds.), *Philosophy and sex*. Buffalo: Prometheus Books, 1975.

Constantinople, A. Masculinity-femininity: An exception to a famous dictum? *Psychological Bulletin*, 1973, *80*, 389–407.

Coughlin, F. E. Religious and lay graduate students in training for helping roles in New York State:

A study of self-concept and attitudes toward feminism and sexuality. *Dissertation Abstracts International*, 1976, *36*, 4682–4683.

Croake, J. W., & James, B. A four-year comparison of premarital sexual attitudes. *Journal of Sex Research*, 1973, *9*, 91–96.

Cutright, P. Illegitimacy in the United States: 1920–1968. In C. F. Westoff & R. Parke (Eds.), *Commission on Population Growth and the American Future: Demographic and Social Aspects of Population Growth* (Vol. 1). Washington: U.S. Government Printing Office, 1972. (a)

Cutright, P. The teenage sexual revolution and the myth of an abstinent past. *Family Planning Perspectives*, 1972, *4*, 24–31. (b)

Davidson, A. R., & Jaccard, J. J. Population psychology: A new look at an old problem. *Journal of Personality and Social Psychology*, 1975, *31*, 1073–1082.

Davidson, A. R., & Jaccard, J. J. Variables that moderate the attitude-behavior relation: Results of a longitudinal survey. *Journal of Personality and Social Psychology*, 1979, *37*, 1364–1376.

Digest. Youngsters served by pediatric clinic. 1974, *3*, 11.

Digest. Carter budget. *Family Planning Perspectives*, 1978, *10*, 114–115.

Eagly, A. H., & Anderson, P. Sex role and attitudinal correlates of desired family size. *Journal of Applied Social Psychology*, 1974, *4*, 151–164.

Elder, R. G. Orientation of senior nursing students toward access to contraceptives. *Nursing Research*, 1976, *25*, 338–345.

Federal Register. Oral contraceptives: Requirements for labeling directed to the patient. 1978, *43*, 4214–4234.

Finkel, M. L., & Finkel, D. J. Sexual and contraceptive knowledge, attitudes, and behavior of male adolescents. *Family Planning Perspectives*, 1975, *7*, 256–260.

Fishbein, M. Attitude and the prediction of behavior. In M. Fishbein (Ed.), *Readings in attitude theory and measurement*. New York: Wiley, 1967.

Fishbein, M. The prediction of behaviors from attitudinal variables. In C. D. Mortensen & K. K. Sereno (Eds.), *Advances in communication research*. New York: Harper and Row, 1972.

Fishbein, M., & Ajzen, I. *Belief, Attitude, intention, and behavior: An introduction to theory and research*. Reading, MA: Addison Wesley, 1975.

Fisher, W. A. *Affective, attitudinal, and normative determinants of contraceptive behavior among university men*. Unpublished doctoral dissertation, Purdue University, 1978.

Fisher, W. A., Fisher, J. D., & Byrne, D. Consumer reactions to contraceptive purchasing. *Personality and Social Psychology Bulletin*, 1977, *3*, 293–296.

Fox, G. L. "Nice girl": Social control of women through a value construct. *Signs*, 1977, *2*, 805–817.

Freedman, R., & Coombs, L. Economic considerations in family growth decisions. *Population Studies*, 1966, *20*, 197–222.

Frieden, B. *The feminine mystique*. New York: Dell, 1963.

Furstenberg, F. F. *Unplanned parenthood: The social consequences of teenage childbearing*. New York: The Free Press, 1976.

Furstenberg, F. F. The social consequences of teenage parenthood. In G. B. Spanier (Ed.), *Human sexuality in a changing society*. Minneapolis: Burgess Publishing Co., 1979.

Furstenberg, F. F., Gordis, L., & Markowitz, M. Birth control knowledge and attitudes among pregnant adolescents: A preliminary report. *Journal of Marriage and the Family*, 1969, *31*, 34–42.

Gagnon, J. H. Sexuality and sexual learning in the child. *Psychiatry*, 1965, 28, 222–228.

Garris, L., Steckler, A., & McIntire, J. R. The relationship between oral contraceptives and adolescent sexual behavior. *Journal of Sex Research*, 1976, *12*, 135–146.

Goldberg, P. Are women prejudiced against women? *Transaction*, 1968, *5*, 28–30.

Goldberg, P., Gottesdiener, M., & Abramson, P. R. Another putdown of women? Perceived attractiveness as a function of support for the feminist movement. *Journal of Personality and Social Psychology*, 1975, *32*, 113–115.

Gough, H. G. Personality assessment in the study of population. In J. R. Fawcett (Ed.), *Psychological perspectives on population*. New York: Basic Books, 1973.

Greeley, A. M., McCready, W. C., & McCourt, K. *Catholic schools in a declining church*. Kansas City: Sheed & Ward, 1976.

Gustavus, S. O., & Nam, C. B. The formation and stability of ideal family size among young people. *Demography*, 1970, *7*, 43–51.

Guttmacher, A. F. The attitudes of 3,381 physicians towards contraception and the contraceptives they prescribe. *Human Biology*, 1947, *12*, 1–12.

Harvey, A. L. Risky and safe contraceptors: Some personality factors. *Journal of Psychology*, 1976, *92*, 109–112.

Himes, N. E. *Medical history of Contraception*. New York: Schocken Books, 1970.

Hunt, M. *Sexual behavior in the 1970's*. Chicago: Playboy, 1974.

Hyde, J. S. *Understanding human sexuality*. New York: McGraw Hill, 1979.

Jaccard, J. J., & Davidson, A. R. Toward an understanding of family planning behaviors: An initial investigation. *Journal of Applied Social Psychology*, 1972, *2*, 228–235.

Jazwinski, C., & Byrne, D. The effect of a contraceptive theme on response to erotica. *Motivation and Emotion*, 1978, *2*, 287–297.

Joestling, J., & Joestling, R. Correlations among women's view of contraception, anxiety, creativity, and equalitarianism measures. *Journal of Psychology*, 1974, *86*, 49–51.

Kantner, J. F., & Zelnik, M. Contraception and pregnancy: Experience of young unmarried women in the United States. *Family Planning Perspectives*, 1973, *5*, 21–35.

Kempe, R. R., & Helfer, C. H. *The battered child*. Chicago: University of Chicago Press, 1968.

King, K., Balswick, J. O., & Robinson, I. E. The continuing premarital sexual revolution among college females. *Journal of Marriage and the Family*, 1977, *39*, 455–459.

Kinsey, A. C., Pomeroy, W. B., & Martin, C. E. *Sexual behavior in the human male*. Philadelphia: Saunders, 1948.

Kinsey, A. C., Pomeroy, W. B., Martin, C. E., & Gebhard, P. H. *Sexual behavior in the human female*. Philadelphia: Saunders, 1953.

Klerman, L. V., & Jekel, J. F. Experiences with psychiatric services in a program for pregnant school-age girls. *Social Psychiatry*, 1973, *8*, 19–20.

Laughlin, C. D., & Allgeier, E. R. *Ethnography of the So of Northeastern Uganda* (2 Vols.). New Haven, CT: Human Relations Area Files, Inc., 1979.

Lindemann, C. *Birth control and unmarried young women*. New York: Springer, 1975.

MacDonald, A. P., Jr. Internal-external locus of control and the practice of birth control. *Psychological Reports*, 1970, *27*, 206.

Masters, W. H., & Johnson, V. E. *Human sexual response*. Boston: Little Brown, 1966.

Masters, W. H., & Johnson, V. E. Major questions in human sexual response. A lecture presented to the Harris County Medical Society, Houston, March, 1967.

Maxwell, J. W., Sack, A. R., Frary, R. B., & Keller, J. F. Factors influencing contraceptive behavior of single college students. *Journal of Sex and Marital Therapy*, 1977, *3*, 265–273.

McCary, J. L. *McCary's human sexuality*. New York: D. Van Nostrand, 1978.

McCormick, N. B., Folcik, J., & Izzo, A. Semi-rural teenagers' values, sex information, sexuality, and contraception. In L. Severy (Chair), *Family planning, contraception, and abortion*. Symposium presented at the meeting of the American Psychological Association, New York, September 1–5, 1979.

Miller, W. B. Psychological vulnerability to unwanted pregnancy. *Family Planning Perspectives*, 1973, *5*, 199–201.

Miller, W. B. *Female role orientation and reproductive behavior*. Paper presented at the American Psychiatric Association Meetings, Detroit, May, 1974.

Millett, K. *Sexual politics.* New York: Doubleday, 1970.

National Center for Health Statistics. Advance report: Final natality statistics, 1975. *Monthly Vital Statistics Report,* 1976, 25.

National Center for Health Statistics. Teenage childbearing: United States, 1966–75. *Monthly Vital Statistics Report,* 1977, 26.

Nye, F. I. School-age parenthood. *Extension Bulletin 667.* Pullman, Wash.: Washington State University, 1976.

Oskamp, S., Mindick, B., Berger, D., & Motta, E. A longitudinal study of success versus failure in contraceptive planning. *Journal of Population,* 1978, *1,* 69–83.

Osofsky, H. J. *The pregnant teenager.* Springfield, IL: Charles C. Thomas, 1968.

Paul, E. W., Pilpel, H. F., & Wechsler, N. F. Pregnancy, teenagers, and the law. *Family Planning Perspectives,* 1976, *8,* 16.

Pohlman, E. *The psychology of birth planning.* Cambridge, MA: Schenkmann, 1969.

Pratt, L., & Whelpton, P. K. Extra-familial participation of wives in relation to interest in and liking for children, fertility planning, and actual and desired family size. In P. K. Whelpton & C. V. Kiser (Eds.), *Social and psychological factors affecting fertility,* Vol. 5. New York: Milbank Memorial Fund, 1958.

Reiss, I., Banwart, A., & Foreman, H. Premarital contraceptive usage: A study and some theoretical explorations. *Journal of Marriage and Family,* 1975, *37,* 619–630.

Ridley, J. Number of children expected in relation to nonfamilial activities of the wife. *Milbank Memorial Fund Quarterly,* 1959, *37,* 277–296.

Robinson, I. E., King, K., & Balswick, J. The premarital sexual revolution among college students. *The Family Coordinator,* 1972, *21,* 189–194.

Roffman, D. M., Speckman, C. E., & Gruz, N. I. Maryland pharmacists ready for family planning initiative. *Family Planning Perspectives,* 1973, *5,* 243–247.

Russo, N. F., & Brackbill, Y. Population and youth. In J. Fawcett (Ed.), *Psychological perspectives on population.* New York: Basic Books, 1973.

Sarrel, P. M., & Davis, C. D. The young unwed primipara. *American Journal of Obstetrics and Gynecology,* 1966, *95,* 722–725.

Schofield, M. G. *The sexual behavior of young people.* Boston: Little Brown, 1965.

Seeley, O. F. Field dependence-independence, internal-external locus of control, and implementation of family-planning goals. *Psychological Reports,* 1976, *38,* 1216–1218.

Settlage, D. S., Baroff, S., & Cooper, D. Sexual experience of young teenage girls seeking contraceptive assistance for the first time. *Family Planning Perspectives,* 1973, *5,* 223–226.

Shah, F., Zelnik, M., & Kantner, J. F. Unprotected intercourse among unwed teenagers. *Family Planning Perspectives,* 1975, *7,* 39–44.

Shpunt, L. Parents and babies. *The New Republic,* Oct. 19, 1974, 28.

Somers, R. L., & Gammeltoft, M. The impact of liberalized abortion legislation on contraceptive practice in Denmark. *Studies in Family Planning,* 1976, *7,* 218–223.

Sorensen, R. C. *Adolescent sexuality in contemporary America: Personal values and sexual behavior, ages 13–19.* New York: World Publishing, 1973.

Stein, A. H., & Bailey, M. M. The socialization of achievement orientation in females. *Psychological Bulletin,* 1973, *80,* 345–366.

Steinlauf, B. Problem solving skills, locus of control, and the contraceptive effectiveness of young women. *Child Development,* 1979, *50,* 268–271.

Stokes, W. R. Control of procreation: A new dimension of freedom. In H. A. Otto (Ed.), *The New Sexuality.* Palo Alto, CA: Science & Behavior Books, 1971.

Tietze, C. Unintended pregnancies in the United States, 1970–1972. *Family Planning Perspectives,* 1979, *11,* 186–188.

Trainer, J. B. *Physiologic foundations for marriage counseling.* St. Louis: Mosby, 1965.

Udry, R. J. *The social context of marriage.* Philadelphia: Lippincott & Co., 1971.

Vessey, M., Doll, R., Peto, R., Johnson, B., & Wiggins, P. A long-term follow-up study of women using different methods of contraception: An interim report. *Journal of Biosocial Science,* 1976, 373.

Vincent, M. L., & Stelling, F. H. A survey of contraceptive practices and attitudes of unwed college students. *Journal of the American College Health Association,* 1973, *21,* 257–263.

Westoff, C., & Bumpass, L. The revolution in birth control practices of U.S. Roman Catholics. *Science,* 1973, *179,* 41–44.

Westoff, C. F., & Jones, E. F. The secularization of U.S. Catholic birth control practices. *Family Planning Perspectives,* 1977, *9,* 203–207.

Wilson, S. J., Keith, L., Wells, J., & Steptoe, R. C. A preliminary survey of 16,000 teenagers entering a contraceptive program. *The Chicago Medical School Quarterly,* 1973, *32,* 26.

Zelnik, M., & Kantner, J. F. Probability of premarital intercourse. *Social Science Research,* 1972, *1,* 335.

Zelnik, M., & Kantner, J. F. The resolution of teenage first pregnancies. *Family Planning Perspectives,* 1974, *6,* 74.

Zelnik, M., & Kantner, J. F. Sexual and contraceptive experience of young unmarried women in the United States, 1976 and 1971. *Family Planning Perspectives,* 1977, *9,* 55–71.

Zongker, C. E. The self concept of pregnant adolescent girls. *Adolescence,* 1977, *12,* 477–88.

9 Emotional Barriers to Contraception

William A. Fisher
The University of Western Ontario

Donn Byrne
State University of New York at Albany

Leonard A. White
*Survey Branch, Army Personnel Center
Alexandria, Virginia*

Editors' Note

Earlier in this book, it was pointed out that contraception is an *active* process which involves learning about birth control, anticipating intercourse, and acquiring, discussing, and using contraception. An adolescent may be motivated to undertake these behaviors, or he or she may be motivated to avoid such contraceptive preparations. In Chapter 9, William Fisher and his colleagues propose that an individual's emotional response to sexuality will generalize and, in part, determine whether the person approaches—or avoids—contraception. To the extent that individuals are comfortable (or uncomfortable) about sex, they should also be comfortable (or uncomfortable) about performing each behavioral step in the contraceptive process. In the present chapter, research which has examined this assumption is discussed, and findings are reported which confirm the proposed link between sex-related emotions and contraceptive behavior. The chapter concludes with a proposal for changing teens' emotional associations to contraception and, by way of such changes, improving adolescents' use of birth control.

Those who are concerned about adolescent pregnancy have tried to understand why sexually active teens so often fail to use contraception. It has been noted, for example, that ignorance of basic contraceptive knowledge may limit teens' use of birth control. Adolescents who "know" that they are too young to get pregnant, or that they will not conceive if they avoid intercourse on the days just prior to menstruation, will be prone to contraceptive neglect. Too, some teenagers hold strongly to belief systems that may act as barriers to responsible contraception. Beliefs that contraception is against one's religion, or is illegal, or will involve social disapproval may inhibit the use of birth control by even knowledgeable teens.

In addition to ignorance and anticontraception beliefs, we propose that adolescents' *emotional responses to sexuality* may affect their use of contraception. Stated in general terms, we believe that an individual's feelings about sexuality will generalize to the realm of contraceptive behavior; a teenager who is somewhat anxious and ambivalent about sex will also be uneasy about acquiring and using contraception, while an adolescent who is emotionally more at ease regarding sex should also be more relaxed about obtaining and using birth control. In the following pages, we propose several hypotheses concerning the link between sex-related emotions and contraceptive behavior. Research that is pertinent to each of these assumptions is described, and possible applications of what we have learned about adolescent contraception are discussed at the end of the chapter.

SEX-RELATED EMOTIONS AND CONTRACEPTIVE BEHAVIOR: SOME HYPOTHESIZED RELATIONSHIPS

It has been pointed out (Byrne, Jazwinski, DeNinno, & Fisher, 1977) that the effective use of contraception is an *active* process—to belabor the obvious, a sexually active teenager who does not want to become a parent must, in some sense, get up, go out, and *do* several important things. As outlined in Chapter 1, an initial step in this process involves *acquiring and retaining accurate information about birth control*. Whatever else is learned about this topic, it seem clear that a sexually active teen must be aware that unprotected coitus may lead to conception, and he or she must also learn the details of at least one appropriate method of birth control.

The contraceptive process, of course, does not end with the mastery of an adequate body of birth control knowledge. A second necessary step involves *self-admission* or awareness by an adolescent that he or she may soon have intercourse. Without acknowledging this possibility, it is unlikely that any contraceptive precautions will be taken. And, once a teen has conceded that he or she might soon be having sex, it is still necessary for the individual to engage in more-or-less *public behaviors to acquire needed contraceptives*. This could involve visiting a physician to get a prescription for the pill, purchasing condoms or spermicidal foam from a clerk in a drugstore, or other such public announcements of sexual intent. In addition to these activities, it is most helpful if sexual partners *communicate with one another about birth control*. Such discussion may range from a discrete inquiry made of a new partner ("Uhhh . . . by the way, are you using . . . anything?"), to encouragement for the successful use of a given method ("I like it when we use condoms and foam, since it's effective and safe and we share the responsibility"), to informed debate between partners regarding birth control alternatives ("I want to go off the pill, I am reluctant to use the I.U.D., and I know that you hate condoms. What shall we do?"). Finally, the last stage in this contraceptive process involves the *consistent use of a chosen method of contraception*. With respect to the methods most often used by teenagers in the U.S. (Zelnik & Kantner, 1977), this involves remembering to take a daily pill, or using a condom on *every* occasion of intercourse.

Ideally, then, a sexually active teenager who does not wish to become a parent needs to learn a fair amount about birth control, and he or she must also anticipate upcoming intercourse, acquire contraception, discuss this matter with a partner, and employ contraception consistently and correctly. This process is not particularly easy or pleasant, and the objective difficulties involved no doubt account for some portion of adolescents' neglect of contraception. Nonetheless, even when many of the usual problems are ameliorated—as in the student oriented contraception clinic studied by Fisher and his associates (Fisher, Byrne, Edmunds, Miller, Kelley, & White, 1979)—many adolescents still do not use birth control. Thus, we are inclined to believe that there are significant internal barriers to adolescent contraception, and we will now discuss just what these psychological obstacles might be.

According to the Sexual Behavior Sequence (Byrne, 1977; see also Chapter 1), individuals are assumed to learn certain kinds of responses to sexual stimuli, and these responses may hinder—or facilitate—effective contraception. One learned response to sex that was discussed earlier involves informational factors such as beliefs (i.e., "My religion opposes contraception") and expectancies (i.e., "If I use the pill, I will incur medical risks") that may prevent teens from using contraception. Over and above the effect of such informational factors, however, the Sexual Behavior Sequence posits that sex-related emotions may help determine contraceptive behavior. Specifically, it appears that people develop a general emotional response to a wide range of sexual topics; such emotional responses may be primarily negative ("erotophobic"), primarily positive ("erotophilic"), or they may fall somewhere in between these emotional extremes (White, Fisher, Byrne, & Kingma, 1977). Thus, emotional responses to sexuality may fall along a negative to positive continuum that we have labeled "erotophobia—erotophilia." We propose that these emotional responses to sexuality will generalize to contraception, since the behaviors involved in birth control use are in many ways *sexual* behaviors. Take, for example, a moderately erotophobic adolescent; while excited about the prospect of having sex, he or she is also somewhat anxious and uneasy about this subject. We would predict that this teenager will not be anxious enough to avoid intercourse, but he or she may well be anxious enough to avoid any of the prerequisite contraceptive behaviors that we have described. The adolescent who is emotionally ambivalent about sex, then, will not be an enthusiastic pupil for contraceptive education; he or she will be relatively unlikely to seek out or retain necessary information about birth control. By the same token, a teenager who is anxious about sex will be less likely to anticipate future intercourse, and should also be reluctant to engage in public behaviors to acquire contraceptives, to speak with a partner about birth control, or to use contraception consistently. In contrast, erotophilic adolescents feel more emotionally comfortable about sex; they should find the prerequisite behaviors to be less aversive and should be more likely to perform each one. To state our case a bit more formally, we hypothesize that relatively erotophobic (versus erotophilic) individuals are:

(1) less likely to possess accurate information about conception and contraception,
(2) less likely to acknowledge the possibility that they may have intercourse in the near future,
(3) less likely to engage in public behaviors to acquire needed contraceptives,
(4) less likely to communicate about contraception with their sexual partners, and
(5) less likely to use contraception consistently.

There is an additional consequence of erotophobia—erotophilia for contraceptive behavior that is worth mentioning. It has been pointed out (Byrne, Fisher, Lamberth, & Mitchell, 1974) that people are not always content simply to note that a particular stimulus makes them feel emotionally good or bad. Rather, individuals often make attributions about the stimulus which help to justify how it has made them feel. Thus, research subjects who responded to erotic slides with feelings of nausea, disgust, and anger were found to label the slides as pornographic; other subjects, who reacted to the same slides with positive feelings, rated them as relatively nonpornographic (cf. Byrne et al., 1974; Fisher & Byrne, 1978). In each case, subjects' evaluations of the stimuli were consistent with their emotional responses. Following the same logic, we propose that emotional responses to sexuality (erotophobia—erotophilia) will generalize and mediate evaluations of contraception. Erotophobic persons are presumed to be uncomfortable about this topic; therefore, they should evaluate contraception negatively and have unfavorable attitudes and opinions about birth control. Erotophilic persons, in contrast, are assumed to be more at ease about contraception and hence should evaluate birth control more positively. This forms the basis for our next hypothesis:

(6) erotophobic (versus erotophilic) individuals have more negative attitudes towards contraception.

At this point, it should be stressed that erotophobia—erotophilia is not regarded as the *sole* determinant of contraceptive behavior. Rather, according to the Sexual Behavior Sequence, individuals' sex-related emotions, as well as their beliefs and expectancies about contraception, will have independent effects on their contraceptive practices. This assumption is expressed in our final hypothesis:

(7) emotional factors (i.e., erotophobia—erotophilia) and informational factors (i.e., relevant beliefs and expectancies) each contribute independently to determining contraceptive behavior.

During the past several years, we and our colleagues have carried out research to explore some of the ideas that have been proposed. First, it was necessary to develop a workable measure of erotophobia—erotophilia. Once such a measure was devised, studies were conducted to investigate the hypothesized relationships of erotophobia—erotophilia and contraceptive behavior. We now turn to a discussion of how we conceptualize and measure erotophobia—erotophilia. Then, research that has used our measure of erotophobia—erotophilia to examine each of the hypotheses is described.

CONCEPTUALIZING AND MEASURING INDIVIDUAL DIFFERENCES IN EROTOPHOBIA—EROTOPHILIA

Becoming Erotophobic or Erotophilic

From the standpoint of the Sexual Behavior Sequence, a person's erotophobic or erotophilic disposition is a result of the individual's learning experiences with respect to sex. In particular, it is assumed that sexual expressions are often accompanied by emotion-producing punishment or reward. After many such pairings, sexual cues themselves may come to elicit the kind of emotion originally caused by the associated punishment or reward. For example, a toddler may be scolded for examining his or her genitals in front of the babysitter; as a 10-year-old, he or she may receive a spanking for bringing mommy's *Playgirl* in for show and tell. As a teenager, the individual may be warned of the dangers of premarital sex, in terms of likely pregnancy, venereal disease, and everlasting shame. As a result of the consistent pairing of sexual cues with punishment, the unfortunate principal in our example should come to respond to such cues with negative emotions. In this way, a relatively uniform history of punishment for sexual expression may sum to form an erotophobic disposition. By analogy, it should be noted that sexual cues can be paired with rewarding, emotionally positive experiences (i.e., a smile, a hug, an orgasm); repeated associations of this sort should result in a relatively positive emotional orientation to sex—erotophilia. Moreover, according to this logic, it ought to be possible to *change* a person's erotophobic or erotophilic disposition by systematically pairing sexual cues with reward or punishment (see Chapter 6).

It is important to stress that—over and above these simple illustrations—an individual's sexual socialization will include a complex mixture of sex-related reward and punishment. Also, while our parents may be the first to teach us emotional responses to sex, we continue to learn such responses from diverse sources (i.e., peers, lovers, spouses, our children, the media, religion, etc.) throughout our lives. The mixure of reward and punishment that we receive for sexuality should be reflected in our erotophobic or erotophilic disposition; an extremely erotophobic person may have received consistent punishment for sexual expression, while a moderately erotophobic individual may have experienced frequent punishment but occasional reward with respect to sex, and an individual at the midpoint of the erotophobia—erotophilia dimension may have experienced sex-related reward and punishment in approximately equal proportions.

Measuring Erotophobia—Erotophilia

In order to test our hypotheses regarding sex-related emotions and contraceptive behavior, it was necessary to develop a valid measure of erotophobia—erotophilia. The first step in this procedure, carried out by White et al. (1977), was to generate scale items which, in the researchers' judgment, would get at an individual's emotional response to a range of sexual stimuli. A pool of 53 such "best guesses" was developed; each described a sexual situation, and respondents were asked to indicate if they would have a particular emotional response to it. For example, one item read:

Almost all pornographic material is nauseating.
I Strongly Agree:__:__:__:__:__:__:__:I Strongly Disagree

Here, subjects use the response scale to indicate whether or not they would react to a sexual stimulus (pornography) with a given negative emotion (nausea). Other items sampled a variety of sexual scenarios (i.e., autoerotic, heterosexual, and homosexual behavior, viewing erotica, etc.) and asked about positive as well as negative emotional responses. Here is an item that introduces a different sexual cue (masturbation) and inquires about a positive emotional response (excitement):

Masturbation can be an exciting experience.
I Strongly Agree:__:__:__:__:__:__:__:I Strongly Disagree

To determine which of the 53 preliminary items constituted valid measures of erotophobia—erotophilia, an item selection procedure was carried out. It was reasoned that, conceptually, erotophobia—erotophilia involves the tendency to respond to sexual cues with positive to negative emotions. Therefore, it was decided to retain only those items that could be shown empirically to predict such emotional responses. In an initial study (White et al., 1977), 195 introductory psychology students (90 males, 105 females at a midwestern U.S. university) responded to the preliminary scale and to a measure of the tendency to answer questionnaire items in a socially desirable (but not necessarily veridical) fashion (Crowne & Marlowe, 1964). Next, the students viewed a series of 19 erotic slides which depicted autosexual, heterosexual, and homosexual acts (Levitt & Brady, 1965). After viewing the slides, subjects completed self-ratings of their positive and negative emotional responses to these erotic stimuli (cf. Byrne et al., 1974; Byrne & Sheffield, 1965). Statistical analyses showed that, for both males and females, 21 of the original items were significantly correlated with emotional responses to the erotic slides. These items were also uncorrelated with the Crowne and Marlowe (1964) measure of social desirability responding.

For further analyses, the 21 items were added to form scores reflecting erotophobia—erotophilia. As can be seen in Table 9.1, this measure of erotophobia—erotophilia was highly correlated with subjects' reports of their emotional responses to the erotic slides (expressed as a proportion of positive to positive plus negative emotional responses). A negligible relationship of erotophobia—erotophilia with the social desirability measure can also be seen in the table. These findings held true, it should be noted, for both male and female subjects considered separately. In addition, cross-validation research (Fisher, 1976) has shown that the 21 items are stable predictors of emotional responses to erotica across different samples of subjects. The items form an internally consistent scale, and split-half reliabilities of .84 or above have been reported (Fisher et al., 1979; White et al., 1977). Our measure of erotophobia—erotophilia has been christened the Sexual Opinion Survey, and it is presented in Table 9.2, along with a scoring key. Normative data for the Sexual Opinion Survey are presented in Table 9.3. In examining the scale, it is worth noting that *not a single item deals directly with contraceptive behavior.* Consequently, relationships that are observed between erotophobia—erotophilia and contraceptive attitudes or practices are not simply attributable to overlapping content.

In addition to these item selection data, we have identified a number of interesting correlates of erotophobia—erotophilia, as measured on the scale. These findings, which are shown in Table 9.4, are based on the responses of 267 introductory psychology students (149 males, 118 females) at a midwestern U.S. university. The students completed the Sexual Opinion Survey and a number of other self-reports, and then they watched a series of erotic slides and indicated their responses to these stimuli. As can be seen in the table, erotophobic (versus

TABLE 9.1

Correlations of Erotophobia-Erotophilia with Emotional
Responses to Erotic Slides and Social Desirability [1]

MALE SUBJECTS	*Proportion of Positive Emotions in Response to Erotic Slides* [2] *(low-high)*	*Social Desirability (low-high)*
Social Desirability (low-high)	.13, n.s. [3]	
Erotophobia-Erotophilia Score	.61**	.05, n.s.
FEMALE SUBJECTS	*Proportion of Positive Emotions in Response to Erotic Slides (low-high)*	*Social Desirability (low-high)*
Social Desirability (low-high)	-.09, n.s.	
Erotophobia-Erotophilia Score	.72**	-.05, n.s.

[1] After White, Fisher, Byrne, and Kingma (1977)

[2] Proportion of positive emotions in response to the erotic slides was computed by dividing subjects' positive emotional responses by the sum of their positive plus negative emotional responses to the slides.

[3] n.s. = not statistically significant

** = Correlation is significant at the .001 probability level. Due to missing data, df (males) = 86, df (females) = 101.

erotophilic) subjects reported somewhat restrictive experiences of socialization to sex; they indicated that, as adolescents, religious training, fear of social disapproval, and the like had inhibited their sexual expression. These findings are consistent with the idea that the association of sex with punishment (i.e., social disapproval) may underlie erotophobia. At the same time, however, it is important to note that these correlations are not high, and they are based on retrospective self-reports; therefore, the findings should be interpreted cautiously.

On the basis of the Sexual Behavior Sequence, erotophobic individuals would be expected to show avoidance responses to sex and to evaluate sexual stimuli negatively. As can be seen in Table 9.4, the data confirm these expectations. Compared to erotophilic students, erotophobic men and women report that they have had less experience with erotica; they dream about sex less often, masturbate less frequently, and have had fewer premarital sex partners. Erotophobic

TABLE 9.2
The Sexual Opinion Survey [1]

Please respond to each item as honestly as you can. There are no right or wrong answers and your answers are completely anonymous.

1. I think it would be very entertaining to look at hard-core pornography.

   I Strongly
   Agree: _____ : _____ : _____ : _____ : _____ : _____ : _____ : I Strongly Disagree

2. Pornography is obviously filthy and people should not try to describe it as anything alse.

   I Strongly
   Agree: _____ : _____ : _____ : _____ : _____ : _____ : _____ : I Strongly Disagree

3. Swimming in the nude with a member of the opposite sex would be an exciting experience.

   I Strongly
   Agree: _____ : _____ : _____ : _____ : _____ : _____ : _____ : I Strongly Disagree

4. Masturbation can be an exciting experience.

   I Strongly
   Agree: _____ : _____ : _____ : _____ : _____ : _____ : _____ : I Strongly Disagree

5. If I found out that a close friend of mine was a homosexual it would annoy me.

   I Strongly
   Agree: _____ : _____ : _____ : _____ : _____ : _____ : _____ : I Strongly Disagree

6. If people thought I was interested in oral sex, I would be embarrassed.

   I Strongly
   Agree: _____ : _____ : _____ : _____ : _____ : _____ : _____ : I Strongly Disagree

7. Engaging in group sex is an entertaining idea.

   I Strongly
   Agree: _____ : _____ : _____ : _____ : _____ : _____ : _____ : I Strongly Disagree

8. I personally find that thinking about engaging in sexual intercourse is arousing.

   I Strongly
   Agree: _____ : _____ : _____ : _____ : _____ : _____ : _____ : I Strongly Disagree

9. Seeing a pornographic movie would be sexually arousing to me.

   I Strongly
   Agree: _____ : _____ : _____ : _____ : _____ : _____ : _____ : I Strongly Disagree

10. Thoughts that I may have homosexual tendencies would not worry me at all.

    I Strongly
    Agree: _____ : _____ : _____ : _____ : _____ : _____ : _____ : I Strongly Disagree

11. The idea of my being physically attracted to members of the same sex is not depressing.

    I Strongly
    Agree: _____ : _____ : _____ : _____ : _____ : _____ : _____ : I Strongly Disagree

12. Almost all pornographic material is nauseating.

    I Strongly
    Agree: _____ : _____ : _____ : _____ : _____ : _____ : _____ : I Strongly Disagree

(Continued)

TABLE 9.2 (Continued)

13. It would be emotionally upsetting to me to see someone exposing themselves publicly.

I Strongly
Agree: _____ : _____ : _____ : _____ : _____ : _____ : _____ :
I Strongly
Disagree

14. Watching a go-go dancer of the opposite sex would not be very exciting.

I Strongly
Agree: _____ : _____ : _____ : _____ : _____ : _____ : _____ :
I Strongly
Disagree

15. I would not enjoy seeing a pornographic movie.

I Strongly
Agree: _____ : _____ : _____ : _____ : _____ : _____ : _____ :
I Strongly
Disagree

16. When I think about seeing pictures showing someone of the same sex as myself masturbating it nauseates me.

I Strongly
Agree: _____ : _____ : _____ : _____ : _____ : _____ : _____ :
I Strongly
Disagree

17. The thought of engaging in unusual sex practices is highly arousing.

I Strongly
Agree : _____ : _____ : _____ : _____ : _____ : _____ : _____ :
I Strongly
Disagree

18. Manipulating my genitals would probably be an arousing experience.

I Strongly
Agree : _____ : _____ : _____ : _____ : _____ : _____ : _____ :
I Strongly
Disagree

19. I do not enjoy daydreaming about sexual matters.

I Strongly
Agree : _____ : _____ : _____ : _____ : _____ : _____ : _____ :
I Strongly
Disagree

20. I am not curious about explicit pornography.

I Strongly
Agree : _____ : _____ : _____ : _____ : _____ : _____ : _____ :
I Strongly
Disagree

21. The thought of having long-term sexual relations with more than one sex partner is not disgusting to me.

I Strongly
Agree : _____ : _____ : _____ : _____ : _____ : _____ : _____ :
I Strongly
Disagree

Scoring the Sexual Opinion Survey

1. Score responses from 1 = "I Strongly Agree" to 7 = "I Strongly Disagree"
2. Add scores from items 2, 5, 6, 12, 13, 14, 15, 16, 19, 20
3. Subtract from this total, the sum of items 1, 3, 4, 7, 8, 9, 10, 11, 17, 18, 21
4. Add 67 to this figure
5. Scores range from 0 (most erotophobic) to 126 (most erotophilic)

[1] After White, Fisher, Byrne, and Kingma (1977)

undergraduates rated their sex attitudes as relatively conservative and, interestingly enough, were more likely to state that *their* sexual attitudes were similar to their *parents'* attitudes. Finally, compared to erotophilic subjects, erotophobic individuals reacted to the erotic slides with more negative and less positive emotions; they were more likely to favor restricting access to such material, and they showed less interest in volunteering to see more erotica in a similar experiment to be held the following week.

The findings discussed in this section provide validating evidence for the Sexual Opinion Survey as a measure of erotophobia—erotophilia. These results are also consistent with our view that erotophobia—erotophilia is a learned disposition that mediates approach—avoidance responses as well as evaluations of sexuality. We are now ready to explore the generality of this conceptualization; to ask whether, as hypothesized, erotophobia—erotophilia may mediate approach–avoidance and evaluative responses to contraception. Discussion will now turn to research that has investigated this topic.

TABLE 9.3
Normative Data for the Sexual Opinion Survey

Student Samples	N	Mean Sexual Opinion Survey Score	Standard Deviation	Note on Sample Characteristics
University males (U.S.A.)	98	75.46	15.55	Introductory psychology students at a midwestern U.S. university.
University females (U.S.A.)	86	52.66	21.61	
University males (Canada)	124	79.66	15.49	Undergraduate psychology students at an Ontario university.
University females (Canada)	143	62.80	17.80	
Adult Samples[1]				
Adult males	116	76.67	22.19	The adult samples were comprised of U.S. parents who were taking part in studies on sex education in the home (average age = 36.2 years). Recruitment of subjects was from community sources (e.g., churches, colleges, mental health centers, etc.).
Adult females	210	65.88	23.91	
Age ≤ 34	195	74.04	34.41	
Age ≥ 35	132	66.04	24.31	
Socioeconomic status relatively *low*	178	64.97	24.59	
Socioeconomic status relatively *high*	149	77.79	35.99	

[1] After Gilbert and Gamache (1982).

TABLE 9.4
Correlates of Erotophobia—Erotophilia

Sexual Socialization Experiences

Erotophobic (versus erotophilic) men and women:
　Rated themselves as being more religious (.26) (.22) (.19)[1]
　Were more likely to report that each of the following had prevented them from freely expressing their sexuality:
　　Fear of social disapproval (.24) (.19) (.16)
　　"Morals" (.37) (.26) (.23)
　　Knowledge that it was "wrong" (.31) (.22) (.23)
　　Religious training (.30) (.32) (.22)

Approach-Avoidance of Sexuality

Erotophobic (versus erotophilic) men and women:
　Have less often seen erotic literature (.57) (.49) (.37)
　Have less often purchased erotica (.52) (.42) (.43)
　Dream about sex less often (.37) (.15) (.38)
　Report that they masturbate less frequently (.46) (.42) (.39)
　Have had fewer premarital sex partners (.25) (.18) (.31)

Attitudes Towards Sex

Erotophobic (versus erotophilic) men and women:
　Are more likely to advocate that legal measures be taken against homosexuals (.30) (.43) (.27)
　Rate their sexual attitudes as relatively conservative (.47) (.36) (.48)
　Rate their sexual attitudes as relatively similar to their parents' sexual attitudes (.22) (.19) (.28)

Reactions to Erotic Slides

Erotophobic (versus erotophilic) men and women were:
　More likely to respond to the slides with emotions of:
　　Disgust (.46) (.48) (.41)
　　Boredom (.20) (.35) (.16)
　　Anger (.30) (.32) (.32)
　　Nausea (.30) (.29) (.29)
　Less likely to respond to the slides with emotions of:
　　Curiosity (.27) (.27) (.32)
　　Excitement (.45) (.47) (.27)
　Were more likely to judge the slides to be "shocking" (.37) (.39) (.31)
　Expressed relative preferences to:
　　Forbid production and sale of movies with similar scenes (.56) (.61) (.49)
　　Forbid display and advertising of movies with similar scenes (.44) (.49) (.36)
　　Prevent unmarried persons from seeing a movie with such scenes (.45) (.50) (.42)
　　Prohibit the showing of such a movie at a local theatre (.46) (.44) (.36)
　　Forbid production and sale of a *magazine* with such pictures (.61) (.55) (.61)
　　Forbid display or advertising of a magazine with such pictures (.49) (.47) (.39)
　　Prevent unmarried persons from buying a magazine with such pictures (.55) (.54) (.52)
　　Prevent teenagers from buying a magazine with such pictures (.43) (.38) (.34)
　　Prevent local libraries from having a magazine with such pictures (.25) (.23) (.23)

TABLE 9.4 (*Continued*)

Indicated that there was less possible benefit that could come from showing movies
with scenes like those just viewed (.42) (.50) (.31)
Indicated that there was more possible harm that could come from showing movies
with scenes like those just viewed (.27) (.29) (.18)
Would be less likely to volunteer for continuation of this experiment the following
week, with additional slides (.38) (.40) (.35)

---

[1] The numbers in parentheses beside each item reflect the magnitude of the correlation of that item with erotophobia—erotophilia for males and females analyzed together, males considered separately, and females considered separately, in this order. All correlations are significant beyond the .05 probability level.

RESEARCH EVIDENCE CONCERNING THE RELATIONSHIP BETWEEN EROTOPHOBIA— EROTOPHILIA AND CONTRACEPTIVE BEHAVIOR

We have hypothesized that, based on their emotional responses to sex, erotophobic persons should avoid the behaviors that are required for effective contraception (i.e., learning relevant information, anticipating intercourse, acquiring, discussing, and using contraception consistently), and they should also hold negative attitudes towards this subject. Erotophilic persons—also based on their emotions—should approach and engage in necessary contraceptive behaviors, and espouse more positive attitudes regarding birth control. In the present section, we report on research that is relevant to each of our hypotheses.

Hypothesis 1: Erotophobic (versus Erotophilic) Individuals are Less Likely to Possess Accurate Information about Conception and Contraception

Before an adolescent may become an effective user of contraception, he or she must know certain specifics about this subject. We have proposed that learning about such matters is in part a function of erotophobia—erotophilia. Erotophobic teens, in particular, feel somewhat uneasy about sex; consequently, they will not be likely to seek out, attend to, or retain sex-related information, including necessary knowledge about contraception. In contrast, erotophilic adolescents are more comfortable with sex and they should be more likely to seek out sexual or contraceptive knowledge and to remember it.

Research evidence concerning this hypothesis comes from an investigation of a "real world" sex education setting. The study, conducted by Fisher (1980), involved 40 male and female students in a human sexuality course that was offered at a large Canadian university. These undergraduates had recently taken a midterm examination on topics that included the history of sex research, theories of sexuality, sexual anatomy and physiology, current patterns of sexual behavior, and the like. A few days after receiving their marks on this exam, the students were asked to complete the Sexual Opinion Survey. When they had finished doing so, they were asked to indicate their grade on the midterm exam, and their overall grade point average for the preceding year. It should be noted that, while these students were not naive—they had also filled out and discussed the Sexual Opinion Survey at the beginning of the term—they did not seem motivated to dissimulate, nor were there many cues as to how to do so systematically.

Statistical analyses revealed that erotophobic students (average grade, 71.16%) did not do as well as erotophilic students (average grade, 78.90%) on the midterm examination in human sexuality. These results were statistically significant even when controlling for past levels of achievement, and the pattern of findings is the same for male and female undergraduates alike. Thus, erotophobia–erotophilia seems to be linked in the hypothesized fashion with difficulty or ease in learning sexual information.

Recently, Yarber and McCabe (1981) have reported data that underscore the role of erotophobia—erotophilia in the acquisition of contraceptive knowledge. These researchers surveyed nearly 20% of all the health educators in the state of Indiana with respect to the teachers' erotophobia—erotophilia, educational background, and teaching experience. In addition, the health educators were asked whether or not they included information on birth control in their public school health classes. As can be seen in Table 9.5, erotophilic (versus erotophobic) health educators were significantly more likely to teach their students about contraception. What is more, the health educators' erotophobia–erotophilia was a better predictor of the sex education topics they chose to teach than any other variable measured, including the teachers' educational background (BA or MA) and number of years of teaching experience. This field research, conducted in "real world" settings, suggests the general importance of emotional orientation to sexuality as a variable that may affect the learning of contraceptive information.

There are a few more studies that—while laboratory based—also bear specifically on learning about contraceptive topics. These investigations have used Mosher's Sex Guilt Scale (Mosher, 1966, 1968) to classify subjects as either high or low in sex guilt—"a generalized expectancy for self mediated punishment for violating . . . standards of proper sexual conduct" (Mosher & Cross, 1971, p. 27). Data that we have collected indicate that scores on the Mosher Sex Guilt Scale and the Sexual Opinion Survey are correlated (about .60), so erotophobia—erotophilia and sex guilt appear to be related constructs.

Using the Mosher Sex Guilt Scale, Schwartz (1973) divided a group of college men and women into those who were relatively high or low in sex guilt. The subjects listened to a 20-minute lecture on birth control topics (e.g., sterilization, abortion), and were then tested for retention of the lecture material. As expected, subjects high in sex guilt remembered less of the lecture information than did low sex guilt subjects. In related work, Mosher (1979) has found that

TABLE 9.5
Inclusion of Sex Education Topics in Public School Health Courses
as a Function of Teachers' Erotophobia—Erotophilia[1]

	Significant Correlations with Teachers' Erotophobia—Erotophilia	
	Grades 6-8 (N = 94)	Grades 9-11 (N = 175)
Contraception and Family Planning		
Family planning (parenthood by choice)		*
Consequences of adolescent pregnancy		*
Pros and cons of each birth control method	*	*
Where to obtain each birth control method	*	*
Effective use of each birth control method		*
Talking with others about sex		*
Abortion		*
Sterilization		*
Overpopulation		*

Note: All correlations (*) are significant at or beyond the .05 level. Each correlation indicates that erotophilic (versus erotophobic) health educators were more likely to teach the topic listed.

[1] After Yarber and McCabe (1981)

high (versus low) sex guilt subjects were more likely to believe in a contraception "myth" (i.e., "conception is most likely to occur if the man and the woman experience simultaneous climax"). And, Mendelsohn and Mosher (1979) report that, in a role playing situation, high (versus low) sex guilt women were more likely to communicate sexual misinformation to others. Taken together, these findings indicate that a negative disposition to sexuality (either erotophobia or high sex guilt) may interfere with the learning of sexual and contraceptive information. These data are in accord with our hypothesis, and they suggest that erotophobic adolescents may have a relatively difficult time learning what they need to know about birth control.

Hypothesis 2: Erotophobic (versus Erotophilic) Individuals Are Less Likely to Acknowledge the Possibility that They May Have Sexual Intercourse in the Near Future

In most cases, adolescents must be aware that they may soon have intercourse before they will take contraceptive precautions. Erotophobic persons, who are emotionally ambivalent about sex, should be relatively unlikely to make this self-admission. Erotophilic persons—who respond to sex with mostly positive emotions—should have no problem acknowledging the possibility of future intercourse; indeed, they are likely to look forward to it. In order to test this reasoning, Fisher (1978) surveyed 145 male undergraduates at a large midwestern U.S. university. These young men completed the Sexual Opinion Survey, and they were also asked to indicate whether or not they intended to have sexual intercourse during the coming month. In addition, the men responded to a number of questions regarding their past sexual behavior. One month after these data were collected, 96 of the undergraduates returned for a follow-up assessment of whether or not they had actually engaged in intercourse during the intervening month; if intercourse had taken place, they were asked if contraception was employed.

Data analyses revealed that erotophobia—erotophilia was reliably correlated with intentions to have sex; erotophobic men were less likely than their erotophilic counterparts to expect to have intercourse during the coming month. This finding held, even when controlling statistically for effects of past frequency of intercourse on intentions for the coming month. To illustrate these findings, subjects who scored in the bottom or top thirds of the Sexual Opinion Survey distribution were classified as "highly erotophobic" or "highly erotophilic," and the percentage of each group who expected to have sex is shown in Table 9.6. It can be seen that only 43% of the erotophobic men—compared to 77% of the erotophilic men—intended to have sex during the coming month. This difference was statistically significant, even when controlling for subjects' past frequency of sexual intercourse.

While it is interesting to note that erotophobic (versus erotophilic) men are less likely to anticipate having intercourse, it is important to examine the *accuracy* of their expectations. In particular, if both groups of men are correct in their projections regarding future intercourse, then the initial difference between erotophobic and erotophilic subjects is not of great consequence. If, on the other hand, erotophobic men underestimate the probability that they will have sex,

TABLE 9.6
Percent of Undergraduate Men Who Expected to Engage in Sexual
Intercourse During the Coming Month, as a
Function of Erotophobia—Erotophilia[1]

	Erotophobic Males (lower third of distribution)	Erotophilic Males (upper third of distribution)
Percent who intend to have sexual intercourse, during the coming month.	43%	77%

[1] After Fisher (1978)

TABLE 9.7

Percent of Undergraduate Men Who Reported Having Sexual
Intercourse During the Preceding Month, as a Function of
Erotophobia—Erotophilia and Intention to Have Intercourse[1]

	Erotophobic Males (lower third of distribution)	Erotophilic Males (upper third of distribution)
Intended to have sexual intercourse during the month	82%	65%
Did not intend to have sexual intercourse during the month	17%	0%

[1] After Fisher (1978).

while erotophilic men do not, this could have crucial implications for contraceptive use: unanticipated intercourse, it would seem, could easily become unprotected intercourse.

Data collected during the follow-up study shed some interesting light on this question. Of the 96 men who returned for the follow-up, 42 reported that they had sex during the month under study. Within this group, we can examine the accuracy of erotophobic and erotophilic men's expectations for intercourse. These data are presented in Table 9.7; since there are relatively small numbers involved, these observations must be regarded as suggestive. It can be seen that 82% of the erotophobic men who intended to have sex actually did so, while 65% of the erotophilic men who intended to have sex did so. What of the subjects who did *not* expect to have sex? About 17% of the erotophobic nonintenders reported that they had intercourse during the month under study, while *none* of the erotophilic nonintenders had sex. What kind of contraceptive precautions were undertaken by the erotophobic men who engaged in unanticipated intercourse? These subjects reported that they either used "rhythm" or were protected because the female used oral contraceptives. Apparently, some of this unanticipated intercourse *was* unprotected intercourse. It should be noted, of course, that not all anticipated sex was protected by birth control either. Thus, thinking ahead about the future probability of intercourse seems to be necessary—but not sufficient—for the use of contraception.

The findings discussed in this section are quite in accord with our hypothesis. Compared to erotophilic men, erotophobic undergraduates were less likely to expect that they would have sexual intercourse in the near future. For erotophobic men, these modest expectations turned out to be underestimates; a few eventually engaged in unanticipated, unprotected intercourse. For their part, erotophilic men tended to overestimate the likelihood that they would have sex, but such great expectations do not seem to hinder (and may actually facilitate) contraceptive preparation.

Hypothesis 3: Erotophobic (versus Erotophilic) Individuals Are Less Likely to Engage in Public Behaviors to Acquire Needed Contraceptives

Assuming that an adolescent does admit to the possibility of future intercourse, he or she must still engage in public behaviors to acquire contraception. And, we have suggested that erotophobic (versus erotophilic) persons will find such public acts aversive and will avoid them. To test this reasoning, we and our colleagues (Fisher et al., 1979) surveyed a group of female undergraduates at a large midwestern U.S. university. Some of these undergraduates were users of a well-publicized campus contraception clinic. The other women were introductory psychology students who had not used the clinic. The participants in the research completed the Sexual Opinion Survey, and they also indicated their attitudes towards the use of contraception in general (and the clinic in particular), their normative beliefs regarding whether significant others (i.e., boyfriends, parents, clinic physicians, etc.) would approve their use of birth control, and they rated the seriousness of their present relationships with members of the opposite sex. The women answered a number of questions about their past sexual and contraceptive practices as well.

Subjects were grouped as consistent or inconsistent users of contraception, or as sexually inactive, on the basis of their responses to a 7-point scale ("In the past, I or my partner 1 = always, 7 = never used a method of birth control; 0 = not applicable; I have never had sexual intercourse"). Women who marked scale points 1, 2, or 3 were classified as "consistent contraceptors," (relatively speaking) while those who checked scale points 4, 5, 6, or 7 were grouped as "inconsistent contraceptors" and those who marked 0 were classified as sexually inactive. The present discussion focuses on the women who stated that they were *inconsistent* users of contraception. Some of these women—the ones who used the contraception clinic—were taking public action to acquire birth control. It is interesting to note how these women may have differed from inconsistent contraceptors who did not use the clinic.

According to our hypothesis, the clinic nonusers should be relatively erotophobic, and the clinic users should be relatively erotophilic; as can be seen in Table 9.8, this was precisely the case. And, compared to clinic users, the nonusers were also relatively negative in their attitudes towards contraception and clinic use, and they were less likely to believe that significant others would approve their use of birth control. In addition, clinic nonusers reported less serious heterosexual relationships. The finding that clinic nonusers are relatively erotophobic confirms our general hypothesis that a negative emotional response to sex may interfere with the public behaviors involved in acquiring contraception. And, results which indicated that clinic nonusers had relatively negative beliefs regarding birth control are consistent with the Sexual Behavior Sequence, which assumes that contraceptive behavior is governed by informational factors as well as by emotions. Finally, the fact that clinic nonusers reported less serious

TABLE 9.8

Erotophobia—Erotophilia, Attitudes, Normative Beliefs, and Seriousness
of Relationship as a Function of Contraception Clinic Use[1]

	Women Who Were Inconsistent Users of Contraception		
	Women Who _Did Not_ Use the Contraception Clinic	Women Who _Did_ Use the Contraception Clinic	Scale Midpoints
Emotional Orientation to Sexuality (0 = most erotophobic, 126 = most erotophilic)	46.95	57.31	63
Attitudes towards Contraception and Clinic Use (low scores = negative attitudes, high scores = positive attitudes)	85.54	103.87	68
Normative Beliefs about Contraception (low scores = little perceived social approval, high scores = much perceived social approval)	20.95	26.90	20
Heterosexual Relationship (low scores = no serious relationship, high scores = serious relationship)	18.88	22.25	16

Note: Each of these differences (clinic users versus clinic nonusers) is statistically significant.

[1] Computed from data collected by Fisher, Byrne, Edmunds, Miller, Kelley, and White (1979).

relationships with men is in accord with similar findings that are discussed in Chapter 2. It seems possible that a certain degree of relationship stability is needed before one may anticipate—and prepare for—future intercourse.

There is one more study to discuss which concerns the role of emotions in contraceptive acquisition. It was pointed out earlier that people often evaluate a stimulus on the basis of how that stimulus makes them feel. Thus, if an adolescent feels particularly anxious when acquiring contraceptives in public (e.g., at a drugstore), he or she may negatively evaluate aspects of this intimidating situation, and this could include negative evaluations of the contraceptive that was just acquired.

To investigate these assumptions, Fisher, Fisher, and Byrne (1977) conducted field research in a drugstore in West Lafayette, Indiana. Forty male volunteers, who were students in an introductory psychology course, took part in the study.

Each subject reported to a local drugstore, where he was informed that the research concerned "male purchasing behavior." Subjects were told that they would be asked to purchase a "male related" product, such as acne cream, a "jock strap itch" preparation, or condoms. A rigged lottery was conducted to determine which product would be purchased, and all subjects drew instructions to buy a three-pack of lubricated condoms. Funds were provided for the purchase, and subjects proceeded to the back of the store and bought the condoms from one of the pharmacists on duty (whose cooperation, of course, had been enlisted beforehand).

Immediately after the condom purchase, subjects were taken to an office at the rear of the store, where they completed a questionnaire measure of their emotional reactions to buying the condoms (i.e., were they anxious or calm? happy or sad? etc.). Then, the undergraduates were asked for their evaluations of condoms in general, and in actual use, for their estimates of how reliable condoms are, for their perceptions of what the pharmacist had thought of them (i.e., did the pharmacist think you were moral or immoral? immature or mature? etc.), for a rating of how much they liked the pharmacist, and for their evaluation of the drugstore where the purchase had taken place. After filling out their questionnaires, the need for the mild deception (i.e., the rigged lottery) was explained to the subjects, as was the purpose of the study, and they were thanked for their participation.

According to our reasoning, subjects who responded to the condom purchase with relatively negative (versus positive) emotions should make the most negative evaluations of the purchase setting. Our analysis of the data, presented in Table 9.9, confirms this assumption. Undergraduate men who reacted to the purchase with relatively negative (versus positive) emotions evaluated condoms, in general, and the use of condoms more negatively, and they rated condoms as being less reliable. In addition, those who responded to the purchase with negative feelings thought that the pharmacist had evaluated them more negatively, they tended to report less liking for the pharmacist who sold them the condoms, and they even tended to evaluate more negatively the *drugstore* where the purchase had taken place! Statistical tests indicated that this pattern of results is significant, but it must be borne in mind that there could be bidirectional links between emotional and evaluative responses to the purchase (i.e., people who experienced negative emotions rated condoms as less reliable, or people who regard condoms as unreliable experienced negative emotions at the point of purchase, etc.). In any event, the findings are consistent with the notion that people may make evaluations of a contraceptive method *based on how it feels to acquire that method*. We can also speculate that negative emotional and evaluative responses to contraceptive purchasing might impede future attempts to acquire birth control. Taken together, then, the data presented in this section suggest that sex-related emotions may help determine whether or not adolescents will "go public" and acquire contraception. And, if they do so, emotions may

TABLE 9.9

Men's Evaluations of the Condom Purchase Situation as a
Function of Their Emotional Response to the Purchase[1]

	Undergraduate Men Who Responded With Relatively _Negative_ Emotions	Undergraduate Men Who Responded With Relatively _Positive_ Emotions	Scale Midpoints
Condoms _in general_ are: (low = negative, high = positive)	17.85	22.55	16
Condoms _in use_ are: (low = negative, high = positive)	11.15	13.55	16
Condom reliability: (low = unreliable, high = reliable)	4.76	5.55	4
Pharmacist's impression of you was: (low = negative, high = positive)	38.80	47.70	40
Did you like the pharmacist? (low = not at all, high = very much)	9.60	10.10	8
The drugstore was: (low = unpleasant, high = pleasant)	48.85	53.45	40

[1] After Fisher, Fisher, and Byrne (1977).

help shape an individual's evaluations of this critical step in the process of contraception.

Hypothesis 4: Erotophobic (versus Erotophilic) Individuals Are Less Likely to Communicate about Contraception With Their Sexual Partners

Unless adolescents discuss birth control with their sexual partners (or better yet, potential partners), they may never know whether contraceptive precautions are adequate. A simple inquiry—"Have you got a condom, Bill?"—could well mean the difference between protected coitus and unwanted pregnancy. Nevertheless, it is apparent that teens do not always feel comfortable enough to initiate such discussion. We propose that a person's emotional orientation to sexuality is one factor that determines whether they will talk about such matters. According to our theory, erotophobic persons should find discussion of birth control (or other sexual topics) to be aversive, and hence they will avoid talking about such subjects. Erotophilic individuals, in contrast, should not respond negatively to such discussion and they should thus be more willing to talk to their partners about birth control.

As of this writing, there has not been a direct test of the relationship between erotophobia—erotophilia and discussion of birth control per se. However, the authors and their colleagues (Fisher, Miller, Byrne, & White, 1980) have studied the role of erotophobia—erotophilia in communicating about sex *in general*. Since the findings of this research are pertinent to our hypothesis, we will consider them in brief detail.

To explore reactions to talking about sex as a function of erotophobia—erotophilia, the investigators created a simplified laboratory analogue of sexual communication. Subjects in the study were introductory psychology students (101 males, 89 females) at a midwestern U.S. university. When they arrived at the lab, they were taken to individual soundproof rooms, and seated in front of a video camera. Subjects were then given a brief prepared speech, and were asked to read this speech into the camera; ostensibly, a videotape of their speech was being recorded and would later be presented to an audience. Half of the subjects were given a sexual speech to record; entitled *Making Love to One Another,* it was approximately 400 words long and described foreplay, intercourse, and orgasm with anatomical and physiological terms. The language was explicit, but not coarse. The other half of the subjects were asked to read a neutral speech entitled *Talking to One Another.* This speech too was about 400 words long, and it described the anatomy and physiology of speech production for a couple who are conversing.

As soon as they had finished giving one of the speeches into the camera, subjects filled out a number of questionnaires. These included scales to measure subjects' perceptions of how the audience would react to the speaker (i.e., to *them*) and how the audience would react to the *speech,* a measure of subjects' emotional responses to giving the speech, and a "release agreement" form on which the undergraduates indicated whether or not they would release their "videotaped" speech for presentation to an audience. Finally, subjects responded to the Sexual Opinion Survey to provide us with a measure of erotophobia—erotophilia. It should be noted that in actuality, no recordings of subjects' speeches were made, and the research participants were apprised of this fact during a postexperimental debriefing.

If our reasoning is correct, erotophobic (versus erotophilic) subjects should show the most negative responses to comminicating the sexual message. And, since we do not expect sex-related emotions to generalize to neutral topics, erotophobic and erotophilic subjects should report equivalent responses to delivering the neutral speech.

The data analysis confirmed our expectations: erotophobia—erotophilia was significantly correlated with reactions to communicating the sexual message, and was not correlated with responses to delivering the neutral speech. To illustrate these effects, we have split the sample at the median into "erotophobic" and "erotophilic" subjects, and their mean responses to communicating are presented in Table 9.10. It can be seen that erotophobic (versus erotophilic) subjects

TABLE 9.10
Responses to Communicating the Sexual and Neutral
Speeches as a Function of Erotophobia—Erotophilia[1]

	Sexual Message		Neutral Message		
	Erotophobic Subjects	Erotophilic Subjects	Erotophobic Subjects	Erotophilic Subjects	Scale Midpoints
The audience will think *I* am: (low scores = most negative evaluation, high scores = most positive evaluation)	56.23	63.85	74.62	74.56	56
The audience will respond to *the speech*: (low scores = most negatively, high scores = most positively)	46.74	51.45	70.68	70.50	52
While giving the speech, *I felt*: (low scores = most negative emotions, high scores = most positive emotions)	55.84	65.79	72.31	70.81	52
Release Agreement: (low scores = I do not agree to release any portion of the videotape; high scores = I agree to the unlimited presentation of the videotape)	2.87	3.78	3.79	3.84	3

Note: The pattern of responses was quite similar for male and female subjects; consequently, their data were combined for the mean scores reported in this table.

[1] Computed from data collected by Fisher, Miller, Byrne, and White (1980).

who delivered the sexual message perceived the audience as evaluating them, and their speech, more negatively, they reported more negative emotional responses to communicating this speech, and they were less willing to release their videotaped speech for future presentation. With respect to communicating the neutral speech, the reactions of erotophobic and erotophilic subjects were, as expected, similar. These results, incidentally, held for male and female subjects alike.

To the extent that this laboratory analogue may be generalized, we would expect that erotophobic teens would find it aversive to discuss birth control with their sexual partners and that they would avoid doing so. Lack of such communication, in turn, may contribute to less-than-optimal contraceptive use by the adolescents in question. Moreover, it will be recalled that erotophobic individuals seem to have difficulty in learning factual information about sex. This problem could be exacerbated by the difficulty that they may have in talking or asking questions about this topic. These issues, of course, must be the subject of further research that bears directly on communicating about birth control as a function of erotophobia—erotophilia.

There is one other bit of anecdotal data that may be worth sharing. We listened in as many of these undergraduates—relatively bright and advantaged students—read their speeches. We were impressed by their frequent inability to pronounce the basic sexual vocabulary which appeared in the sexual speech. For these students, vagina was occasionally transformed into "virginia," clitoris became "cleotoris," and scrotum was delivered as "scrotum" once or twice. One can speculate that, over and above the emotions involved, such vocabulary deficiencies make it even more difficult for adolescents to talk to one another about sex or contraception.

Hypothesis 5: Erotophobic (versus Erotophilic) Individuals Are Less Likely to Use Contraception Consistently

In view of the fact that erotophobic (versus erotophilic) young adults seem to have difficulty with each of the prerequisites, it should not be surprising to find that they are inconsistent users of birth control. Data that we have collected provide clear-cut support for this assumption. For instance, the university women who were studied by Fisher et al. (1979) were classified as consistent or inconsistent contraceptors, or as sexually inactive, on the basis of their questionnaire responses. Measures of erotophobia—erotophilia, attitudes about using birth control or about using a birth control clinic, normative beliefs about birth control, and seriousness of present heterosexual relationship were compared across the three groups of women. These data are presented in Table 9.11, where it can be seen that erotophobia—erotophilia neatly, and significantly, differentiates the groups: consistent contraceptors are relatively erotophilic, inconsistent contraceptors are relatively erotophobic, and sexually inactive women are most erotophobic. Presumably, a person's feelings about sex may be negative enough to preclude sex entirely (i.e., the sexually inactive women), they may be just negative enough to inhibit the planning but not the sex itself (i.e., the inconsistent contraceptors), or they may be positive enough to allow for both the planning and the sex (i.e., the consistent contraceptors). It can also be seen in the table that consistent users of birth control tend to have more positive attitudes and normative beliefs about birth control than do inconsistent contraceptors or sexually inactive women. In addition, it is interesting to note that consistent contraceptors report significantly more serious heterosexual relationships than do inconsistent contraceptors. On one hand, this again suggests that relationship stability—perhaps because one has more opportunity to plan—is associated with better contraceptive practice. On the other hand, the women who were inconsistent contraceptors were obviously more in jeopardy of unplanned pregnancy, and in the absence of a highly stable relationship it might be harder for them to cope with such an eventuality.

TABLE 9.11
Womens' Emotions, Attitudes, Normative Beliefs, and Seriousness of
Relationship as a Function of Consistency of Birth Control Use[1]

	Consistent Contraceptors	Inconsistent Contraceptors	Sexually Inactive	Scale Midpoints
Emotional Orientation to Sexuality (0 = most erotophobic, 126 = most erotophilic)	61.70$_a$	52.13$_b$	45.93$_c$	63
Attitudes towards Contraception and Clinic use (low scores = negative attitudes, high scores = positive attitudes)	101.76$_a$	94.71$_b$	92.20$_b$	68
Normative Beliefs about Contraception (low scores = little perceived social approval, high scores = much perceived social approval)	27.64$_a$	23.93$_b$	21.82$_c$	20
Heterosexual Relationship (low scores = no serious relationship, high scores = serious relationship)	22.00$_a$	20.56$_b$	18.66$_c$	16

Note: Means with common subscripts do not differ significantly from one another at the .05 probability level.
[1] After Fisher, Byrne, Edmunds, Miller, Kelley, and White (1979).

It is worth noting that the relationship of erotophobia—erotophilia and consistency of contraception has been observed among men as well as among women. For example, Przybyla (1979) surveyed 142 undergraduate men at a U.S. university and found that about 80% reported having had sexual intercourse. Among those who were sexually experienced, the erotophobic (versus erotophilic) men were more likely to indicate that they or their partner did not always use contraception. In an additional test of the hypothesized relationship, Fisher (1978) reported that erotophobic (versus erotophilic) men were less likely to indicate that they had always used condoms, if they had intercourse during the preceding month. Thus, the link between erotophobia—erotophilia and consistency of contraception seems to be a fairly general one, holding for both sexes and across several independent studies. (For related research which has linked high sex guilt and contraceptive neglect, see Gerrard, 1982).

Hypothesis 6: Erotophobic (versus Erotophilic) Individuals Have More Negative Attitudes Towards Contraception

According to the Sexual Behavior Sequence, emotional responses to sexuality should generalize and mediate positive or negative evaluations of birth control.

Thus—based on their emotional responses—erotophobic persons should have relatively negative attitudes about contraception, and erotophilic individuals will have more positive attitudes in this regard. Data that we and our associates have collected support this reasoning consistently. In the sample of college women studied by Fisher et al. (1979), for example, erotophobia—erotophilia was significantly correlated, in the expected direction, with a wide range of attitudes about birth control. To highlight these relationships, we have contrasted the attitudes of highly erotophobic and highly erotophilic women (i.e., the top and bottom thirds of the distribution of Sexual Opinion Survey scores); these findings are presented in Table 9.12. As you can see in this table, erotophobic (versus erotophilic) women thought it was *relatively* more probable that using birth control would lead to major negative side effects, that it would negatively affect their sexual morals, be unnatural and unreliable, might result in guilt feelings and decreased sexual pleasure, etc. Such relationships have been found in samples of men, as well. For instance, Przybyla (1979) observed that erotophobic (versus

TABLE 9.12
Women's Attitudes towards Contraception as a
Function of Erotophobia—Erotophilia[1]

Attitudes towards Birth Control	Highly Erotophobic Women[2]	Highly Erotophilic Women
Using birth control leads to *major negative side effects* (except where noted, 1 = probable, 7 = improbable	3.92	4.61
Using birth control would have a *negative effect on my sexual morals*	5.41	6.51
Using birth control methods *is unnatural,* (1 = true, 7 = untrue)	4.97	5.82
Birth control methods *are unreliable*	4.66	5.81
Using birth control would *give me guilt feelings*	5.41	6.64
Using birth control would *decrease my sexual pleasure*	5.86	6.48
Using birth control would *remove the worry of becoming pregnant*	2.37	1.72
Using birth control would *make sex less romantic*	5.91	6.46

[1] Computed from data collected by Fisher, Byrne, Edmunds, Miller, Kelley, and White (1979)

[2] "Erotophobic" and "erotophilic" women scored in the bottom and top thirds of the distribution of Sexual Opinion Survey scores, respectively. Each of these differences is statistically significant.

erotophilic) men were relatively more likely to indicate that using birth control would result in guilt feelings or in decreased sexual pleasure, and erotophobic men were also less convinced that using contraception was "good" or "right," or indeed that using birth control helps regulate family size.

There are several points that might be discussed in connection with these findings. First, the erotophobic—erotophilic differences in attitudes were not enormous, nor would we expect them to be in more-or-less liberal college samples. Nevertheless, Fisher et al. (1979) found that precisely such differences in attitudes were related to variations in contraceptive acquisition and use. Specifically, analyses suggested that erotophobia—erotophilia may mediate attitudes towards contraception, which in turn affect behavior. Speculating beyond these relationships, it seems possible that contraceptive behavior that results from this emotional—attitudinal chain could eventually reinforce one's erotophobic or erotophilic disposition. Thus, an erotophobic adolescent, who may regard contraception as unreliable and unnatural, will probably not use birth control consistently. To the degree that this results in gut-wrenching teenage distress over a late period or other sex-related anxiety, the individual in question may become even *more* erotophobic and by extension more attitudinally negative about contraception. In contrast, an erotophilic teen who has more positive attitudes about contraception and uses it more consistently may well end up enjoying sex more. Consequently, he or she may become increasingly erotophilic and perhaps develop more positive attitudes and become an even more effective user of contraception. This logic suggests that emotions, attitudes, and behavior may comprise a self-maintaining, self-reinforcing system. The presence of such a self-reinforcing chain might be quite advantageous for erotophilic teens, but it could prove to be quite disastrous for their erotophobic counterparts. Confirming the existence of this mediational network might become a topic for future research. If it is found to be implicated in contraceptive behavior, appropriate strategies for intervention could be sought.

Hypothesis 7: Emotional Factors (i.e., Erotophobia— Erotophilia) and Informational Factors (i.e., Relevant Beliefs and Expectancies) Each Contribute Independently to Determining Contraceptive Behavior

Until this point, we have focused exclusively on emotional determinants of contraceptive behavior. According to the Sexual Behavior Sequence, however, contraception is governed by *both* emotional factors (i.e., erotophobia—erotophilia) and informational variables (i.e., beliefs and expectancies). This possibility, of course, has implications for understanding—and improving—adolescent contraception. If adolescents' birth control practices are purely a function of sex-related emotions, or purely a result of their beliefs and expectancies, then interventions should justifiably deal with this sole determinant of behavior. If, as we propose, emotional and informational factors contribute independently to explaining adolescent contraception, then interventions must deal with both determinants.

In order to study this question, it is necessary to employ both emotion-based and information-based predictors, and to clarify whether they may independently be related to contraceptive behavior. Fisher (1978) has conducted such a study, using the measure of erotophobia—erotophilia as the emotion based predictor, and using behavioral intentions—a component of Fishbein's model (Fishbein & Ajzen, 1975; see also Chapter 8)—as the information-based predictor. Readers may recall from the discussion in Chapter 8 that, according to Fishbein, contraceptive behavior is a function of an individual's *intention* to perform such behavior. Behavioral intentions, in turn, are regarded as a function of four components: beliefs about the consequences of using contraception, evaluations of these consequences, beliefs about whether significant others want the person to use contraception, and the individual's desire to comply with these wishes. Thus, intentions can be thought of as information-based predictors of contraceptive behavior in two senses. First, intentions are based in part on the individual's beliefs and expectancies about contraception. Second, behavioral intentions themselves can be viewed as beliefs or expectancies about one's future use of birth control.

To examine whether emotional and informational factors may contribute independently to contraceptive behavior, Fisher (1978) surveyed a group of 145 undergraduate males at a U.S. university. These men were asked to complete the Sexual Opinion Survey in order to measure erotophobia—erotophilia. They also stated whether of not they intended always to use condoms during sexual intercourse in the coming month. Approximately 4 weeks after this initial assessment, most of these men reported back for a follow-up study, where those who had intercourse indicated whether or not they had always used condoms.

An analysis of these data revealed three main findings, which are presented graphically in Figure 9.1. First, it can be seen that erotophobia—erotophilia was moderately correlated with condom use; erotophobic (versus erotophilic) men were less likely always to use condoms. Second, behavioral intentions were also correlated with condom use; men who intended to do so were most likely to report that they had always used condoms during intercourse in the intervening month. Finally, it can be seen that while erotophobia—erotophilia and intentions are both related to condom use, these predictor variables are *not* related to one another. Further statistical analyses showed that erotophobia—erotophilia and behavioral intentions contributed *independently* to explaining variations in condom use. The linear combination of these two variables was a significantly better predictor of condom use than was either factor taken singly. These results confirm our hypothesis that emotional and informational factors may be independent but complementary determinants of contraceptive behavior. Thus, interventions may seek to change both general emotional factors (i.e., erotophobia—erot-

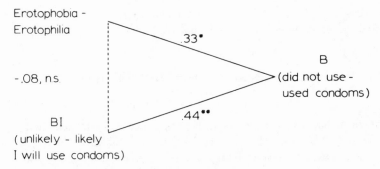

FIG. 9.1. Correlations of erotophobia—erotophilia, behavioral intentions (BI), and reports of condom use behavior (B) across a month's time. (After Fisher, 1978). The multiple correlation of erotophobia—erotophilia and intentions with condom use was $R(40) = .57, p < .001$.
* = correlation is significant at the .05 probability level
** = correlation is significant at the .01 probability level

ophilia) as well as contraceptive intentions and the belief and expectancy factors upon which these intentions are based.

Beyond Contraception: Erotophobia—Erotophilia and Sex-Related Health Care

A central theme in our discussion has been that sex-related emotions may generalize and mediate approach–avoidance responses to contraception. In addition, it seems reasonable to us to assume that erotophobia—erotophilia may mediate approach or avoidance of *other* important behaviors that are sexual in nature. Sex-related health care activities, such as electing to get a gynecological checkup or to self-examine one's breasts, provide cases in point. These behaviors require that the individual perform active, approach responses to a sexual object—one's own body. Hence, we would predict that erotophobic (versus erotophilic) persons would be less likely to engage in either of these elective behaviors.

To test this reasoning, we analyzed the questionnaire responses of 543 women from two U.S. universities. Each woman had completed the Sexual Opinion Survey, and each had indicated how recently she had gotten a gynecological checkup and how often she self-examined her breasts. Data analyses revealed small but significant relationships: erotophobic (versus erotophilic) women were less likely to report that they had a recent gynecological checkup, and erotophobic women also reported less frequent breast self-examination. Interestingly enough, the same kinds of emotions which seem to inhibit adolescents' use of contraception may also act as barriers to sex-related health care. Thus, it appears that there may be a rather general relationship of erotophobia—erotophilia and approach—avoidance of sexuality, over and above the specific relationships that we have observed with contraceptive behavior.

CONCLUSIONS AND DIRECTIONS FOR FUTURE ACTION

What, then, have we learned about the link between sex-related emotions and contraceptive behavior? The data suggest that persons with a negative emotional response to sex may have difficulty in learning what they need to know about conception and contraception. Findings also indicate that erotophobic young adults may not accurately anticipate future intercourse, and this may prevent them from taking contraceptive precautions in advance. Moreover, the erotophobic individuals that we have studied seem to be reluctant to engage in public behaviors to acquire contraception, they appear to find discussion of sexual topics aversive, and they hold relatively negative attitudes about birth control. And, at what must be our "bottom line," erotophobic (versus erotophilic) young men and women are inconsistent users of contraception. In sum, across a series of studies, erotophobic individuals seem to be less likely to engage in each behavior that is required for effective contraception. Finally, there is evidence that erotophobia—erotophilia may have quite general effects on approach or avoidance of sexuality: disturbingly enough, the negative emotions which seem to inhibit the use of contraception also seem to inhibit performance of sex-related health care practices.

This research suggests directions for future study and for interventions. There are, in particular, at least three strategies that we might pursue in efforts to improve adolescent contraception, and we will consider each in turn.

Educating for Change In Erotophobia—Erotophilia

According to all of the evidence that we have collected, erotophobic persons avoid a number of important, sex related behaviors, ranging from the learning of sex information, to the use of contraception, to the performance of sex-related health care activities. Assuming that our theory is correct, general changes in erotophobia—erotophilia should "trickle down" and mediate general changes in approach or avoidance of sexuality. Thus, as an adolescent becomes more erotophilic, he or she should begin to acquire improved knowledge of birth control, to use contraception more regularly, to engage in sex-related health care, and to perform other such approach responses to sexuality.

How, then, are we to educate for change in the direction of more positive emotional responses to sex? Conceptually, there are really two tasks involved. First, it is necessary to desensitize persons—to alleviate their negative emotional responses to sex—and it seems possible that the desensitization procedures that have been worked out by Wolpe (1958) might be useful in this regard. Basically, this method involves learning to remain at ease in the presence of stimuli that formerly were aversive, and variations of these procedures could be adapted to the classroom with the aim of increasing teenagers' tolerance for their own and others' sexuality. It is not enough, however, simply to remove a person's aversion for his or her own sexuality—it is necessary to *replace* such feelings with more positive, erotophilic responses. Thus, the second part of educating for change in erotophobia—erotophilia involves the systematic association of sexual cues with positive emotions in order to foster the development of an erotophilic disposition. Possible methods for using these principles in sex education settings are described in some detail in Chapter 12.

Changing the Emotional Tone of Contraceptive Learning, Acquisition, and Use

In addition to fostering general change in adolescents' emotional response to sexuality, we think it is also necessary to change their feelings about the specific behaviors that are required for effective contraception. We now have grounds to suspect that many adolescents avoid learning about sex and are reluctant to acquire, discuss, or use contraception because they find it emotionally aversive to do so. Hence, interventions are needed to make each of these prerequisite behaviors a source of *positive* (or at least less negative) emotions. If contraceptive cues could be made to provoke pleasure instead of anxiety, teens would likely be more motivated to employ birth control. Thus, we must develop imaginative strategies to make the acquisition of sex and contraceptive knowledge fun, and as those who have turned away eager students from overcrowded sexuality classes can attest, it is not difficult to make learning about sex enjoyable. Beyond the acquisition of knowledge, we must find ways of associating positive emotions with anticipating intercourse and discussing contraception. Whether through role playing, desensitization, or otherwise, we must make prerequisite contraceptive behaviors part of an extended process of "foreplay." In addition, we must engineer more emotionally positive ways for teens to acquire contraception. Such innovations might involve contraceptive boutiques (similar to the "Rubber Tree" in Seattle, Washington), mail order or vending machine access to contraception, or student-oriented clinics like the one described in Chapter 10. Finally, we need to condition positive emotions to the use of birth control per se. The advertisements of a shapely young nurse in a starched white uniform selling ribbed condoms ("for extra pleasure"), or a nude female on a horse indicating that with a particular brand of condoms the male reader will "come with me" are excellent prototypes for making the regular use of contraception a source of positive emotions.

In general, then, we propose that to the degree that interventions make each of the prerequisite behaviors pleasurable (or at least less aversive), they will facilitate adolescents' use of contraception. Such interventions, we feel, will complement efforts to change adolescents' general emotional response to sexuality. These specific changes cannot, however, replace the broader emotional changes suggested earlier. Unless adolescents are helped to feel good about sex in general, it will be hard to convince them that *contraception* is good.

Changing Beliefs and Expectancies

Research discussed in this chapter suggests that informational factors as well as emotions may govern contraceptive behavior. Therefore, we advocate interventions that focus on changing relevant beliefs and expectancies, in addition to the emotional changes discussed earlier. A promising framework for such intervention has been provided by Fishbein and his colleagues (see Chapter 8). Using this approach, it should be possible to identify particular beliefs and expectancies that govern contraceptive intentions and behavior in specific target populations. Educational interventions could then be developed in efforts to change such beliefs and expectancies and through such changes, improve adolescents' practice of contraception.

In Conclusion

Based on our research, we propose fairly wide-ranging interventions that are aimed at changing teens' emotions, beliefs, and ultimately their contraceptive behavior. These are obviously long term objectives that will require much work and will likely engender resistance. Nevertheless, it should be made clear that *inaction* is also a decision of sorts. That is, failure to attempt interventions promotes, by default, a status quo that has literally millions of U.S. teenagers at risk of unwanted pregnancy. Therefore, despite the costs involved, it seems clear to us that positive change is needed.

REFERENCES

Byrne, D. Social psychology and the study of sexual behavior. *Personality and Social Psychology Bulletin*, 1977, *1*, 3–30.

Byrne, D., Fisher, J. D., Lamberth, J., & Mitchell, H. E. Evaluations of erotica: Facts or feelings? *Journal of Personality and Social Psychology*, 1974, *29*, 111–119.

Byrne, D., Jazwinski, C., DeNinno, J. A., & Fisher, W. A. Negative sexual attitudes and contraception. In D. Byrne and L. A. Byrne (Eds.), *Exploring human sexuality*. New York: Harper and Row, 1977.

Byrne, D., & Sheffield, J. Response to sexually arousing stimuli as a function of repressing and sensitizing defenses. *Journal of Abnormal Psychology*, 1965, *70*, 114–118.

Crowne, D. P., & Marlowe, D. *The approval motive; Studies in evaluative dependence*. New York: Wiley, 1964.

Fishbein, M., & Ajzen, I. *Belief, attitude, intention, and behavior: An introduction to theory and research.* Reading, Massachusetts: Addison Wesley, 1975.

Fisher, W. A. *Individual differences in behavioral responsiveness to erotica: Cognitive labeling, transfer of arousal, and disinhibition considerations.* Unpublished master's thesis, Purdue University, 1976.

Fisher, W. A. *Affective, attitudinal, and normative determinants of contraceptive behavior among university men.* Unpublished doctoral dissertation, Purdue University, 1978.

Fisher, W. A. *Erotophobia—erotophilia and performance in a human sexuality course.* Unpublished manuscript, University of Western Ontario, 1980.

Fisher, W. A., & Byrne, D. Individual differences in affective, evaluative, and behavioral responses to an erotic film. *Journal of Applied Social Psychology,* 1978, *8,* 355–565.

Fisher, W. A., Byrne, D., Edmunds, M., Miller, C. T., Kelley, K., & White, L. A. Psychological and situation-specific correlates of contraceptive behavior among university women. *Journal of Sex Research,* 1979, *15,* 38–55.

Fisher, W. A., Fisher, J. D., & Byrne, D. Consumer reactions to contraceptive purchasing. *Personality and Social Psychology Bulletin,* 1977, *3,* 293–296.

Fisher, W. A., Miller, C. T., Byrne, D., & White, L. A. Talking dirty: Responses to communicating a sexual message as a function of situational and personality factors. *Basic and Applied Social Psychology,* 1980, *1,* 115–126.

Gerrard, M. Sex, sex guilt, and contraceptive use. *Journal of Personality and Social Psychology,* 1982, *42,* 153–158.

Gilbert, F. S., & Gamache, M. C. The Sexual Opinion Survey: Structure and use. Manuscript submitted for publication, 1982.

Levitt, E. E., & Brady, J. P. Sexual preferences in young adult males and some correlates. *Journal of Clinical Psychology,* 1965, *21,* 347–359.

Mendelsohn, M. J., & Mosher, D. L. Effects of sex guilt and premarital sexual permissiveness on role-played sex education and moral attitudes. *Journal of Sex Research,* 1979, *15,* 174–183.

Mosher, D. L. The development and multitrait-multimethod matrix analysis of three measures of three aspects of guilt. *Journal of Consulting Psychology,* 1966,, *30,* 25–29.

Mosher, D. L. Measurement of guilt in females by self-report inventories. *Journal of Consulting and Clinical Psychology,* 1968, *32,* 690–695.

Mosher, D. L. Sex guilt and sex myths in college men and women. *Journal of Sex Research,* 1979, *15,* 224–234.

Mosher, D. L., & Cross, H. J. Sex guilt and premarital sexual experiences of college students. *Journal of Consulting and Clinical Psychology,* 1971, *36,* 27–32.

Przybyla, D. *Survey of midwestern U.S. students' sexual attitudes and contraceptive behavior.* Unpublished manuscript, State University of New York at Albany, 1979.

Schwartz, S. Effects of sex guilt and sexual arousal on the retention of birth control information. *Journal of Consulting and Clinical Psychology,* 1973, *41,* 61–64.

White, L. A., Fisher, W. A., Byrne, D., & Kingma, R. *Development and validation of a measure of affective orientation to erotic stimuli: The Sexual Opinion Survey.* Paper presented at the meeting of the Midwestern Psychological Association, Chicago, Illinois, May, 1977.

Wolpe, J. *Psychotherapy by reciprocal inhibition.* Stanford: Stanford University Press, 1958.

Yarber, W. L., & McCabe, G. P. Teacher characteristics and the inclusion of sex education topics in grades 6–8 and 9–11. *Journal of School Health,* 1981, *51,* 288–291.

Zelnik, M., & Kantner, J. Sexual and contraceptive experience of young unmarried women in the United States, 1976 and 1971. *Family Planning Perspectives,* 1977, *9,* 55–71.

POSSIBLE SOLUTIONS

Perhaps the most important goal of this book is to explore potential solutions to the problem of teenage pregnancy. To provide a foundation for such solutions, we have discussed theory and research which help explain the mechanisms that govern teens' sexual behavior and their use—or neglect—of contraception. Now, it is time to consider strategies for controlling the epidemic of adolescent pregnancy. The present section begins with a description of what is in many ways a model contraception clinic and educational program for college students. The health educator who was based at this clinic discusses its history, its methods, and some of the successes and difficulties that have been encountered in delivering contraceptive care to thousands of young persons. Next, two social psychologists report on a series of in-depth interviews that were conducted with young men and women who have engaged in unprotected coitus. It is pointed out that certain social arrangements that are common in adolescence predispose teens to pregnancy risk, and specific suggestions are proposed for dealing with these "social traps." In the concluding chapter, one of the theories that was discussed earlier—the Sexual Behavior Sequence—is used as a conceptual framework for organizing and interpreting many of the findings that are reported in this volume. Based on this analysis, systematic recommendations are made for a new kind of sex and contraceptive education that is directed at reducing the incidence of teenage pregnancy. Let us now consider some of these possible solutions to the problem of adolescent pregnancy.

10 Providing Contraceptive Care on a College Campus

Marilyn Edmunds
The Pathfinder Fund
Boston, Massachusetts

Editors' Note

Part of the reason that adolescents neglect to use contraception is that birth control services are either unavailable to them or are perceived as being in some way unsatisfactory. In Chapter 10, Marilyn Edmunds outlines a two-component approach that is geared to providing attractive, accessible contraceptive care for college youth. The medical facet of this strategy utilizes the expertise of gynecological nurse clinicians as well as physicians to examine patients, answer questions, and prescribe contraception. The educational component of this approach includes peer health educators who conduct outreach programs on contraceptive education, as well as an obligatory contraceptive counseling session for each person who wishes to obtain birth control at the campus clinic. Limitations of this method with respect to involving males in the contraceptive process are discussed, and applications of this approach in settings other than universities are also considered. The chapter closes with the script of a contraceptive education movie—*No Choice But to Choose*—that was developed especially for use in the clinic's programs. As you read the script, it is worth noting how the similarity of the actors to the intended audience emphasizes the relevance of the contraceptive message to viewers' own lives. The film presents a more-or-less explicit behavioral script concerning how viewers may acquire and use contraception, and the movie's recommendations are phrased in such a way as to motivate the audience to avoid unwanted pregnancy by using contraception responsibly.

BACKGROUND—INDIANA UNIVERSITY AND THE I.U. STUDENT HEALTH SERVICE

Indiana University at Bloomington is the largest campus of the eight campus state-wide system. It is situated on a 1,250 acre campus in the northeast section of Bloomington, a city of approximately 40,000 located in south central Indiana. The student body numbers approximately 30,000 including part-time and full-time undergraduate and graduate students. Although no student is required to live on campus, about 12,500 students, or 41%, do live in University housing. Another 3,600 or 11% live in the 51 fraternities and sororities. More than half the total number of students, then, live on campus. (Report of a Survey of the Health Program of Indiana University conducted by the American College Health Association, October, 1975, p. 2).

A four-story independent facility, the Student Health Service serves all I.U. students, full-time and part-time. Comprehensive health services are available, including physician and nurse visits, clinical laboratory services, x-rays, physical therapy, health education, dietary counseling, pharmacy, an in-patient unit, and counseling and psychological services. Care provided by nurses with a physician on-call is available after hours. Between appointments and walk-ins, the Student Health Service sees approximately 450–500 patients a day during the academic year. Financial support of the Student Health Service comes primarily from the University general fund, which in turn, comes from tax monies and tuition fees. Prepaid fees and fees collected by the Student Health Service for care rendered comprise less than 20% of the total Student Health Service budget.

HISTORY OF CONTRACEPTIVE CARE AT I.U. SHS

Contraceptive care has been available to I.U. students in varying degrees for over twenty years. In the mid-1950s a woman could have a pelvic exam performed by a clinic physician and discreetly obtain a birth control method if she knew which physician to see. Only a few staff physicians felt comfortable prescribing birth control methods at that time, and even those who did were reluctant to publicize the fact. As a result, most students assumed that contraceptive care was not available on campus and thus sought care elsewhere, if at all. Some I.U. students sought contraceptive care from OB/GYN specialists or other physicians in town. Many, no doubt, either did not use contraception or relied upon methods they could obtain without a physician visit.

With the increased student activism and awareness of the 1960s, the demand for gynecological care on campus increased. Students no longer felt apprehensive or hesitant about requesting contraceptive services. Gynecological care, including the prescription of birth control methods, was simply another aspect of comprehensive medical care which should be readily available to students. In the spring of 1971 an effort was made to make comprehensive contraceptive care more accessible to I.U. women. The local Planned Parenthood affiliate began operating a weekly evening contraceptive clinic held for students in the Student Health Service. Although Student Health Service facilities were used, Planned Parenthood personnel staffed the clinic. This arrangement mutually suited the Planned Parenthood affiliate and the Student Health Service. Since Student Health Service medical staff could not meet all the student contraceptive needs at that time, many students were already going to Planned Parenthood. The student population, added to Planned Parenthood's regular community patients, overloaded their daytime clinics. Thus, the opening of an evening clinic specifically for I.U. students solved problems for both agencies. In the first full year of operation (1972), 2,575 women were seen in the Planned Parenthood/Student Health Service clinic. Operation of this clinic continued for the next 5 years with utilization increasing annually.

In the fall of 1974, the Student Health Service initiated a Prepayment Fee Plan for general health care. Students could elect to pay a flat fee per semester at registration, which would then entitle them to extensive 'free' care at the Student Health Service throughout the semester, and to reduced rates for those services which were not covered by the Prepaid fee. Students electing not to enroll in the Prepayment Plan were still eligible for care at the Student Health Service, but on a fee-for-service basis. With the implementation of the Prepaid Plan, students could receive much of their medical care at reduced cost. Under this plan, physician and nurse visits were free, as were many lab tests, etc. Although the Prepaid Plan offered students a great savings on most types of medical care, one significant area was *not* covered by this plan: contraceptive care provided through the Planned Parenthood/Student Health Service clinic.

Women students who utilized the Planned Parenthood clinic paid anywhere from $10.00 for a Pap test and pelvic exam to $15.00 or $20.00 for a Pap test, pelvic exam, and a contraceptive method. The same services, had they been covered by the Prepaid Plan, would presumably have cost significantly less. Many students, both female and male, complained about the inequity of this arrangement. In addition, students disliked the inconvenience of only being able to obtain contraceptive care one night a week. Although the Student Health Service administration agreed with the students philosophically, it was not in a financial position to incorporate contraceptive care into the general outpatient clinic. However, in 1976, after the Prepaid Plan had been in effect for 2 years, the Student Health Service was able to expand programming in several areas, including contraceptive care. Two gynecological nurse clinicians were hired, thus enabling the Student Health Service to provide the majority of contraceptive care required by students. Thus, in January 1977, the Planned Parenthood clinic was discontinued and contraceptive care became available through the regular outpatient clinic, with coverage through the Prepaid Plan. If a student paid the prepaid fee at registration, she could now obtain a pelvic exam at no cost, the processing of her Pap test would cost only $1.00, and the only other cost to her would be the price of her contraceptive method. Women students are now saving financially on their contraceptive care, and these services are regularly available to them. Although the Prepaid Plan has now increased, I.U. students still receive contraceptive care at low cost as compared with the cost of such care in the community.

In the fall of 1977, 31,884 students enrolled in classes at I.U., either full-time or part-time. Forty-seven percent of these were female. In the same year, at the I.U. Student Health Service, approximately 5,600 pelvic exams were performed, approximately 700 diaphragms were fitted, and over 3,300 new oral contraceptive prescriptions were filled. (The I.U. Student Health Service did not at that time perform IUD insertions. Women students interested in IUDs were referred to either the local Planned Parenthood affiliate, or to a private physician in town.)

Usage of Contraceptive Services

In a setting such as the I.U. Student Health Service, it is difficult to present precise statistical breakdowns regarding usage of individual contraceptive methods, since most figures kept refer to specific medical procedures performed (such as pelvic exam, Pap test, diaphragm fitting, etc., and not to care received by particular patients). Many women who come to the Student Health Service to have a pelvic exam and/or Pap test do not necessarily obtain a contraceptive method, while similarly, some women have more than one pelvic exam and Pap test in a given year. Thus, problems arise in attempting to extrapolate data on specific contraceptive method use from figures which are coded by procedure. As a result, we encounter a figure of 5,600 pelvic exams and 2,800 Pap tests as compared with the filling of 3,300 new pill prescriptions and 700 diaphragm fittings. Another bias in the figures involves the woman who comes in initially to obtain one method, and after a period of use, returns to switch to a different method. Probably the most accurate assessment of total new contraceptive patients can be drawn from figures referring to the number of individuals who view a film on contraception (a prerequisite for obtaining an appointment with a clinician for birth control) in a given period of time. In a typical month during the academic year, 95 people view the film. On an academic annual basis then, approximately 760 individuals seek first-time contraceptive care at the I.U. Student Health Service.

Despite the accessibility of contraceptive services on the campus of Indiana University at Bloomington, and despite widespread publicity of these services, a significant number of pregnancies occurs each year. In the 1977–78 academic year, Student Health Service clinicians diagnosed 289 pregnancies (Indiana University, 1978). However, 1047 pregnancy tests were conducted the same year, which indicates that in addition to the approximately 300 pregnancies diagnosed, another 700 I.U. women experienced a pregnancy scare severe enough to warrant having a pregnancy test. According to the Fisher et al. (1979) research, 43% of the female students who were surveyed had experienced a pregnancy scare at one time or another since becoming sexually active, and 3% had an actual pregnancy terminated by abortion. How many of these pregnancy scares result from contraceptive method failure and how many result from irregular or complete nonuse of contraception remains a question, although the data indicate that 60% of those sampled do not always use a contraceptive method. Nonetheless, with over 1,000 pregnancy tests being conducted in a given year, and with the actual number of pregnancies increasing from year to year, it is clear that some Indiana University women in need of contraceptive care are not receiving it.

One hypothesis suggests that young women do not feel comfortable acknowledging to themselves and to others that they are sexually active. However, when the women in the Indiana University sample were questioned about whether or not going to the Student Health Service for birth control would alert others that they were engaging in intercourse, 41% responded that this was improbable. Similarly, 50% stated that they would *not* be embarrassed to seek birth control at the Student Health Service. When asked if they felt that physicians at the Student Health Service disapproved of providing birth control to unmarried women, only 11% responded that they believed this to be probable.

Research indicates that young, unmarried women who *do* use birth control regularly tend to use less effective methods than their older and/or married counterparts. Our study bears this out. Women coming to the clinic for first-time contraceptive care reported previous method use in the following breakdowns:

no method used	40%
birth control pills	6%
condoms	29%
withdrawal	13%
contraceptive foams	10%
rhythm	2%

The combined total for use of contraceptive methods with less than 90% user-effectiveness (withdrawal, condoms alone, foams alone, rhythm) was 54%. Forty per cent reported *no* method use, and only 6% reported consistent use of a method with greater than 90% user-effectiveness rates. These data indicate clearly that a significant number of sexually active I.U. women are not consistently effective contraceptors.

Procedure for Obtaining Contraceptive Services

If a woman wishes to obtain a contraceptive method from the I.U. Student Health Service, she must attend a contraceptive education session prior to being given an appointment for her exam. Partners are also encouraged to attend this session, although few do. The education, at this point, consists of a film entitled "No Choice But To Choose", which describes the various medically-approved contraceptive methods, pointing out advantages and disadvantages to each (see the Appendix to this chapter). Film viewers also receive various handouts outlining the procedures for use of each different method. Afterward, a health educator answers any questions raised by the film, and provides some additional information not covered in the film, including instructions for making an appointment. If, after viewing the film, some remain uncertain about their choice of contraceptive, they are referred to a contraceptive nurse for counseling. Finally, the health educator gives each woman a gynecological history form which she must fill out and hand in before leaving. After noting on each history form that the woman has attended the educational session, the health educator forwards the histories to the Medical Records Department, where they are filed in the individual's medical chart.

Women who choose the diaphragm and contraceptive cream or jelly are instructed to make an appointment with one of the gynecological nurse clinicians or one of the staff physicians for a pelvic exam, Pap test, and diaphragm fitting. Similarly, women who wish to use oral contraceptives are referred directly to one of the nurse clinicians or physicians for a pelvic exam, Pap test, and oral contraceptive prescription. Women who choose to use contraceptive foam and condoms for their method are referred to the pharmacy where they can purchase the necessary supplies. Although contraceptive foam and condom users are not required to have a Pap test and pelvic exam in order to obtain this method, they are strongly encouraged to do so for general preventive health reasons.

EDUCATIONAL COMPONENT OF CONTRACEPTIVE SERVICES

The evolution of the contraceptive care educational session warrants some attention at this point. Prior to the establishment of the Planned Parenthood/Student Health Service clinic in 1971, all contraceptive education occurred privately between physician and patient. With the opening of the evening clinic, and the first publicized effort at providing contraceptive care, came a need for a more efficient operation in order to accomodate the increased number of women seeking contraceptive methods. Although one-to-one patient/physician education might be most desirable, it was no longer feasible in terms of time. Some type of group education/instruction seemed appropriate. Initially, patients were separated into small groups according to their preferred contraceptive choice, where they received instruction for the particular method in question. Although this arrangement solved the immediate time problem, it did not accommodate the woman who was still undecided about her contraceptive choice, or the woman who, after initially choosing one method, changed her mind and switched to a different choice.

Another problem arose with women who came to the clinic asserting, "I want to go on the pill", when they were seemingly unaware of other contraceptive alternatives. In keeping with the prevalent medical philosophy of the time, Student Health Service staff clinicians preferred to educate new potential contraceptors about all the medically-approved birth control methods, in order that each woman might then make an informed choice regarding use of a particular method.

From 1971, when the Planned Parenthood/Student Health Service clinic opened, until 1975, when the Health Service hired a health educator, the medical staff experimented with several educational techniques. First, an attempt was made to present the contraceptive information verbally. However, the need for repetition of the same material several times a week soon created a problem for the physicians—how to present essentially the same content over and over without losing enthusiasm for the subject. The next approach involved the staff in the creation of a contraceptive education videotape, which eliminated the problem of boredom for the presenters, yet seemed to create the same problem for the audience. Although the videotape was far from the perfect solution, it proved to be a sufficient step in the right direction.

In 1975, the Student Health Service hired a professional health educator who would be responsible for the education segment of the contraceptive services. At about the same time, the videotape broke, once again necessitating repeated verbal presentations on contraception instruction. Positive student response to the live presentation versus the videotape raised some question about the desirability of resurrecting the damaged tape. While the health educator continued to present the contraceptive method instruction verbally, four times a week, inquiries were made into other media alternatives. The Student Health Service staff previewed several contraceptive education films, but found most available ones geared to high school rather than college students. Finally, a film created by the UCLA Student Health Service in 1975, "IF YOU CARE, YOU'RE CAREFUL", was singled out as the most appropriate choice for use at the Student Health Service. One disadvantage of this film was that it covered both contraception and venereal diseases, which meant an abundance of information in a relatively brief film. However, using the film solved problems which outweighed the inconvenience of having a potential overload of information.

The use of this film continued until such time as resources became available for the Student Health Service staff to produce its own contraceptive education film. In early 1976, plans progressed into action. Student Health Service physicians collaborated with students on the Student Health Service Student Advisory Board and came up with a workable script. Technicians from the I.U. Audio-Visual Center agreed to direct and produce the film, and student members of the Student Advisory Board and Student Health Service staff agreed to be the "actors". The end result, titled, "NO CHOICE BUT TO CHOOSE", premiered in August, 1976. The movie centers around a young student couple who are faced with a pregnancy scare. They go to the Health Service to have a pregnancy test done, and while waiting for the test results, they see the health educator for contraceptive information. The health educator begins by reviewing the anatomy and physiology of intercourse and conception, and then proceeds to describe each medically-approved contraceptive method, noting their respective advantages and disadvantages. Once all the information has been presented, the health educator encourages the couple to choose the method which is most appropriate to their needs.

Student Reactions to the Educational Component

Student reactions to the educational film are generally positive. In the survey discussed earlier, the women who came to the Student Health Service for contraceptive care were asked specific questions about the film. Sixty-eight per cent of the clinic users felt that having to attend the film prior to making an appointment for birth control was *not* inconvenient. When asked how helpful they found the information contained in the film, 91% reported finding the information at least somewhat helpful. Eighty-two per cent reported that they did not feel the plot interfered with their ability to absorb the educational information. Interestingly, while 91% found the information helpful, 50% reported that their decision regarding which contraceptive method to use was not really influenced by the film. These findings indicate that although students find the contraceptive information in the film helpful, half of them have already decided which birth control method they want to use before they come to the Student Health Service for care.

The successful incorporation of a relevant educational film into the services provided by the Indiana University Student Health Service contributes to an increased awareness of the contraceptive alternatives available on campus. In addition to showing the film to prospective contraceptors within the Student Health Service, peer health educators arrange contraceptive film showings within their residence units. In the fall semester of 1977 alone, 35 birth control programs *outside* the Student Health Service were presented by peer health educators and Student Health Service Health Education Department staff. Following the film, presenters conduct a question/answer session and conclude by telling students about the contraceptive services available at the Student Health Service.

Our survey finding that 82% of the clinic non-users knew that contraception could be obtained at the Student Health Service provides evidence of the high level of student awareness of birth control availability on campus. However, the additional finding that over 50% of those clinic non-users do not always use contraception suggests that comprehensive contraceptive education alone does not assure consistent contraceptive use. Other variables including positive or negative emotional orientation to sexuality, attitudes towards the clinic and towards birth control in general, and degree of involvement in a serious heterosexual relationship seem to affect the consistency and effectiveness of university women's contraceptive behavior as well. Although providing detailed information about the various birth control methods is crucial, it seems broader efforts at changing individuals' emotional orientation to sexuality must precede or accompany the educational effort in order to facilitate more effective contraception among university women.

I.U. Student Health Services as a Model for a Delivery of Contraceptive Health Services

The unique nature of a university health service—an ambulatory clinic offering a wide array of preventive outpatient services—provides an ideal setting for delivery of comprehensive contraceptive care. With a team of physicians, GYN nurse clinicians, and health educators, patients have multiple opportunities to receive complete and accurate information about contraception. Ideally, the basic information about advantages and disadvantages of medically-approved birth control methods can be given through some means of audio-visual instruction—videotape, slide/tape cassette, 16 mm film, etc. The next step could include informal discussion groups for interested men and women led by a nurse clinician/ health educator team. Different sessions could be scheduled to accomodate couples, women alone, and men alone. Such sessions would give students a chance to ask specific questions regarding any aspect of sexuality including contraception. At this point, emotions, attitudes, and values about birth control could be emphasized and explored in more detail than the instructional media program permits. Values clarification exercises could be used to help students identify their feelings and attitudes about sexuality, prior to choosing a specific type of contraception. Additionally, these sessions would offer couples a chance to discuss their reactions to the information obtained in the media program. Perhaps a woman who initially thought she wanted to use foam and condoms would discover that her partner felt uncomfortable about using condoms. A couple might, upon learning of the exact time elements critical to effective diaphragm use, choose a method with less restriction. Similarly, those students who tend to be erotophobic may not effectively use a contraceptive method which is directly related to intercourse, such as foam and condoms, diaphragm and jelly, etc. Informal discussion groups, designed as follow-up to the information presentation could focus on interactions between sexual orientation and effective contraceptive use. Attempts could be made in these groups to reassess individuals' emotional orientation to sexuality by linking emotions of sexual pleasure with performance of necessary contraceptive behaviors.

Male participation in the process of contraceptive education poses a specific, although not uncommon, problem. Men who do attend the educational program tend to be involved in more serious relationships with their partners—precisely those women who tend to be the more effective contraceptors. As a result, any efforts to involve men in contraceptive education must take special care to reach those males who are not necessarily a partner of specific women patients. A reasonable approach might be to meet with members of various campus men's groups—Inter-Fraternity Council, athletic clubs and teams, etc. to publicize the contraceptive education program, stressing the dual role of the primary male contraceptive: condoms are the only birth control method which simultaneously aid in the prevention of sexually-transmitted disease. Given the current state of male contraceptive technology, it seems unrealistic to envision thorough integration of men into contraceptive education programs, particularly those geared to adolescents and young adults. After all, the majority of birth control methods require action by the female which may, but does not necessarily, involve the male, just as it is the woman who will experience pregnancy if it occurs. However, to the degree that men express interest in contraceptive education, and are willing to share in the responsibility for consistent birth control use, whether through use of condoms or by patiently encouraging use of their partner's chosen method, they can take an active role in contraceptive education.

The above mechanism for delivery of contraceptive services, audio-visual instructional session combined with informal groups designed to explore sexual feelings and attitudes, followed by comprehensive clinical care can be used as a model in settings other than university health services. Many hospital based family planning clinics or free-standing specialty clinics can provide contraceptive care in a similar manner. Even those facilities which do not enjoy the luxury of physician/nurse clinician/health educator teams can implement contraceptive services following this model. Nurses can be trained to fulfill the health educator role, and physicians can function as both clinicians and discussion group leaders with some additional training. The key to successful incorporation of comprehensive contraceptive care lies more in the philosophy of those delivering the care than in their specific titles. A true commitment to the need for dissemination of complete information about the various contraceptive methods, coupled with professionally led groups to explore patients' sexual attitudes and feelings prior to their receiving clinical contraceptive services, should facilitate more consistent and effective use of contraception by most clinic populations.

SCRIPT—CONTRACEPTIVE FILM

FIRST SCENE: Dorm room or apartment; small single room; stereo; empty bottle of wine, glasses half-filled.

Don: Why didn't you tell me last night?

Kathy: Well, if I am then it doesn't make any difference about last night.

Don: Yeah. Guess you're right. What do you want to do?

Kathy: I don't know. (Silence) Where are you going?

Don: Back to my room.

Kathy: Will you call me later?

Don: Yeah. Yeah, I guess so.

(Don departs down hall.)

SECOND SCENE: College student's room; student reading book, but not really interested. (Don walks in.)

Roommate: Hi, Don. I was beginning to wonder if I still had a roommate. Do you still pay rent around here?

Don: Why don't you just shove it? (Silence) I'm sorry. It's Kathy. She thinks she's pregnant.

(Male #1 enters the room abruptly.)

Male #1:   This is an emergency!

Roommate: What's wrong now?

Male #1:   I'm out of deodorant.

Roommate: In the bathroom.

(Male #1 enters the bathroom.)

Male #1:   Have you got anything for zits?

Don: *(to roommate)* Can you get him out of here?

(Roommate shows Male #1 to door. Male #1 walks out and mutters.)

Male #1:   Everytime I get a date my face breaks out like a Latin American Revolution.

Roommate: She thinks she's pregnant? You mean you weren't using anything?

(Don shakes head)

Roommate: You've been sleeping with this girl and you haven't been using any contraceptives.

Don: Well, I assumed she was.

Roommate: But you didn't talk to her about it?

Don: The subject never came up.

Roommate: Aren't you majoring in . . .

Don: Yeah, I'm majoring in Biology and I know all about not getting V.D. from toilet seats and I know a girl can get pregnant at any time of the month. That's not the point. The point is I don't know what the hell to do.

THIRD SCENE: Reception area of Student Health Center.

Nurse: Dr. Barnes is in room 108, right over there. While you're waiting for the results of the pregnancy test, we recommend both of you go upstairs for some birth control information.

Don: No, listen. I already . . .

(Don is interrupted by the nurse deliberately tearing off the visit form and handing it to him.)

FOURTH SCENE: Health Educator's office.

*Health
Educator:*   Hello.

Don: We want her to go on the pill.

H.E.:   The doctor has prescribed the pill for you then? (Looking at Kathy)

Kathy: No, not exactly.

H.E.:   Well, contraception involves a lot more than just the pill. Before we can issue you any contraceptive method, you'll have to receive a review of all the methods we recommend. Then you can decide for yourself which method best suits your need.

Don: Look, I've heard this before. How about if I just come back when you're finished?

H.E.:   No, we feel that birth control is never the responsibility of just one person. I think you should stay and listen.

Contraception is designed to prevent conception. Conception takes place when the egg of a female and sperm of a male unite in the female's fallopian tube. At this point, perhaps we'd better back up and examine how these two specialized cells get together in the first place.

An egg, or ovum, is released from the ovary about once a month, or every 28 days, although this can and does vary.

Kathy: It does with me.

H.E.   Once released, the egg travels through the fallopian tubes to the uterus. If sperm reach the egg when it's in the fallopian tubes, the sperm can penetrate and fertilize the egg.

Don: So the sperm meets the egg in the tube and the girl gets pregnant, right?

H.E.:   No, in order for pregnancy to take place, the fertilized egg must implant itself in the lining of the uterus. Here, growth occurs.

Kathy: And if fertilization doesn't occur or the egg doesn't implant, then the egg and the uterine lining are lost during menstruation.

H.E.:   That's right. Now about the man's role.

Don: Look, if you're going to talk about the part where sperm gets to the egg, that's the part I know really well. How about if I just . . .

H.E.:   Sperm cells are produced in the testicles of the male and are then passed through the vas deferens to the seminal vesicles where secretions are added. When sexually stimulated, the penis of the male fills with blood and becomes erect. At the peak of sexual excitation, sperm flows through the urethra and is ejaculated.

The strongest sperm can make the journey through the vagina, cervix, and uterus to the fallopian tubes in about an hour. These sperm which do get through the uterus to the fallopian tubes can live for up to four days, while those that remain in the vagina generally die within about eight hours.

I should also mention that fertilization can take place even if ejaculation occurs on the moist mucosa surrounding the vagina. This explains how someone can become pregnant when technically they have never had intercourse.

Don: Well, if the physiology lesson is over, maybe we can jump right ahead to the part about preventing pregnancy?

Kathy: You know, you're being really obnoxious. Why don't you just listen?

Don: O.K., I'm sorry.

H.E.:   Pregnancy is effectively prevented by keeping the egg and sperm from meeting. Unfortunately, there is no perfect way to accomplish this—there are drawbacks to every method.

Don: But the pill is the best.

H.E.:   No, actually the surest way of preventing pregnancy is to abstain from sexual intercourse altogether.

(Don and Kathy look at each other and then back to the Health Educator)

Don: No, I don't think so.

H.E.:   There are several effective and safe methods in use today to meet the needs of many different people. The first type of contraceptives I'll show you are designed to work against the sperm—these methods keep the sperm from reaching the egg.

The condom effectively does this. The condom or ''rubber'' is a thin sheath rolled over the erect penis prior to intercourse. The condom should fit tightly, although space should be left at the tip for sperm collection at ejaculation. Most condoms in use today have a built-in reservoir for this purpose. The condom is an extremely convenient method as it doesn't require a doctor's prescription, and no side effects have been reported, except for some psychological effects.

Kathy: Psychological effects?

H.E.: Yes, some men report a loss of sensation during intercourse when using a condom, and sometimes the time taken to roll on the condom is blamed for "breaking the mood".

Kathy: How effective is the condom?

H.E.: With 100 couples using this method for a year, you could expect about 15 pregnancies. In other words, the condom is 85% effective. However, when used in conjunction with spermicidal foam, its effectiveness can be raised to 98%.

Kathy: The foam takes care of any sperm which escape the condom?

H.E.: That's right. The foam, which is inserted no more than one half hour before intercourse, coats the vaginal walls and cervical entrance with a chemical designed to kill sperm. The foam comes in a container which is used with an applicator. The applicator fits on top of the bottle, when tilted to the side, the applicator fills with foam. The applicator is then inserted into the vagina, and the plunger is plunged, coating the vaginal walls and the cervical entrance with foam. The foam is a very convenient method too. It doesn't require any doctor's prescription and no side effects have been reported, except some allergic reactions in some people.

Kathy: You mentioned foam, but what about jellies or creams?

H.E.: We recommend the foam over the jellies and creams since it most effectively lines the vaginal walls.

Kathy: What about the diaphragm? My mother used one of these after I was born.

H.E.: The diaphragm was the most popular birth control device in this country from the turn of the century until the advent of the pill in the 1960s.

The device is simple—just a rubber dome stretched over a metal ring. It is positioned so as to "cap" the cervical entrance and provide an actual physical barrier to the invading army of sperm. It's used in conjunction with a spermicidal cream or jelly. The cream is put on the inside and the outside of the dome, so as to kill any sperm which slip past the diaphragm. Some is also put around the rim, then it is smeared into place with the finger. The diaphragm is then folded in half and inserted into the vagina. Insertion should take place no more than 2 hours before intercourse, and after intercourse has occurred, the diaphragm should be left in place for at least 8 hours.

The diaphragm is over 90% effective, but it does require a doctor's prescription. The proper fit of this device is extremely important to its effectiveness and therefore periodic checks by a physician are required. Also, a woman should have her diaphragm refitted if she has a child, a miscarriage, an abortion, or gains or loses 10 lbs. or more.

Don: Doesn't the diaphragm kind of get in the way?

H.E.:   No, if properly fitted the only thing the diaphragm blocks is the sperm.

After speaking about ways of sidetracking the sperm on its journey to the oviducts—condoms, spermicidal foam, creams, jellies and the diaphragm—there is one more method I'd like to mention. The method is withdrawal, or removal of the penis from the vagina prior to ejaculation. Even if used properly, this method has drawbacks—the largest one being a 20% risk of pregnancy due to some sperm release prior to ejaculation.

Don: It's also the cause of a lot of broken promises. . . .

H.E.:   Next, I'd like to tell you about methods that are designed to work against the egg. Rhythm is the first method which uses this strategy. Rhythm is simply abstinence from sexual intercourse during those times when the egg has been ovulated and is traveling down the oviducts. The problem here is to accurately determine when ovulation occurs. This can be done by keeping track of one's menstrual cycles for at least eight months, and then estimating the unsafe period. It can also be done by taking daily body temperature readings since the body temperature is slightly higher just after ovulation than before.

Kathy: Is this the method you recommend for physics majors?

H.E.:   Only if they have regular periods, and are willing to take a big chance.

Don: How effective is it?

H.E.:   Well, that depends on how accurately the day of ovulation, and therefore, the ''unsafe'' period can be calculated. At best this method is only 80% effective and like withdrawal, it's not one we highly recommend.

Now, I'd like to tell you about a method which is second only to abstinence in preventing pregnancy; that's the pill, or oral contraceptive. The birth control pill is designed to prevent ovulation. If ovulation doesn't occur, there is no egg to be fertilized and therefore, pregnancy cannot take place. In addition to preventing ovulation, the pill also causes a thickening of the mucus around the cervical entrance which would prevent the sperm from reaching an egg even if one should be released. This double action of the pill makes it well over 99% effective.

Don: Then the pill is the closest to the "perfect" contraceptive?

H.E.: It may be, but you must remember that the pill is a powerful drug which requires a doctor's prescription. It contains two synthetic hormones which are similar to the estrogen and progesterone found in the human body. Taking the pill creates a hormonal balance in the woman similar to the balance present during a pregnancy. In a sense, the pill creates a false pregnancy in the woman.

Kathy: But you don't have periods when you're pregnant, and when you're on the pill you do have periods.

H.E.: That's right. That's because the pill is taken for 21 consecutive days and then for seven days no pills are taken. During these 7 days the period occurs. So that in addition to preventing pregnancy, the pill also regulates the menstrual cycle and in some cases relieves cramping and heavy periods.

Unfortunately, this powerful drug is not without its negative side effects. The most common side effects include nausea, breakthrough bleeding, weight changes, and breast tenderness. Nausea, which can be accompanied by vomiting, most often occurs in the first few days of the first few cycles. Generally, this will go away with continued use of the pill. Breakthrough bleeding can be either just spotting or heavy flow. This too will usually go away with continued use of the pill. Weight changes can occur as a result of the two hormones in the pill. The estrogen causes water retention and a bloated feeling which can lead to a weight gain. The progesterone is thought to stimulate the appetite, which if isn't checked, will cause a weight gain as well. Breast tenderness is another common side effect which will generally disappear within the first few months of pill usage.

Kathy: Those side effects sound more like inconveniences. What about the blood clots I've been reading about?

H.E.: In the late 1960s it was discovered that women taking the pill faced a greater risk of developing blood clots in the legs and pelvic region that could lead to serious and even fatal complications. This condition of blood clotting is known as thromboembolism. It is thought to be caused by the estrogen in the pill. It is estimated that about 1 woman in 66,000 pill users would die as a result of estrogen-induced blood clotting. Hospitalization rates for women using the pill were found to be nine times greater than for women who didn't use the pill. Another serious side effect of the pill is that it can cause an increase in blood pressure. It's been suggested that the increase of blood pressure may be related to a higher risk of strokes in women who use the pill. Although this hasn't yet been proven, it's still thought that women using the pill do face a slightly higher risk of developing strokes than women who don't use the pill.

Don: If the pill is so dangerous, how come the government allows it to be used?

H.E.: Well, you have to look at the risk statistics in perspective. For example, there's no doubt that the risks involved in use of aspirin and penicillin are far greater than those involved with the pill.

Kathy: I've heard the pill causes cancer. Is that true?

H.E.: As yet there's been no evidence to link the pill to cancer, although this question is still being studied. But I think you should both remember that the risk due to complications from pregnancy is many times greater than the risk of death due to complications from taking the pill. Still, some women shouldn't use the pill. These are women who have had any blood clotting disorders, a stroke, severe endocrine disorder, heart disease, or cancer. The pill can also worsen some existing conditions. These would include: liver disease, kidney disease, migraine headaches, hypertension, diabetes, epilepsy, asthma, extreme menstrual irregularity, or varicose veins. A woman with any of these conditions should consult a physician to decide whether her individual case will allow for the use of oral contraception.

Don: Well, we've stopped the sperm from getting to the egg, and the egg from getting to the sperm, so if that's about everything. . . .

H.E.: No, there is one more method I'd like to tell you about. It's the Intrauterine Device.

Kathy: The IUD?

H.E.: Yes, that's right. The IUD is a plastic object of various shapes which is inserted into the uterine cavity by a physician or a trained nurse clinician. Some of the IUDs have chemical elements such as copper which increase their effectiveness. The IUD is inserted during menstruation since at that time the cervix is softer and there is no question of a pre-existing pregnancy. The IUD is inserted with an introducer, which has the device inside. The introducer is passed through the cervical opening and the plunger is plunged which pushes the IUD into place in the uterine cavity. No one is exactly sure at this time how the IUD works, although there are some theories. One theory suggests that the IUD interferes with muscle coordination necessary for egg transport down the oviduct and sperm transport up the oviduct. Another theory suggests that the presence of the IUD in the uterus alters the lining so that implantation of the fertilized egg is impossible. Although no one is certain how the IUD works, there is absolute certainty that it is an effective birth control device—up to 97% effective.

Kathy: Aren't there some pretty serious side effects with the IUD? I remember reading about an IUD that had to be removed from the market because it was dangerous.

H.E.:   That's right. The Dalkon Shield was removed from the market recently. The Dalkon Shield was used largely in women who had never been pregnant because its expulsion rates were lower than those of other IUD's. However, it was discovered that a number of women using the Dalkon Shield were developing pelvic infections after having the device in place for a few months. Extensive studies were done and the trouble was finally tracked down to being the tail of the device. The tails of the Dalkon Shield had a double-stranded filament twisted together to form a single strand. All of the other IUD's had only a single-stranded filament. For some reason the

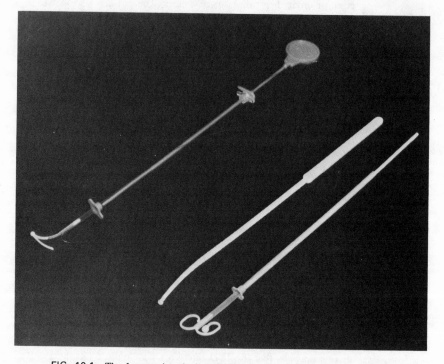

FIG. 10.1   The Intrauterine device (IUD) is made of plastic in a variety of shapes. It is inserted in the uterus during menstruation. Its presence serves to interfere with the transportion or implantation of the egg. (Photo: Marilyn Edmunds)

double twisted nature ot the Dalkon Shield's tail proved to be a good spawning ground for bacteria. Thus, naturally-present bacteria multiplied in out-of-proportion numbers, causing pelvic infection.

Currently, all of the IUD's on the market have only the single-stranded string. However, there are some other problems with IUD's on the market. Some of the common side effects include cramps, bleeding, and heavy periods. These are usually worse for women who have never been pregnant, although they can also bother women who have been pregnant.

Serious side effects of the IUD include pelvic infections, and in some very rare cases, perforation of the uterine lining. Such uterine perforation generally occurs about 1 in 2500, although in some cases surgery has been required to remove an IUD which has perforated the uterine lining. Perhaps the greatest problem with the IUD is that many women expel the device without even knowing it. For this reason, there is a nylon string which hangs down into the vagina and can be felt by the user. This string should be felt for periodically, preferably just after the menstrual period, in order to ensure that the IUD is still in place.

As you can see, there are many different ways of preventing pregnancy, and it takes a thoughtful, responsible decision to decide which method best suits your needs.

Kathy:	With all this information, it's difficult to decide at all. How do you suggest we go about making a choice?
H.E.:	Well, first of all, I would evaluate the type of contraceptive need you have. This means evaluating your sexual relationship, and asking questions like "How often do we sleep together?"
Kathy:	And how many side effects are we willing to put up with.
H.E.:	Exactly. Each method I've mentioned has both good points and bad points. It's up to each couple who wishes to avoid pregnancy to weigh both the good and bad points of each method and then decide for themselves which method best meets their individual need.
Kathy:	You mean like if a couple only slept together every third weekend then the diaphragm might be better than the daily hassle of taking a pill.
H.E.:	That's right. And it's also a good idea to consult a physician since individual health peculiarities often play an important role in the choice of the proper contraceptive. The decision to have sex should be made responsibly. So should the decision to use contraception.
Don:	Yeah. Thanks. That does us a lot of good right now.
H.E.:	Have you considered what you will do if the test is positive. (*Silence*)

FIFTH SCENE: Same as Second Scene - Don's room; two males are seated in the room talking. Roommate is at his desk with book studying.

Male #2:   Then what'd she do?

Male #1:   Well, you know, she kind of scooted up near me, rubbed up against me . . .

Roommate: Look, you guys, can you keep it down? I've got a test tomorrow!

Male #2:   Relax, relax! Take a break!

Roommate: I don't have time for a break. This is important!

Male #1:   OK, alright, we'll be quiet.

Male #2:   What'd she do then?

Male #1:   What'd she do? Then she got real close and whispered in my ear, "I gotta go home—my mother's waiting up!"

Male #2:   You know something: I think you're full of horseshit!

Roommate: Get out now. Get out!
(Two males get up and leave; Don enters. Roommate closes book and orients himself to Don.)

Roommate: How'd it go?

Don: After the test, they made us sit through some bullshit contraceptive lecture.

Roommate: Well what about the results of the test?

Don: She was going downstairs to find out. She told me she'd call as soon as she knows—it should be any time now.

Roommate: Well what will you do if she's pregnant?

Don: Listen, one problem at a time, OK?

Roommate: Sure. Listen, I gotta lot of work to do. I'm going to the library. See you in a little while, OK?

Don: Yeah.

(Roommate gets up and walks out of room. Phone rings. Don looks at it and picks it up.)

Don: Kathy?

Credits.

11

A Social Psychological Approach to Reducing Pregnancy Risk in Adolescence

Alan E. Gross
University of Maryland

Martha Bellew-Smith
St. Louis University

Editors' Note

In Chapter 11, Alan Gross and Martha Bellew-Smith propose that we must understand the social context of teenage sexuality if we are to develop ways to reduce pregnancy risk in adolescence. To begin with, the authors point out that the social conventions that govern teenagers' sexual behavior may predispose them to contraceptive neglect. For example, a traditional sexual goal for young men involves more-or-less subtle attempts to seduce a female, and such attempts could be irretrievably botched if contraceptive preparations became known to the female in question. Similarly, many teenage women do not wish to appear as if they have planned to have sex, and this desired image is also inconsistent with the discussion, acquisition, or use of contraception. In addition to such conventions, Gross and Bellew-Smith note that teenagers' sexual relationships have a social history which may affect the use of contraception. For instance, at the beginning—or the end—of a relationship, intercourse may be quite unpredictable, and this makes it difficult for teens to take contraceptive precautions. In the present chapter, the authors report on a series of interviews with young men and women who have engaged in unprotected coitus, and identify social factors that are associated with contraceptive neglect. Gross and Bellew-Smith then propose a detailed list of objectives for sex education to help teens deal with social arrangements of adolescence that may lead to pregnancy risk.

Today's adolescents are better informed, more worldly, and more sophisticated than ever. They are also responsible for approximately one million unwanted pregnancies annually and for an even greater number of pregnancy risks. We define an instance of pregnancy risk as any act of heterosexual intercourse that occurs without use of contraception at a time when either the male of the female does not want to conceive a child. The glaring paradox of an act performed willingly by people who may incur the negative consequences of that act is evident even in this brief definition. On the one hand we are baffled, incredulous, and sometimes appalled when we are informed that a couple has weighed the high costs of an unwanted pregnancy against the relatively brief pleasures of sexual intercourse, and then decide to take a risk. On the other hand, we suspect that a great many sexually active teenagers and adults (including one of the present authors) have taken at least one such poor gamble.

As social scientists we are curious about why such seemingly self-defeating behavior takes place. As concerned citizens we are interested in discovering how to prevent or lessen pregnancy risk, especially among adolescents and young adults who may be most vulnerable to risk and least prepared to cope with unwanted pregnancy.

In an attempt to begin answering both the "why it happens" and the "how to prevent it" questions, we decided to interview and distribute questionnaires to a number of sexually active young men and women who have reported at least one incident of risk. Rather than directly asking them why they took the risk (a question we believe they would find difficult to answer without inventing rationalizations and justifications), we quizzed them about circumstances in which the unprotected sex act occurred. Thus, although we will offer a few general speculations about why people take pregnancy risks, most of the ideas presented in this paper are distilled from summaries of the circumstances surrounding the events reported by our respondents.

Moreover, because this paper is based on information obtained from only 90 open-ended interviews and questionnaires, and because most of the respondents were mid-western, white, single, heterosexual undergraduate men and women, we are not confident that the responses summarized here are either comprehensive or generalizable to all adolescents. Nonetheless, many of the interviews were extensive (1–2 hours), rich in detail, and strong in feeling. Although this paper does not attempt to classify or quantify the responses systematically, we hope to stimulate research which can lead to developing programs for the reduction of adolescent pregnancy risk.

Because we are social psychologists, we attempted to elicit descriptions of the social context in which risks occurred; we were less concerned about demographic characteristics, contraceptive technology, and the physiology of the sexual act itself. Specifically, our interviews focused on the interactions between sexual partners as reflected by the individual respondents. Our survey included questions related to discussion between partners about sex and contraception, circumstances leading to incidents of unprotected sex, differences in these factors between short-term and long-term relationships, etc.

It will become evident that a social analysis of sexual behavior which is difficult even when there are shared long-term goals as in a mature cooperative marriage, becomes even more difficult when the goals of potential sex partners are not similar or even complementary, as is often the case in adolescent hetero-sexual interaction. The most frequent theme related to dissimilar goals that emerged in our interviews is that males and females often develop differing expectations stemming from their distinctive sex-role socialization experiences.

In the following paragraphs, we discuss a number of common social behaviors that we believe are closely related to the high incidence of unwanted pregnancy among today's teen population. It will be seen that these behaviors are all related to the general reluctance to acknowledge sexuality as a legitimate and important personal quality for adolescents in our society. We then suggest how awareness of social factors can reduce risk, and finally we offer some general and specific suggestions for implementing educational programs aimed at reducing the incidence of unprotected sexual intercourse and associated unplanned pregnancies.

Few couples talk about sex before they do it.   Many writers (Gagnon & Simon, 1973; Gross, 1978) have suggested that men and boys often view sex and sexual conquest as an instrumental act related to obtaining recognition from peers. In our survey, whether males sought sex for peer recognition, for personal satisfaction, or both, many of them believed that a frank discussion of sex or contraception could reduce chances of "success." For example, one man believed that discussion before having sex for the first time with a woman would cause her to interpret his intentions as too physical or sexual. And, a number of men viewed *any* discussion related to sex before a point where the partners are virtually committed to sexual intercourse as alerting the woman to sexual intentions which in turn would cause her to retreat.

Another man reported his hesitancy to suggest that a potential sex partner begin using contraceptive pills because she might misinterpret his intentions as more serious than they were. His concern was that his partner might understand his suggestion that she start using pills, daily on a month by month basis, as signifying a relationship of relatively long duration.

These kinds of comments reveal an ambivalence that plagues male adolescents in relation to contraception and sexuality. On the one hand, they want sexual activity; on the other hand, they are concerned that openly expressing their desire to contracept might (1) lower probabilities of "scoring," and (2) be misunderstood as signifying an unwanted serious or long-term relationship. In attempting to avoid both lowering the probability of sex and creating misunderstandings, these men resolved their ambivalence by engaging in a great number of incidents of unprotected sexual intercourse.

The male perception that early discussion of sex or contraception will reduce sexual opportunities is not wholly inaccurate in that it is corroborated by some of our female informants. When asked if they had discussed sex or contraception with their partners before engaging in sexual activity, some of our female adolescents insisted that many sexual acts "just happened to them" without forethought. Of course it is difficult, if not impossible, to have discussions about behaviors that "just happen" before they occur. This spontaneous view of sex thus becomes a frequently used female rationale for not taking contraceptive precautions.

The general phenomenon of failing to discuss sex before participating in it may be subsumed under a cultural "sexual mystique" which functions to reduce female (and some male) sex guilt by creating an illusion of unintentional sex. This sexual mystique includes a strong preference for impulsiveness and spontaneity as contrasted with careful planning. In compliance with the mystique that sex, like chemical reactions, just happens, most seduction artists fastidiously avoid any explicit mention of the proposed sexual activity. Although the seducer is most often male, his partner may collude by failing to acknowledge the sexual content of their interaction (even to herself), preferring instead to be "swept off her feet."

A norm which prescribes male responsibility for sexual initiation (Carlson, 1976; Peplau, Rubin, & Hill, 1977) undoubtedly contributes to the failure to communicate before intercourse. It effectively removes one of the potential communicators, the female, because it is often considered appropriate for her (although she stands most to gain by the use of contraception) to stand mute rather than be perceived as taking the sexual initiative. The traditional male role also requires men to be in control and to be knowledgeable, especially about sex (Masters & Johnson, 1966, p. 87; Gross, 1978). Because talking about contraception may reveal their ignorance, some males are probably inhibited from broaching the topic.

Finally, the general inappropriateness of talking about sex in our culture (Baron & Byrne, 1977, pp. 454ff.) certainly includes an obviously sex-related topic such as contraception. All of these forces conspire to inhibit potential sex partners from talking about and planning for contraception at precisely the time when they most need it, and explains why less than one-third of our respondents reported that they discussed sex before actually "doing it."

Social pressures for acceptance and fear of rejection lead to risk taking. Real or imagined social pressures impinging on teenage men and women often tip the scales in favor of "taking a chance" with unprotected sexual intercourse. As previously noted, men may believe (correctly) that if they do not take advantage of an immediate sexual opportunity, there is reduced chance that the woman will willingly participate in sex after a cooling-off period during which contraception is considered and obtained.

FIG.11.1.   Few couples talk about sex before they do it. (Photo by Clark Brown).

Women face similar pressures. An adolescent woman confronted with a sexually assertive and socially desirable male may fear (perhaps accurately) that continuation of an incipient relationship with him is contingent on fulfilling his sexual expectations even before contraception has been secured. For example, one female in our survey told us she worried that the man she was seeing would drop her if she didn't have sex with him. In these circumstances, fear of losing a potential social relationship or being excluded from a social group may predominate over the dangers of "taking a chance."

For teens who are especially vulnerable to fear of rejection, this results in a very unpleasant avoidance-avoidance conflict. One unsatisfactory means of resolving this conflict is to distort and enhance the safety of such inferior "contraceptive" techniques as rhythm and withdrawal. These kinds of concerns were especially prevalent among respondents involved in the earliest stages of a relationship.

Young adults are reluctant to identify themselves as sexually active.   A common scenario in fiction about adolescent boys is the purchasing of unneeded condoms with the intent of flaunting them to peers as false symbols of sexual maturity. However, adolescents are often extremely reluctant to display such bravado to others, especially parents. Our respondents, especially females, often expressed fear that their possession of contraceptive pills, diaphragms, condoms, or other paraphernalia would be discovered and lead to their unmasking as sexually active. This fear, which may have a basis in fact, tends to reduce the likelihood that contraceptives will be purchased, and, if they are purchased, they may be hidden in inaccessible or inconvenient locations. The tense scene in Roth's *Goodbye Columbus* where Brenda's mother discovers her daughter's diaphragm in a dresser probably depicts one of our respondents' worst fears.

For example, one young man was apprehensive about hiding contraceptives in his room which was regularly cleaned by his mother. He was even unwilling to carry condoms in his wallet because they produced an unmistakable circular impression which was visible through the leather. He considered storing contraceptives in his own car, but feared his mother might, by accident, discover them there. Although this man's plight may seem extreme, we interviewed many teens who, though sexually active, typically concealed or at least did not voluntarily reveal this fact to family members with whom they lived. Worry about discovery was a frequently cited reason for not purchasing contraceptive devices.

It has been suggested that female ambivalence about sex sometimes becomes focused on contraception. Because planning contraception is clearly an acknowledgment of anticipated sex, it forces women to consciously define themselves as sexual beings. Because women traditionally have not been viewed, even by themselves, as sexual beings until after marriage, considering contraception may engender a good deal of guilt. Unfortunately, a common means of dealing with such guilt is to avoid actual consideration of contraception and to therefore maintain an untarnished, sexually inactive self-image, often until it is too late. When asked about factors leading up to unprotected sex, several of our female respondents answered that they usually did not premeditate or anticipate sexual experiences even though they had engaged in sex in the past. Some individuals seem to perceive each sexual act as an exception; therefore they fail to devise an appropriate contraceptive program. These survey responses reveal a reluctance to acknowledge sexuality as an integral or worthy part of the self.

Risk taking varies with developmental stages of relationships.   As might be expected, our respondents reported that they were more likely to talk about contraception and to avoid pregnancy risks in the context of a long-term intimate relationship. Both men and women admitted that they were especially likely to be irresponsible when engaging in sexual relationships with casual acquaintances. To follow up on these interview responses, Bellew-Smith and Orlofsky (unpublished) administered a measure of relationship depth to a separate sample of college males. They found that this measure was significantly and positively related to self-reported contraceptive behavior. (See also Fisher, Byrne, Edmunds, Miller, Kelley, & White, 1979; Foreit & Foreit, 1978).

In a number of subjects, contraceptive behavior differed depending on the stage of development of their relationships. Contraception was used least often at the beginning and end of relationships. These low levels of contraceptive practice seem to be associated with inhibitions about discussing sexuality and contraception in the early stages and with emotional turmoil in the later stages of a relationship. Ironically, new and ending relationships are usually least well equipped for dealing with unwanted pregnancy.

Awareness of social factors can reduce risk.   A primary reason for extracting the social themes noted above is that we believe that increasing *consciousness* of the social factors that can lead to unprotected sex can substantially reduce pregnancy risk. Although people tend to speak in conscious decision-making metaphors when describing a couple who chooses to engage in sex, we know that a choice to have sex is not always carefully weighed. In fact, especially among teens, such choices are sometimes not even premeditated or "conscious." The term "mutually consenting" which is often applied to sexual interaction does not necessarily mean that both partners are aware of their individual or social motives for relating sexually.

It is not enough to simply understand some of the social phenomena and pressures that lead teens to take unacceptable pregnancy risks. An essential step is to design effective educational and informational programs aimed at junior and senior high school students (and in some cases their parents). Many school districts already include family and sex education in their curricula, and most of today's teenagers somehow have managed to acquire the basic sexual facts of life before they reach puberty. Unfortunately, however, the teachers, parents, and others who transmit these facts often limit instruction to purely mechanical and physical aspects of sexual intercourse and conception.

It is true that sex education is not always strictly limited to simple birds and bees descriptions, but our point is that in the home and in the classroom, physical facts are emphasized when sex is discussed. Sometimes, it is almost as if sex acts were analytically removed from the human beings who are involved in sexual expression and communication. When pregnancy risk and contraception are introduced into sex education, a physical-mechanical emphasis remains the rule.

Many sex education programs do include units dealing with ethical and social issues. And many teens are at least somewhat aware that the chances of engaging in unplanned and unprotected sex increase with certain physical situational factors: e.g., use of alcohol, marijuana, drugs; absence of parents from home; late in the evening when tired.

While we endorse the continuation and expansion of these existing programs, we recommend that more of them include discussions of social contexts in which sex is likely to occur. It may be obvious to adults that there is much more to heterosexual interaction than the connection of penis and vagina; yet the complex social transactions that may lead to unprotected sexual intercourse are often omitted when adolescents are socialized into the sexual world.

Goals of an educational program.   Thus, a major goal of educational programs that include social factors should be to increase sensitivity to the situations in which unplanned sex may occur. But a program designed to reduce pregnancy risk must go beyond sensitizing adolescents to the kinds of general social psychological variables outlined above. A number of specific suggestions, not necessarily in order of importance, about topics which can augment general consciousness-raising follow:

1. Establishing the legitimacy of pre-sex talking about sexuality *and* contraception. Role playing and other techniques may be used to develop skills which enhance direct communication, but avoid presumptuousness or intrusiveness.
2. Helping individuals to acknowledge their own sexuality and the possibility that they may be vulnerable to pregnancy risks in certain circumstances. Emphasizing that pregnancy risk is not something that happens only to "other" more careless people—it can and probably will happen to anyone in given situations.
3. Rejection of seduction as a legitimate activity. Encouraging direct assertive communication about sex including the possibility of saying "no" or "wait" and learning how to accept "no" or "wait" from a partner.
4. Legitimizing regular purchase, carrying, and convenient placement of contraceptives even in periods of sexual dormancy; keeping contraceptives close to places where sexual activity is likely to occur. In cases where concealment is an issue in a family environment, it may be desirable to educate parents.
5. Provide intellectual concepts to help explain to teens just how a person can weigh an unwanted pregnancy (with its attendant responsibility of nine months of gestation and eighteen years of child rearing) or abortion against a relatively brief act of sexual intercourse and then still decide to take a risk. Behaviorists have demonstrated that in many areas of human activity immediate reinforcers are more powerful than serious negative long-term consequences. These concepts can be related to specific incidents in adolescent social-sexual experience.

6. Debunking myths about male sexuality, especially the myth that men "need" sex and will "suffer" if frustrated. This myth may be held widely by both men *and* women.

7. Sanctioning and destigmatizing means of sexual satisfaction other than intercourse during vulnerable periods, e.g., oral sex, mutual masturbation. Sanctioning autoerotic activities including masturbation.

8. Encouraging male partners to share responsibility for contraception and prevention of unwanted pregnancies including, but not limited to, joint medical appointments, joint participation in contraceptive techniques such as injecting foam or placing condom, male responsibility for purchasing medication, verbal checking on whether or not nonvisible contraceptives, e.g., diaphragm, are in use, allowing/encouraging female partner to discontinue a method which is convenient for him but may be contraindicated, bothersome, or dangerous for her, e.g., IUD or contraceptive pill.

FIG. 11.2.   Encouraging male partners to share responsibility for contraception is an important educational goal, and these eye-catching posters of pregnant men make this point quite clearly. (Reproduced courtesy of Pharmacists Planning Service, Inc., P. O. Box 1336, Sausalito, CA. 94965. Posters are available upon request. © Pharmacists Planning Service, Inc.).

ACKNOWLEDGMENTS

We are grateful to Susan K. Green for helpful suggestions and comments.

REFERENCES

Baron, R. A., & Byrne, D. *Social psychology: Understanding human interaction.* Boston: Allyn & Bacon, 1977.

Carlson, J. E. The sexual role. In F. I. Nye (Ed.), *Role structure and analysis of the family.* Beverly Hills, CA: Sage Publications, 1976.

Fisher, W. A., Byrne, D., Edmunds, M., Miller, C. T., Kelley, K., & White, L. A. Psychological and situation-specific correlates of contraceptive behavior among university women. *Journal of Sex Research,* 1979, *15,* 38–55.

Foreit, K. G., & Foreit, J. R. Correlates of contraceptive behavior among unmarried U.S. college students. *Studies in Family Planning,* 1978, *9,* 169–174.

Gagnon, J., & Simon, W. *Sexual conduct: The social sources of sexuality.* Chicago: Aldine, 1973.

Gross, A. E. The male role and heterosexual behavior. *Journal of Social Issues,* 1978, *34,* 87–107.

Masters, W. H., & Johnson, V. E. *Human sexual response.* Boston: Little, Brown, 1966.

Peplau, L. A., Rubin, Z., & Hill, C. T. Sexual intimacy in dating relationships. *Journal of Social Issues,* 1977, *33,* 86–109.

12 Adolescent Contraception: Summary and Recommendations

William A. Fisher
The University of Western Ontario

Editors' Note

A great deal of theory and research on adolescent contraception has been discussed in this volume. In our concluding chapter, William Fisher summarizes a number of the major findings that have been reported, and provides research-based recommendations for a new kind of sex and contraceptive education that is directed at controlling teen pregnancy. Throughout this paper, however, it is stressed that the problem of adolescent pregnancy will require political as well as pedagogical solutions. In fact, while many believe that all that is needed is a breakthrough in sex education technology (on the order of a "silver bullet"), Fisher suggests that what is needed just as much are political breakthroughs to permit and encourage sex education programs to combat teenage pregnancy. The chapter ends with a note on the desirability of researchers and practitioners joining their efforts to understand and improve adolescent contraception.

Thus far in our discussion, it has been established that American adolescents now engage in premarital intercourse in greater numbers and at an earlier age than ever before. Although few wish to conceive, the majority of these sexually active teens do *not* always use effective means of contraception. Predictably enough, this results in large numbers of unplanned teenage pregnancies each year—pregnancies that lead to hundreds of thousands of abortions, out-of-wedlock births, and hasty marriages annually, as well as elevated levels of child abuse by teenage parents, maternal suicide, and the like. What is more, the problem of adolescent pregnancy is part of a global population explosion that may threaten our planet with Malthusian disaster.

In an effort to understand and ultimately reduce the problem of adolescent pregnancy, our contributors have presented theory and research that deal with teens' use (or nonuse) of contraception. Now, it seems useful to conclude this discussion with a summary of some of the major findings, and with recommendations for change. Following the general outline of the Sexual Behavior Sequence (discussed in Chapter 1), we will consider how contraceptive behavior may be affected by informational, emotional, and imaginative factors. In the context of each, existing barriers to teens' use of birth control are reviewed, and interventions are proposed to remedy contraceptive neglect. Finally, a general strategy is suggested which combines research and intervention to help understand and improve adolescent contraception.

INFORMATIONAL BARRIERS TO CONTRACEPTION

Summary of the Findings

Developmental issues.   In Chapter 5, George Cvetkovich and Barbara Grote pointed out that "A major task of the adolescent years . . . is the achievement of psychosexual maturity and competence. This achievement involves the ability to think about one's sexuality in an objective and rational manner" (p. 110). According to evidence that was reviewed, however, many teens appear to become sexually active before they become capable of the sort of rational thought that is required for the practice of contraception. Thus, adolescents may deny their own or others' sexual activity, they may arrange to be "overcome" by lust or by liquor, and they may be certain that they are immune from pregnancy— even as they have sex without using contraception. The information that young teens can accept about their own sexuality may lag far behind their precocious behavior. It seems to take time for adolescents to formulate a new self-image which accepts the fact that they are sexually active. When this happens, and teens begin to think about their sexuality in an objective way, their contraceptive practices improve greatly. Until teens are able to think about themselves as sexual beings, however, they may be developmentally unprepared for responsible contraception.

Ignorance as a barrier to contraception.   It is obvious that many adolescents are ignorant of the facts about contraception. Data reported in preceding chapters show that some teenagers cannot identify the fertile days in a woman's menstrual cycle, others insist that the diaphragm must be removed *immediately* after coitus, and still others have never learned even a basic vocabulary of sexual terms. Moreover, some adolescents are so misinformed as to believe that contraception is unnecessary, or that it is too expensive, too hard to get, or illegal. Such ignorance does not, in general, prevent teens from having intercourse. Added to the effects of psychosexual immaturity, however, ignorance does seem to limit the effectiveness of teens' use of contraception.

Despite the fact that teenagers may be dangerously uninformed, parents are quite ambivalent about providing sex education in the home. For example, a near majority of teens state that they would prefer to learn about sex from their parents, but very few of them ever get the opportunity to do so. And, although most Americans claim to favor sex education in the schools, such courses are often so restricted in scope as to be ineffective, or they are offered long after teens first need them, or they are absent altogether.

The evidence reported in this volume converges to suggest two tentative conclusions about sex education. First, the personal and societal costs of sexual ignorance are enormous, whether calculated in human or financial terms. Second, research shows that existing methods of sex education are effective in increasing teens' knowledge about sex and contraception. And, as pointed out by A. R. Allgeier (Chapter 7) and Stuart Oskamp and Burton Mindick (Chapter 4), teens who are knowledgeable about sex tend to have intercourse at a *later* age and to be more effective users of contraception. Nonetheless, research is still needed to establish a direct link between sex education and teens' use of birth control.

Ideological barriers to contraception.   Many adolescents have personal beliefs or opinions that are inconsistent with responsible contraception. For example, in Chapter 3 Paul Abramson discussed the formation of sex- and contraception-inhibiting principles, formed early in life, that may have rather general negative effects on adolescents' use of birth control. And, in Chapter 8, Elizabeth Allgeier identified the components of an "anticontraception ideology." Some teens, for instance, believe that the use of contraception will mark them as promiscuous, or will ruin their relationships with the opposite sex, or will destroy their spontaneity in sex, or their physical pleasure, etc. Other adolescents may be opposed to contraception because their religion forbids most forms of birth control (ignoring, for the moment, that their religion also forbids premarital sex). And, teens may have beliefs that are not directly sexual in nature, but which nonetheless have implications for contraception. For example, some teenagers have a general belief that they have little control over what happens to them. Such persons, it seems, would be unlikely to use contraception to try to control their reproductive destiny, or that of a partner. Anticontraception ideology, then, involves subjectively held beliefs that may work against adolescents' use of contraception.

Recommendations for Change

The findings that we have reviewed suggest that, from the standpoint of teens' information and expectancies, there are several barriers to adolescent contraception. First, younger teens may not be mature enough to think of themselves as sexually active, and consequently they cannot make rational decisions about contraception. Second, many adolescents appear to lack adequate knowledge about reproduction and birth control. Finally, some teenagers have anti-contraception beliefs that are incompatible with teens' use of birth control. The consequences of this situation are familiar: contraceptive neglect, teen pregnancy, and a constellation of related problems.

What, then, can be done to overcome these barriers to responsible contraception? The solution that we propose involves a new kind of sex and contraceptive education in the public schools. The object of such education is to help teens become well informed and responsible sexual decision makers. It goes without saying, of course, that we are not the first to suggest an educational solution to the problem of teen pregnancy. Nevertheless, adequate sex and contraceptive education is still *not* available to most teenagers, and until it becomes available, teens will remain in jeopardy and books such as this will continue to argue for educational reform.

Efforts to introduce sex education in the schools seem to involve at least two separate issues. First, sex education is a *political question,* in the sense that instituting—or denying—such programs is subject to the public will. Thus, our recommendations must consider arguments that can be used to persuade citizens that sex education is desirable and that the status quo is deplorable. In our society, it is clear that political approval must be secured before large scale sex education can begin.

Beyond the politics of sex education, we must also consider *pedagogical issues* related to this question. Specifically, it is necessary to identify what is to be taught, as well as when and how this material is to be communicated, etc. Moreover, procedures for monitoring and adjusting the effects of sex education must be built into each such intervention. With these issues in mind, let us consider the political and pedagogical requirements of sex education.

Contraceptive Education: Political Issues

In the United States and Canada, contraceptive education has always been a politically and legally volatile issue. For example, when the physician Robert Knowlton published the first American book about birth control in 1832, he was sent to jail for 3 months at hard labor (Guttmacher, 1973). Later, as we learned, the Comstock laws made contraceptive education in the U.S. virtually illegal until 1936. At present, however, legal restrictions have eased, sex education has become more widely accepted, and a case can now be made for instituting contraceptive education in the public schools on a large scale.

In common with most interventions that are proposed in this chapter, political advocacy of contraceptive education involves a two-part strategy. First, existing barriers—in this case, political opposition to sex education—must be removed. Then, favorable conditions—in this case, political support for sex education—must be instated. We will now discuss the removal of political barriers to contraceptive education, and some of the arguments that can be used to create political support for such education.

Removing political barriers to contraceptive education. There are at least two political arguments against sex education that can now be dismissed on the basis of research evidence. First, many believe that the family—not the schools—is the appropriate setting for sex education of any kind. The research findings on this topic may be made clear to all parties concerned: most teens simply do *not* learn about sex at home. This does not seem to limit their sexual activity, although it may well interfere with teens' use of contraception. In essence, the home is now part of the problem of teenage sexual ignorance, and it may be unrealistic to believe that it can quickly become part of the solution. While parental input must be sought out and valued, school based programs may, for the present, be the most efficient means of providing sex education to teenagers.

There is a second argument against sex education that we can also judge in light of research evidence. Many are concerned that teens who know about contraception will become promiscuous, since they are equipped to avoid the consequences that are thought to deter other teens from having sex. Several kinds of data have been adduced to show that this is *not* the case. First, in Chapter 8, Elizabeth Allgeier noted that most teens have sex first, and seek contraceptive information later. Thus, sex education could help prevent unwanted pregnancies among the many teens who are already sexually active but who remain uninformed about contraception. Moreover, studies of teens who have obtained contraception show increases in frequency of intercourse, but *not* in the number of partners with whom they have sex.

A second line of evidence concerning the presumed knowledge—promiscuity link comes from research that has directly examined the effect of sex education on students' sexual behavior. For example, Zuckerman and his associates (1976) found that college men who took a course in human sexuality increased somewhat their level of sexual activity. It is worth noting, however, that these men were *already* more permissive than a comparison group before the course began, they were quite a bit older (in their early 20s) than our intended public school clientele for sex education, and they had deliberately chosen to take the course in question. For these reasons, the Zuckerman, Tushup, & Finner findings may be quite limited in their generality. What, for example, might be the effects on sexual behavior of a *high school* course on family planning? Since this is precisely the intervention that we have in mind, the question is a critical one. Fortunately, a doctoral dissertation by Norman West (1976), cited in Chapter 7, focused on just this issue. Because it is one of the only studies to examine the effects of contraceptive education on the sexual behavior of high school students, we will discuss this investigation in some detail.

In his doctoral research, West surveyed some 2,214 high school students in

London, Canada. This sample included nearly 80% of all students then enrolled in the high schools that were chosen for study. About half of these students had taken a year long course in Physical and Health Education which, incidentally, included a "Family Planning Unit." As part of this unit, detailed instruction concerning birth control was provided, and in many cases actual devices (I.U.D.s, condoms, etc.) were passed around the classroom. In addition to the Family Planning Unit, it should be noted, quite a few of the students had also received some sex education in elementary school.

West classified each student in the survey with respect to whether they had taken the Family Planning Unit, or had received elementary school sex education. Self-reports were then obtained concerning the number of persons with whom students had sexual intercourse during the past 6 weeks. These figures are presented in Table 12.1, as a function of students' sex education background.

Data analysis showed that students who took the Family Planning Unit—compared to those who did not—had more sexual partners in the last 6 weeks. Does this mean that contraceptive education causes promiscuity among high school students? We think not, for two reasons. First, although the observed differences were statistically significant, practically speaking the differences seem to be trivial. All in all, students who took the Family Planning Unit reported something like .06 "more" sexual partners across a month and a half. Second, even the miniscule differences that did surface may well have been exaggerated by a tendency for permissive students to take the course, and for sexually conservative pupils to stay away. Whatever the ultimate cause of these differences, West's large-scale study provides an important piece of information. *At worst,* it seems that explicit contraceptive education may have only quite trivial effects upon high school students' sexual behavior. In light of such objective evidence, concern that sex education causes promiscuity seems to be unwarranted.

Creating a political climate that favors contraceptive education.   It may not be enough to remove political barriers to contraceptive education. Rather, it also seems necessary to obtain legislative and community support to *favor* such education actively. There are a number of ways to work toward this kind of political climate, and we believe that a case in favor of contraceptive education can be made in terms that have traditionally appealed to citizens of democratic societies. In particular, it can be argued that access to contraceptive education is consistent with the highest principles of democracy, and it can also be pointed out that contraceptive education could lead to economic benefits for the public and private sectors. Now, let us briefly consider each line of reasoning.

One rationale that favors contraceptive education emphasizes that this is a highly democratic way to deal with the problem of teenage pregnancy. Specifically, it is assumed in most western democracies that individuals have a right to the facts about matters that affect their lives. It is thought that persons so informed may freely make intelligent decisions about such issues. In contrast,

TABLE 12.1

High School Students' Sexual Behavior as a Function of Their Sex Education Background[1]

		Students Who Had Sex Education in Elementary School		Students Who Did Not Have Sex Education in Elementary School	
	Grade	*Students Who Had Family Planning Unit in High School*	*Students Who Did Not Have Family Planning Unit in High School*	*Students Who Had Family Planning Unit in High School*	*Students Who Did Not Have Family Planning Unit in High School*
Question: With how many different people did you have sexual intercourse in the last six weeks? (1 = none, 2 = one, 3 = two, 4 = three, 5 = more than three)	11	2.150	1.826	2.182	1.650
	12	1.656	1.712	1.688	1.471
	13	1.819	1.529	1.486	1.636
	11-13 Average	1.795	1.753	1.670	1.593

Note: This table presents the responses of 662 students, of the 2,214 sampled, who indicated nonvirgin status.

[1] After West (1976)

restricting access to information is generally frowned upon, and such practices are associated with totalitarian regimes. Indeed, Thomas Jefferson said of the free diffusion of knowledge that "No other sure foundation can be devised, for the preservation of freedom and happiness."

Does present day education provide teens with the facts about contraception, so that they can make informed judgments about a matter that is of great importance to them? The data discussed in Chapter 7 suggest emphatically that—democratic principles notwithstanding—most teens do not have access to contraceptive education. This may occur as the result of action, as when a school board decides against sex education, or it may occur as the result of inaction, through failure to change the status quo. Either way, the result is sexual ignorance and the problems that derive from such ignorance.

It might also be mentioned that democratic principles would seem to require full and fair presentation of *all* relevant facts. The sex education which is available to teens, however, does not always conform to such standards. In fact, while curriculum guides for most subjects prescribe what *must* be taught, those for sex education classes may prescribe what must *not* be taught. Often enough, the verboten material involves information on birth control. For example, it was reported in Chapter 7 that of those few teens who had sex education in high school, most were taught about sexual intercourse but most did *not* learn about contraception. This curious selection of topics is not unlike teaching student drivers about the accelerator, but avoiding all mention of brakes.

There is a second line of reasoning that advocates contraceptive education, and it focuses on the economic benefits to be derived from such action. It is a truism that present levels of contraceptive neglect are enormously costly. For example, in 1974 there were about 1,000,000 pregnancies to teenage women in the U.S. Some 210,000 of these pregnancies led to out-of-wedlock births, 280,000 were conceived before marriage but resulted in marital births, and about 270,000 pregnancies—mostly to unmarried teens—ended in abortion (Alan Guttmacher Institute, 1976). These pre-marital conceptions, out-of-wedlock births, and abortions may be assumed to represent unwanted pregnancies. At $1,000 per birth and $250 per abortion, the total cost of dealing with these unwanted pregnancies in 1974 comes to $557,500,000 for medical procedures alone. This estimate is conservative, in that it does not include work days lost, the cost of complications, the expense of raising to maturity 490,000 children who were conceived before marriage, welfare costs, etc.

It is interesting to compare this staggering expense to the cost-per-year for an equivalent number of women to be protected from pregnancy by oral contraceptives ($30,400,000), the diaphragm ($22,800,000), the I.U.D. ($38,000,000), or condoms and foam ($68,400,000; all cost projections are based on estimates given by Hyde, 1979). Theoretically, the effective practice of contraception could have saved at least $489,000,000 in 1974 alone. Needless to say, neither the limited resources of most teens nor the public coffers can easily bear this kind of excess expense. Thus, citizens and elected officials can be made aware of two facts. First, the status quo with respect to adolescent contraception involves extraordinary—and needless—expense. Second, educational programs which improve teens' use of contraception may ultimately save vast sums of money for individuals and for public institutions.

The cost saving potential of contraceptive education, incidentally, need not be used only as a general political argument that may one day lead to change. The same reasoning can be used to persuade specific health care institutions—who bear much of the excess cost just discussed—to take a more active role in contraceptive education. For example, if statistics were collected to show an insurance company or health maintenance organization that abortions were costing it X million dollars a year, they might be motivated to include contraceptive counseling as part of preventive health care for teens. What is more, the consumers of health care—to whom excess costs are also passed—may support contraceptive education as a cost saving measure.

Finally, it is worth noting that contraceptive education would expand the youth market for birth control products and result in profits for manufacturers, distributors, and retailers. Members of the private sector may thus be encouraged to support—politically and financially—programs in contraceptive education. In fact, it could be suggested that contraceptive neglect is largely a marketing problem that can be solved for the personal benefit of millions of teens and the corporate benefit of private industry.

In summary, we have proposed arguments for removing political barriers to contraceptive education, and for creating instead support for these programs. It was pointed out that contraceptive education does not seem to have the deleterious effects that are often ascribed to it, and that teenagers in our democracy may be entitled to such education. Moreover, programs of this nature could save vast sums of money for health care providers and consumers, and contraceptive education may expand the birth control market and result in profit for the private sector. These arguments are examples of the sort of case that may be made to favor contraceptive education. They reflect our belief that eliminating sexual ignorance is a political as well as an educational task. It would be naive, however, to think that the issues involved will be settled by the weight of any particular argument. Rather, political strategy and commitment—as well as the merits of the case—will determine whether education is used to help solve the problem of adolescent pregnancy.

Contraceptive Education: Pedagogical Issues

In addition to securing political approval, it is necessary to decide just what should be included in contraceptive education programs. In this regard, our discussion of informational barriers to contraception suggests at least three problems that education may help to remedy. First, developmental limitations seem to exist with respect to teens' ability to see themselves as sexual beings with contraceptive needs. Second, many adolescents are ignorant of crucial facts about sex and contraception. Third, many teenagers have acquired beliefs that are inconsistent with the use of contraception. In the next few pages, we will discuss educational strategies that are designed to overcome each of these informational barriers to contraception.

✗ *Dealing with psychosexual immaturity.*   Adolescents may have intercourse long before they are able to deal with their own sexuality on a rational basis. Contraception is not used, for this would require self-admission of teens' sexual involvement. This may continue until teens form a self-image which accepts their sexual activity and allows for contraceptive planning. What kind of educational strategy can be devised to overcome this developmental lag? Since we are concerned with what happens when sexual activity precedes psychosexual maturity, two possibilities are apparent. Education may seek to postpone teens' initiation to intercourse, or it can try to help teens think about sex rationally at an earlier age. A few examples of programs that work towards these goals are described next.

One way to insure that teens handle sex and contraception responsibly is to encourage them to postpone intercourse until they are older (i.e., 17 or 18 instead of 13 or 14). As noted in Chapter 5, the older teens are at first intercourse, the more likely they are to use contraception, presumably because older teens accept their sexuality and can plan for birth control in advance. How can teens be encouraged to "wait until later"? Obviously, such encouragement must come before most teens in a particular locale have begun to have sex. Beyond timing interventions appropriately, teens must be convinced that there are disadvantages to early sexual involvement and that there are advantages to delay. It can be suggested that the more mature teens are when they begin a sexual relationship, the better able they will be to handle interpersonal, sexual, and contraceptive demands. And, from their own point of view, teens may have good reasons for delaying intercourse. Educational programs could benefit by eliciting such rationales from adolescents. After all, teens may be most impressed with their own advice. Finally, it can be made clear to younger teenagers that advice to delay intercourse is not the same as traditional warnings against ever having premarital sex. The former can be presented as counsel to help teens run their own sex lives, while the latter is often dismissed as someone else's attempt to control teens' affairs.

Pointing out the virtues of mature sexual relationships is not all that we can do to help teens delay intercourse. They also need to become aware of certain "social traps" that can work against the postponement of intercourse. Such traps may include dishonest seduction strategies, the custom of bartering sex for affection (and vice versa), the convention of never talking about sex beforehand, and other practices that are discussed in Chapter 11. Once teens can recognize such pressures to have sex, they need a great deal of social finesse to tell a potential lover "no" or "not yet." Educational programs must help teens acquire the skills that are needed to decline sex assertively. Thus, teaching adolescents to recognize and deal with social pressures to have sex may provide an additional means to help them postpone intercourse.

A second way of dealing with the lag between onset of sexual intercourse and onset of maturity is to design interventions that, in effect, hasten psychosexual maturation. According to Cvetkovich and Grote, if teens are helped to accept their own sexuality, they will be able to deal with it more rationally, and this would facilitate responsible contraception. On the other hand, if teens remain afraid of their sexuality, then denial and contraceptive neglect will result. Therefore, it would seem desirable to help teenagers to accept themselves as sexual beings. Educational programs may accelerate this process in a number of ways. First, teens need to be given accurate information about sex so that they can form concepts and think about this subject with some facility. Next, information on the normativeness of different types of sexual behavior—whether abstinence, wet dreams, petting, or intercourse—should help assure teens that their own sexuality is not deviant. The object of such exercises is straightforward: to help make adolescents more comfortable with their sexuality. Teens who can accept their sexual natures, we feel, will be best equipped to make adaptive decisions about sex and contraception.

A final tactic for hastening psychosexual maturity involves working out, with teens, just what mature, responsible sex is. Whatever else may be concluded, it can be stressed that mature sex is sex that is noncoercive, nonexploitative, *and sex that is adequately protected by contraception.* Once such criteria for mature sex have been established, teens may be encouraged to monitor their own relationships to see that these standards are met. Teenagers who decide upon standards for responsible sex and try to comply with them are bringing a good deal of psychosexual maturity to their relationships.

In summary, we have suggested a kind of holding action. The goal of this strategy is to insure that teens become psychosexually mature *before* they become sexually active. Mature teens, who can make rational judgments about their own sexuality, will likely use contraception responsibly in their sexual relationships. In order for them to do so, however, they must also become knowledgeable about birth control, and it is to this subject that we now turn our attention.

Dealing with ignorance about contraception.   In a sense, teenagers' ignorance about sex and contraception is a problem that is very easy to solve. Ignoring for the moment the political difficulties of sex education—weighty though they are—we find that effective means for teaching adolescents about sex already exist. To illustrate this point, we will discuss in detail two studies that were mentioned earlier.

In research that was conducted at Indiana University, Parris Watts (1977) compared the effectiveness of three different methods of sex education. All of the students in Watts' study first took a test of their sexual knowledge. Then, one group of students heard a series of lectures on sexual anatomy and physiology, birth control, and the like; a second group of students studied readings and took part in group discussion on these topics, while a third group of students learned the same material from audiovisual sources (i.e., slides, tape recordings, etc.). Afterwards, the students' sexual knowledge was tested again, and their pre- and posttest scores are presented in Table 12.2. It can be seen that *all* of the methods employed led to appreciable gains in sex knowledge, although the lecture method had a statistically significant edge over the audiovisual approach. Thus, traditional pedagogical methods such as lecture, independent study, or small group discussion may be useful tools for teaching facts about sex, at least at the college level.

The second investigation that we will discuss is the one conducted by Norman West (1976). It will be recalled that West surveyed some 2,000 Canadian secondary school pupils, some of whom had a Family Planning Unit in high school or a sex education course in elementary school. What were the effects of this education? To find out, West gave these students a test of sexual and contraceptive knowledge. Students' scores on this test, as a function of their sex education background, are presented in Table 12.3. Statistical analyses showed that boys who had sex education in elementary school (compared to boys who did not) had greater sexual and contraceptive knowledge. Moreover, both boys and girls who took the Family Planning Unit in high school (compared to those who did not) had greater sexual and contraceptive knowledge. Thus, it appears that high school and even grade school sex education may lead to gains in sexual and contraceptive knowledge.

TABLE 12.2
Sexual Knowledge Before and After Exposure to Three
Methods of Sex Education[1]

Method of Instruction	Pretest of Sexual Knowledge	Posttest of Sexual Knowledge
Lecture	36.61	43.48
Individual Study and Small Group Discussion	38.35	42.65
Audiovisual	36.63	41.06

Note: Higher scores indicate greater sexual knowledge.

[1] After Watts (1977)

TABLE 12.3

High School Students' Scores on a Contraception and Sexual
Knowledge Test, as a Function of Their Sex Education Background[1]

	Students Who _Had_ Sex Education in Elementary School				Students Who _Did Not Have_ Sex Education in Elementary School			
	Students Who _Had_ Family Planning Unit in High School		Students Who _Did_ Not Have Family Planning Unit in High School		Students Who _Had_ Family Planning Unit in High School		Students Who _Did_ Not Have Family Planning Unit in High School	
Grade	Boys	Girls	Boys	Girls	Boys	Girls	Boys	Girls
11	12.84	13.06	10.46	11.24	13.23	13.41	9.90	10.77
12	13.00	13.55	12.16	12.23	12.18	13.50	11.83	10.69
13	14.41	14.84	14.05	14.43	13.91	14.86	13.24	12.25
11-13 Average	13.64	13.83	11.28	11.82	13.01	13.87	11.29	11.06

Note: Scores may range from a possible 0 (no items correct on the sex knowledge test) to 22 (perfect
score on the sex knowledge test).

[1] After West (1976)

There is one more critical issue that must be considered. Given that sex
education seems to increase students' knowledge about sex, is this knowledge
translated into more responsible sexual behavior? For example, in the study just
discussed, students who took the Family Planning Unit were exposed to detailed
information about birth control. Did these students become more consistent users
of contraception? West has analyzed this question, and his results are not encouraging. The sexually active high school students in West's survey were asked
whether they or their partner always used a method of contraception. Students'
responses, as a function of their sex education background, are presented in
Table 12.4. Disappointingly, it can be seen that taking a high school unit that
dealt specifically with birth control did *not* improve students' use of contraception. In fact, the only variable that was associated with better contraceptive
practice was grade level. In line with our earlier discussion of immaturity and
contraceptive neglect, it was found that students in lower grades were the least
consistent users of contraception.

Thus far, it seems that while sex education generally leads to gains in knowledge, this knowledge does not automatically produce desired changes in behavior. Upon reflection, this may not be too surprising. First, it must be realized that
what is taught in sex education courses may have very limited applicability to
teens' immediate needs. Explaining to teenage women how the pill works, for
example, is less useful than teaching them where they may obtain it cheaply and

TABLE 12.4
High School Students' Self-Reports of Contraceptive Use,
as a Function of Their Sex Education Background[1]

	Students Who *Had* Sex Education in Elementary School		Students Who *Did Not Have* Sex Education in Elementary School	
Grade	Students Who *Had* Family Planning Unit in High School	Students Who *Did Not Have* Family Planning Unit in High School	Students Who *Had* Family Planning Unit in High School	Students Who *Did Not Have* Family Planning Unit in High School
11	2.00	1.920	1.818	1.700
12	2.123	2.237	2.188	1.882
13	2.284	2.147	1.942	2.318
11-13 Average	2.173	2.035	2.053	1.983

Note: This table presents the responses of 662 sexually active students (out of the total sample of 2,214). The question read, "Did you and your partner use any method of contraception?" (during the past six weeks); 1 = no, 2 = sometimes, 3 = always.

[1] After West (1976)

confidentially, how to talk to the doctor, etc. To be effective, contraceptive education must provide a behavioral script that clearly lays out for teens exactly what steps must be taken to obtain and use birth control. Second, it should be apparent that coexisting with whatever knowledge teenagers do glean are powerful motives *not* to use contraception. Sex education programs rarely consider factors such as anticontraception ideology, not wanting to admit to one's self that one may soon have intercourse, etc., and such factors may prevent teens from putting their knowledge into practice.

The challenge for sex education, then, is to develop instructional techniques that will affect *both* knowledge and behavior. To achieve such effects, a carefully planned intervention is required. Initially, it is necessary to decide upon the goals of the program. What, for example, are the particular behaviors that are targeted for change? These goals, of course, will determine the particular strategies that are used to bring about change. In addition, however, two overriding principles should be kept in mind. First, the information that is imparted should be easily translated into the desired behavioral change. Second, motivational factors must be dealt with, such that inhibitory forces are replaced with conditions that promote the desired behavior. Finally, careful evaluations must be conducted to monitor the effects of the intervention on the target behavior. Based on such evaluations, changes may be made to improve the intervention.

In the case of contraceptive education, the process we just outlined might look something like this. A school board, in conjunction with the parent-teacher group, decides that something must be done about teen pregnancy in a local high school. The behavioral change that is desired involves the consistent use of birth control by sexually active students; abstinence as a target behavior was rejected as too difficult to achieve. Based on the objective of increasing contraceptive use, programming is developed to provide teens with information that can be easily converted into appropriate action. Lectures about how to use the various forms of birth control are presented, as well as information about how and where each method may be obtained. Students also role-play scenarios in which they discuss contraception with simulated doctors, pharmacists, and sex partners. Motivational blocks to the use of contraception (i.e., not wanting to admit one is sexually active, etc.) are discussed, and positive reasons for using birth control are highlighted.

After the experimental program has been in place for a time, students who have participated may be compared to a random sample of students who have not, with respect to target behavior: consistent use of contraception. Based on this evaluation, needed adjustments may be made to increase the program's effectiveness. Following sufficient refinement, the program may be introduced as a regular part of the high school health curriculum. By focusing on relevant informational and motivational factors, this intervention would hope to affect teens' knowledge *and* their behavior with respect to contraception.

Dealing with anticontraception ideology.   It was pointed out earlier that many teens possess beliefs that are inconsistent with responsible contraception. In dealing with such anticontraception ideology, it is necessary to respect the right of individual teens to believe exactly what they wish. Nonetheless, it does seem reasonable to help teens become aware of the beliefs and values that may be guiding their behavior. When adolescents are able to reflect upon their beliefs, they may well choose to reject those which lead them into contraceptive neglect. Together with making teenagers aware of anticontraception beliefs, it may also prove useful to expose adolescents to a *procontraception* ideology, some of whose tenets they may decide to accept.

There are a number of methods that can be used to make teens aware of their own beliefs—and alternatives—about contraception. For example, in Chapter 8, Elizabeth Allgeier provided an excellent summary of anticontraception beliefs that teenagers may hold. Some of these beliefs, together with related pro-contraception sentiments, are presented in Table 12.5. This outline could serve as the basis for values-clarifying discussions between teens and sex educators. Hopefully, the teens involved would decide to reject values that foster contraceptive neglect, and to accept those that foster contraceptive responsibility. Reflection on anticontraception values, their implications for teens' lives, and on alternative values may become an effective means for dealing with belief systems that work against contraception.

There is an additional strategy, mentioned in Chapter 8, that may also be employed to counter the effects of anticontraception beliefs. It will be recalled

TABLE 12.5
Anti- and Procontraception Beliefs:
Suggestions for Values Clarifying Discussion[1]

Anticontraception Beliefs	*Procontraception Beliefs*
I. Contraception *is Not* Really Necessary.	I. Contraception *is* Really Necessary.
A. Pregnancy *can't* happen to me .	A. Pregnancy *can* happen to you if you don't use birth control.
B. I have little control over what happens to me, so why should I worry about contraception.	B. I can have nearly *total* control over contraception, although one good way to lose control over my life is to become a teenage parent.
C. If I get pregnant (or get someone pregnant), it's simple to get an abortion.	C. If I get pregnant (or get someone pregnant), it's *not* that simple to get an abortion—nor is it that cheap, and there are certain risks involved as well.
II. Contraception is Immoral.	II. Contraception is *Not* Immoral.
A. Free availability of contraception causes teens to be sexually active.	A. Most teens begin having sex long before they begin using contraception, so how can birth control be responsible for their sexual behavior?
B. My religion forbids contraception.	B. If my religion forbids contraception, I really have three choices: (1) Change my religious beliefs; (2) Change my sexual practices to abstinence; (3) Do neither (1) or (2), and run the risk of conceiving a child. If I ignore the whole issue, incidentally, I have chosen (3) by default.
III. Contraception is Difficult to Acquire.	III. Contraception is Easy to Acquire.
A. I do not know where to go to get birth control, and besides its illegal (because I'm under 16) and too expensive for me.	A. Contraception can be obtained at my local Planned Parenthood (it's listed in the phone book), or at a pharmacy and it is both legal and cheap.
B. Doctors and pharmacists will disapprove of me if I approach them for contraception.	B. Doctors and pharmacists will probably not sneer at me if I approach them for contraception but they might well disapprove of a pregnant teenager.
C. If I get contraceptives, it's like admitting that I'm really responsible for having sex.	C. If I get contraceptives, it may be like admitting that I'm responsible for having sex, and that's a perfectly acceptable feeling to have.

TABLE 12.5 (*Continued*)

IV.	Using Contraception Causes Problems.	IV.	Not Using Contraception Causes Problems.
	A. If I use contraception, my partner will think I'm plotting to have sex, or that I don't love him/her.		A. If my partner has such a response, I'd better consider carefully whether my partner really cares for me.
	B. Contraception threatens my health, and causes a reduction in my future fertility.		B. Pregnancy or abortion are greater health threats than contraception, and abortion is a greater danger to my future fertility.
V.	Pregnancy is Good.	V.	Pregnancy is Good—In its Time
	A. Pregnancy proves that you are normal.		A. Pregnancy during the teen years would make me abnormal.
	B. Having children is the most important thing a woman can do.		B. Women can do many important things, such as helping to plan for children that are wanted and can be cared for properly.
	C. Regardless of timing, the birth of a child is always a blessed event.		C. If born during the teen years, a baby may suffer and so may its parents.

[1] After Allgeier (Chapter 8).

that, according to Fishbein's theory (Fishbein & Ajzen, 1975), contraceptive behavior is viewed as a function of a person's *intention* to behave in a particular way (i.e., to begin to use condoms). Behavioral intentions, in turn, are assumed to be related to four underlying factors:

(1) *beliefs about the consequences of the behavior* (i.e., using condoms will ruin the spontaneity of sex),
(2) *evaluations of these consequences* (i.e., all in all, reduction of spontaneity is moderately bad),
(3) *normative beliefs* about what respected others wish one to do (i.e., my girlfriend is only mildly in favor of my using condoms),
(4) *motivation to comply* with these other's wishes (i.e., I don't really care to do what my girlfriend wants me to do).

Fishbein's theory suggests that these basic psychological underpinnings must be identified for specific contraceptive behaviors (i.e., use of condoms, the pill, etc.) within defined populations (i.e., middle class teens in a particular school system). Once these underlying factors have been identified, changes in each in a procontraception direction should lead to intentions to use birth control, and changes in contraceptive behavior. With regard to the example for condom use that was just discussed, for instance, the young man in question could be persuaded that (1) condom use doesn't reduce spontaneity if it is made a part of foreplay, (2) any remaining interference is trivial, when compared to an unplanned pregnancy, (3) his girlfriend probably *does* want him to use condoms, and (4) he should cooperate with his girl friend's wishes about contraception. If these and other salient beliefs shifted to favoring the use of condoms, the young man would be expected to form an intention to start using condoms, and actually to behave in this way. Thus, the Fishbein model has the advantage of bringing organized psychological theory to the question of anticontraception beliefs, and it can provide a specific listing of targets for persuasive attempts. While research is still needed to establish the utility of this approach to changing behavior, it would seem useful to conduct such research in the area of adolescent contraception.

EMOTIONAL BARRIERS TO CONTRACEPTION

Summary of the Findings

Developmental Issues.   Earlier in this book, it was proposed that childhood experiences with sexuality can have important effects on adolescents' sexual behavior. For example, in Chapter 6, Kathryn Kelley pointed out that our first "sexual" experiences usually involve masturbation. Infants and children who masturbate, of course, generally receive some kind of negative feedback for engaging in this behavior. If punishment is repeatedly paired with genital exploration, a child may come to associate fear and anxiety with touching his penis or her vulva. Such classically conditioned emotional responses seem to remain with many persons as they enter adolescence.

What might be the effect of such ambivalent emotions, in terms of teenagers' use of contraception? According to Kelley's reasoning, persons who are uncomfortable about masturbation should dislike the methods of birth control that require genital manipulation—methods such as the diaphragm, vaginal foam, or condoms. And, those who are ambivalent about sexual intercourse should show general disapproval for the use of contraception. Kelley's research confirmed both of these propositions. Thus, emotional responses to sexuality that are learned in childhood may later affect teens' dispositions to use birth control.

Emotional barriers to adolescent contraception.   In Chapter 9, Fisher, Byrne, and White discussed further the link between sex-related emotions and teens' use of contraception. It was pointed out that there are wide individual differences in emotional responses to sexual cues. At one end of a hypothetical dimension, erotophobic teens have learned to react to sexual content with mostly negative emotions, while at the other end of the dimension, erotophilic teens have learned to respond to sexuality with positive feelings. And, it was proposed that an individual's positive or negative emotional response to sexuality will generalize to his or her contraceptive behavior. Erotophobic teens, who feel ambivalent about sex, should find it difficult to engage in the preparatory behaviors that are required for effective contraception. Erotophilic teens, on the other hand, feel generally positive about sex, and they should have less difficulty acquiring and using contraception.

According to research discussed in Chapter 9, sex related emotions do seem to play an important role in determining adolescents' contraceptive behavior. Results suggest that erotophobic (versus erotophilic) persons may not learn efficiently about sex and contraception, and erotophobic individuals may also fail to anticipate upcoming intercourse, they seem reluctant to engage in public behaviors to acquire contraception, they may find it aversive to discuss this subject with others, and they do not use contraception consistently. In short, erotophobic individuals seem less likely to engage in each behavior that is necessary for effective contraception. For this reason, erotophobic teens may be at relatively great risk of unplanned conception.

Recommendations for Change

It seems clear that ambivalent feelings about sex are a major obstacle to teens' use of contraception. In essence, it appears that large numbers of adolescents are comfortable enough to have intercourse, but they are not comfortable enough to plan for it in advance. Moreover, the origins of this disposition seem to lie in early childhood socialization. Thus, we cannot easily prevent the development of negative emotional responses to sex. What, then, can be done to remove emotional barriers to contraception?

To ensure that negative feelings about sex do not interfere with contraception, a two-stage intervention is needed. First, it is necessary to *desensitize* teens and alleviate their anxiety about each step in the contraceptive process—learning about birth control, anticipating intercourse, acquiring, discussing, and using contraception (see Chapter 1). Second, it is necessary to *countercondition* positive emotional responses to each of these behaviors, to help teens to feel *good* about contraception. This combination of desensitization and counterconditioning is intended to replace strong motivational barriers to contraception with strong incentives for using birth control. A speculative example of how these goals might be accomplished is presented next.

Desensitization.   To improve adolescent contraception, sex education must reduce teens' anxiety about this subject. Anxiety reduction may be achieved through the use of some variant of the systematic desensitization procedures that were developed by Wolpe (1958). For example, young teenagers might be instructed to relax, shut their eyes, and listen to an audio tape that will guide them in imagining the steps of the contraceptive process, arranged from least to most anxiety provoking. First, students imagine that they are in a sex ed class, learning basic facts about reproduction and birth control. Next, they imagine that at some point in the future, they are contemplating intercourse, and they realize that they must do something about contraception. The fantasy sequence then turns to acquisition; now the students are phoning Planned Parenthood for an appointment . . . next they are speaking with a doctor . . . next a purchase is being made from a pharmacist.[1] The next scenario involves discussing birth control with a partner, and the last imagined scene involves the actual use of different methods of birth control.

The purpose of this exercise is simply to help teens "walk through," in fantasy, each behavior that they would need to perform in order to use contraception effectively. By going through the contraceptive process in fantasy, with no untoward effects, teens' anxieties about using contraception may be reduced considerably. At that point, incidentally, it might be worthwhile to *actually* walk through as many of the behaviors as possible—phoning for an appointment and then visiting a contraception clinic, visiting a pharmacy, role playing discussion of birth control, etc. If care is taken so that "practicing" contraceptive behavior does not arouse anxiety, these procedures may help diminish teens' fears about contraception.

Counterconditioning.   Desensitization exercises should remove some emotional obstacles to contraception, but that is not the same as creating *incentives* for teens to use birth control. To do so, it is necessary to associate each behavior in the contraceptive process with positive feelings. When contraception becomes a source of pleasure instead of a source of anguish, teens will be more motivated to use birth control consistently.

A number of techniques—all involving the association of positive feelings with contraception—might be used to improve teens' emotional response to this issue. Learning about contraception, for example, ought to be *fun*. Sex educators seem to be in the enviable position of teaching a subject that students find inherently interesting. This situation can be exploited by careful selection of personnel and instructional aids so as to make sex education a positive experience. By creating a pleasant atmosphere, students may be encouraged to learn what they need to know about sex and contraception, and to continue learning even after the course has ended.

In addition to making it fun to learn about birth control, other phases of the contraceptive process may also be associated with positive feelings. Using the guided imagery technique that was discussed earlier, for example, students could

---

[1]While this example is most relevant to females, parallel procedures relevant to males could also be developed.

National Condom Week

February 14-21

Sponsored by

Pharmacy Planning Service

P.O.B. 1336
Sausalito
California
94965
415/332-4066

SECOND PRIZE

Excuuuse Us!

PPSI VD/Family Planning Program is pleased to announce the NATIONAL CONDOM COUPLET CONTEST. Stretch your imagination and come up with a rubber rhyme!!

The rules of the contest are simple. Just send us a rhymed couplet having to do with condoms, or any kind of contraception, and win yourself a valuable prize and a warm spot in the heart of America.

First prize is a GOLD CONDOM!!!
Second prize is a BRONZED WALLET WITH THE CHARACTERISTIC INDENTATION!!
Third prize is a GROSS OF CONDOMS (144)!
In addition, the winning entries and any others we feel are deserving of special attention will be printed on t-shirts and recited on radio stations around the country.

For those of you who have forgotten your English lessons, a rhymed couplet is simply two lines of verse with the same number of syllables, and rhyming last syllables. What could be simpler? For instance:

*"From using a condom you will learn
No deposit means no return"*

*"Rubberizing Copulation
Puts a cap on population"*

OR

"When you rise.......Condomize"

Come on. You can do better than that!

FIG. 12.1.   The organizers of National Condom Week—an annual event—have gone to extraordinary lengths to make learning about contraception enjoyable. On one campus, National Condom Week celebrations involved the release of thousands of multicolored helium filled condoms, as well as an ice sculpture contest. In addition, the National Condom Couplet Contest was held, with the first prize (a gold condom) going to the author of the best verse advocating condom use. (Reproduced courtesy of Pharmacists Planning Service, Inc., P.O. Box 1336, Sausalito, CA. 94965. Posters are available upon request. © Pharmacists Planning Service, Inc.).

learn to associate contraceptive planning with other pleasurable preparations for a heavy date—borrowing the car, selecting one's clothes, making reservations for a romantic dinner, and buying a three-pack of condoms. Guided fantasy could also seek to link the discussion and use of birth control with other types of foreplay. Here, the object is to turn birth control into a minor fetish object—a source of sexual arousal. Such feelings, in turn, may make it pleasant for teens to use contraception.

Before concluding this section, let us note that desensitization and counterconditioning procedures may well arouse political opposition, on at least two grounds. First, these techniques may appear to be highly manipulative. In fact, they are, but these methods are no more manipulative than teaching children to salute the flag, or drilling multiplication tables, and they are no more manipulative than is the *denial* of contraceptive education to teens. A second potential objection to these procedures is that they make contraception look too good. While we do not expect virginal teenagers to rush out and have intercourse just to sample the sweet pleasures of birth control, it is possible that these procedures might result in some increase in sexual activity. It may be necessary to choose between having large numbers of sexually active teens who are poor contraceptors, as is now the case, and having slightly more sexually active teens who are much better contraceptors.

IMAGINATIVE BARRIERS TO CONTRACEPTION

Summary of the Findings

In Chapter 1, Donn Byrne proposed that sexual fantasy may have both motivational and informational effects on adolescents' sexual behavior. The scripts that teenagers play out in fantasy can provide imagined incentives for acting in a particular way, and fantasy content may provide information about how to behave as well. Perhaps because teens lack models for responsible contraception, their sexual fantasies do not include the use of birth control. Consequently, teens' sexual fantasies provide neither imagined incentives for contraception, nor fantasy scripts that describe how to engage in this behavior.

There has not been a great deal of research on the relation of fantasy and contraceptive behavior. Nevertheless, scattered throughout this book are bits of evidence that bear on this question, and we will summarize a few of these points. In Chapter 11, for instance, Alan Gross and Martha Bellew-Smith alluded to the fact that teens have no fantasy scripts for pre-sex discussion of birth control. They *can*, however, imagine the horrors that would result from such an indelicacy. This "anticontraception fantasy," from a male's point of view, might involve visions of a seduction that fails the instant contraception is mentioned. Women may imagine that, if they bring up contraception, they will appear to be too forward or too wanton. Teens' anticontraception fantasies can also include a "fear of purchasing" script (*Summer of '42*), and one for fear of discovery (*Goodbye, Columbus!*). Added to such specific anticontraception fantasies, incidentally, are other imaginative processes that are not conducive to the use of birth control. For example, it was pointed out in Chapter 4 that some adolescents simply cannot imagine a future time perspective; they may fail to anticipate either the need for contraception or the consequences of unprotected coitus. By and large, then, it seems that teens do not have fantasies that involve responsible contraception, and their imaginations may actually interfere with the use of birth control.

Recommendations for Change

It seems clear that more research needs to be done to clarify the link between fantasy and contraceptive behavior. Nonetheless, it is possible to speculate about educational programs that influence teens' fantasies and lead to improved contraceptive practices. We propose that such interventions must have two goals: to remove anticontraception fantasy, and to replace it with *procontraception* imagery.

To reduce the influence of anticontraception fantasy, we must first learn just what the content of this imagery is. Once fantasy content has been identified for a particular group of teens, it may be subjected to the sort of values-clarifying discussion that was mentioned earlier. For example, teens can consider whether it is legitimate to let imagined fears of rejection prevent them from asking a sex partner if he or she is using contraception. In this way, adolescents may come to reject fantasy-based constraints that promote contraceptive neglect.

In addition to reducing anticontraception imagery, it is necessary to establish procontraception fantasy to guide teens' behavior. One way to instate such fantasy involves providing models of responsible contraceptive behavior for teens to emulate. Exposure to such models may lead teens to imagine incentives for responsible contraception, and they may acquire a behavioral script for doing so. An excellent example of this kind of intervention is provided in Chapter 10, where Marilyn Edmunds describes a contraceptive education film that was produced at Indiana University. The movie—''No Choice But to Choose''—realistically portrays an undergraduate couple who have had sex without using birth control. The action follows the hapless duo from the worry over a late period, to the campus health clinic for a pregnancy test. While waiting for the results, the couple have a highly informative discussion about contraception with a health educator, and the film ends with the couple thinking over which of the methods of birth control is right for them. The portrayal of college student models who are quite like the intended audience stresses the relevance of the problem—and the advocated solution—for viewers. And, not only does the audience learn a script for exactly how to acquire contraception on campus, but motivational factors are treated as well. Teens may imagine the anguish associated with contraceptive neglect, and the peace of mind occasioned by responsible contraception. Such procontraception fantasy, it is hoped, may lead to improved use of birth control.

Beyond providing procontraception imagery, there is one other fantasy based intervention that could be undertaken. In particular, it might be useful to provide teens with models that establish the legitimacy of *not* having sex. It might never cross the mind of many teens that they can say ''no, thanks'' to a sexual overture and still remain popular. From many quarters—the media, peers, and even ''enlightened'' sex education—teens are urged to ''get with it'' and become sexually active. Despite such ubiquitous pressure to have sex, however, educators have generally not provided teens with models of socially competent young people who decide to remain virgins. Where in our world of media hype are the

WHAT KIND OF WOMAN BUYS PROPHYLACTICS?

Today's kind of woman. Because there's no longer any old fashioned prudery or stigma attached to women buying what was once an exclusive male purchase. At one time prophylactics were hidden from view in drug stores and had to be specifically asked for by the customer. It was often a furtive and embarrassing experience. But not any more. Today, prophylactics are on display right beside the vitamins and cold remedies. And there's nothing tacky or smutty about purchasing them.

It's just a simple every-day transaction that more and more women are engaging in; for a lot of good reasons.

Because today, a woman is more aware, concerned and knowledgeable about her body than ever before.

She realizes that birth control is something that should not be her responsibility alone.

And she is aware of the controversy surrounding the pill.

That's why more and more women are choosing prophylactics as a trusted and reliable alternative method of contraception.

Also, apart from birth control, use of the prophylactic is the only method

officially recognized and accepted as an aid in the prevention of transmission of venereal disease.

At Julius Schmid we sell the most popular brands of prophylactics in Canada. They're the brands most women choose; because they are all electronically tested to assure dependability and quality.

And you can only buy them in Drug Stores.

RAMSES REGULAR

SHIK

Fiesta

NuForm
Sensi-Shape

FOUREX
NATURAL SKINS

JULIUS SCHMID OF CANADA LIMITED

32 Bermondsey Road
Toronto, Ontario M4B 1Z6

FIG. 12.2. By providing attractive models for responsible contraception, this advertisement helps establish procontraception imagery. Here, adolescent women may begin to imagine that they, too, might be the kind of person who buys prophylactics. (Reproduced courtesy of Julius Schmid of Canada Limited).

with-it teenagers who dress well, play tennis, drive sports cars, date like crazy, and refrain from intercourse? In order to make abstinence a viable option, sex education must provide teens with attractive models who display successful strategies for stopping short of sexual intercourse. Exposure to such models may help teens imagine incentives for abstinence, and teens may also acquire a behavioral script for pursuing this option. Part of such a script could involve learning how to say "no" successfully, and another variant could involve imagery for satisfying activities like petting to climax or oral sex that do not involve intercourse or the need for contraception. Fantasies that help establish these options as acceptable means of "contraception" may become another strategy for reducing teen pregnancy.

To summarize our discussion, then, it was proposed that teens' sexual fantasies may influence their contraceptive behavior. Interventions were suggested to reduce the effects of anticontraception imagery, and to establish fantasies with procontraception themes. In this way, teens may learn fantasies that provide incentives for responsible contraception, and scripts for carrying out such behavior.

Before closing this review of informational, emotional, and imaginative barriers to contraception, two additional points must be mentioned. First, while we have advocated separate interventions to overcome each barrier to contraception, it seems likely that these interventions will have interactive effects that reverberate throughout the Sexual Behavior Sequence. Thus, an educational program which improves contraceptive knowledge may make teens' emotional response to this topic more positive and promote development of procontraception fantasy. Similarly, a change to more positive feelings about contraception could dispose teens to learn about this topic more efficiently, and increase their readiness to entertain procontraception fantasies. And, it seems probable that the behavioral outcome of these interventions will reinforce the changes that have been introduced into the system. A teenager who becomes more favorable to contraception in terms of information, emotions, and fantasy should become a more effective user of birth control. And, the security and peace of mind occasioned by responsible contraception should strengthen the changes in information, emotions, and fantasy that brought about this new behavior. Thus, the interventions that have been proposed may form a self-reinforcing, self-perpetuating system.

The second point to consider is really a call for further research on a specific aspect of contraceptive behavior. For the most part, contraception has been studied by examining the dispositions of *individuals* to use (or not use) birth control. In many ways, however, contraception is also an *interpersonal* behavior that occurs in the context of an evolving relationship. For example, as John DeLamater proposed in Chapter 2, the intimacy of one's relationship, frequency of intercourse, and other dyadic factors may help determine teens' use of contraception. Too often, research has neglected to study the crucial interpersonal aspects of contraception, and this oversight needs to be rectified. It seems to be a good bet that both individual dispositions and interpersonal relationships must be considered if we are to understand adequately the process of adolescent contraception.

IN CONCLUSION

The evidence that we have gathered shows that teens may be negatively disposed to contraception for several reasons. On the level of information and expectancies, teens may be too immature to accept the fact that they need birth control, they may be misinformed about this subject, and they may embrace beliefs that are inconsistent with responsible contraception. On an emotional level, teens may be ambivalent about acquiring and using contraception. And on the level of fantasy, teens cannot imagine incentives for responsible contraception or behavioral scripts for doing so. In view of such obstacles, it is a bit easier to understand why most sexually active adolescents do not always use contraception.

What can be done to encourage teenagers to use contraception responsibly? The solution that we propose involves a new kind of sex and contraceptive education in the schools. To implement such programs, it will be necessary to resolve contentious political problems. It will also be necessary to devise educational methods to affect teenagers' contraceptive *behavior* as well as their knowledge.

With respect to the political question, we have presented cases that may be made in favor of contraceptive education. These arguments will not magically eliminate dispute. They do acknowledge, however, that sex education will require political as well as pedagogical solutions.

With respect to educational programs, we suggested a number of strategies to promote responsible contraception. These approaches involve modifying teens' informational, emotional, and imaginative dispositions to use birth control. Such modifications will result in basic *cognitive changes,* or changes in what teens think about contraception, and *motivational changes,* or changes in the incentives that teens associate with contraception. In terms of cognitive change, motivational change, and several other characteristics, let us now summarize the main elements of our proposal for contraceptive education.

Cognitive change. To improve adolescent contraception, younger teens must be helped to overcome developmental limitations which prevent them from thinking rationally about their own sex lives. Teens must be provided with information about contraception that is both accurate and positive. This information should, in effect, provide adolescents with a complete and well rehearsed behavioral script for the acquisition and use of birth control.

Motivational change.   To improve adolescent contraception, it is necessary to reduce inhibitions that teens feel about birth control and to increase the perceived incentives for responsible contraception. To this end, desensitization procedures may be used to extinguish anxiety about contraception, and counter-conditioning may help teens develop positive feelings about this subject. In addition, values-clarification techniques can be used to make teens aware of the implications of anticontraception ideology and fantasy, and procontraception alternatives can be presented for teens to consider. In this fashion, adolescents may acquire the motivation to practice what they have learned about contraception.

Timing Contraceptive Education.   The kind of education that we propose must be offered to teenagers *before* they need it—that is, before many of them begin to have sex. The age at which this occurs varies from place to place, and research is needed to determine the appropriate timing for contraceptive education in different locations. It would also seem useful to provide contraceptive education on a more-or-less continuing basis, in order to reinforce past learning and to provide new information as it is needed by increasingly mature students.

Changing Persons Versus Changing Situations.   Most of the suggestions that we have made are directed at changing teens' *internal dispositions* to use contraception—their information, emotions, and fantasies. We believe that such educational efforts are essential. Nonetheless, it is also true that *situational changes* can and should be made to facilitate each step of the contraception process. In addition to motivating teens to learn about and acquire contraception, for example, contraceptive education and purchase *settings* themselves can and should be made more appealing. Thus, changing personal dispositions as well as altering contraception-relevant situations may prove to be complementary means for improving the practice of adolescent contraception.

An Evaluation Component.   It cannot be assumed that procontraception interventions will succeed automatically. Rather, the effects of such programs must be monitored carefully. Based on these evaluations, programs may be adjusted and improved.

THE NEED FOR RESEARCH AND THE NEED FOR SERVICE

Our knowledge about adolescent contraception is not complete. Most research, for example, has been correlational in nature. The co-incidence of dispositional factors (i.e., age, sexual ignorance, etc.) and contraceptive neglect has been described, and the evidence seems to be clear. Nevertheless, for scientific and pragmatic reasons we still need to establish, where possible, cause-and-effect relations between dispositional factors and contraceptive behavior. Too, as noted earlier, interpersonal aspects of *couples'* contraceptive behavior remain largely unexplored. Thus, while it is a cliche, it is also true that more research is needed to help understand adolescent contraception.

At the same time that researchers call for further investigation, educators and health care workers have an immediate need to provide the best contraceptive services possible to the maximum number of teens. How can these diverse interests be reconciled? We propose that interventions be undertaken to improve adolescent contraception, and we advocate studying these interventions for further clues as to determinants of contraceptive behavior. By doing research within ongoing interventions, we can answer important theoretical questions at the same time that we bring much needed services to our teenage constituency. Thus, researchers and practitioners can work together to understand and improve adolescent contraception.

REFERENCES

Alan Guttmacher Institute. *11 million teenagers. What can be done about the epidemic of adolescent pregnancies in the United States.* New York: Alan Guttmacher Institute, 1976.

Fishbein, M., & Ajzen, I. *Belief, attitude, intention and behavior: An introduction to theory and research.* Reading, Massachusetts: Addison Wesley, 1975.

Guttmacher, A. F. *Pregnancy, birth and family planning.* New York: Signet, 1973.

Hyde, J. S. *Understanding human sexuality.* New York: McGraw-Hill, 1979.

Watts, P. R. Comparison of three human sexuality teaching methods used in university health classes. *Research Quarterly,* 1977, *48,* 187–190.

West, N. W. *The effect of instruction in family planning on knowledge, attitudes and behavior of London (Ontario) senior secondary school students.* Unpublished doctoral dissertation, The Ohio State University, 1976.

Wolpe, J. *Psychotherapy by reciprocal inhibition.* Stanford: Stanford University Press, 1958.

Zuckerman, M., Tushup, R., & Finner, S. Sexual attitudes and experience: Attitude and personality correlates and changes produced by a course in sexuality. *Journal of Consulting and Clinical Psychology,* 1976, *44,* 7–19.

Author Index

Numbers in *italics* indicate pages with bibliographic information.

H

Hagelis, J. P., 71, *105*
Hamilton, E., 9, *29*
Hand, D., 24, *29*
Hansson, R. O., 162, *168*
Harvey, A. L., 178, 195, *203*
Heaton, E., 148, *167*
Heilbroner, R., 8, *29*
Helfer, C. H., 5, *29*, 196, *203*
Henry, W. E., 70, 72, *105*
Herold, E. S., 130, *141*
Hill, C. T., 114, *123*, 266, *272*
Himes, N. E., 49, *60*, 184, *203*
Hite, S., 166, *168*
Hochreich, D. J., 23, *30*
Hodgson, R. J., 20, *30*
Hofferth, S. L., 110, *123*
Hopkins, J. R., 4, *29*
Hornstein, S., 157, *168*
Hoyt, M. F., 129, *141*
Hunt, M., 4, 24, *29*, 181, *203*
Hyde, J. S., 151, 155, *168*, 176, 177, 179, 181, 186, 193, *203*, 280, *300*

I

Ibrahim, Y. M., 8, *29*
Inazu, J. K., 130, *141*
Izzo, A., 174, 185, *203*

J

Jaccard, J. J., 23, 24, *28*, *29*, 75, *104*, *105*, 198, *202*, *203*
James, B., 181, *202*
Jazwinski, C., 21, 22, *28*, 114, *122*, 164, *167*, 190, 192, 199, *201*, *203*, 208, 209, *238*
Jekel, J. F., 5, *30*, 49, *60*, 194, *203*
Jessor, R., 67, 69, 73, 74, 87, *105*, 118, *123*
Jessor, S. L., 67, 69, 73, 74, 87, *105*, 118, *123*
Joestling, J., 195, *203*
Joestling, R., 195, *203*
Johnson, B., 191, *205*
Johnson, V., 26, *30*, 166, *168*, 190, *203*, 266, *272*
Jones, E. F., 184, 185, *205*
Jones, W., 162, *168*

K

Kane, F. J., Jr., 71, 73, *105*, 162, *168*
Kantner, J., 5, *29*, 33, 35, 37, 47, *48*, 66, 68, 74, 87, *105*, *107*, 110, 111, 112, *123*, 154, 162, 166, *168*, 172, 173, 174, 175, 176, 177, 180, 182, 183, 185, 190, 195, *203*, *204*, *205*, 209, *239*
Kar, S. B., 70, 72, 74, 75, 87, *105*
Keith, L., 182, *205*
Keller, A. B., 70, 72, *105*
Keller, J. F., 173, 174, 184, 189, *203*
Kelley, K., 16, 18, 21, 22, 24, 26, *28*, *29*, *30*, 129, 130, 132, 134, *140*, *141*, 162, *167*, 209, 213, 224, 225, 230, 231, 232, 233, *239*, 269, *272*
Kempe, R. R., 5, *29*, 196, *203*
Kilmann, P. R., 156, *168*
Kim, Y. J., 110, *123*
King, K., 173, 181, *203*, *204*
Kingma, R., 21, *31*, 209, 212, 213, 214, 216, *239*
Kinsey, A. C., 4, *29*, *30*, 166, *168*, 173, 181, *203*
Kirkendall, L., 156, *168*
Klerman, L. V., 5, *30*, 49, *60*, 194, *203*
Koch, P. B., 153, *168*
Kohlberg, L., 134, *141*
Kolberg, L., 5, *30*
Kothandapani, V., 74, 75, 87, *105*
Kramer, B., 8, *30*
Kreitler, H., 153, *168*
Kreitler, S., 153, *168*
Ku, L., 24, *29*
Kulik, J. A., 77, 87, *107*
Kutner, S. J., 22, *30*

L

Lachenbruch, P. A., 71, 73, *105*, 162, *168*
Ladner, J. A., 137, *141*
Lamberth, J., 20, 22, *28*, 164, *167*, 210, 213, *238*
Laughlin, C. D., 195, *203*
Lawless, J., 157, *168*
Lebel, K., 5, *30*
Lehfeldt, H., 71, 73, *106*
Levine, G., 5, *30*
Levitt, E. E., 213, *239*
Lewin, K., 72, *106*

Subject Index